Excel 4 for Windows
Made Easy

Excel 4 for Windows
Made Easy

Martin S. Matthews

Osborne **McGraw-Hill**

Berkeley   New York   St. Louis   San Francisco
Auckland   Bogotá   Hamburg   London   Madrid
Mexico City   Milan   Montreal   New Delhi   Panama City
Paris   São Paulo   Singapore   Sydney
Tokyo   Toronto

Osborne **McGraw-Hill**
2600 Tenth Street
Berkeley, California 94710
U.S.A.

For information on translations or book distributors outside of the U.S.A.,
please write to Osborne **McGraw-Hill** at the above address.

Excel 4 for Windows Made Easy

34567890 DOC 998765432

ISBN 0-07-881807-9

Publisher

Kenna S. Wood

Acquisitions Editor

Bill Pollock

Associate Editor

Vicki Van Ausdall

Technical Editor

Stephanie Seymour

Project Editor

Judith Brown

Copy Editor

Marcia Baker

Proofreading Coordinator

Kelly Barr

Proofreaders

K.D. Sullivan
Audrey Johnson

Indexers

Phil Roberts
Peggy Bieber-Roberts

Quality Control Specialist

Bob Myren

Computer Designer

Lance Ravella

Cover Design

Mason Fong

Contents

Acknowledgments

Stephanie Seymour has been a major contributor to this book since the first edition. She has written various parts of it and read and technically edited all of it, now three times. In this edition she also wrote Chapter 11, an excellent chapter on the Solver and other analysis tools. Working with Stephanie is always a joy and her work is greatly appreciated.

John Cronan joined the team for this edition, doing much of the revision for version 4.0 of Excel and producing most of the screen shots. Against a very tight schedule, John made every deadline and did excellent work. John's work is also greatly appreciated.

Introduction

Microsoft Excel, which runs in the Windows graphical environment, is an integrated business software package for producing worksheets, databases, and charts. Each of these products contributes to your ability to increase productivity and make better decisions in your business or profession. By doing this in a graphical environment, Excel adds real ease of use to a high degree of capability, allowing you to easily do the tasks you need.

About This Book

Excel 4 for Windows Made Easy supplements Microsoft's own documentation by continuing where that documentation leaves off. Whereas the Microsoft documentation presents you with short and simple explanations designed to help you find answers to immediate questions, *Excel 4 for Windows Made Easy* provides more substantial examples designed not only to get you started, but also to guide you in building your skills so that you can perform more advanced business tasks—all with clear, step-by-step instructions.

How This Book Is Organized

Excel 4 for Windows Made Easy was written the way most people learn Excel. The book starts by reviewing the basic concepts. It then uses a learn-by-doing method to demonstrate the major features of the product. Next, the book provides examples and clear explanations of many advanced features.

Introducing Windows and Excel

The book begins by introducing Windows and Excel and providing the basic concepts needed to use them. This section includes four chapters. The first explains the features and functions of Windows and the mouse that are needed to use Excel. Included are all parts of the screen, windowing, menus, the mouse buttons and moves, and using the keyboard.

The second chapter describes each of the three components of Excel, worksheets, databases, and charts, with particular attention to worksheets. It also quickly introduces cells, ranges, formulas, functions, commands, and macros. For Excel 4 users, Chapter 2 introduces the Shortcut menus, toolbars, and Wizards.

The third chapter looks at how Excel uses the Windows graphical environment and the mouse to build and maintain worksheets. Each of the menus is described, as are the keystrokes and mouse moves necessary to utilize them. This chapter introduces the Standard toolbar and all of its tools, and tells you how to switch to one of the other eight toolbars or create a custom toolbar of your own.

Chapter 4 focuses on how to create and modify a worksheet, including using the menus, mouse, and keyboard to enter and edit information, save the worksheet, and leave Excel. Excel 4's Shortcut menus and Zoom feature are demonstrated in this chapter.

This first part of the book provides the foundation for the rest of the book. This section is slower paced due to the importance of building a firm foundation. If you are a new user of Excel, the first four chapters are vital to your success. If you have some experience with Excel, you need them to a lesser extent. At the very least, you should skim these chapters to assure that you have an understanding of the terms and concepts.

The Fundamentals of Excel

Next, the book covers the fundamentals of Excel—creating and manipulating worksheets, producing charts, and using a database. This section includes four chapters.

Chapters 5 and 6 are companions. Chapter 5 shows you how to create a worksheet. Included are planning, placing text and headings, entering numbers and formulas, copying formulas, inserting and deleting rows, and saving the worksheet. The spelling checker, centering text across columns, and using drag and drop to copy formulas are all demonstrated. In Chapter 6 you format, change, and print the worksheet. Included are loading the worksheet, formatting numbers and headings, moving, deleting, erasing, and setting the parameters for and printing the worksheet. You also learn about the Formatting toolbar, AutoFormat, and audio note capabilities of Excel 4.

Chapter 7 looks at producing charts, including three-dimensional charts. It describes all chart types and includes selecting the type of chart, determining the worksheet ranges to plot, adding legends and titles, viewing, and printing. Both the ChartWizard and manual chart creation methods are used.

In Chapter 8 you learn how to build and use a database. The chapter includes sorting a database and selecting and analyzing information from a database. In analyzing information, you are shown how statistical functions and data tables are used and how the Crosstab Wizard is used to build a crosstab that summarizes the database.

These chapters should be read by all levels of users. For new users it provides the experience with which you can create your own worksheets, charts, and databases. For intermediate and advanced users, Chapters 5 through 8 provide a refresher course that also provides considerable insight into Excel.

Advanced Uses of Excel

The last four chapters discuss the advanced features of Excel. The pace of presentation quickens here; the focus is almost entirely on the advanced topics, with little or no time spent on building the worksheets used to demonstrate the topics. You may, if you wish, continue to follow along on your computer. The detailed steps for building the underlying worksheet, however, are left up to you.

Chapter 9 describes linking worksheets and using external files. Included are setting up links and transferring information among worksheets as well as combining worksheets, exporting and importing text files, dividing or parsing a text file, and saving related documents in a workbook. Linking worksheets is one of the most powerful features of Excel.

Chapter 10 looks at worksheet and macro functions. The section on worksheet functions ties together the work already done on functions in previous chapters. It provides a general discussion on using them as well as discussion and examples of the types of functions not previously discussed. Most important here are date and time functions and text functions. The macro section looks at macro functions in general, discusses how they are built, used, and debugged, and provides a number of examples.

Chapter 11 demonstrates how to use the very powerful analysis tools included in Excel 4: Goal Seek, the What If macro, the Scenario Manager, and the Solver. The tools are used both independently and in various combinations. They provide the means of finding optimal solutions as well as keeping track of solutions as you generate them.

Chapter 12 guides you through all of the steps needed to automate a sophisticated worksheet. Included are automatic loading, custom menus, and updating of a database from a custom data entry dialog box, all operated by a set of macro commands. Chapter 12 shows you the full power of Excel.

Rather than reading these last four chapters immediately, new users may want to wait until they have completed several spreadsheets of their own and know they want more of the capability of the product. Intermediate users probably will want to continue on immediately; it is the next logical step in their Excel education. If you are an advanced user—this is what you've been waiting for!

All readers are encouraged to go through these chapters at some point. The "booster rockets" of Excel are discussed here. Such things as linking worksheets, functions, and macros are not as hard to use as you might think, and they significantly increase the power of Excel.

Installing Windows and Excel

Appendix A provides both the background and detailed steps to install Windows and Excel. It describes what equipment you need and how to start and use both the Windows and Excel Setup programs. In addition, it discusses how you prepare to store the data you will create with Excel and how to leave Windows and Excel.

Appendix B describes each of the nine toolbars and their tools. Additionally, the appendix discusses how to customize an existing toolbar by adding and removing tools, how to create a new toolbar, and how to attach your own macro to a new tool.

Using Various Versions of Excel

Excel, for the most part, has maintained an upward compatibility among its versions. In other words, the majority of the commands and functions available in older versions can be used in newer versions.

In writing this book for version 4 of Excel, most of the features new to version 4 have been identified. Therefore, if you stay away from these new features you can use the book with version 3.*x*. There are two caveats on this: first, the version is usually identified only when a feature is first introduced, and that is generally not in the exercises; second, the toolbar discussed throughout this book is the Excel 4 toolbar, and it differs from the Excel 3 toolbar without any notice of that in the text.

Conventions Used in This Book

Excel 4 for Windows Made Easy uses several conventions designed to make the book easier for you to use. These are as follows:

- **Bold** type is used for text you are instructed to type from the keyboard.

- Keys on the keyboard are presented in key-shaped boxes; for example, (RIGHT ARROW) and (ENTER).

- When you are expected to enter a command, you are told to *press* the key(s). If you enter text or numbers, you are told to *type* them.

Disk Order Form

The worksheets, databases, and charts produced in this book are available on disk. The disk is not required to use the book, but by using the disk you can save the time and effort of typing the input and also eliminate the possibility of introducing errors.

The files are available on 360K 5 1/4-inch disks for the IBM PC or AT, or 720K 3 1/2-inch disks for the IBM PS/2 and 100 percent compatible computers.

Be sure that your input is accurate and avoid the inconvenience of typing the detail by purchasing this disk. Save time and explore Excel now.

To order, complete the following form and return it to Matthews Technology with your payment. Please allow four to six weeks for delivery.

To:

Matthews Technology
P.O. Box 967
Freeland, WA 98249

Please send me the disk indicated for *Excel 4 for Windows Made Easy*. My check for $15 in U.S. funds and drawn on a U.S. bank is enclosed. (Washington state residents add 7.8% sales tax for a total of $16.17.)

____ 360K 5 1/4" disk   ____ 720K 3 1/2" disk

Name: _____
Company: _____
Street: _____
City:_____State: ____ ZIP: _____
Telephone: _____

RETURN POLICY: Returns are accepted only if a disk is defective. In that case, return the disk within 15 days and you will be sent a replacement disk immediately.

Osborne/McGraw-Hill assumes no responsibility for this offer. This is solely an offer of Matthews Technology and not of Osborne/McGraw-Hill.

1

The Windows Environment

Excel is a Windows application. This means that Excel requires Microsoft Windows for it to run. Windows provides the interface between you and Excel—the way Excel tells you on the screen what it is doing, and the way you tell Excel what to do. Though Excel 4 requires Windows 3.0 at a minimum, this chapter introduces you to some of the essentials of Microsoft Windows 3.1. You may never use all of the capabilities and tools available in Windows, but when you become acquainted with them, you will appreciate the additional power in the Excel environment.

This chapter is more of a tutorial than the rest of the book. It proceeds more slowly in order to establish a common ground for using this book and Excel. If you are already familiar with Windows and using a mouse, simply scan the chapter to verify that you know the vocabulary used here and the basic operating procedures used in Windows 3.1.

Introducing Windows

Excel is designed to run "under" Microsoft Windows, an extension of the MS-DOS operating system. This is desirable for several reasons, but primarily because Windows offers a standard environment for all of the programs, or *applications*, that run under it. This environment consists chiefly of a standard screen display, or *visual interface*, that you use to communicate with Windows applications. Once you learn to use Windows, you will find that working with the various applications, including Excel, that run under Windows is very similar.

Windows also provides a way to transfer information among applications, such as from Excel to Word for Windows or to PageMaker. Through this feature, called the Clipboard, you can easily move a portion of an Excel worksheet or an Excel chart to a word processing document.

Windows allows you to load more than one application into memory simultaneously and to switch among them with minimal effort. You can work with a word processor, a graphics application, and Excel all at the same time. Of course, the degree to which this can be done depends on the amount of memory in your computer.

Finally, Windows provides a set of applications that are handy accessories. These include the following:

Calculator	A calculator program for adding, subtracting, dividing, and multiplying numbers
Calendar	A scheduling program for jotting down your appointments and commitments
Cardfile	A list-management program
Character Map	A table of available characters not found on most keyboards
Clock	A clock that can be displayed on the screen at all times
Notepad	A program that lets you keep notes, reminders, and other memos handy
Media Player	A program to control media hardware and software such as CD ROMs and sound boards

Object Packager	A program that lets you embed or link a full or partial document (in the form of an icon) into another document
Paintbrush	A graphics program
Recorder	A means of recording and playing back sets of keystrokes to produce macros
Sound Recorder	A program that lets you play, edit, and record sound files when applicable hardware is installed
Terminal	A communications program that lets you connect via a modem and telephone lines to another computer
Write	A word processing program

As a result of operating under Windows, Excel has all these accessories available to it on demand.

The quickest way to learn about Windows is to start using it. If you have not already done so, turn on your computer now and start Windows. If you have not already installed Windows, refer to Appendix A. When you complete the installation and your mouse is connected, return here.

The Windows Screen

When Windows 3.1 is started, you first see a screen similar to the one shown in Figure 1-1, if you installed Windows with the instructions in Appendix A. (Depending on how you installed Windows and if you have non-Windows applications or other Windows applications, your screen may look different.) The screen in Figure 1-1 shows two windows, both with several standard features that appear in most windows of Windows 3.1. The top line, or *Title bar*, of a window contains its title. The two windows in the figure are the Program Manager and Microsoft Excel 4.0. On the left end of the Title bar is the *Control-menu box*. You use this box to access the *Control menu*, which contains window options that allow you to perform such operations as moving, sizing, or closing a window.

Figure 1-1.   *Windows 3.1 startup screen*

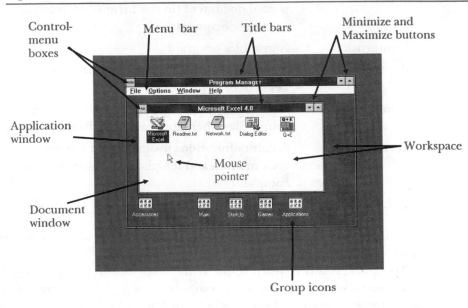

On the right end of the Title bar are the *Minimize* and *Maximize* buttons, which are used for changing the size of the window.

Below the Title bar in the Program Manager window is the *Menu bar*. The menus available (File, Options, Window, and Help) apply only to the Program Manager. The menus displayed in the Menu bar change as the window changes.

Below the Menu bar is the *workspace*, which contains, at the top, the Excel group document window. At the bottom of the workspace, as shown in Figure 1-1, are graphic symbols, called *group icons*, that represent five groups of programs you can use. Inside the Excel group window are five *application icons* that represent three Excel-related programs and two information files that you can run. As you saw in Appendix A, double-clicking on an application icon starts that program. When you start an application such as Excel, and then temporarily set it aside while you do something else, the application becomes an icon again, but now it is at the bottom of the screen in the icon area. An application icon in the icon area can be reactivated, moved around the screen, or deactivated. Whatever you were doing in the application remains frozen just as you left it, until it is reactivated or the application is closed.

Several indicators show where you are on the screen. First, the *active window*—the one you are currently working in—is indicated by a Title bar and border that are filled in normally with a dark color and light letters. Both the Program Manager and Excel group windows are active in Figure 1-1. Second, the *selected object* or objects—what your next action will effect—is highlighted. In Figure 1-1 the Microsoft Excel program icon is the selected object, and the program name is reversed with white or light-colored letters on a black or dark-colored background. The third indicator is the *mouse pointer,* which, in this case, is an arrow that tells you where the mouse is pointing. In Figure 1-1 the arrow is in the Excel group window. All three indicators change as you work. The varying symbols tell you something about the task being done. You'll see examples later.

Using the Mouse

Although Windows allows you to use either the mouse or the keyboard to enter commands, using a mouse will greatly increase the power of Windows for you. Most instructions in this book assume that you'll use a mouse. The keyboard occasionally does offer shortcuts, so these shortcuts and some general rules for using the keyboard are covered later in this chapter.

The mouse is used to move the pointer on the screen. You can *select* an object by moving the mouse until the pointer is on top of it (pointing *on* it) and then pressing the mouse button. Using the mouse in this way allows you to choose, for example, an option on a menu. A mouse can have one, two, or three buttons. Normally, Windows and Excel use only one button, called the *mouse button* in this book. By default the left button is used, but you can change the default to another button, which you may want to do if you are left-handed. (You'll see how later in this chapter.)

Mousing Around

If you move the mouse across a flat surface such as a table or desk, the mouse pointer (the arrow on the screen) also moves. Practice moving the mouse as follows:

1. Place your hand on the mouse. The button(s) should be under your fingers with the cord leading away from you.

2. Move the mouse now, without pressing the mouse button, and watch the pointer move on the screen.

    If you run out of room while moving the mouse, simply pick it up and place it where there is more room. Try experimenting with this now.

3. Move the mouse to the edge of your work surface; then pick it up and place it in the middle of your work surface, and move it again.

    Watch how the pointer continues from where the mouse was picked up. When you point on the border of the window, the arrow changes to a double-headed arrow. This tells you that the pointer is on the border. If you press the mouse button here, you can size the window, as you will see shortly.

This book uses the following standard Windows terminology to describe your actions with the mouse:

Term	Action
Press	Hold down the mouse button
Release	Quit pressing the mouse button
Point on	Move the mouse until the tip of the pointer is on top of the item you want
Click	Quickly press and release the mouse button once
Click on	Point on an item and click
Double-click	Press and release the mouse button twice in rapid succession

Term	Action
Drag	Press and hold the mouse button while you move the mouse (to move the highlight bar within a menu to the desired option, to move an object in the work area, and to highlight contiguous text you want to delete, move, or copy)
Select	Point on an item and click the mouse button (same as "click on")
Choose	Drag the pointer (and the corresponding highlight bar) to a menu option and release the mouse button

After the upcoming demonstrations of these terms, this book assumes that you know them. For example, the instruction "Select the File menu and choose the Run option" indicates that you should point on the word File in the Menu bar, press and hold the mouse button while moving the mouse toward you to drag the highlight bar down to the Run option, and then release the mouse button. Practice using the mouse to perform some of these actions:

1. *Point on* the Q+E icon by moving the mouse (and the corresponding pointer) until the pointer is resting on it.

2. *Select* the Q+E icon by *clicking*–quickly pressing and releasing the mouse button while pointing–on it. The Title bar beneath the icon is highlighted, indicating it is selected.

3. *Drag* the Q+E icon to the lower-left corner of the Excel group window. First point on the icon, and then press and hold the mouse button while you move the mouse until the pointer and the icon move to the lower-left corner of the window, as shown in Figure 1-2.

4. *Drag* the Q+E icon back to its original position.

5. *Click* on the Minimize button–the downward pointing arrow in the upper-right corner of the Excel group window. The window closes and becomes another group icon, as shown in Figure 1-3.

Figure 1-2.   *Q+E icon moved to the lower-left corner of the window*

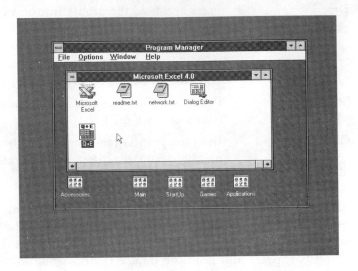

Figure 1-3.   *Excel group window closed to a group icon*

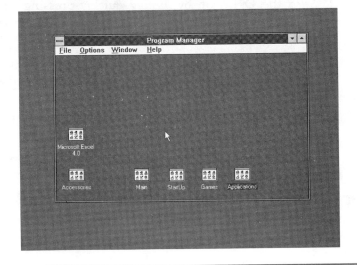

Figure 1-4. Accessories window open

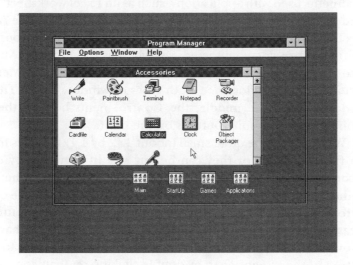

6. *Double-click* on the Accessories group icon in the lower part of the Program Manager window. The Accessories window opens, as shown in Figure 1-4.

7. Double-click on the Control-menu box in the upper-left corner of the Accessories window. The Accessories window closes.

8. Double-click on the Accessories icon again to reopen the Accessories window.

It sometimes takes a couple of tries to get the rhythm of double-clicking. A frequent problem is double-clicking too slowly. You will see later in this chapter how to adjust the speed of double-clicking.

Using Windows

A window is an area of the screen that is assigned a specific purpose. There are two types of windows: *application windows*, which contain running programs or applications such as Excel, and *document windows*, which contain documents used with applications, such as an Excel worksheet. An application window may contain one or more document windows. The Accessories and Excel group windows that you have been looking at on your screen and in the figures are document windows, whereas the Program Manager window is an application window. An application window has a Menu bar while a document window does not. Both types of window have a Title bar with the window title in the middle, the Control-menu box on the left, and the Minimize and Maximize buttons on the right.

Windows can be quite small (about 1/2 by 1 1/2 inches minimum), they can fill the screen, or they can be any size in between. By clicking on the Maximize button, you can make a window fill the screen. When you maximize a window, a new button—the *Restore button*—appears in place of the Maximize button. If you click on the Restore button, the window is returned to the size it was just before you clicked the Maximize button. As you have already seen, if you click on the Minimize button, the window shrinks to an icon at the bottom of the screen. Then by double-clicking on that icon you can return it to an open window that is the size it was when you minimized it.

You can make an open window that is not maximized any size by dragging on the border of the window. When you place the mouse pointer on top of the border around the window, the mouse pointer becomes a double-headed arrow. By pressing the mouse button while you see the double-headed arrow and dragging the border, you can change the window size. By dragging on any side, you can change the size of the window in one dimension. By dragging on a corner, you can change the size in two dimensions—for example, you can enlarge a window upward and to the right by dragging the top-right corner.

Finally, both an open application window and an application icon can be dragged anywhere on the screen. A document window can be dragged only within its application window. To drag an open window, point on the Title bar of the window (anywhere except on the Control-menu box or the Minimize or Maximize buttons) and drag it where you want. To drag an icon, point anywhere on the icon and drag it.

Practice using some of the window-sizing features with these instructions:

1. Click on the Maximize button in the upper-right corner of the Accessories window. The Accessories window expands to fill the Program Manager window.

1

Notice that the Title bar has changed. The title is now "Program Manager - [Accessories]", which tells you that the Accessories window has filled the Program Manager window. Also note that the Control-menu box in the Title bar is for the Program Manager, while the Control-menu box in the Menu bar is for the Accessories window.

2. Click on the Restore button that now appears just under the Program Manager's Maximize button. The Accessories window returns to its former size.

3. Click on the Maximize button of the Program Manager window. It expands to fill the screen.

4. Click on the Restore button of the Program Manager window, and the window shrinks to its former size.

5. Point on the lower-right corner border of the Accessories window. A double-headed arrow appears if you are precisely on the border.

6. Drag the lower-right corner toward the bottom right until the Accessories window is about one and a half times its former size.

7. Drag the lower-right corner toward the upper left until the Accessories window is about one-quarter of the size it was before you enlarged it, as shown in Figure 1-5.

8. Point on the Title bar of the Accessories menu, anywhere but the Control-menu box and the Minimize and Maximize buttons.

9. Drag the Accessories window to the lower-right corner of the Program Manager window. Notice that you cannot get out of the Program Manager window.

10. By pointing on the Program Manager's Title bar, drag it around the screen.

11. Click on the Minimize button of the Program Manager window. It closes to an icon at the bottom of the screen.

12. Double-click on the Program Manager icon. Notice how the Program Manager and Accessories windows open in the same location in which they closed.

13. Drag both the Accessories window and the Program Manager window back to their original positions, as shown in Figure 1-5.

Figure 1-5.   *Shrunken Accessories window*

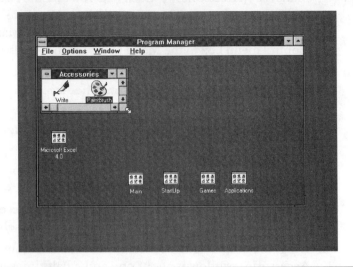

Using Scroll Bars

A window on the screen is just that—an opening through which you can see something displayed. If what is displayed is very small, a small window adequately displays it all. If what is displayed is very large, the largest window you can create (one that covers the entire screen) may not be large enough to display it all. In that case, you can horizontally or vertically move, or scroll, what the window contains.

Imagine that you are reading a billboard by looking through a stationary knothole in a high fence close to the billboard. You must move the billboard from left to right to read a full line on it, and you must move the billboard up to read all of the lines. The scroll bars perform the same function for a Windows window. The *scroll bars* move the *area being displayed* (not the window itself) up or down (that is, vertically) or left or right (horizontally).

Each of the two scroll bars has three mechanisms for moving the area being displayed. First, there are four *scroll arrows,* one at each end of each scroll bar. By clicking on one of the scroll arrows, you can move the display area in the direction of the arrow by a small increment—one line vertically.

Second, there are the two square *scroll boxes* in the scroll bars. By dragging a scroll box, you can move the display area by a corresponding proportional amount. Third, there are the scroll bars themselves. By clicking on the scroll bars (in areas other than the scroll arrows and scroll boxes), you can move the display area by the height or width of one window in the direction corresponding to where you clicked.

Use the reduced Accessories window and the following instructions to try out the scroll bars:

1. Click on the down scroll arrow at the bottom of the vertical scroll bar. Notice that the display area moved up to display the information below that previously shown. Notice also that the scroll box has moved down in the scroll bar.

   The position of the scroll box in the scroll bar represents the approximate position of the portion of the file displayed within the total file. When the vertical scroll box is at the top of its scroll bar, you are looking at the top of the file. When the horizontal scroll bar is at the left end of its scroll bar, you are looking at the left edge of the file. When both scroll boxes are in the middle of their scroll bars, you are looking at the middle of the file.

2. Click on the right scroll arrow several times until the scroll box is at the far right of the horizontal scroll bar. Your screen should look like Figure 1-6.

3. Click on the horizontal scroll bar, on the left of the scroll box, until the scroll box is at the far left of the scroll bar. Notice how it takes fewer clicks to move over the length of the scroll bar.

4. Drag the vertical scroll box a small amount toward the middle of the scroll bar. Note how this allows you to move the display area in very precise increments.

The three scrolling mechanisms give you three levels of control. Clicking on the scroll bar moves the display area the farthest; dragging the scroll box can move the display area in the smallest and most precise increments; and clicking on the scroll arrows moves the display area a small to intermediate amount.

Figure 1-6.   *Accessories window scrolled to the lower-right corner*

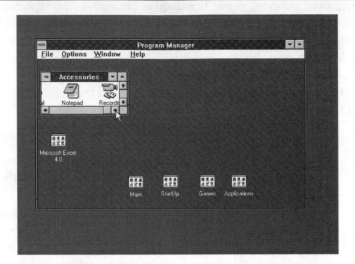

Now that you can scroll the Accessories window, your next step is to use it to select an application.

Starting Applications

The Accessories window contains the icons for the various accessories available in Windows. Each of these accessories is an application that runs under Windows just like Excel. To start an application you simply double-click on its icon. Do that now to work with several application windows.

1. Scroll the Accessories window until you can see the Clock icon.
2. Double-click on the Clock icon. The Clock application starts and opens a window entitled Clock, as shown in Figure 1-7.

    Notice how the Clock window's Title bar and border are dark with light letters while the Program Manager's Title bar and border have become light with dark letters. This means that the Clock is now the active application while the Program Manager is inactive. (There

Figure 1-7. Clock window open

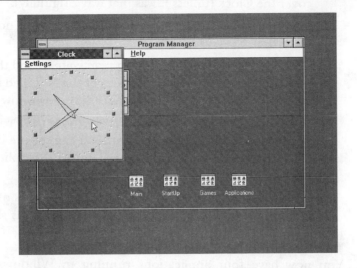

may be some differences between your screen and the figures and illustrations shown in this book. That is due to the differences in displays, display adapters, and in the options you selected during Windows installation.)

3. Click on the Clock's Maximize button. The Clock window expands to fill the screen.

4. Click on the Restore button, and the Clock window returns to its original size.

5. Drag the Clock window (by dragging on the Clock window's Title bar anywhere except the buttons or the Control-menu box) to the lower-right corner of the screen.

6. Click on the Accessories window to activate the Program Manager, scroll the Accessories window until you can see the Notepad icon, and then double-click on it. The Notepad application starts; its window opens and becomes the active window, as shown in Figure 1-8.

7. Drag the Notepad window until it overlaps but does not completely cover the Clock (unless it was that way originally).

8. Click on the Clock to activate it. Notice how it now overlaps the Notepad.

9. Click on the Notepad window to reactivate it, and then drag on the upper-left corner to reduce the size of the Notepad to about half its original size so you can see the Accessories window.

10. Click on the Accessories window to activate the Program Manager, scroll the Accessories window until you can see the Paintbrush icon, and then double-click on it. The Paintbrush application starts; its window opens and becomes the active window.

11. Size the Paintbrush window so you can see parts of the Clock, the Notepad, and the Program Manager windows, as shown in Figure 1-9.

You now have four applications running in Windows: the Program Manager, the Clock, the Notepad, and Paintbrush. Move them around, size

Figure 1-8.   Notepad window open

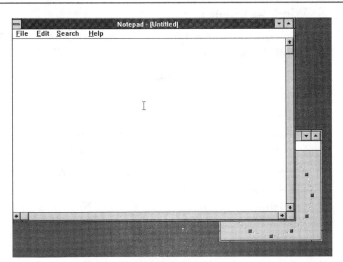

Figure 1-9. *Paintbrush window added*

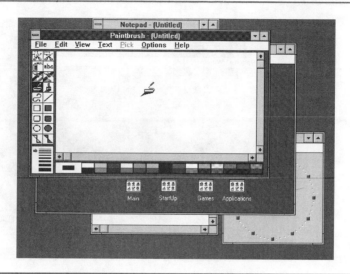

them in various ways, and activate first one and then another. Continue this until you are comfortable working with these windows.

Notice that as you move the mouse among these windows the mouse pointer changes. In the Paintbrush window the mouse pointer can be a paint roller, a dot, a crosshair, or several other shapes; in the Notepad window the pointer is an I-beam; and in the Clock and Program Manager windows the pointer is the familiar arrow. The pointer is telling you what can be done when it is in the various windows. With the dot in Paintbrush you can draw, while the crosshairs are for cutting away a part of a drawing. The I-beam is used with text; its skinny nature allows you to insert it between characters. When you click an I-beam you are establishing an *insertion point,* which determines where text you type is placed.

12. Click on the Minimize button of the Notepad, Clock, Paintbrush, and Accessories windows. The first three become application icons at the bottom of the screen while the Accessories window becomes the now familiar group icon at the bottom of the Program Manager window, as shown in Figure 1-10.

Figure 1-10.   *Application windows turned into icons*

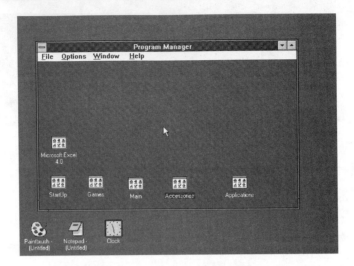

Notice how the clock still tells time even though it has turned into an icon. This is generally true about application icons—they are running programs that are just temporarily inactive. The only difference between an inactive window and an application icon is the amount of the screen they use and that you must double-click on an icon to activate it while you need only click once on an inactive window.

13. Drag the three application icons to reorder them, and place them in other locations on the screen just to see how you can do it. When you are done, drag them back to their original location and order, as shown in Figure 1-10.

Manipulating windows and their icons—by selecting, dragging, maximizing, minimizing, sizing, and scrolling—is one of the primary functions of the Windows environment. Practice these techniques until they are second nature. You will use them often. Another primary function of the Windows environment is the use of menus.

Using Menus

A menu is the primary device you use to give instructions to Windows and its applications. MS-DOS, by itself, is command oriented—you type commands at a system prompt. Within Windows, you give a command by making a choice on a menu. The menus available to you at any given time are shown in the Menu bar. By clicking on a menu name—*selecting* a menu—you open the menu. By clicking on a menu option—*choosing* an option—you make the option perform its function.

Menu options can represent several different functions. Often when you choose a menu option you are telling the application to carry out a command, such as saving a file or copying something. Other menu options allow you to set parameters or defaults for the items you are working on, like selecting the size of a page to be printed or the color of an object. Still other menu options are themselves menus—in other words, selecting a menu option opens another menu. This is called *cascading menus*.

Look at several menus now and get a feel for how they operate.

1. Click on the Program Manager's File menu. It opens as shown here:

The Program Manager's File menu has eight options. Notice that some of the options (Move and Copy, for example) are dimmed while others are not. Dimmed options are not available in the context of what you are doing. For example, if you do not have a selected object in the current window's workspace, you cannot move an object in that window; therefore, the Move option is dim. Many of the options, such as New, Copy, and Run, have an ellipsis (...) after them. When you select such an option, a dialog box opens.

A *dialog box* is a place for you to provide further information or answer questions about the option you selected. For example, if you ask to save a file but you never provided the application with a filename, a dialog box opens asking you for the filename.

2. Click on New in the File menu.

    A dialog box opens asking if you want to add a new group or a new application to a group and what to name the group or application.

3. Click on Cancel to close the dialog box.

4. Click on the File menu again. Then click on Properties and then Run to look at their dialog boxes. Click on Cancel in each case to close the dialog boxes.

5. Click on the Options, Window, and Help menus in succession to look at each of them.

Notice in the Window menu that one of the listed windows has a check mark to the left of it. This means that window is currently active. One of the options of the Window menu allows you to choose the active window. When you click on your choice, a check mark is placed beside it so that the next time you open the menu you can tell which is active.

Notice also that a menu option may have a series of keystrokes to the right of the option name. These are *shortcut keys*. By pressing these keys you can choose the menu option directly without first opening the menu.

Using Dialog Boxes

As you have seen, dialog boxes are a means of providing information about an option you have chosen. The dialog boxes you just looked at are rather simple, with only a couple of items. Dialog boxes can be very complex, with many different components. Windows uses several types of components to gather different types of information. These components are shown in the dialog boxes displayed in Figures 1-11, 1-12, and 1-13. These Excel dialog boxes are used for opening files, setting up a printer, and setting up a page to be printed, respectively.

1

Figure 1-11.   *File Open dialog box*

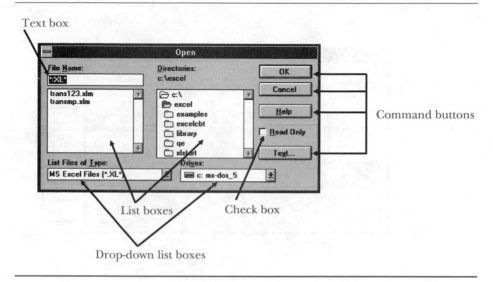

Figure 1-12.   *Printer Setup dialog box*

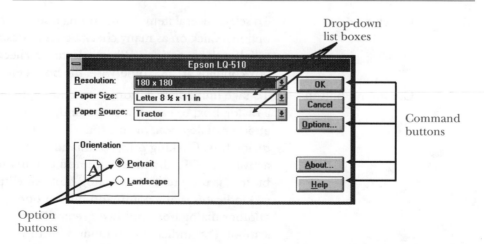

Figure 1-13.   *Page Setup dialog box*

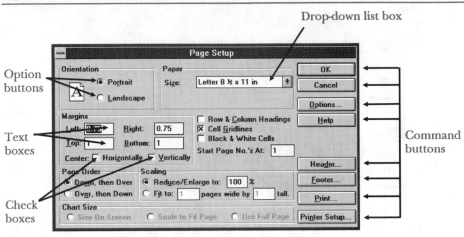

The various dialog box components, as well as their uses, are as follows:

Component	Usage
Check box	To select several items from among a series of options. Click on as many check boxes as desired to select those options. When selected, a check box contains an "X"; otherwise, the box is empty.
Command button	To take immediate action; for example, to close a dialog box, to cancel a command, to open another dialog box, or to expand the current dialog box. Clicking on a command button activates it. OK, the most common command button, is used to close a dialog box. An ellipsis (...) indicates that a command button opens another dialog box, and two greater-than symbols (>>) indicate a command button expands the current dialog box.

Component	Usage
Drop-down list box	To select usually one item from a list in a constrained space. The current selection is shown. Clicking on the arrow to the right opens the drop-down list box. Click on the option desired, possibly using the scroll bar first.
List box	To select usually one item from a list. The current selection is highlighted. Click on the option desired, possibly using the scroll bar first.
Option button	To select one item from a set of mutually exclusive options. A selection is changed by clicking on another option.
Text box	To enter text, such as a filename. The mouse pointer turns into an I-beam in a text box. Clicking the mouse in a text box places an insertion point, and any text typed will follow the insertion point. Without clicking an insertion point, any existing text in a selected text box is replaced by anything typed. The (DEL) key removes existing selected text in a text box.

Dialog boxes provide a very powerful and fast means of communicating with Windows and its applications. It is important that you know these terms and are comfortable using dialog boxes.

Using the Keyboard

You can do almost everything (except enter text) with a mouse, but in several instances the keyboard provides a useful shortcut. You have seen how several of the menu options have direct shortcut keys. You can also choose any of the other menu options with a general keyboard procedure. You can open any menu by pressing (ALT) (you do not have to hold it down) followed by the underlined letter in the menu name. After pressing (ALT) you can also use (LEFT ARROW) and (RIGHT ARROW) to highlight a menu name, and then (DOWN ARROW) to open the menu and highlight an option. After a menu is open you can choose an option by typing the underlined letter in the option name or highlighting the option with the direction keys and pressing (ENTER). (ENTER) can also be used to open a menu once you have highlighted the menu name, and the (F10) function key can be used in place of (ALT) to initiate the process. To cancel a menu selection and return to the workspace, press (ALT) or (F10) a second time. To cancel a menu selection but stay in the Menu bar so that another menu selection can be made, press (ESC).

Give the mouse a rest for a moment and access several Menu options using the keyboard.

1. Press (ALT)-(F) to open the Program Manager's File menu.

2. Type **R** to select the Run option. The Run dialog box opens.

3. Press (TAB) to move among the various fields in the dialog box, and then press (ESC) to cancel the dialog box, close the File menu, and deactivate the Menu bar.

In general, to move around in a dialog box you first press (TAB) to move through the major groups of options, normally from left to right and top to bottom, or use (SHIFT)-(TAB) to reverse the direction. Alternatively, press and hold (ALT) while typing the underlined letter in the option or group name to move directly to that option or group. Then use the direction keys to highlight an option within a group, and use (SPACEBAR) to make the final selection of the option. Finally, press (ENTER) to complete and close the dialog box.

4. Press (F10) to reactivate the Menu bar.

5. Press (RIGHT ARROW) twice to move to the Window menu.

6. Press (ENTER) to open the Window menu, and then press (DOWN ARROW) four times to highlight the second group of applications.

7. Press (ENTER) to select the highlighted menu item and open the selected group window.

8. Press (ALT)-(-) (hyphen) to open the Control menu of the open group window and then type **N** to minimize it once again to an icon.

Using the Control Menu

The Control menu, located in the upper-left corner of most windows and icons and some dialog boxes, allows you to perform many other Windows functions with the keyboard that you have previously learned to perform with the mouse. There is some difference among Control menus but, for the most part, the options are the same.

Click on the Control-menu box or press (ALT)-(SPACEBAR) to open the Program Manager's Control menu shown here:

The options available in this Control menu and their functions are as follows:

Option	Function
Restore	Restores the window to the size it was prior to being minimized or maximized
Move	Allows moving the window with the keyboard
Size	Allows sizing the window with the keyboard
Minimize	Minimizes the window size to an icon
Maximize	Maximizes the window size, normally, to fill the screen
Close	Closes the window
Switch To	Switches among the currently running applications and allows rearrangement of their icons and windows

The following additional options are available on other Control menus:

Option	Function
Edit	Opens an Edit menu with four options (non-Windows applications in 386 enhanced mode only):

    Mark   Allows selection of text to be copied to the Clipboard

    Copy   Copies text to the Clipboard

    Paste   Copies the contents of the Clipboard to the insertion point in the active document window

    Scroll Scrolls the active document window

Next	Switches to the next open document window or document icon (on document windows only)
Paste	Copies the contents of the Clipboard to the insertion point in the active document window (real and standard mode only)
Settings	Allows entering settings for multitasking (non-Windows applications in 386 enhanced mode only)

Now try several of the Control menu options using the keyboard.

1. Press (DOWN ARROW) to highlight Move and press (ENTER) to choose it. The pointer becomes a four-headed arrow.

2. Press one or more of the direction keys to move the window in the direction you choose. An outline shows you where you are going.

3. When the outline of the window is where you want it, press (ENTER). Should you want to cancel the move, press (ESC) before pressing (ENTER).

4. Press (ALT)-(SPACEBAR) to reopen the Program Manager's (the active window) Control menu.

5. Press (DOWN ARROW) twice to highlight Size, and press (ENTER) to choose it. The pointer becomes a four-headed arrow.

6. Press one arrow key to select one side whose size you want to change, or press two arrow keys simultaneously to select two sides whose sizes you want to change. (Pressing two arrow keys simultaneously is the same as selecting a corner with the mouse.)

7. Press one or two arrows until the window is the size you want it. Then press (ENTER). If you want to cancel the sizing, press (ESC) before pressing (ENTER).

8. Press (ALT)-(SPACEBAR) to reopen the Program Manager's Control menu.

9. Type **X** to choose Maximize. The Program Manager window expands to fill the screen.

10. Press (ALT)-(SPACEBAR) to open the Program Manager's Control menu, and press (ENTER) to choose Restore. The Program Manager window returns to its original size.

11. Press (ALT)-(SPACEBAR) again, and type **N** to choose Minimize. The Program Manager window shrinks to an icon.

12. Press (ALT)-(ESC) to cycle through the various application icons (or windows if any were open). When you have reached the Program Manager again, press (ALT)-(SPACEBAR) to open the Control menu.

13. Press (ENTER) to choose Restore. The Program Manager window reopens at its last size and location.

14. Press (CTRL)-(F6) or (CTRL)-(TAB) to cycle through the various document (group) icons (or windows if any were open).

15. When you reach Main, press (ALT)-(-) (hyphen) to open the Main group's Control menu.

16. Choose Restore by pressing (ENTER), since Restore is already highlighted. Your screen should look like that shown in Figure 1-14.

Notice that for application windows and document windows you use different key combinations to open their Control menus and to cycle through windows and icons. Use (ALT)-(SPACEBAR) to open an application window Control menu, and use (ALT)-(ESC) to cycle through the application windows

Figure 1-14.   *Main group displayed in the Program Manager window*

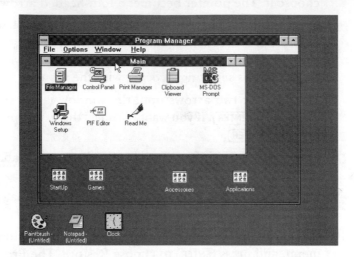

and icons that are running (on the screen). Use (ALT)-(-) (hyphen) to open a document window Control menu, and use (CTRL)-(F6) or (CTRL)-(TAB) to cycle through the document windows and icons in the active application window.

One important Control menu option you have not tried yet is Close. In most windows, Close simply closes the window. With the Program Manager, Close closes Windows and returns you to DOS. You will do that later in the chapter. Once the Control menu is open, you can choose Close in the normal ways: by clicking on it, by highlighting it and pressing (ENTER), or by typing **C**. You can choose Close with the Control menu closed by double-clicking on the Control-menu box or by pressing (ALT)-(F4). The other Control menu commands (Switch To, Edit, Next, Paste, and Settings) are not relevant to Excel and thus are beyond the scope of this book.

The keyboard and the Control menu are important adjuncts to the mouse. But they should be viewed as that and not the other way around. With Windows and Excel the mouse is by far the most effective and expeditious way to do most things. For that reason, this book usually has instructions for the mouse. Keyboard instructions normally are given only for shortcut keys when you are already typing on the keyboard.

Using the Main Group Applications

The Main application group, which should currently be displayed on your screen, includes eight applications that have the following functions:

Application	Function
File Manager	To view and manipulate files.
Control Panel	To set defaults such as color, double-click speed, and date and time.
Print Manager	To manage the queuing and printing of files.
Clipboard Viewer	To display the contents of the Clipboard.
DOS Prompt	To provide a DOS command-line prompt at which any DOS command can be entered. Type **exit** to return to Windows.
Windows Setup	To make changes to the hardware and software configuration you are using with Windows.
PIF Editor	To edit PIF files.
Read Me	To display notes on Windows 3.1. Supplements written documentation.

Take a brief look at two of these applications: the Control Panel and the File Manager.

Setting Defaults with the Control Panel

The Control Panel is the primary place in Windows where you set the parameters or defaults that tell Windows how you want a number of different functions handled. Open the Control Panel now and look at the options.

Double-click on the Control Panel icon. The Control Panel opens as shown here:

The Control Panel consists of the following functions, each with its own icon, for which you can set defaults.

Icon	Function Set
Color	Colors associated with the various parts of the screen
Fonts	Fonts available for both screen and printer(s)
Ports	Communications parameters used with serial ports
Mouse	Behavior of the mouse, including the double-click rate, the speed the pointer moves across the screen, and whether the left or right mouse button is primary
Desktop	Characteristics of the screen or "desktop," including the cursor blink rate, the presence or absence of a "magnetic" grid to better align objects, and the patterns used for various areas
Keyboard	Keyboard repeat rate
Printers	Parameters applicable to your printer(s), including ports assigned, paper size and orientation, graphics resolution, and the identification of the default printer

Icon	Function Set
International	Formats for numbers, currency, dates, and times
Date/Time	System date and time
386 Enhanced	Sharing of peripheral devices and system resources in multitasking environment (available only if you are using 386 enhanced mode)
Drivers	Addition, removal, and configuration of drivers for audio and video equipment
Sound	Presence or absence of the warning sound or beep
Network	Parameters applicable to your network (available only if you are using a network)

You can set any of the functions by selecting the appropriate icon (by clicking on it) and then entering the necessary parameters in the dialog box that opens. Try that now by setting the double-click rate of the mouse.

1. Double-click on the Mouse icon in the Control Panel. The Mouse dialog box opens as shown here:

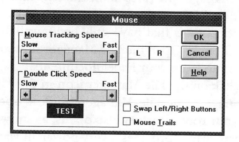

2. If you are left-handed and want to make the right mouse button the primary mouse button, click on the Swap Left/Right Buttons check box at the bottom middle of the screen.

3. Double-click on the Test command button. If the button darkens, the double-click speed is set correctly.

4. If the Test button does not darken, you need to change the speed. Click on the Slow or Fast scroll arrow, whichever is correct for you, and try double-clicking again.

5. Repeat steps 3 and 4 until the double-clicking speed is set correctly.

6. When you are done with the mouse settings, click OK to close the dialog box and return to the Control Panel window.

On your own, look at the other Control Panel functions. You'll find you can do a lot to tailor Windows to your tastes. Unless you want to change something, click on Cancel in each dialog box so you won't change anything inadvertently.

7. When you are done with the Control Panel, double-click on the Control Panel's Control-menu box in the upper-left corner. This closes the Control Panel and returns you to the Main group window of the Program Manager.

Creating a Directory with the File Manager

The File Manager provides all of the customary DOS file-handling commands, such as COPY, DELETE, and RENAME, as well as a number of file-manipulation tools that have only been available with such packages as XTree and PC Tools. Open the File Manager now and create a new directory named SHEET to store your Excel documents.

Double-click on the File Manager icon in the Main group window of the Program Manager. The File Manager window opens, and a directory tree window for your root directory also opens, as shown in Figure 1-15.

The directory tree provides a very powerful way of viewing and working with your directories and their files. The initial view shows you an alphabetical list of all the subdirectories under your root directory in a Tree window on the left, and a directory of all contents (both subdirectories and files) within the root directory on the right. Each subdirectory is represented by a file folder. Files are displayed either by a single sheet (data files) or by an index card (.COM, .EXE, and other executable files). You can choose to display

Figure 1-15.   *File Manager and root directory tree*

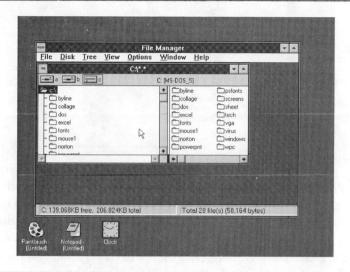

either the tree or the directory, or both; indicators to show whether a file folder contains subdirectories; and other options. For example:

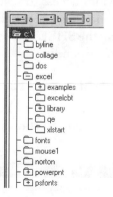

You may open and list the files and subdirectories in any directory by double-clicking on the folder icon. If you were to double-click on the Excel directory folder (c:\excel) you would get this directory window:

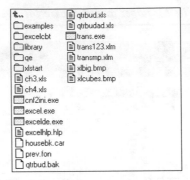

In the Directory window you can select or highlight files you want to move, copy, rename, or delete. To move a file, drag its icon from the current directory on the right to a new directory or subdirectory in the Tree window on the left. To copy a file, press and hold (CTRL) while you drag the file icon. If you wish to move, copy, rename, or delete several files at one time and the files are listed sequentially, click on the first filename, and then press and hold (SHIFT) while you click on the last filename in the sequence. If you want to select several files that are not in sequence, press and hold (CTRL) while you click on each of the items. To cancel a selected item, press and hold (CTRL) while you click on the item. To delete or rename files, select the files and then choose the appropriate command from the File menu.

The File menu provides access to several other file functions, as you can see in Figure 1-16. Among these is creating a directory. Use that command now to complete creating the SHEET directory to store your Excel worksheets if you did not do this in Appendix A.

1. Click on the File Manager's File menu to open it.
2. Click on Create Directory to choose that option. The Create Directory dialog box opens, as shown here:

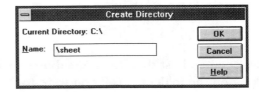

Figure 1-16.   *File Manager's File menu*

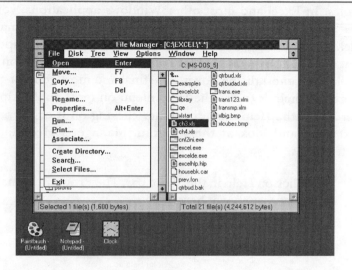

If you had correctly selected the directory under which you wish to create a new subdirectory, all you would need to enter is the new directory's name. Otherwise you need to type the full pathname of the new directory. (If you already did this in Appendix A, you won't be able to do it here.)

3. Type **sheet** or, if necessary, precede it with the pathname you want to use, for example typing **\sheet**, as shown in the illustration.

4. Press (ENTER) to close the dialog box, create the directory, and return to the File Manager window.

5. When you are done with the File Manager, double-click on its Control-menu box to close it and be returned to the Main group window of the Program Manager.

Getting Help

Windows online help is very extensive and context sensitive—it tries to provide specific help about what you are doing. You can get help by several methods. The fastest method is to press $\boxed{F1}$. You'll get an index of help topics. In Excel and most other Windows applications, you can also press $\boxed{SHIFT}$-$\boxed{F1}$. The mouse pointer will become a question mark that you can click on something, a menu option for example, to get specific help about that option. The second method of getting help is to click on the Help button available in most dialog boxes. The final and most general–purpose method of getting help is to use the Help menu on most application windows. You can access the Help menu by either clicking on it or pressing $\boxed{ALT}$-$\boxed{H}$. Do that next and look at the Program Manager's Help facility with these instructions:

1. Click on Help in the Menu bar. The Program Manager's Help menu opens, as shown here:

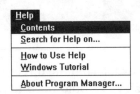

Most Help menus within Windows have the same set of options. These options, with the information they provide, are as follows:

Option	Information Provided
Contents	Topic summary
Search for Help on	Quick access to Help contents
How to Use Help	Tutorial on how to use Help
Windows Tutorial	Starts the Windows tutorial
About	Information about the application and your system resources

If you want information about the keys used with menus you would proceed with these steps:

2. Click on Contents. A window appears, as shown in Figure 1-17. In the help window you make a choice by clicking on an underlined

Figure 1-17. Contents for Program Manager Help

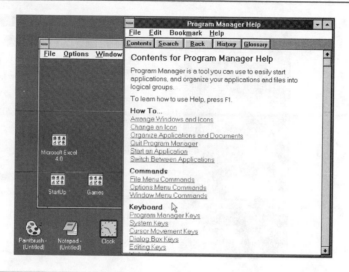

topic. When the pointer is pointing on a topic that can be chosen, it becomes a grabber hand, as shown in Figure 1-18.

3. Click on the downward-pointing arrow box on the scroll bar at the lower-right corner of the window until you see the full Keyboard topics listing.

4. Click on Menu Keys. The Menu Keys help window opens, as shown in Figure 1-19.

The command buttons at the top of a help window return you to Contents, allow you to search for a topic, retrace the path you have taken to get to the current help window, see a listing of your previous help choices, or see topics covered in alphabetical order.

5. Use the Help command buttons on your own to review the Windows Help facility.

6. When you are done reviewing Help, double-click on the Control-menu box to close Help. You will be returned to the Main group window of the Program Manager.

Figure 1-18.   *Mouse pointer turned into a grabber hand*

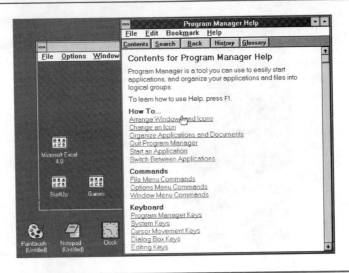

Figure 1-19.   *Menu Keys help window*

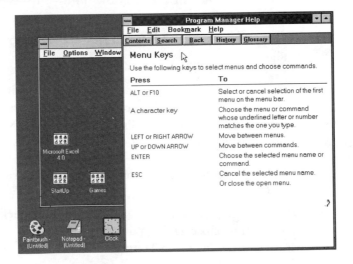

Leaving Windows

Windows and many of the applications, like Excel, that run under Windows use temporary files to store intermediate information as the program is running. If you leave the applications and Windows in the correct manner, not only are these temporary files erased, but you are reminded to save any files you have not saved. The correct manner to leave any window is to double-click on its Control-menu box. Simply do this until you reach the DOS prompt and you have correctly left Windows. Then, and only then, can you safely turn off your computer.

Arrange your Program Manager window the way you want it to be when you next use Windows—with the Excel group open—and then leave Windows with these steps:

1. Double-click on the Control-menu box of the Main group window to close it.

2. Double-click on the Excel group icon to open it.

Figure 1-20. *Program Manager and Windows' application windows in final positions*

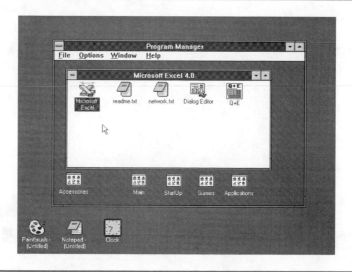

3. Size and position the two windows and icons in those windows (not the icons at the bottom of the screen) so they look approximately like Figure 1-20.

4. Double-click on the Program Manager's Control-menu box. You are asked to confirm that you want to leave Windows. Click on OK to leave Windows. You are returned to the DOS prompt.

This chapter has laid a foundation on which you can now begin to add specific knowledge of Excel. Windows is not a simple subject, but it provides a very powerful framework that is fully utilized by Excel. You now have enough knowledge of that framework to use it in Excel, which you will do in Chapter 2.

2

The Components of Excel

This chapter explains the three components of Excel—worksheets, databases, and charts—paying particular attention to worksheets. It also quickly introduces cells, ranges, formulas, functions, commands, and macros.

Excel is considered a worksheet program, yet it really has three components that perform three different tasks: the *worksheet* component displays and analyzes text and numbers in rows and columns; the *database* component manipulates lists of information; and the *chart* component produces charts.

Each component is really just a different way of looking at and interacting with data that has a common structure based on rows and columns. This common structure is the worksheet. It may contain data from one or more of the three components, but underlying the different components, all data is contained in the same row and column structure. This common data structure makes Excel *integrated*—able to transfer and manipulate data easily among the three components.

Worksheets

The easiest way to think of a worksheet is to consider an accountant's multicolumn paper worksheet—a piece of paper that is divided into rows and columns. Generally there is a wide column on the left for text labels that describe what is in each row. To the right of the label column are several columns for entering numbers. Paper worksheets are used for manually listing sales or expenses, for preparing budgets or financial plans, or any other similar task.

The worksheet component of Excel, shown in Figure 2-1, is an electronic multicolumn worksheet far more flexible than its paper namesake. Excel provides 256 columns and 16,384 rows. Each column can be between 0 and 255 characters wide, and words and numbers can be intermixed as needed. Excel allows many types of calculations over rows and columns, and copying and moving information from one column or row to another is easy with Excel.

Worksheets and Files

Both the paper worksheet and Excel's are a means of analyzing data by organizing it into rows and columns. Excel's worksheets, however, are stored on your computer's hard disk in *files*. When you build a worksheet, you do so in your computer's temporary memory, called *RAM*, for random access memory. When you load another program, or turn off your computer, what is in RAM is lost. You must save your worksheet in a file on disk for it to be permanent. A file that has been stored on disk can be read back into Excel, reviewed, altered, and saved again. Also, a worksheet file on disk can be run on another computer running Excel, which means you can share your work. The only outwardly distinguishing feature of an Excel file is the name you give it. Like a manila file folder, an Excel file is just a collection of information with a name.

Figure 2-1. *Excel's worksheet*

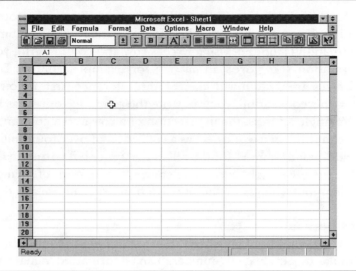

Rows and Columns

The row and column structure of the Excel worksheet provides a powerful framework for financial analysis. Consider a company's financial plan or budget, as shown in Figure 2-2. Each row is an account—an element of revenue or expense. Each column is a period of time—months, quarters, or years. Summing across columns you get the total for an account, and summing down rows you get the total for a time period.

The horizontal rows and vertical columns make a two-dimensional grid. The rows are numbered 1 through 16,384, while the 256 possible columns are labeled A through IV (A through Z, then AA through AZ, BA through BZ, and so on through IV). With this grid, you could build a formula that, for example, adds column C from row 24 through row 32, or you can graph row 15 from column AC through column AH.

Addresses, Cells, and Ranges

When information is entered into a worksheet, it is stored in a specific location. You know what that location is by the row and column in which the information is located. Using Excel's row and column grid, you can give the information you stored an *address*; for example, column D, row 7. Excel addresses are written with the column reference first, followed by the row. Using this convention, you can write the example address as D7.

A single address, the intersection of a row and a column, is called a *cell*. You can think of a worksheet as a collection of over four million cells. These are addressed from A1 for the cell in the upper-left corner to IV16384 for the cell in the lower-right corner. Of course, the amount of memory you have in your computer limits the number of these you can use at a time.

Numbers and Text

A cell may contain either numbers or text. Numbers, which include formulas that evaluate to numbers, can be formatted in many ways, including

Figure 2-2.   *A financial plan*

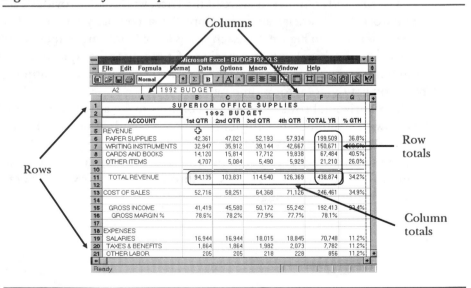

dollars, percentages, dates, or time. Text can include numbers and can be used as titles, row and column labels, and notes on a worksheet.

The primary difference between numbers and text is that you can do arithmetic on numbers but not on text. Think of numbers as arithmetic values and text as everything else.

Based on what you type, Excel determines whether your entry is a number or text. If you type only numbers (0 through 9) or these numeric symbols,

$$+ \quad - \quad (\quad) \quad . \quad , \quad : \quad \$ \quad \% \quad / \quad E \quad e \text{ (in scientific notation)}$$

Excel considers your entry a number. If you enter a date or time value in one of Excel's built-in formats, it is considered a number. Finally, a recognizable formula that results in a number is treated as a number. Everything else is text.

You can enter numbers that range from $2.225E^{-307}$ to $1.789E^{305}$ and format them in several ways. For example, you can enter **3.25**, **3.25%**, **$3.25**, **3 2/5**, **32.5E-1**, or **3,250,325.25**. In other words, you can include commas, dollar signs, fractions, and percent signs in numbers and Excel will interpret them correctly. The entry of formulas, which are also numbers, is discussed below, as is more about entering, formatting, and aligning text and numbers.

Ranges and Range Names

A rectangular group of adjacent cells is called a *range*. Figure 2-3 shows the four kinds of ranges that can exist on a worksheet: a row of cells, a column of cells, a rectangular block of cells, or a single cell. A range cannot be an L-shaped or otherwise nonrectangular arrangement of cells; it must be a complete rectangle.

Ranges are used in many Excel commands to specify a group of cells you want Excel to work on. To specify a range in a command, you may use the pair of addresses representing the first and last cells in the range (the upper-left and lower-right corners, respectively) separated by a colon, as in B11:G18. Or, you may highlight the range on the screen or you may use a *range name* that you have previously given to that particular range of cells.

A range name is a text string that begins with a letter and can be as long as 255 characters. A range name such as Salaries is often used because it is easier to remember and more meaningful than a range address such as G16:T16. Many of Excel's arithmetic functions use ranges as arguments and, when a range name is substituted for the address, they become very descrip-

Figure 2-3.   Types of ranges

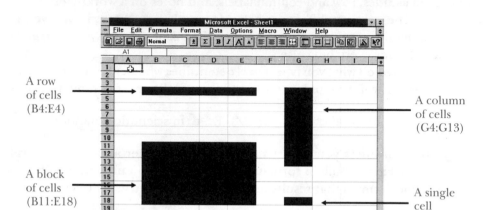

A row
of cells
(B4:E4)

A column
of cells
(G4:G13)

A block
of cells
(B11:E18)

A single
cell
(G18:G18)

tive. For example, to total a group of salaries you would use the Excel function =SUM(Salaries) if you had previously defined the range name Salaries.

Formulas and Functions

The ability to enter text and numbers is not very useful unless you can do something with them. You need to be able to total columns of numbers, calculate percentages, and perform numerous other mathematical operations. Formulas are the means of doing this. Formulas may operate on numbers, other formulas, or text. When a formula uses text it is called a *text formula* and may contain the text operator (&) for *concatenation* (combining two text strings). Formulas that contain the arithmetic operators

$$+ \quad - \quad * \quad / \quad \wedge \quad \%$$

are *numeric formulas*, and formulas that contain the comparison operators

$$= \quad < \quad > \quad <= \quad >= \quad <>$$

are *logical formulas* which produce the logical values True or False.

Formulas use standard algebraic notation with nested parentheses, if necessary, and they always begin with an equal sign (=). You may also enter a formula beginning with an @ symbol, a plus sign (+), or a minus sign (-). Excel will automatically replace an @ symbol or a plus sign with an equal sign and add an equal sign in front of a minus sign. Formulas may be up to 255 characters long but may not contain spaces, except within a *literal*—a set of letters, numbers, or symbols enclosed in quotation marks. Formulas usually use data in other locations on a worksheet by referencing either a cell address, a range of cells, or a range name.

Examples of formulas are shown here:

If the Formula Is	Contents of the Cell Containing the Formula Will Be
=B5	The contents of B5.
=C6-C7	The result of subtracting the contents of C7 from the contents of C6.
=.45*1590	The product of 0.45 times 1590.
=subtotal*tax	The product of the ranges named Subtotal and Tax.
="Dear "&D5	The combination of the literal string "Dear " with the contents of D5. (Quotation marks define a literal string, character for character.)
=date<=today()	The logical value True if a range named Date is less than or equal to a function named TODAY() that produces the current date; otherwise, the logical value False.

Order of Calculation

Excel calculates or evaluates a formula in a particular order determined by the *precedence number* of the operators being used and the parentheses placed in the formula. The following table describes each operator and gives its precedence number. Operators with a lower precedence number are performed earlier in the calculation. When two operators in a formula have the same precedence number, Excel evaluates them sequentially from left to right.

Operator	Description	Precedence
:	Range of cells	1
(a space)	Intersection of cells	2
,	Union of cells	3
-	Negation	4
%	Percentage (/100)	5
^	Exponentiation	6
*	Multiplication	7
/	Division	7
+	Addition	8
–	Subtraction	8
&	Concatenation	9
=	Equal to	10
<	Less than	10
>	Greater than	10
<=	Less than or equal to	10
>=	Greater than or equal to	10
<>	Not equal to	10

Parentheses in a formula change the order of calculation. For example, to add two amounts before multiplying them by a third, you cannot use the formula =A+B*C because the multiplication is performed before the addition, in accordance with the order of calculation. When you put parentheses around the addition operation, the formula becomes =(A+B)*C, and the addition is performed first. Excel performs the calculation within the inner-most parentheses first. Parentheses must always be added in pairs and may be nested more than 20 levels deep. Excel has a very handy feature that shows the matching left parenthesis as you enter the right parenthesis. That way you know your parentheses match without having to count them.

Functions

Excel has a number of built-in formulas, called *functions*, that can be used within other formulas or can be used alone. Functions always begin with an equal sign and include mathematical, informational, date and time, lookup, logical, database, text, financial, and statistical calculations. A function can be either text or a number, depending on whether it is operating on text or numbers. Here are some examples of functions and their uses:

=SUM(A4:A7,A9)	Adds A4, A5, A6, A7, and A9
=NOW( )	Produces the current date and time
=PI( )*G3^2	Calculates the area of a circle whose radius is in G3
=PV(C4,F6,B1)	Calculates the present value of a series of equal payments at an interest rate contained in C4, for the number of periods in F6, and with the payment amount contained in B1
=RIGHT(T22,5)	Displays the rightmost five characters of a text string contained in T22

Functions are discussed throughout this book, but they get an in-depth treatment in Chapter 10.

Commands

You can give Excel commands in six ways: by choosing options from a menu presented on the screen, by choosing an option from the pop-up Shortcut menu, by clicking on a tool in a toolbar, by clicking or dragging the mouse on the worksheet, by pressing particular keys on the keyboard, and by activating a set of commands you have stored on a special worksheet. In this book, *command* refers to one of the first five methods: those implemented with the mouse by itself, with a toolbar, or with a menu, and those implemented by pressing keys on your keyboard. Commands stored on a worksheet are called *macro functions* or *macros*.

Commands from a Menu

The primary means of giving Excel a command is by choosing an option from a menu presented to you on the screen. When you use menus to choose an option, you sometimes are asked for more information with a dialog box, or you may be presented with a secondary menu. As you saw in Chapter 1, you can begin menu selection in several ways: by clicking with the mouse on the name of the menu you want to use or by pressing (ALT), (F10), or (/) (slash). This book assumes that you usually use the mouse, but you should become familiar with all of the menu selection techniques. For the most part, the instructions in this book state "Select the File menu" or "From the File menu." Whether you use the mouse or the keyboard is up to you.

    If you use the keyboard, the (ALT), (F10), or (/) key only gets you to the Menu bar; you must still select the menu you want to use (which is one of many good reasons why using the mouse is preferable). Once the Menu bar is activated there are two methods to select a menu with the keyboard: you can type the underlined letter in the menu name you want, or you can use the direction keys to highlight the menu name and then press either (DOWN ARROW) or (ENTER) to open the menu.

    Once a menu is open, you can choose a menu option in one of three ways: click on the menu option with the mouse, type the underlined letter in the option name, or use the direction keys to highlight the option and press (ENTER) to choose it. Examples of the three methods follow, in which you select the Edit menu and choose the Copy option, as shown in Figure 2-4. The message area on the left side of the Status bar at the bottom of the Excel window displays an explanation of the highlighted menu or menu option. No other change appears on the screen as a result of these steps.

Mouse Method
1. Click on the Edit menu.
2. Click on the Copy option.

Keyboard Method 1
1. Press (ALT), (F10), or (/).
2. Type **e**, (you can use upper- or lowercase), the underlined letter in Edit.
3. Type **c**, the underlined letter in Copy.

Keyboard Method 2
1. Press (ALT), or (F10), or (/).
2. Press (RIGHT ARROW) one time.

2

Figure 2-4. *Choosing Copy from the Edit menu*

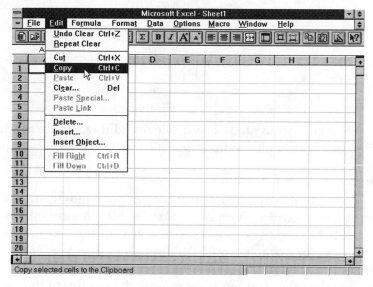

3. Press (DOWN ARROW) four times.

4. Press (ENTER).

Because you will be using the menu system extensively as you work with Excel, menu commands are a primary subject of this book. Chapter 3 introduces each Excel menu.

Commands from the Shortcut Menu

By using your right mouse button, Excel 4 will open a Shortcut menu that gives you direct access to most commonly used commands. For example, clicking your right mouse button on the active cell will give you a pop-up menu of editing and formatting options, as shown here:

Shortcut menus are also available for editing and formatting charts and databases, as you will see in chapters 7 and 8.

Direct Mouse Commands

In addition to its function in choosing commands from menus, the mouse can also be used directly on the worksheet. Most importantly, you can use the mouse to highlight a range of cells on which you want to operate—copy, move, or format, for example. You do this by pointing on a cell in one corner of the range, pressing the mouse button, and dragging the mouse (pressing and holding the mouse button while moving the mouse) to the opposite corner. For example, the highlighted range in Figure 2-5 was created by pointing the mouse on C7 and dragging the mouse to E13.

Other direct mouse commands within Excel include placing an insertion point in a formula or text string, selecting an entire row or column by clicking on the row or column headings, widening a column or heightening a row by dragging on the intersection of two columns or two row headings, and dividing the window into panes by dragging the horizontal or vertical split bar. (The parts of the Excel window are discussed in Chapter 3.) Of course, you can also use the mouse with the scroll bars to change what is being displayed and to size and move the window, as you learned in Chapter 1.

A large portion of this book focuses on using the mouse. Therefore, you will see many examples of using the mouse directly on the worksheet and have ample opportunity to practice such maneuvers.

Commands from a Toolbar

Excel normally has a *toolbar* as the third bar on the screen. The toolbar has a series of buttons that you can simply click on to accomplish a task that would otherwise take several steps with a menu or the keyboard. For example,

Figure 2-5.   *Highlighted range*

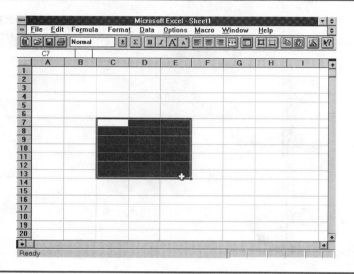

to make a title bold with the toolbar, you select the title and click on the B button (two steps). With the menu, you would select the title, then select the Format menu, choose the Font option, click on Bold, and then click on OK (five steps).

The Standard toolbar also allows you to enter the most used function—the =SUM function—by clicking on a button, as shown in Figure 2-6. Otherwise, you would have to type it on the keyboard or select it from the menu. Additionally, a toolbar is the only means for selecting a drawing tool.

There are actually nine toolbars in Excel 4. Each toolbar contains special tools for various activities. The Standard toolbar, shown on the screens in this chapter, is displayed unless you select one of the other eight toolbars. More than one toolbar can be displayed on the screen at the same time and you can customize each toolbar by adding and deleting tools and selecting the order in which the tools appear. Also, you can create a totally new toolbar, which you can name and add tools of your choice. Finally, you can position and change the shape and orientation of an individual toolbar or multiple

Figure 2-6.   *Entering a =SUM formula using the toolbar*

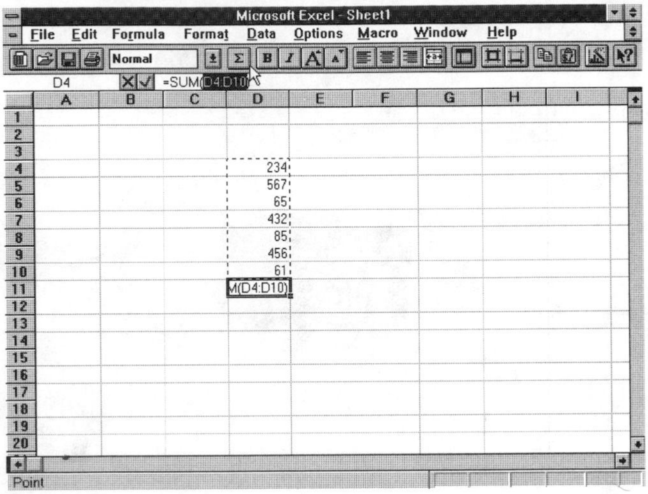

toolbars. Chapter 3 describes each of the functions you can perform with the Standard toolbar, and Appendix B describes all of the nine toolbars and their tools as well as how to customize both tools and toolbars.

Commands from the Keyboard

Most of the keys on the keyboard that are not standard typewriter keys can be used to give Excel commands. Microsoft provides a keyboard template that lists many of these keys.

Many of the keyboard commands are implemented with the *function keys* (F1) through (F10) or (F12) on the top or left of most keyboards. On the right of most keyboards are the *direction keys*—the keys marked with the four arrows and (HOME), (END), (PGUP), and (PGDN). Use these keys to move around the screen, from cell to cell, or through a menu.

Some Excel commands are implemented through the use of two or more keys. Just as the (SHIFT) key is used with the normal typewriter keyboard to produce alternate characters, the (CTRL) and (ALT) keys are used with other keys to produce alternate commands.

Chapter 3 describes these keys in more detail. Also, there is a card in the back of this book that lists keys that are shortcuts for menu options—called *shortcut keys*.

Wizards

A new feature in Excel 4, Wizards, provides an optional menu of step-by-step procedures to walk you through the choices involved in creating and editing a chart (ChartWizard), or summarizing and comparing data contained in the fields of a database (Crosstab Wizard). The ChartWizard tool, located on the Standard toolbar, is shown in Figure 2-7. You will learn more about how to use the ChartWizard in Chapter 7 and the Crosstab Wizard in Chapter 8.

Macro Functions

A macro function is one or more commands, stored on a macro sheet, that behave like automatic menu, mouse, and keyboard commands when executed. You can have Excel execute a macro function, or macro, by pressing two keys. For example, you can format a number with a macro that

Figure 2-7.   Cursor pointing to ChartWizard tool

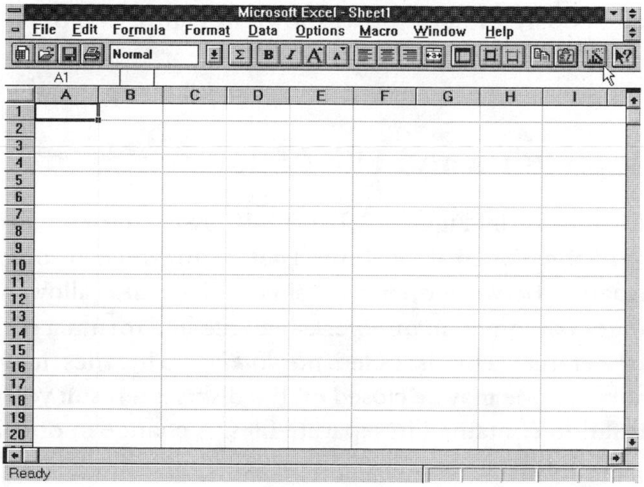

accomplishes six or more keystrokes with two. Macros are used to automate or speed up repetitive procedures.

Almost all commands that you can perform with a menu, the mouse, the toolbar, or the keyboard can be stored on a macro sheet in a macro function and can be activated as you choose. In addition to menu, mouse, toolbar, and keyboard commands, a set of macro functions can be used to perform built-in programming functions, such as repeating a sequence or accepting input from the keyboard. With these additional macro functions you can build custom menus and automate a worksheet. Chapter 10 discusses macros in depth, and Chapter 12 demonstrates worksheet automation with macros.

Worksheet Windows

The Excel worksheet window, as it appears in Figure 2-6, uses as much of the screen as possible to display a single portion of one worksheet. With the scroll bars or direction keys you can change the rows and columns being displayed, but the view is similar. In addition to this basic view, Windows and Excel provide several other views that give you a different look at one or more worksheets.

By splitting the window into *panes*, vertically, horizontally, or both, you can look at two or four parts of the same worksheet at the same time, as shown in Figure 2-8. With multiple windows, you can look at several worksheets simultaneously, either *tiled*, as shown in Figure 2-9, or *overlapping*, as shown in Figure 2-10.

Multiple Files and File Linking

As implied by Figures 2-9 and 2-10, Excel allows you to have more than one worksheet open at one time. That means you can compare, copy, or move information between open worksheets. Excel also allows you to refer to cells or ranges contained in one worksheet file in a formula contained in a second worksheet file. This is called *file linking*. The files may both be open in memory, or one may be closed on the disk. As a result you can easily combine information contained in separate files. A change in one linked file automat-

Figure 2-8. *A single worksheet window split into four panes*

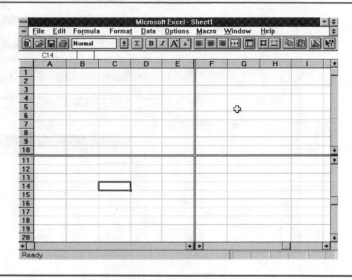

Figure 2-9. *Three worksheet windows, tiled*

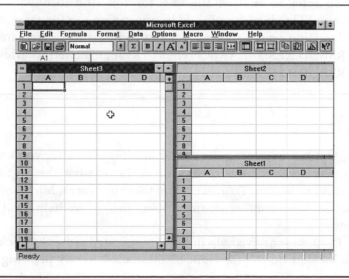

Figure 2-10.   *Three worksheet windows, overlapping*

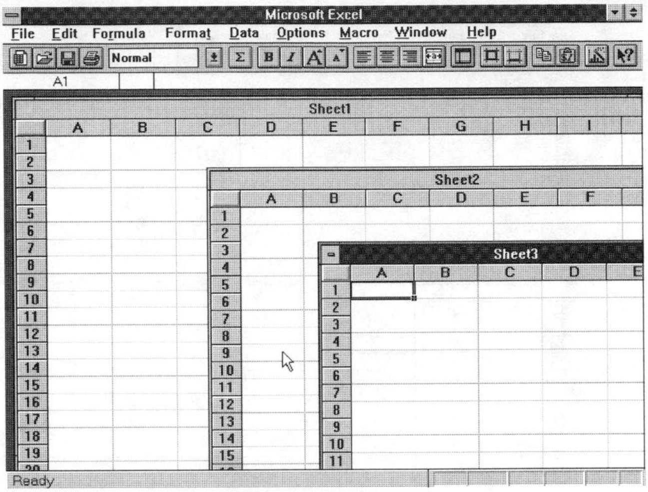

ically is reflected in the second file. If the second file is on the disk, it must be loaded and recalculated before the change is apparent.

To refer to another file in a formula, the formula must contain the filename. This is accomplished by appending the filename, followed by an ! (exclamation point), to the front of an address or range name. For example, QTR3BUD.XLS!SALARIES refers to a range named Salaries in a file named QTR3BUD.XLS.

Help

As you are learning Excel, and possibly even after you know it fairly well, you may forget how a command works or what the arguments are for a function or macro. To assist you in these instances, Microsoft provides three types of help: context-sensitive help, dialog box help, and a help table of contents.

Context-sensitive help in Excel is activated either by clicking on the Help tool located on the far right of the toolbar or by pressing (SHIFT)-(F1). The

Figure 2-11.   *Help window for the Edit Cut command*

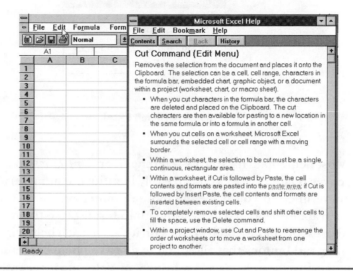

mouse pointer then becomes a question mark and, when clicked on any command or object, you will get information in a help window describing that command or object. For example, if you have a question on the Edit Cut option, click on the Help tool or press (SHIFT)-(F1) to get the question mark, and then click on the Cut option located on the Edit menu. You will get information in a help window describing the Edit Cut option, as shown in Figure 2-11. Additionally, when you get an alert or error message, you can press (SHIFT)-(F1) and get a help window describing the message.

Secondly, help is available by clicking on the Help button in any Excel dialog box. Information on the function of that particular dialog box will appear in a help window. You can accomplish the same thing by pressing (SHIFT)-(F1) while a dialog box is open.

Finally, the Help menu on the far right of the Menu bar provides a number of Help options, including a listing of the help table of contents, a topic-sensitive searching procedure, answers to commonly asked questions received by Microsoft's product support staff, tutorials on using Excel 4 and learning its new features, and help for Lotus 1-2-3 and Multiplan users. The Help menu is shown here:

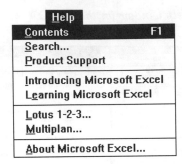

Most help topics have cross-references, or *jump terms,* to other help topics that cover related areas. You can easily identify the jump terms because they are underlined. If you place the mouse pointer on them, the pointer turns into a grabber hand. To look at the jump term, place the mouse pointer on it and press the mouse button (click on it). Also, each help window has a series of command buttons that allow you to go to the help contents list, conduct a topic-sensitive search, or see a history of your most recently selected help topics.

Databases

The row and column structure of a worksheet is excellent for storing lists of information. Consider the phone list shown in Figure 2-12. Each entry in the list is called a record and is stored in a single row of the worksheet. Each part of an entry—the name, company, or phone number in Figure 2-12—is called a *field* and is stored in a column. You therefore have a natural and common relationship between records and fields in a list and rows and columns in a worksheet.

A list of related information organized in a consistent, logical manner is called a *database*. A database must be completely contained on a single worksheet, but a single worksheet can contain more than one database.

Figure 2-12. *Phone list on a worksheet*

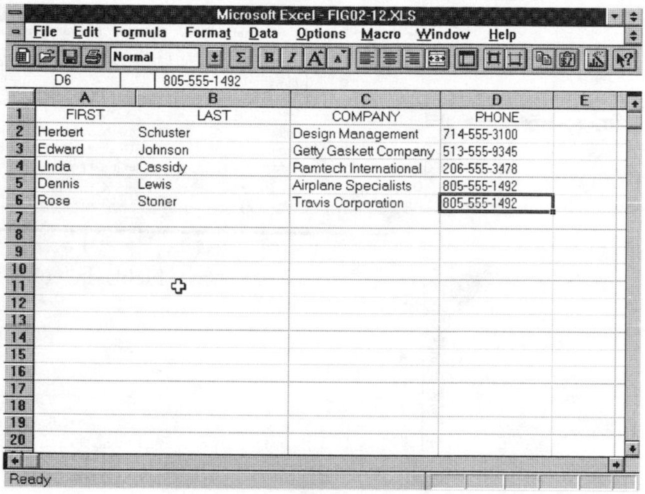

	A	B	C	D	E
1	FIRST	LAST	COMPANY	PHONE	
2	Herbert	Schuster	Design Management	714-555-3100	
3	Edward	Johnson	Getty Gaskett Company	513-555-9345	
4	Linda	Cassidy	Ramtech International	206-555-3478	
5	Dennis	Lewis	Airplane Specialists	805-555-1492	
6	Rose	Stoner	Travis Corporation	805-555-1492	

Rows and Records

Each row of a database, other than the first row, is a record representing a single entry. The first row of a database must contain the names of each field, one per column. These *field names* are used to identify the fields in commands and functions. All rows after the first in a database are data records. They can be blank or contain a divider line, for example, but they are still considered data records. A database can contain a maximum of 16,383 records (one less than the number of rows in a worksheet).

Columns and Fields

Each column of a database is a field representing a common data element in all records. For example, the company name in Figure 2-13 is a field. Each field can contain a number, text, or a formula. A database can contain a

Figure 2-13.   *Parts of a database*

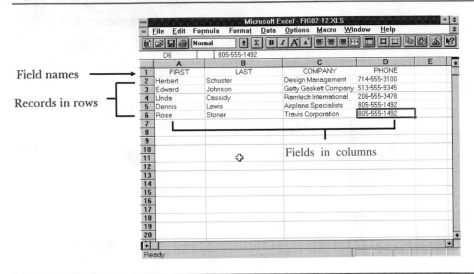

maximum of 256 fields, one for every column in a worksheet, but you cannot have two fields with the same field name in one database.

The parts of a database are shown in Figure 2-13.

Using Databases

You can use a database any time you need a list of items. Examples of databases, in addition to the phone list, are stocks in a portfolio with dates and prices, parts of a machine with the part number and supplier, salespeople with their quotas and commissions, and products with their prices and margins.

Within Excel there is a set of commands that let you manipulate databases. These commands are called *data commands* because they are all accessed through the Data menu shown here:

2

The primary functions of these commands are sorting databases, extracting information from them, and analyzing them. For example, you can sort the phone list by company, extract stocks that are performing below your expectations, find the machine parts from a given supplier, and analyze the change in sales commissions that would result from changes in quotas. Database-related commands and functions are explored in chapters 7 and 8.

Charts

If a picture is worth a thousand words, a chart is worth at least a thousand numbers. A chart allows you to give visual meaning to a set of numbers, to show the differences or similarities between them, and to show the patterns produced. Many people find they absorb information faster and easier from charts, or even that they see things in charts they do not see in the numbers that produce the charts.

An Excel chart is a pictorial representation of one or more ranges on a worksheet. If you have a range on a worksheet that contains company sales by month, you can produce a line chart that would make it easy to show fluctuations in monthly sales. Given ranges for expenses and earnings by month, you can produce additional lines on the same chart and tell not only if they are going up or down, but also show how any trends relate to each other. Figure 2-14 shows such a line chart.

Figure 2-14.   *A line chart of sales, expenses, and earnings*

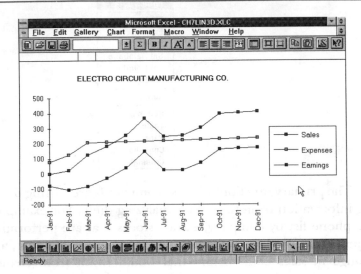

The three-dimensional pie chart shown in Figure 2-15 shows the proportion each product line contributes to total company sales by charting a range containing the sales by product. Given ranges containing sales by quarter for each of four regions, the chart shown in Figure 2-16 can be produced.

Excel provides eight two-dimensional types of charts: Area, Bar, Column, Line, Pie, Radar, Scatter, and Combination; and six three-dimensional types of charts: Area, Bar, Column, Line, Pie, and Surface; plus several alternatives for each type. As a result you have many ways to chart information on a worksheet.

To produce these charts, Excel provides a unique set of menus in the chart window opened with a new chart. Through these menus you select the type of chart you want to produce and identify the ranges on the worksheet that will generate it. You can add titles and annotations, as well as specify the color and fonts to be used. Charts can be named, saved, and printed on most printers. The production of charts is discussed in detail in Chapter 7.

Figure 2-15.   *A three-dimensional pie chart showing product contribution to sales*

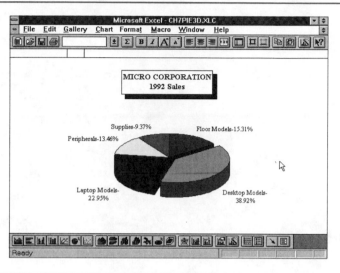

Figure 2-16.   *A two-dimensional bar chart of plant sales by quarter*

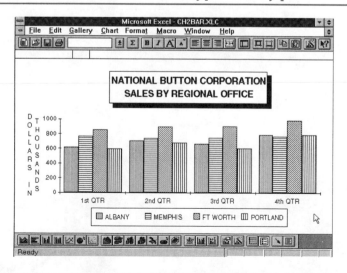

3

The Excel Environment

This chapter and the remainder of the book are written with the assumption that you follow along on your computer as you read. This allows you to see for yourself what a keystroke does and how the screen looks as a result. Most people find that they learn much faster by doing while reading than by reading alone.

To use Excel on your computer, you must first install Windows and then Excel. This process is discussed in Appendix A. If you have not installed Windows or Excel yet, turn to Appendix A and complete the installation, including the startup procedure. When you are done, you can return to this chapter.

If you have already installed Windows and Excel, start them now, following the procedure described in Appendix A.

Excel's Screen and Menus

When you first start Excel, after briefly seeing the Microsoft copyright message, you'll see a blank worksheet on your screen like the one shown in Figure 3-1. The worksheet screen contains two windows. On the outer perimeter of the screen is the Excel application window. This contains Excel's menus, the toolbar, the address of the currently active cell, the Formula bar, and the Status bar. Within the Excel window is a single worksheet document window. The worksheet window is the primary working area in Excel. The Excel application window may contain several worksheet windows as well as one or more chart, macro, and information document windows. The two primary windows, Excel and worksheet, are discussed in the following sections.

The Worksheet Window

Initially, Excel opens a single worksheet window. As you saw in Chapter 2, you can open additional worksheet windows as well as chart and other types

Figure 3-1.   *Blank worksheet screen*

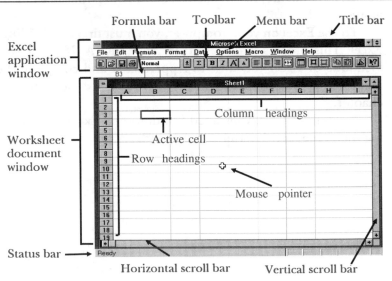

of windows. You use a single worksheet window most often and open other windows only for special purposes.

The worksheet window in which you are currently working is called the *active window.* You may have other worksheets open, but they are not active until you click the mouse on them or choose a different window from the Window menu. You can tell which worksheet is active because its Title bar and an active cell are highlighted. In Figure 3-2, Sheet2 is the active window.

A worksheet window provides the area for you to enter numbers, text, and formulas to build what you want. The worksheet's inherent structure—its rows and columns—allows you to enter and organize your work easily.

Rows and Columns

The blank worksheets in Figures 3-1 and 3-2 show the row and column nature of the worksheet: the row and column headings are across the top and down the left side, and the two-dimensional grid forms individual cells. The intersection of one row and one column, a *cell,* is where you enter numbers, text, or a formula. Only one cell at a time is active and available for entry or editing. You know which cell is active because it has a heavy border around

Figure 3-2.   *Sheet2 is the active window*

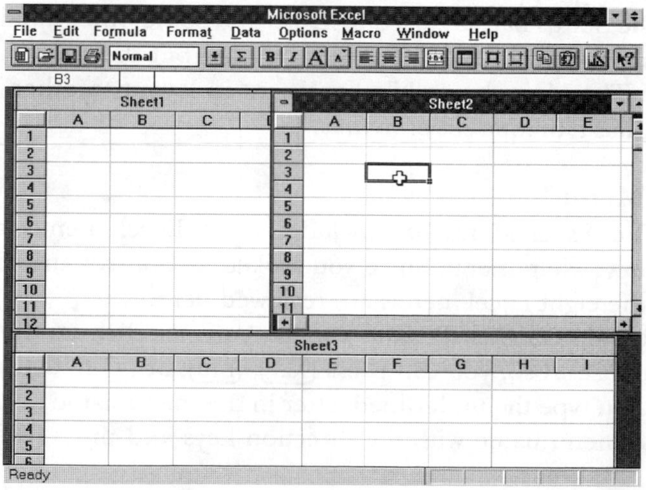

it. In Figure 3-1, cell B3 is active. This is the cell formed by the intersection of column B and row 3. Cell H3 of Sheet2 is active in Figure 3-2. The address of the active cell can be seen in the upper-left corner of the spreadsheet, just under the toolbar, in the reference area.

You can make a different cell active by either clicking on it with the mouse (moving the mouse pointer to the new cell and pressing the mouse button) or by using the direction keys on the right side of your keyboard to move the active cell border to the new cell. You will do that shortly.

By clicking on the scroll bars on the right and bottom of the worksheet window, or by using the direction keys, you can look at and work on other areas of the active worksheet. Compared to Excel's total potential area, the area actually displayed on your screen is quite small—20 out of 16,384 rows and 9 out of 256 columns (the number of rows and columns depends on your monitor and graphics card). Of course most applications in Excel also use only a small amount of the total area but often are larger than what you initially see on the screen.

The Excel Window

The Excel window contains five bars—four at the top and one at the bottom. The top two bars, the Title bar and the Menu bar, are common to all Windows applications. The other three bars, the toolbar, the Formula bar, and the Status bar, are used by Excel and some other applications. The Title bar is standard in Windows, with nothing but the name it contains to set it apart. The Menu bar, while consistent in layout to other Windows applications, has a unique set of menus.

The Menu Bar

The Excel Menu bar includes eight Excel menus and the standard Windows Help menu. Since you looked at Control and Help in Chapter 1, only the eight Excel menus are reviewed here.

Remember that to open a menu you can click on the menu name with the mouse. Also, you can press (ALT), (F10), or (/) to activate the Menu bar, and then type the underlined letter in the menu name or move the highlight to the menu name with the direction keys and press (ENTER). With a menu open you can look at another menu by either clicking on the menu name or by using the direction keys to move to the other menu. If you want to close a menu without choosing an option, you press (ESC).

File Menu   The File menu provides the means of creating new worksheets, charts, and macro sheets; opening existing worksheets, charts, and macro sheets stored on disk; and closing, saving, and deleting worksheets, charts, and macro sheets. The file menu allows you to save any combination of worksheets, charts, and macro sheets in a single document called a Workbook, to more easily organize and manage related information.

     The File menu also allows you to set up the page you will print, set up your printer, print a worksheet or chart, and exit Excel. Near the bottom of the menu, there is a list of the last four files you have used. If you would like to open one of these files, simply click on the one you want or type its number on the keyboard. The File menu is shown here:

Edit Menu   You use the Edit menu to copy, move, and clear (delete) the contents of a cell or range of cells; to undo or repeat the last thing you did; and to insert and delete rows and columns. The Fill options at the bottom of the menu allow you to quickly copy to a range of cells. The Edit menu is shown here:

Formula Menu   The Formula menu is used to build and maintain formulas. This includes creating, using, and deleting range names, adding functions, and switching between absolute and relative references. Also, through the Formula menu you can add notes to cells, go to a particular cell, find cells based on their contents, search and replace text, and select cells of a specified type. Finally, the Formula menu provides access to Excel's Outline, Goal Seek, Solver, and Scenario Manager functions. The Formula menu is shown here:

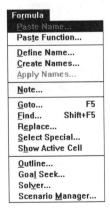

Format Menu   Through the Format menu you determine how a cell entry looks. If it contains a number, you can format it as dollars or percents, with or without commas, and set the number of decimal places. For both text and numbers you can left, right, or center align them in a cell; place a border around or shade them; protect a cell from being overwritten; and determine a cell's width and height.

Excel 4 introduces AutoFormat, an option which you can use to automatically format a selected range. The AutoFormat option provides 14 formatting styles within five categories: classic, financial, colorful, list, and 3-D effects. Each style has an example of how it will look. Autoformatting is discussed further in Chapter 6. Finally, with the Format menu, you can justify text in a range of cells and manipulate graphic and text objects placed on the worksheet. The Format menu is shown here:

Data Menu   The Data menu is used with databases to define them; to determine selection criteria; to find, extract, or delete selected records based on the criteria; to view and maintain them as a form instead of a table; and to sort them. The Data menu is also used to fill a range of cells with a series of numbers or dates, to create a table, to divide a text string into individual cells (that is, to *parse*), to consolidate several data ranges on one or multiple worksheets, and to quickly summarize data with crosstab data tables. The Data menu is shown here:

Options Menu   The Options menu is the catchall menu for options that do not fit in any other menu. It provides the means of specifying the area of the worksheet to be printed and to identify repeated titles on a printout. The Options menu also allows you to set manual page breaks, to determine how your screen will look, to select toolbars, to display a color palette, and to protect a document (worksheet, chart, or macro sheet) or window from being overwritten. New to Excel 4, the Options menu also provides the Add-ins feature, which shows current macro programs loaded into Excel and allows for macro programming additions and deletions. Additionally, you can set how Excel calculates a worksheet; force the recalculation of a worksheet at any time; change overall defaults, like the display of the Status bar, scroll bars, and Formula bar; and change the type of menu.

The Workspace option introduces another new feature with Excel 4, *drag and drop*. This allows you to copy and move the active cell contents with a mouse, without using a menu. When drag and drop is activated, the lower-right corner of the active cell will contain a small box. Point on the small box with the mouse pointer and the pointer will change as shown in Figure 3-3. As you drag the small box, the contents of the cell are copied to adjacent rows or columns. If you drag the active cell border instead of the small box while drag and drop is activated, you move the contents of the active cell to another cell location instead of copying it.

Finally, with the Options menu you can start a Spelling checker; make changes to a number of documents at a time; and access a number of analysis tools. The Options menu is shown here:

Macro Menu   The Macro menu is used to record and run macro functions. Macro functions, you remember, are Excel commands that have been stored on a macro sheet. The Macro menu allows you to record functions on the macro sheet as you carry out the related commands on a regular worksheet, to run a macro once it has been recorded, and to set several options for recording macros.

Figure 3-3.   *Mouse pointer changes when drag and drop is activated*

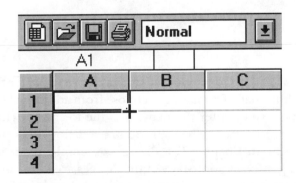

Here is the macro menu:

Window Menu   The Window menu allows you to open another window on the active worksheet, to arrange all open windows so they can be seen on the screen, to save a particular view of a worksheet by saving various display and print settings, and to hide or unhide a window. Additionally, you can split a worksheet into different size horizontal and vertical panes; freeze a pane so that, for example, column headings remain in place while the rest of the worksheet is scrolled; and enlarge or reduce a view of a worksheet. Finally, you can select from among open windows. The Window menu is shown here:

Dialog Boxes   Menu options with an ellipsis (...) after them require that you enter additional information or choose from additional options. For example, you may have to enter the name of a file to save or choose the type of cell alignment you want. When this occurs, a dialog box opens for this purpose. As you saw in Chapter 1, a dialog box employs one or more devices for collecting information. Many of the devices are illustrated in the Save As and Alignment dialog boxes shown in Figure 3-4 and the Font dialog box shown in Figure 3-5.

You will have many opportunities in the chapters that follow to become more familiar with Excel's menus and their related dialog boxes.

The Toolbar

The third bar down, the one under the Menu bar, is the toolbar. The Standard toolbar is shown in Figure 3-6.

A toolbar provides a number of tools and buttons to quickly do tasks that would take several steps with the menus, or could not be done at all. A toolbar

3

Figure 3-4.   *Save As and Alignment dialog boxes*

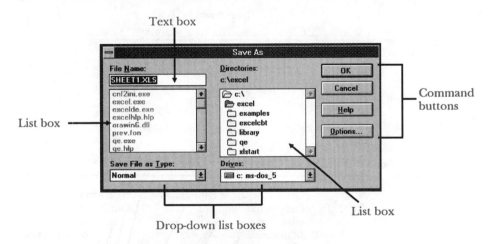

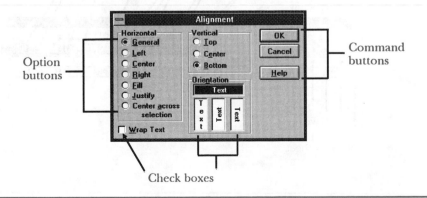

Figure 3-5.   *Font dialog box*

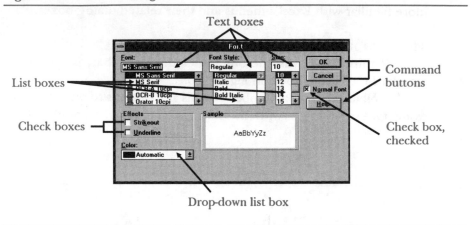

Figure 3-6.   *The Standard toolbar*

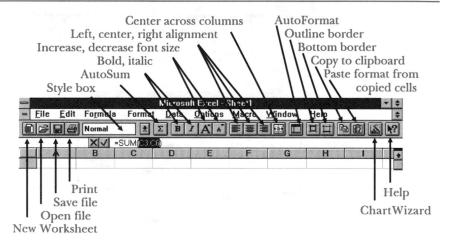

is used with a mouse, so if you don't have a mouse, you can turn off (Hide) the toolbar with the Options Toolbars option.

The nine toolbars provided by Excel 4 are: standard, formatting, utility, chart, drawing, Microsoft Excel 3.0, macro, macro recording, and macro pause. You can display one, none, or multiple toolbars, as you choose.

To select a toolbar different from the standard one, choose Toolbars from the Options menu; the Toolbars dialog box will appear. Alternately, you can open the Toolbars Shortcut menu by clicking on the toolbar with your right mouse button. The dialog box lists the nine available toolbars and provides a button to create customized toolbars.

A customized dialog box provides a list of tool categories and allows you to drag individual tools within each category, either to add to an existing toolbar, or place anywhere on the application sheet. Microsoft Excel provides over 130 tools; most tools are displayed in the nine toolbars, the remainder are displayed in the tools categories.

Toolbars can be moved, sized, and arranged to suit your individual needs. They provide a fast and flexible means to make working in Excel as efficient as possible. A complete listing of tools by toolbar can be found in Appendix B. The Standard toolbar tools and their functions are listed here:

Tool		Function
	New worksheet	Creates a new worksheet
	Open file	Allows you to open an existing document; displays the Open dialog box
	Save file	Saves the active document
	Print	Prints the active document
Normal	Style box	Selects and applies styles to selected cells or defines a new style based on the style of the selected cells

Tool		Function
Σ	AutoSum	Creates a SUM function in the active cell with a reference to the contiguous range of numbers either in the column above or in the row to the left
B I	Bold and italic	Applies or removes bold or italic type styles to selected cells
A▲	Increase font size	Increases the selected text by one font size
A▼	Decrease font size	Decreases the selected text by one font size
▤▤▤	Alignment	Applies left, center, or right alignment to selected cells
+a+	Center across columns	Horizontally centers text from one cell across selected columns
▥	AutoFormat	Applies cell formatting to ranges of cells
▢	Outline border	Applies a border around selected cells
▭	Bottom border	Applies a border on the bottom edge of selected cells
▤	Copy to Clipboard	Copies the selected range to the Clipboard

Tool		Function
	Paste format	Pastes the formatting of a copied range
	ChartWizard	Assists you in creating or editing charts
	Help	Changes the mouse pointer to a question mark. When clicked on a command or screen area, context-sensitive help is provided

The Formula Bar

Beneath Excel's toolbar is the Formula bar, which is shown in Figure 3-7. On the left side of the Formula bar is the *reference area*, which contains the address of the currently active cell on the worksheet. For example, when the cell address C7 is displayed, this tells you that the currently active cell is in the third column (column C) and the seventh row. While you are in the process of selecting a range of cells—C3:E4, for example—the reference area tells you the number of rows and columns being selected—2RX3C in the example, for 2 rows by 3 columns. The reference area also has some specialized uses with charts and during several operations. These are discussed later in this book with the related topics.

On the right side of the Formula bar is the *edit area*, where you enter and edit text, numbers, and formulas for the active cell. If you are entering or editing a cell's contents, two boxes appear to the right of the reference area: the Cancel box with an "X" in it and the Enter box with a check mark in it. Clicking on the Cancel box cancels any changes you made in the edit area and returns a cell's original contents. The Cancel box is similar to pressing (ESC). Clicking on the Enter box is like pressing (ENTER). It transfers the edited contents of the edit area to the active cell.

When you begin typing in an empty cell, the letters or numbers that you type go into both the cell itself and the edit area of the Formula bar. In many instances the cell is not wide enough to display all of what you type, but the edit area expands to the 255 maximum characters a cell can hold. After completing the entry and pressing (ENTER), the edit area still displays the cell's contents. If you move to another cell and then come back, the edit area again displays the cell's contents.

If you want to change or edit the contents of a cell, you do so in the edit area of the Formula bar. First make the cell you want to edit active by clicking on it or by using the direction keys. You then click on the Formula bar, or you can press the (F2) function key to activate the edit area. While you are entering or editing a cell's contents, a vertical line appears in the edit area, as shown in Figure 3-7. You'll remember from Chapter 1 that this line is called the insertion point. Characters you type are added to the immediate left of the insertion point. When the mouse pointer is in the edit area, it becomes an I-beam. The I-beam is thin enough to be inserted between characters in the edit area. By placing the I-beam between two characters and clicking, you move the insertion point to where you clicked. This allows you to insert new characters between existing characters.

While you are making an entry, what you see in the edit area and what you see in the cell are the same up to the cell width. Once you complete a formula entry, the formula is displayed in the edit area, while the cell displays the value resulting from the formula. If the entry is a number or text, it is displayed in both the Formula bar and the cell. Figure 3-7 shows a formula in the edit area.

Figure 3-7.   *Elements of the Formula bar*

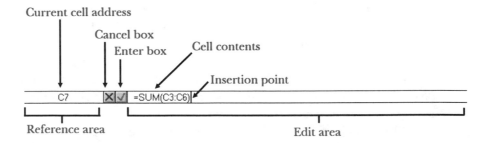

The Status Bar

The Status bar, at the bottom of the Excel window, displays messages on the left and up to six keyboard indicators on the right, as shown here:

Edit	EXT CAPS NUM SCRL OVR FIX

Message Area   The message area has several uses depending on what you are doing. If you highlight a menu name or a menu option, the message area displays a brief description of the menu or option. When you are using a dialog box or have an alert message on the screen, the message area tells you how to get help. At other times the message area serves as a mode indicator that tells you what Excel is doing. The most common mode is Ready, meaning that Excel is ready for you to make an entry or use a menu. The 12 other modes are shown with their meanings in the following table:

Mode	Meaning
Calculate	With manual calculation, this indicates that a change has been made to the worksheet and it needs to be recalculated.
Circular	A circular reference has been detected where, through whatever route, a cell is referencing itself. One of the cells in the circular path will be identified.
Copy	A copy operation has started, and a destination needs to be selected.
Cut	A cut operation has started, and a destination needs to be selected.
Edit	An entry is being edited in the Formula bar.
Enter	Data is being entered into the active cell.
Find	A database record matching the stated criteria has been found and is being highlighted.
Help	A help window is being displayed.
Point	You are being asked to highlight a cell or range for use in a formula.
Ready	Excel is ready for a command or entry.
Recording	The macro recorder is recording what you are doing with Excel.

3

Mode	Meaning
Split	A window is being split. Use the direction keys to complete it.

Keyboard Indicators   The keyboard indicators on the right of the Status bar tell you that a certain key has been pressed or that a certain condition exists. The status indicators and their meanings are as follows:

Indicator	Meaning
ADD	The Add key, (SHIFT)-(F8), has been pressed to make multiple selections.
CAPS	(CAPS LOCK) has been pressed for uppercase letters.
END	The (END) key has been pressed. When an arrow key is pressed, the active cell will go to the last occupied cell in the direction of the arrow.
EXT	The Extend key, (F8), has been pressed to extend a selection.
FIX	The Fixed Decimal option has been chosen from Options Workspace. This adds a fixed number of decimal places on all numeric entries, similar to an adding machine.
MI	The Macro Interpreter has been started.
NUM	The (NUM LOCK) key has been pressed, enabling the numeric keypad to be used for the entry of numbers.
OVR	The (INSERT) key has been pressed while a cell is being edited, turning on overtype mode instead of the normal insert mode.
SCRL	The (SCROLL LOCK) key has been pressed, causing the direction keys to move the entire worksheet instead of just the active cell.

Excel's Use of the Keyboard

You may find looking at the screen interesting, but to accomplish anything you must use the mouse and the keyboard. Excel's use of the mouse is fairly straightforward and is covered in Chapter 2. This section covers how Excel uses the special-purpose keys surrounding the typewriter keyboard.

Most keyboards can be divided into three areas. On the left or along the top are a set of function keys, (F1) through (F10) or (F12). You use these keys to give Excel commands, such as to recalculate the worksheet or display a help screen. In the center of all keyboards are the normal typewriter keys, and on the far right of most keyboards is a set of direction keys, either superimposed on or separate from the numerical keypad. The direction keys can move the active cell around the worksheet and the highlight bar down a menu. These three regions of the keyboard are discussed in the following sections.

3

Direction Keys

Eight keys comprise the direction keys: the four arrow keys (DOWN ARROW), (LEFT ARROW), (RIGHT ARROW), and (UP ARROW) plus (HOME), (END), (PGUP), and (PGDN). These keys, either alone or in combination with (CTRL) and (SHIFT) on the typewriter keyboard, can move you quickly and easily anywhere on the worksheet. Also, the same keys can move you within the menus and dialog boxes and within the Formula bar for cell editing. With the mouse, the use of the direction keys is not as important as it might be otherwise. Nevertheless it is important to understand how the direction keys can be used.

The direction keys have a two-dimensional task in moving the active cell vertically (up or down a column) and horizontally (left or right along a row). Excel has ways to do this one cell at a time, one screen at a time, to the beginning or end of contiguously occupied cells, or to the first or last cell in an active worksheet.

Using Direction Keys on a Worksheet

The easiest way to learn about the direction keys is to use them. Try them now with the following instructions. Your computer should be turned on, Excel should be loaded (see Appendix A if not), and you should be looking at the blank worksheet screen shown in Figure 3-1, with cell A1 selected as the active cell. If your Scroll Lock light is on, press (SCROLL LOCK) to turn it off.

Moving One Cell at a Time   The simplest way to move about the work-sheet is to go cell to cell. The four arrow keys perform this task, as shown with the following instructions:

1. Press (RIGHT ARROW). The active cell moves one cell to the right, to cell B1.

2. Press (DOWN ARROW). The active cell moves down one cell, to cell B2.

3. Press (LEFT ARROW). The active cell moves one cell to the left, to cell A2.

4. Press (UP ARROW). The active cell moves up one cell, to cell A1—where you started from.

The four arrow keys are the most heavily used of the direction keys. Their function is to move you one cell in any direction, as you saw in the one-cell square you just made.

Moving One Screen at a Time   Moving one cell at a time can be slow if you have very far to go. The next set of direction keys move you a screen at a time. (Depending on the type of display and display adapter you have and the mode you are running them in, one "screen" may be different than that described here—it may be larger or smaller.) Make a larger square now with these keys.

1. Press (PGDN). The active cell and the portion of the worksheet shown in the window moves down one window height to the first cell in column A beyond that originally shown—cell A20 (depending on the type of monitor you have, you may go to a different row).

2. Press (CTRL)-(PGDN) (press and hold (CTRL) while pressing (PGDN)). The active cell and the portion of the worksheet shown in the window move to the right one window width to the first cell in row 20—cell J20 (again, yours may be different).

3. Press (PGUP). The active cell and the portion of the worksheet shown in the window moves up one window height to cell J1.

4. Press (CTRL)-(PGUP) (press and hold (CTRL) while pressing (PGUP)). The active cell and the portion of the worksheet shown in the window moves to the left one window width to cell A1.

You have completed another square, one window high and one window wide. (PGDN) and (PGUP) are used frequently, but (CTRL)-(PGDN) and (CTRL)-(PGUP) are forgotten by many people.

Moving Around the Periphery of the Active Worksheet   The set of keystrokes used to move around the periphery of the active worksheet requires that you first enter some information on the worksheet to establish what is "active." Simply type the information in one cell using the typewriter keyboard, and then press one of the arrow keys to go to the next cell. You can then use a set of direction keys to move around the periphery of the worksheet. Try that now.

1. Type **a** and press (RIGHT ARROW). The letter "a" is placed in cell A1, and the active cell moves to B1.

2. Do the *combination* of typing **a** and pressing (RIGHT ARROW) six more times. The final active cell is H1.

3. Type **a** and press (DOWN ARROW) The letter "a" is placed in cell H1, and the active cell moves to H2.

4. Do the combination of typing **a** and pressing (DOWN ARROW) nine more times. The final active cell is H11. Your screen should look like Figure 3-8. Now use the direction keys to jump around the information you just entered.

Figure 3-8.   *Screen after entries*

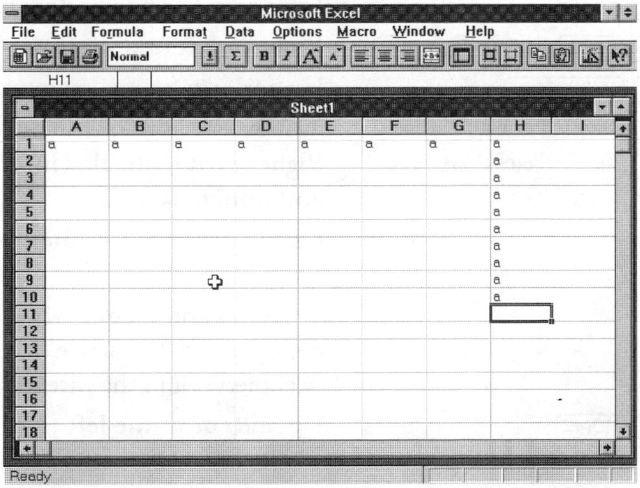

5. Press (HOME). The active cell jumps to cell A11.

6. Press (UP ARROW), (END), and (LEFT ARROW). The active cell jumps to H10.

7. Press (CTRL)-(UP ARROW). The active cell jumps to cell H1.

8. Press (CTRL)-(LEFT ARROW). The active cell jumps to cell A1.

9. Press (CTRL)-(RIGHT ARROW). The active cell jumps to cell H1.

10. Press (CTRL)-(DOWN ARROW). The active cell jumps to cell H10.

11. Press (CTRL)-(HOME). The active cell jumps to cell A1.

12. Press (CTRL)-(END). The active cell jumps to cell H10.

13. Press (CTRL)-(HOME). The active cell returns to cell A1.

The (CTRL) plus direction key combinations are not only very powerful but also extremely useful. You will use them often if you do not have a mouse.

Direction Key Summary

The following table summarizes the direction keys:

Key	Moves the Active Cell
(RIGHT ARROW) or (LEFT ARROW)	Right or left one column
(UP ARROW) or (DOWN ARROW)	Up or down one row
(PGUP) or (PGDN)	Up or down one window height
(CTRL)-(PGDN) or (CTRL)-(PGUP)	Right or left one window width
(CTRL)-(UP ARROW) or (CTRL)-(DOWN ARROW)	Up or down to the first intersection of blank and nonblank cells
(CTRL)-(RIGHT ARROW) or (CTRL)-(LEFT ARROW)	Right or left to the first intersection of blank and nonblank cells
(HOME)	Left to column A in the row with the active cell
(END)	Turns on end mode. When a direction key is next pressed, the active cell moves to the last occupied cell in the direction of the arrow
(CTRL)-(HOME)	Up and/or to the left to cell A1

CTRL-END   Down and/or to the right to the lowest and
                                            rightmost occupied cell

Function Keys

The function keys (F1) through (F10) or (F12) are located on the top or left
of most keyboards. With function keys you can give Excel special commands
using one or several keystrokes (when you press the key itself, or press and
hold (SHIFT), (CTRL), or (ALT) while pressing a function key). Many of the
commands performed by the function keys are used only in certain circumstances and are not easy to demonstrate here. Try several that can be easily
demonstrated now with the instructions that follow. You will use many of the
others later in the book. Following the instructions is a table that summarizes
each function key.

Using Function Keys

The following instructions assume that you are picking up where you left
off in the previous section. The active cell is A1, and the worksheet is the one
in which you entered the "a"s. Excel is in ready mode. Also, from your
previous work, cell A1 should contain the letter "a." If you do not have an "a"
in A1, type it now and press (ENTER).

1. Press (F1) (Help). A help window opens with the Help Contents
   screen shown in Figure 3-9. From this window you can select subjects
   on which to get help.

2. Double-click on the help window Control-menu box or press (ALT)-
   (SPACEBAR) and type **c** to return to the worksheet. A1 is still the active
   cell.

3. Press (F2) (Edit). The letter "a" appears in the edit area of the
   Formula bar, with the insertion point just to the right of the letter.

4. Press (BACKSPACE). The "a" is removed.

5. Type **b** and press (ENTER). Excel is returned to ready mode, and "b"
   replaces "a" in cell A1.

6. Press (ALT)-(BACKSPACE) (Undo). The contents of cell A1 are again "a."

3

7. Press (F5) (Goto). A dialog box appears, asking for the address to jump to.

8. Type **e14** and press (ENTER). The active cell jumps to cell E14.

9. Press (CTRL)-(HOME). The active cell returns to cell A1.

10. Press (F12) (Save As) or (ALT)-(F2) if you have only ten function keys. The File Save As dialog box opens.

11. Type **ch3** (for Chapter 3) and press (ENTER) to save the active worksheet with the filename CH3.XLS (the .XLS extension is automatically added by Excel).

12. Press (SHIFT)-(F11) (New Worksheet) or (ALT)-(SHIFT)-(F1) if you have only ten function keys. A new worksheet opens, probably entitled Sheet2.

Both (F2) (Edit) and (F5) (Goto) will get increasingly heavy use as you learn Excel. Also useful, although not a function key, is (ALT)-(BACKSPACE) (Undo). The Undo command reverses many commands if they were the last thing you did. You can even undo an undo. Note that Undo *cannot* undo File and Data commands, especially File Delete, Data Delete, or Data Extract.

Figure 3-9.   *Help Contents screen*

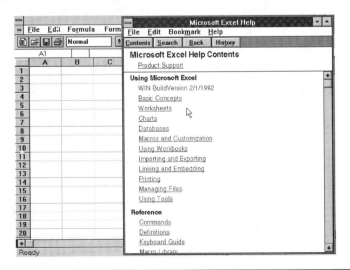

Several function keys are shortcut keys for menu options. For example, (F3) is the Formula menu Paste Name option, (F4) is the Formula menu Reference option, and (F12) is the File menu Save As option.

Function Key Summary

The following table provides a summary of the function performed by each function key. The keys are discussed further with the particular subject to which they apply. For example, (F11) (New Chart) is discussed in Chapter 7 with charting.

Key	Name	Function
(F1)	Help	Opens a help window
(SHIFT)-(F1)		Displays context-sensitive help
(ALT)-(F1)	New	Creates a new chart window
(ALT)-(SHIFT)-(F1)		Creates a new worksheet window
(ALT)-(CTRL)-(F1)		Creates a new macro sheet window
(F2)	Edit	Activates the Formula bar for editing
(SHIFT)-(F2)	Note	Allows entering, editing, or deleting a note that is to be attached to the active cell
(CTRL)-(F2)	Info	Displays a window containing information about the active cell
(ALT)-(F2)	Save	Opens the File Save As dialog box
(ALT)-(SHIFT)-(F2)		Saves the active document
(ALT)-(CTRL)-(F2)		Opens the File Open dialog box
(ALT)-(CTRL)-(SHIFT)-(F2)		Opens the File Print dialog box
(F3)	Name	Opens the Formula Paste Name dialog box
(SHIFT)-(F3)		Opens the Formula Paste Function dialog box
(CTRL)-(F3)		Opens the Formula Define Name dialog box
(CTRL)-(SHIFT)-(F3)		Opens the Formula Create Name dialog box

3

Key	Name	Function
(F4)	Absolute	Makes a cell address or range name absolute, mixed, or relative
(CTRL)-(F4)	Close	Closes the active document window
(ALT)-(F4)		Closes the application window (Excel)
(F5)	Goto	Moves the active cell to the cell address, range name, or file entered
(SHIFT)-(F5)	Find	Opens the Formula Find dialog box
(CTRL)-(F5)	Restore	Restores the size of the active document window
(F6)	Pane	Moves the active cell clockwise to the next pane
(SHIFT)-(F6)		Moves the active cell counter-clockwise to the previous pane
(CTRL)-(F6)	Window	Moves the active cell to the next document window
(CTRL)-(SHIFT)-(F6)		Moves the active cell to the previous document window
(F7)	Next	Finds the next cell matching the specified contents
(SHIFT)-(F7)	Previous	Finds the previous cell matching the specified contents
(CTRL)-(F7)	Move	Sets up the active document window to be moved with the direction keys
(F8)	Extend	Toggles the extension of the current selection
(SHIFT)-(F8)	Add	Allows adding to the current selection
(CTRL)-(F8)	Size	Sets up the active document window to be sized with the direction keys
(F9)	Calculate	Recalculates all open documents

Key	Name	Function
(SHIFT)-(F9)		Recalculates the active document
(F10)	Menu	Activates the menu bar
(CTRL)-(F10)	Maximize	Maximizes the active document window
(F11)	New	Creates a new chart window
(SHIFT)-(F11)		Creates a new worksheet window
(CTRL)-(F11)		Creates a new macro sheet window
(F12)	Save	Opens the File Save As dialog box
(SHIFT)-(F12)		Saves the active document
(CTRL)-(F12)	Open	Opens the File Open dialog box
(CTRL)-(SHIFT)-(F12)	Print	Opens the File Print dialog box

Alternate Keys Similar to 1-2-3

With Excel 4 you can choose to use a set of alternate keystrokes that are similar to those used by 1-2-3. This choice can be made either at the time of installation of Excel or by clicking on the Alternate Navigation Keys check box in the Options Workspace dialog box. The use of alternate keystrokes can be turned off by clicking again on the Alternate Navigation Keys check box. The alternate keystrokes, their functions, and the normal Excel key-strokes for the same functions are as follows:

Alternate Key	Function	Normal Key
(CTRL)-(LEFT ARROW)	Left one window width	(CTRL)-(PGUP)
(CTRL)-(RIGHT ARROW)	Right one window width	(CTRL)-(PGDN)
(HOME)	Up and/or to the left to cell A1	(CTRL)-(HOME)
(END)-arrow keys	First intersection of blank/nonblank cells	(CTRL)-arrow keys or (END)-arrow keys

For further assistance, the Introducing Microsoft Excel option of the Help menu has a tutorial that helps 1-2-3 users switch to Excel.

Quitting Excel

You are done with Excel for this chapter. Use the following instructions to leave it:

1. Double-click (click twice in rapid succession) on the Excel Control-menu box in the upper-left corner of the Excel application window. (From the keyboard, press (ALT)-(SPACEBAR)-(C).)

2. Click on No (or type **n**) to not save the worksheet again. You return to the Windows Program Manager window.

3. If your Program Manager is an icon, restore it and double-click on the Program Manager's Control-menu box, and click on OK to end the Windows session. You will return to DOS.

4. If you desire, you can now shut off your computer following your normal shutdown procedure.

4

Entering and Editing Information

In several examples in Chapter 3, you practiced entering and editing information. Entering text and numbers is a simple matter of typing what you want in each cell. You can edit as you type or, after you have completed the entry, you can come back and edit it. These operations are more subtle than they first appear, however, and their considerable power demands further study.

Typing on the Worksheet

All information that you type on a worksheet is stored in cells. While there are a lot of cells, each cell can hold only 255 characters. The normal practice is to place only a single number or a short text string (usually much smaller than 255 characters) in a cell and spread most of the information over many cells, using the row and column structure to organize it.

A cell on a worksheet can hold either a number or text, but not both. You therefore must decide what a cell will contain before you make an entry. If you decide an entry is text, you must then decide if it will be left, right, or center aligned in the cell. If an entry is a number, you must not only decide alignment but also formatting, such as dollars, percents, and dates. Finally, when you complete an entry, you must determine what you want to do next so you can move the active cell to accomplish that.

Entering Text Versus Numbers

Whether you enter numbers (including dates, times, and formulas) or text (letters as well as numbers) depends on what you type. If your entry contains only numbers or these numeric symbols

    + - = . , ( ) % $ E e / :

then the entry is a number. If the entry contains anything other than a number or numeric symbol, or the symbols are not in the proper context, the entry is text. For example, if you start an entry with the letter "E", Excel will interpret the entry as text, whereas "1.25E + 2" will be considered a number since the letter "E" is a numeric scientific notation symbol.

General Alignment

When Excel recognizes that text is being typed, it automatically left aligns the text in the cell (meaning that it pushes text up against the left side of the cell). When you enter a number, Excel automatically right aligns it in the cell (pushes it up against the right side). This default alignment—left-aligned text and right-aligned numbers—is called *general alignment*. General alignment also aligns logical values (TRUE or FALSE) and error values (#NUM!, for example) in the center of a cell. With either the Format or Shortcut menu **Alignment** option you can align text, numbers, and logical or error values on the left, in the center, or on the right as you choose. You can also change the horizontal or vertical alignment of your cell contents, or even change the orientation of how your data is displayed.

Figure 4-1 shows some of the various types of alignment.

Typing Text

Try entering some text now, following these instructions:

1. Load Windows and Excel as discussed in Appendix A. A blank worksheet should appear on the screen. (If you still have the work you did in Chapter 3 on your screen, double-click on the worksheet's (not Excel's) Control-menu box to close the worksheet. Then from the File menu choose New and click on OK to create a new worksheet.)

2. Type **This is some text.** As you type you will see the letters go into the edit area of the Formula bar as well as into cell A1. If you make

Figure 4-1. *Types of alignment*

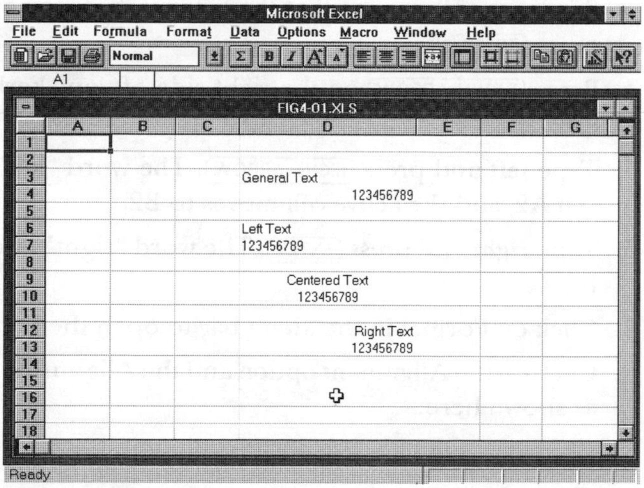

a mistake, press (BACKSPACE) to correct it. The top of your screen should look like this:

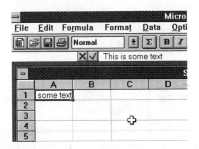

Notice that the text is in both the edit area and cell A1. You can see only the last two words in the cell. Also notice the blinking line in the edit area. This is the insertion point.

3. Press (ENTER). The edit area is deactivated (the insertion point, Cancel box, and Enter box disappear). Also, the text in A1 adjusts itself so you can see it all, although it does not fit completely in a single cell. The active cell remains in A1.

   If your active cell moves to A2, then the Move Selection after Enter setting has been changed in the Options Workspace dialog box. It's your choice whether or not to change this back to the default, but this book will assume that the active cell does not move when you press (ENTER).

4. Press (DOWN ARROW) on the right side of your keyboard. The active cell moves to A2.

5. Type **left** and press (RIGHT ARROW). The word "left" is left aligned in cell A2, and the active cell moves to B2.

6. Type **right** and press (ENTER). The word "right" also is left aligned in B2.

7. Click on Format in the Menu bar to open the Format menu.

8. Click on the Alignment option and the Alignment dialog box opens, as shown here:

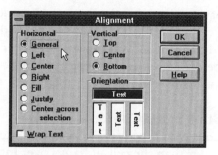

4

9. Click on Right in the dialog box and then click on OK to close the dialog box. The word "right" in cell B2 is right aligned. Press (RIGHT ARROW) to move to C2.

10. Type **center** and press (ENTER). Click on the Center tool in the toolbar, as shown here:

The word "center" is centered in C2. Press (RIGHT ARROW) to move the active cell to D2.

11. Type = and press (ENTER). Move the mouse pointer to the cell area of the worksheet and click the right mouse button to get the Shortcut menu. Click on Alignment, Fill, and OK. The = is repeated to fill D2, less one space. Press (RIGHT ARROW).

12. Type **555-1234** and press (RIGHT ARROW). Cell E2 contains a left-aligned text string in the format of a phone number.

13. Type **=555-1234** and press (ENTER). The equal sign turns this into a formula, and the cell contains the number -679 (the results of 555 minus 1234). In other words, to make this a number you must tell Excel it is a formula.

Your screen should now look like Figure 4-2. The contents of F2 look different in the edit area and in the cell. Unless you or someone else changed the default, the text in A1 is left aligned, as shown in the figure. You did not align it; it is left aligned because of Excel's general alignment default.

You may have noticed that the Format Alignment option is cumbersome. The new Shortcut menu and the Left, Center, and Right tools in the toolbar help this considerably. Also, you can align a larger range of text by highlighting the range before selecting the Alignment option from either the Shortcut or Format menu, or by clicking on an Alignment tool.

Column Width Versus Contents Width

The first entry you typed in the previous exercise, shown in cell A1 in Figure 4-2, is wider than the cell—it hangs over into cell B1. Because there is nothing in B1, the full text from A1 is displayed. If you enter something in B1, the text in A1 would appear truncated, based on the width of column A. Try that now:

1. Press (CTRL)-(HOME) (RIGHT ARROW). The active cell moves to B1.

2. Type **new text** and press (ENTER). The words "new text" fill B1 and, on the screen, truncate the text from A1. The full original entry is still in A1; you just can't see it all.

Figure 4-2.   *Text entries*

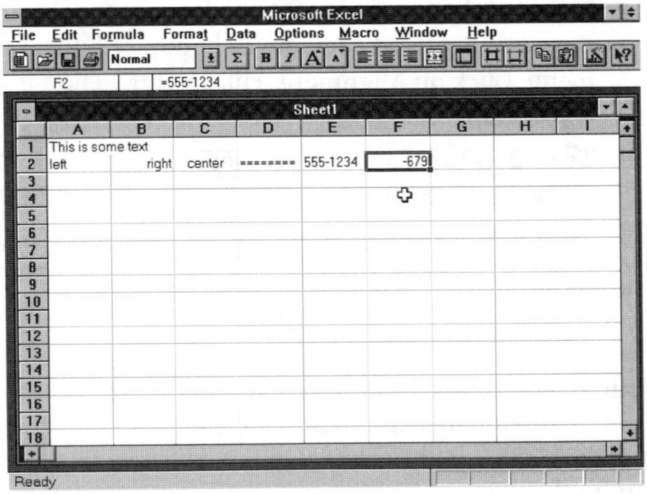

The top portion of your screen should look like this:

The width of a worksheet area is considered in terms of column width, not cell width. You cannot adjust the width of an individual cell, only the width of the column that contains the cell. In Chapter 5 you will see how to change the width of both individual columns and a range of columns.

Entering Numbers

Excel gives you a lot of flexibility in entering numbers. You can enter numbers with commas, dollar signs, percents, and scientific notation. Excel converts your entry into a number with up to 15 significant places. You can then format the cell to display the number in any way you choose, no matter how you entered it.

Try entering several numbers now:

1. Press (HOME) and then press (DOWN ARROW) four times. The active cell moves to A5.

2. Type **1,234,567**. The number appears in the edit area.

3. Press (DOWN ARROW). The number disappears from the edit area, and 1,234,567 appears in A5. If you added another digit to 1,234,567 (for example, 1,234,567.8) it would be too wide to fit in the standard column width. The cell would fill with a series of number signs (#). The edit area would display the full number, with the exception of the commas. Unlike text, numbers do not hang over the adjacent cell when they are too big for the column they are in. The column must be widened for the number to show.

4. Type **3.25** and press (RIGHT ARROW). The number 3.25 appears in A6 as entered.

5. Type **$3.25** and press (RIGHT ARROW). The number $3.25 appears in
   B6.

6. Type **3.25%** and press (RIGHT ARROW). The number 3.25% appears in
   C6.

7. Type **3 1/4** and press (RIGHT ARROW). The number 3 1/4 appears in
   D6.

8. Type **32.5E-1** and press (RIGHT ARROW). The number 3.25E+00 appears in E6.

9. Type **=e6** and press (ENTER). The number 3.25E+00 appears in F6.
   You entered a formula by placing = in front of a cell reference, and
   you used it to pick up the contents of cell E6 in cell F6.

Figure 4-3 shows how your screen should look when you have completed
these entries.

Being able to enter commas, dollar signs, percents, and fractions is an
important capability, even if you must change them later. When you enter

Figure 4-3.   *Text and numbers on the worksheet*

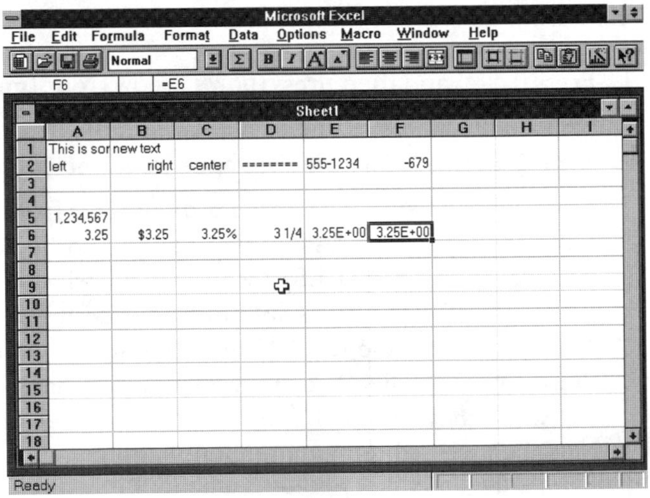

numbers that you are copying from a source that has dollar signs, commas, and so on, without thinking you may type the symbols as well as the numbers. In some worksheet packages you would get an error with such an entry. Excel gives you the flexibility to enter numbers with or without symbols.

Using the Numeric Keypad

While you were not given directions to that effect, it is likely that you entered the numbers in the previous exercise using the numeric keys at the top of the typewriter keyboard. Unless you are using a laptop or notebook computer, you also have a numeric keypad on the right of your keyboard. The numeric keypad performs two functions: movement of the active cell when (NUM LOCK) is off and numeric entry when (NUM LOCK) is on. The (NUM LOCK) key is at the top of the numeric keypad. Most keyboards have a light to tell you if it is on or off, and Excel has a status indicator, NUM, that appears at the bottom of the window to tell you when (NUM LOCK) is on.

When (NUM LOCK) is on, the numeric keypad can be used for numeric entry like a 10-key adding machine. The direction keys on the numeric keypad are no longer available when (NUM LOCK) is on, unless you press and hold down (SHIFT) while pressing a direction key. Enhanced keyboards have a set of direction keys, separate from the numeric keypad, that can be used at any time. Throughout your work with Excel, you may use either set of keys for numeric entry without affecting the results.

Fixing the Number of Decimal Digits

If you are experienced using a 10-key adding machine or calculator and like the ability to enter numbers with a fixed number of decimal digits without typing the decimal point, you can do that with Excel. To set up a fixed number of decimal digits, follow these steps:

1. Select the Options menu and choose Workspace.

2. Click on the Fixed Decimal check box. An "X" appears in the box.

3. If you want to change the number of decimal digits, press (TAB) to move the highlight to the Places text box and type the number you want to use. Your Workspace dialog box should look like that shown in the following illustration:

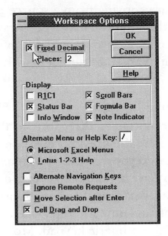

4. Click on OK to close the dialog box and return to the worksheet.

Remember that when you turn on this setting you have a fixed number of decimal digits in every number you type. Typing **6** gives you .06, and typing **3500** gives you 35. Excel remembers this the next time you start it up—it is a permanent setting until you turn it off. There is a status indicator, FIX, that appears in the Status bar to remind you that you have fixed the number of decimal digits.

Completing an Entry and Moving to the Next Cell

As you saw in the previous examples, you can complete an entry either by pressing (ENTER) or by pressing one of the direction keys, depending on where you want to go next. If you use (ENTER), the active cell remains the cell in which you made the entry (unless you change a setting in Options Workspace). After using (ENTER) you can then use one of the direction keys to move where you wish. If you want to go directly to another cell, you can save one keystroke by pressing a direction key to complete the entry.

You are not limited to the arrow keys. You can complete an entry using (HOME) (END), or even (PGUP) (PGDN) (CTRL)-(PGUP), or (CTRL)-(PGDN)—it just depends on where you want to go next.

Making Changes

Making changes to the information you are entering or have entered into Excel is a task at least equal to making the initial entry. One of the beauties of an electronic worksheet is that changes can be made easily and often. You can make changes in four ways. First, you can replace a completed entry in a cell by typing over the original entry. The original entry disappears and the new entry takes its place. Second, you can edit an entry as you are entering it. Third, immediately after completing an entry you can remove it and restore the previous contents of the cell by pressing the Undo key, (ALT)-(BACKSPACE), or by choosing Undo from the Edit menu. Fourth, you can edit a completed entry by pressing the (F2) key. The next several sections explore the last three of these methods.

Editing During Entry

Editing during entry has a simple mode that uses the (BACKSPACE) or (ESC) key and an edit mode using the (F2) (Edit) key. In the simple mode you press (BACKSPACE) to erase one or more characters to the left of the insertion point, or you press (ESC) to erase the entire entry. After pressing one of these keys, you can continue to type the corrected or new entry. When you press (F2) (Edit) the mode indicator in the Status bar becomes EDIT, and you have full use of the edit keys. The edit mode of editing is the same during and after entry, so it is explained in the "Editing After Entry" section coming up shortly. Now try simple mode editing:

1. Select the File menu, choose New, and click on OK to create a new worksheet.

2. Type **Spring 91**. Spring 91 appears in the edit area.

3. Press (BACKSPACE) and type **2**. Spring 91 changes to Spring 92 in the edit area.

4. Press (ESC) and type **Fall 91**. Spring 92 changes to Fall 91 in the edit area.

5. Press (ENTER). The edit area closes and Fall 91 is the final contents of cell A1.

Simple mode editing is just that, simple. You will use it constantly to correct the many small errors made during data entry.

Using Undo

The Undo option from either the Edit menu or from its shortcut keys (ALT)-(BACKSPACE) is a great lifesaver. It lets you remove the last thing you did and restore the worksheet to the way it was before you did it. The definition of "the last thing you did" is usually whatever happened between two ready modes, but there are exceptions. Two important things you cannot undo are File Delete and Data Delete. Also, you cannot undo a file operation, and you cannot undo the effect of recalculating the worksheet. You can undo an Undo. When you are editing, you can use Undo to reverse the last change you made to a cell. Try that now:

1. Make sure the active cell is still the cell in which you last entered Fall 91.

2. Type **Spring 92** and press (ENTER). Spring 92 replaces Fall 91 in A1.

3. Press (ALT)-(BACKSPACE) (Undo). Fall 91 is restored in A1.

When you make a mistake that requires retyping, immediately choose Undo from the Edit menu, or press (ALT)-(BACKSPACE) (Undo) and see if it restores the worksheet to its condition before the mistake. It cannot make the situation worse.

Editing After Entry

To edit a cell entry after it is completed, highlight the cell and press (F2) (Edit). The edit mode indicator is displayed, and the cell entry is moved to the edit area with the insertion point blinking on the right of the entry. The (LEFT ARROW), (RIGHT ARROW), (HOME), and (END) keys all move the pointer within the entry so that individual characters can be changed. Pressing (BACKSPACE) removes the character to the left of the insertion point, and (DEL) removes the character to the right of the insertion point. Also, you can press (INS) to switch from *insert mode*, which pushes existing characters to the right of new characters, to *overtype mode*, which replaces existing characters with new ones at the insertion point. Try editing now:

1. Make sure the active cell still contains Fall 91.

2. Press (F2) (Edit). The edit area is activated (the Cancel box, Enter box, and insertion point appear) with the insertion point to the right of 91.

3. Press (HOME). The insertion point moves to the left of Fall.

4. Type **Summer/**. The entry becomes Summer/Fall 91.

5. Press (LEFT ARROW) four times. The insertion point is between the two "m"s in Summer.

6. Press (INS). The OVR mode indicator is displayed in the Status bar.

7. Type **.** (period). The . replaces the second "m" in Summer.

8. Press (DEL) twice. The "e" and "r" are removed from Summer.

9. Press (END) and then (LEFT ARROW) three times. The insertion point moves to the right of the second "l" in Fall.

10. Press (INS). The OVR mode indicator is removed, and Excel returns to insert mode.

11. Type **/Win.**. The entry now reads Sum./Fall/Win. 91.

12. Press (END). The insertion point moves to the right end of the entry.

13. Type **/92**. /92 is added to the right end of the entry. The top part of your screen should look like this:

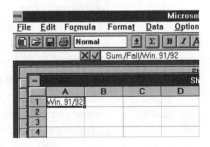

14. Press (ENTER). The edit area closes and A1 reflects the final entry. Unlike in enter mode, where you can press a direction key to finish editing a cell and move to a new cell, edit mode requires you to press (ENTER) and then press a direction key to move to another cell.

Edit Keys

The functions of the keys you can use while editing are summarized here:

Key	Function
(BACKSPACE)	Deletes the character to the left of the insertion point
(CTRL)-(LEFT ARROW) or (CTRL)-(RIGHT ARROW)	Moves the insertion point one word to the left or right in the entry
(CTRL)-(DEL)	Deletes text from the insertion point to the end of the current line
(CTRL)-(END)	Moves the insertion point to the right of the last character in the edit area
(CTRL)-(HOME)	Moves the insertion point to the left of the first character in the edit area
(CTRL)-(')	Inserts the formula in the cell above the active cell at the insertion point
(CTRL)-(")	Inserts the value in the cell above the active cell at the insertion point
(CTRL)-(;)	Inserts the current date in your computer at the insertion point
(CTRL)-(:)	Inserts the current time in your computer at the insertion point
(DEL)	Deletes the character to the right of the insertion point
(END)	Moves the insertion point to the right end of the current line of the entry
(ENTER)	Completes editing, closing the edit area, and leaving the active cell where it was originally
(ESC)	Cancels any changes made during editing, closes the edit area, and returns the original contents to the active cell

Key	Function
(F2)	Activates the edit area so you can do a character-by-character edit on the active cell
(HOME)	Moves the insertion point to the left end of the current line of the entry
(INS)	Switches between insert mode, in which newly typed characters push existing characters to the right, and overtype mode, in which newly typed characters replace existing characters
(LEFT ARROW) or (RIGHT ARROW)	Moves the insertion point one character to the left or right in the entry
(UP ARROW) or (DOWN ARROW)	Moves the insertion point between lines in the edit area if the entry occupies more than one line; otherwise does nothing

Editing with the Mouse

Editing with the keyboard is effective and often preferred if you are doing a lot of typing. However, the mouse has two benefits: you can jump immediately to the characters you want to change by clicking on the spot, and you can easily highlight characters to be deleted or otherwise changed by dragging across them. These benefits often make it worthwhile to take your hands off the keyboard to use the mouse. Try it now:

1. The worksheet that you have on your screen should have Sum./Fall/Win. 91/92 in cell A1.

2. Click on E12. The active cell moves to E12.
   Assume that you want to edit cell A1. If it were not in the home position, it would take at least two keystrokes to get there. With the mouse, it only takes one movement.

3. Click on A1. The active cell moves to A1.

4. Drag across Sum./ in the edit area. (Place the mouse pointer on the "S" in Sum in the edit area, not in cell A1. Press and hold the mouse button while dragging the mouse pointer across Sum./, then release the mouse button.) Sum./ in the edit area is highlighted.

Notice that the mouse pointer becomes an I-beam when you move it into the edit area. This allows you to click between characters to place the insertion point. Notice, also, that you activated the edit area as soon as you pressed the mouse button while pointing anywhere in the edit area.

5. Press (DEL). The edit area contains Fall/Win. 91/92.

6. Drag across the period following Win. Type **ter**. The edit area now reads Fall/Winter 91/92, as shown here:

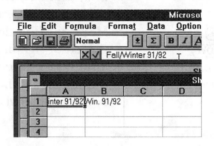

7. Click on E12 to carry on where you started.

The ability to jump quickly to a cell, make a change by clicking and dragging in the edit area, and then jump back to where you started is powerful. Use it for a while and you will agree.

Using Menus

Menus are the primary means of having Excel perform tasks such as opening a file, copying a range, printing a worksheet, or creating a chart. All menu operations begin in one of three ways:

- Clicking on a menu name
- Clicking the right mouse button to access the Shortcut menu
- Pressing (ALT), (F10), or (/) and then either highlighting the menu name with the direction keys and pressing (ENTER) or typing the underlined letter in the menu name

Any of these methods cause the selected menu to be displayed. Once a menu is displayed, you have two ways to choose an option:

- Clicking on an option name.
- Using the direction keys to highlight an option and pressing (ENTER). Additionally, when using a menu from the Menu bar, an option can be chosen by typing the underlined letter in the option name.

Once you have selected a menu and chosen an option, either the option immediately executes (as does Save in the File menu or Copy in the Edit menu, for example) or a dialog box opens. When you choose a menu option with an ellipsis (...) after it, a dialog box opens. Excel (and all Windows applications) uses a dialog box to get further information. Dialog boxes give you additional choices and provide the means for you to type in a name or some other information.

Take a look now at how the menu system works. In the following instructions the keyboard and mouse methods are intermixed to give you experience with both.

1. Press (ALT). The File menu name in the Menu bar is highlighted. Notice that the Status bar at the bottom of the window gives you a brief description of the File menu.

2. Press (ENTER). The File menu opens.

3. Press (DOWN ARROW), and then press it several more times. Notice that the Status bar provides a description of each option as you highlight it.

4. Press (RIGHT ARROW). The File menu closes and the Edit menu opens.
    Some of the options in the Edit menu are light gray or dimmer than the other options. These options are not available because they are not applicable to the current situation. The light gray options in the current Edit menu all deal with pasting (copying something from the Clipboard to the worksheet). To paste you must first cut or copy, both of which place something from the worksheet onto the Clipboard.

5. Press (RIGHT ARROW) slowly seven more times. Look at each of the menus in succession. Use (DOWN ARROW) to explore some of the options that interest you. Look at the Status bar to see the description of the option.

6. Press (RIGHT ARROW) three more times. The highlight wraps around and opens first the Excel Control menu, and then the worksheet Control menu, and finally returns to the File menu where you started.

   If you continue to press (RIGHT ARROW), you continue to move around the set of menus. If you press (LEFT ARROW) you move the other way. If you press (UP ARROW) or (DOWN ARROW), you move up or down through the options in the menu that is currently open. The direction keys provide a sure way to move through the menu system.

7. Press (ESC) twice. The Menu bar is deactivated and you return to the worksheet.

8. Click on A1, and it becomes the active cell. A1 should still contain Fall/Winter 91/92. If it doesn't, type anything in it (your first name, for example) so you have something to work with in the next set of instructions.

9. Click on Edit in the Menu bar. The Edit menu opens.

10. Click on Copy in the Edit menu. The Edit menu closes, and a blinking *marquee* appears around the active cell, A1, telling you that a copy of the contents of A1 is ready to be placed in some other cell on the worksheet.

11. Click on C5 to select it as the destination of the copy. Press (ENTER) to complete the copy. C5 now contains a copy of A1's contents.

12. Press (F10) to activate the Menu bar.

13. Type **e** to open the Edit menu.

14. Type **t** to choose the Cut option. The Edit menu closes and again a blinking marquee forms around the active cell, in this case C5. The contents of C5 are placed on the Clipboard.

15. Click on E9 and press (ENTER). The contents of C5 are moved to E9. In other words, the contents of C5 are removed (cut) and placed (pasted) in E9.

16. Drag on the Edit menu until Undo Paste is highlighted (point on the Edit menu name in the Menu bar, press and hold the mouse button while dragging the highlight bar down to the Undo Paste option, and then release the mouse button). The contents of E9 are restored

to C5 and a blinking marquee reappears. With Edit Undo Paste you have completely undone step 15 and you are back where you were when you completed step 14, except that E9 is the active cell.

17. Drag to highlight cells C5, C6, C7, and C8 (place the mouse pointer on C5, press and hold the mouse button while dragging the mouse pointer over C6, C7, and C8, and then release the mouse button). Cells C5 through C8 are highlighted.

18. Click on the Edit menu to select it, and then click on Fill Down to choose it. The contents of C5 are replicated in cells C6 through C8, as shown in Figure 4-4.

19. With the mouse pointer in the C5 through C8 highlighted range, click the right mouse button to display the Shortcut menu. Click on Clear. The Clear dialog box appears. Click on All and OK. The contents of C5 through C8 are cleared from the screen.

20. Click on the Edit menu to select it, and then click on Undo (the word Clear is added to the Undo option to let you know which command you are restoring).

Figure 4-4.   *Results of choosing Fill Down from the Edit menu*

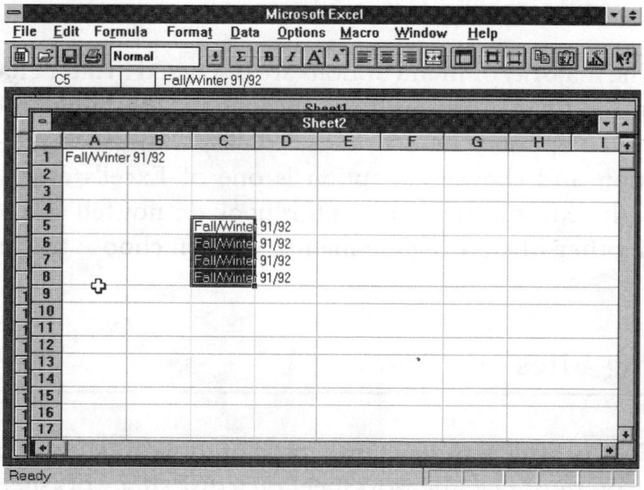

21. The screen returns to its original look, as in Figure 4-4.

Using Zoom

Another new feature provided by Excel 4 is Zoom. Much like a camera lens, Zoom allows you to increase or decrease the magnification of the worksheet. You can choose from five magnifications provided by Excel or create your own, anywhere from 10 to 400 percent of normal (normal being 100 percent). Zoom only changes the size of the worksheet; the window that contains the worksheet stays the same. Try some zooming exercises now.

1. Click on the Window menu, and then click on the Zoom option. The Zoom dialog box appears. Choose 200 percent magnification by clicking on its option button, and then click on the OK button. The worksheet is enlarged as shown in Figure 4-5.

2. Again, click on the Window menu, choose Zoom, but this time choose the Custom option button. Type **40** and click on the OK button to display the worksheet in Figure 4-6.

3. Return to the original worksheet by clicking on the Window menu, Zoom, 100%, and OK. The worksheet returns to its normal magnification as in Figure 4-4.

The majority of menu options are discussed in later chapters of this book. The same procedures are used throughout the book to open a menu and choose an option. The ease and flexibility with which you can make a menu selection and choose an option is one of Excel's and Windows' greatest strengths. Most instructions in this book do not tell you to use one method or the other when using the menus; you can choose the method you prefer.

Using Files

Files provide a permanent record of the worksheets you build. To create a file you must save the worksheet on a disk. If a worksheet is not saved, it is

Figure 4-5. Worksheet enlarged in size

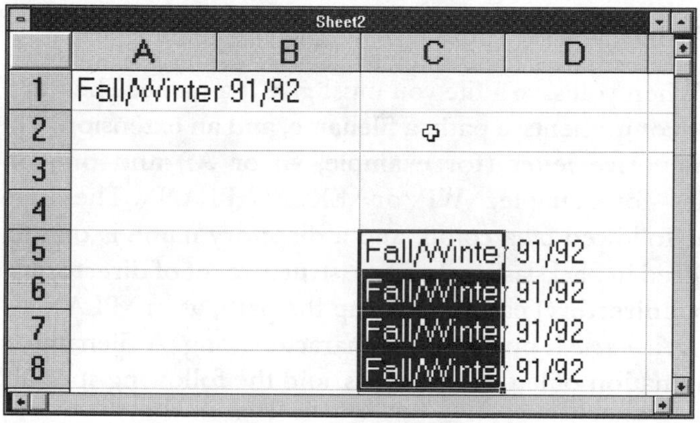

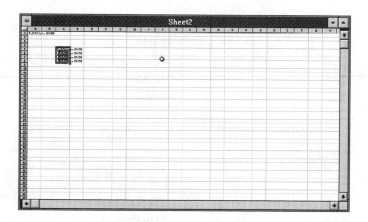

Figure 4-6. Worksheet reduced in size

lost when you leave Excel or turn off the computer (although you will receive a warning if you try to leave Excel without saving an open worksheet).

Naming Files

When you save a file you must give it a name. The full name of a file has three components: a path, a filename, and an extension. The *path* is made up of the drive letter (for example, C: or A:) and one or more directory names—for example, \WI\ or \EXCEL\PLAN\. The drive letter is a single letter followed by a colon, and a directory name is one to eight characters enclosed in backslashes. In a tree structure set of directories, several directory (or subdirectory) names make up the path, as in \PLAN\SALES\1992\.

A *filename* is one to eight characters long. A filename can consist of any combination of letters, numbers, and the following special characters:

~ ' ! @ # $ % ^ & ( ) - _ { } '

A filename may not include blanks.

The filename *extension* is optional but highly recommended. It begins with a period and can be up to three characters long. Unless you override it, Excel automatically adds an extension to all files. The extensions and the types of files they are applied to are as follows:

Extension	File Type
.BAK	Backup
.CSV	Comma-separated values
.DBF	dBASE II/III/IV
.DIF	VisiCalc
.TMP	Temporary
.WKS, .WK1, .WK3, .FMT, or .FM3	Lotus 1-2-3
.XLB	Toolbar
.XLC	Chart
.XLM	Macro sheet
.XLS	Worksheet
.XLW	Workbook

Saving Files

You already saved a file when you worked through some steps in Chapter 3. That example included minimal explanation, so use the following instructions to save another file now (even though there is not much on the worksheet to save):

1. Click on File. The File menu opens, as shown here:

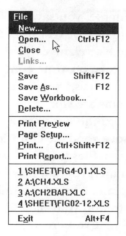

2. Click on Save As. The Save As dialog box opens, asking for the name of the file you want to save, as seen here:

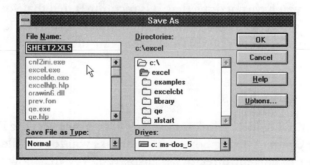

3. Type **ch4**. The name CH4 goes into the filename text box of the Save As dialog box. Excel automatically adds the worksheet exten-

sion .XLS, and for now you are using the current drive and directory
(see the next section, "Using Directories").

4. Click on OK. The worksheet is saved in a file named CH4.XLS, and
   Excel returns to ready mode.

Using Directories

In the previous example, you saved a file without specifying a drive or
directory. When you do that, Excel uses the current drive and directory.
Unless you or someone else changes your default drive and directory, the
current drive and directory on your computer are the ones in which you
installed Excel. In other words, you store your worksheet files in the same
directory as your programs are stored.

While there is nothing inherently wrong with using the program directory
to store data files, it is not a good idea for files that are important. You should
not keep data and program files together because you can end up erasing the
data files along with all the program files you want to erase when you get a
new release of the program. Also, the number of Excel program files in the
directory make it hard to find your data files.

It is recommended that you create one or more separate directories to
hold your data files. You can then specify one of these directories when saving
files. Appendix A describes creating a subdirectory named SHEET under your
Windows directory in which you can store the sample files created in this
book. If you have not done that, it is recommended that you turn to Appendix
A now and do it. In the remaining chapters of this book, it is assumed that
you are using a path of \SHEET\ for your files.

Retrieving Files

Retrieving files is similar to saving files. You select the File menu and then
choose Open. A dialog box opens that asks you for the filename, and a list of
files in the current directory is displayed. Try that now with the following
instructions:

1. Click on the File menu. The File menu opens.

2. Click on Open. The Open dialog box opens, as shown here:

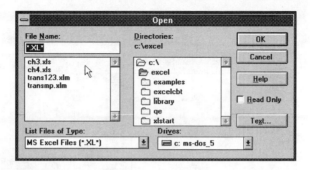

3. Double-click on ch3.xls in the files list box. The file CH3.XLS opens.

If you don't know a filename, you can use the two *wildcard characters*, ? and *. To replace a single character, use ?; to replace any number of consecutive characters, use *. For example, ?QTRPLAN.XLS refers to 1QTRPLAN.XLS, 2QTRPLAN.XLS, 3QTRPLAN.XLS, and so on, while *.XLS refers to all files with an .XLS extension.

It is important to note that when Excel opens a file, it creates a new worksheet window that is added to the other worksheet or document windows you have open. You can find out what document windows are open by opening the Window menu, as shown here:

You can see that you currently have three windows open. If you want to go to another window, choose that window from the Window menu or click on the window if you can see it on the screen. To display all windows currently

Figure 4-7.   *Effect of choosing Tiled from the Window Arrange dialog box*

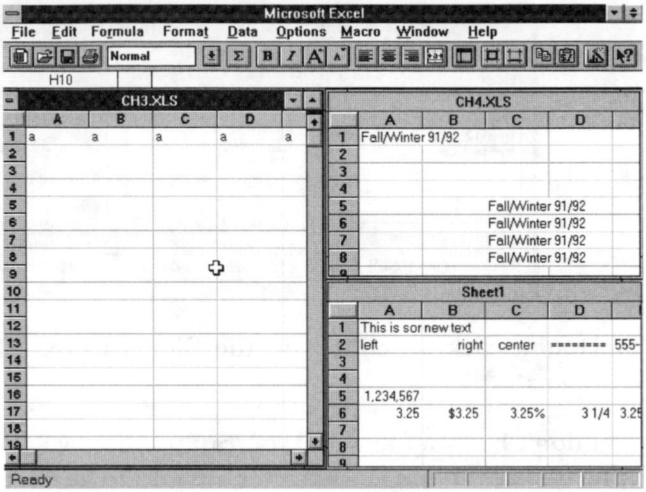

open, choose Arrange from the Window menu, click on the Tiled option button, and then click on the OK button. With the current windows available, this will produce a screen that looks like Figure 4-7.

Quitting Excel

When you are done using Excel you should formally leave it with the Close option from Excel's Control menu, rather than just turning off your computer. The main reason for this is that if you have forgotten to save a file, Excel's Close option reminds you as part of the quitting process. Also, with the Close option, Excel erases any temporary files it has written, thus keeping your hard disk from getting filled with them. Use the following steps to leave Excel:

1. Double-click on Excel's Control-menu box. A "Save changes" dialog box opens, as shown here:

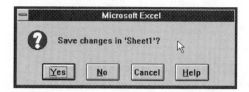

The dialog box asks if you want to save changes in Sheet1 and gives you four command buttons to choose from: Yes, No, Cancel, and Help. Choosing Yes saves Sheet1 in a file named SHEET1.XLS in the current directory. Choosing No exits Excel without saving Sheet1—in essence throwing away Sheet1. Choosing Cancel interrupts the quitting process and puts you back in ready mode. Choosing Help provides a Help menu that explains the features of the command buttons. You can then look at Sheet1 and determine if you want to save it. Since you want to throw away Sheet1, choose No.

2. Click on No to leave Excel without saving Sheet1.

3. Double-click on the Program Manager's Control-menu box to leave Windows and return to DOS.

4. Click on OK to end your Windows session.

Excel and Windows shut themselves down, erasing any temporary files and returning you to the DOS prompt.

4

5

Creating a Worksheet

Creating a worksheet is the central focus of Excel—its reason for being—and it is the one thing every user of Excel does. The importance of learning how to do this well, and becoming familiar with as many tricks and shortcuts as possible, cannot be overemphasized. This chapter provides the foundation for that learning process by taking you through the actual construction of a worksheet to demonstrate how it is done. Chapter 6 builds upon this foundation to demonstrate additional worksheet capabilities in Excel.

You will benefit from following along on your computer as you read this chapter. It is not absolutely necessary to do this—there are plenty of figures and illustrations to show you what is going on—but you will learn far more by actually seeing for yourself what is happening as the worksheet progresses. More importantly, you will learn how to untangle yourself from the many small mistakes that everyone makes but are impossible to predict in a book.

Creating a worksheet has a number of steps. This chapter covers the planning phase: placing headings and titles, entering numbers and formulas, copying formulas, and completing and saving.

Planning a Worksheet

You *could* start building a worksheet by simply entering the necessary headings, labels, and numbers or formulas. If you need an extra row or column, you could just insert it and delete those you do not need. A great number of worksheets—probably the majority—are built that way. As with most things, however, a little planning up front saves considerable time as you go along. Planning involves simply visualizing what the worksheet will look like and sketching it out so you have a layout to follow as you build the worksheet. This takes only a few minutes and can save more time later.

Figure 5-1 shows a layout for a third-quarter budget worksheet that you will build in this chapter. This layout was done using Excel, but most are simply sketched on a scrap of paper. To construct this layout you first need to answer three questions: How many revenue, cost of sales, and expense accounts are to be included? How many time periods are covered? What assumptions are involved?

The answers to these questions allow you to make the following decisions regarding the layout in Figure 5-1:

- A title will appear at the top of the worksheet with a blank line under it.

- There will be three assumptions, one each for the growth of revenue, cost of sales, and expenses. Each requires a row, and there will be a blank line following the third assumption.

- Each column heading will take 2 rows and have a blank line below it.

- The row headings will be in columns A and B and take 17 rows, 10 through 26 (five for revenue, four for cost of sales and gross income, six for expense, and two for net income).

- The data area will occupy six columns: C through H (two for quarters, three for months, and one for the percent growth).

If you cannot visualize the worksheet from the layout in Figure 5-1 and these decisions, don't feel bad. Sneak a look at the finished product in Figures 5-18 and 5-19 at the end of the chapter. As you build more worksheets you will be able to visualize them more easily before you start them.

That's all there is to the planning process: constructing a rough layout of what will go where on the worksheet after making a series of decisions about what is to be included and how much room it will take. Use the plan to begin building the worksheet by placing headings and other elements where you have decided they belong.

Figure 5-1. *Layout for a third quarter budget worksheet*

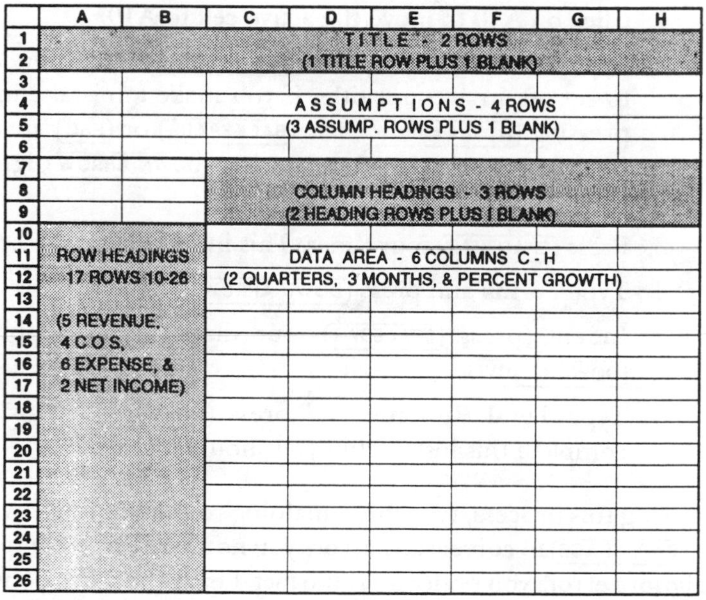

5

Placing Labels, Headings, and Titles

Where you begin a worksheet probably has as much to do with how you visualize or create it in your mind as anything else. It is important to minimize the number of keystrokes and therefore the traveling you must do around the worksheet, but trying to reach the absolute minimum path is more trouble than it's worth and does not allow for possible errors. Therefore, start where you like and don't worry about it. Here you will start with the row labels, knowing that you will have to go back and enter the title and assumptions.

Entering a Column of Labels

If it is not on already, turn on your computer and load Windows and Excel. With a blank worksheet on your screen, use the following instructions to enter a column of labels:

1. Click on A10 to move the active cell to A10.
2. Type **REVENUE** and press (DOWN ARROW). All capital letters are used to set off an account title. If you make a mistake in typing before pressing (DOWN ARROW), use (BACKSPACE) or (ESC) or to correct it. If you notice a mistake after pressing (DOWN ARROW), ignore it. You will come back later and edit the labels.
3. Press (SPACEBAR) four times. This indents a detail account.
4. Type **Forms** and press (DOWN ARROW).
5. Indent (press (SPACEBAR) four times), type **Supplies**, and press (DOWN ARROW).
6. Type **Total Revenue** and press (DOWN ARROW) twice. When you complete this instruction you should be in A15.

Using this process, type the remaining row labels as shown in Figure 5-2. Use (BACKSPACE) to correct any errors you notice prior to completing an entry, but ignore errors you notice after the fact. Leave the space between P/R Taxes and Other Expenses to allow for its use later. Press (ENTER) when you complete Net Income since it is the last account.

Figure 5-2.   *Row labels completed*

Read over the row labels carefully for any typing errors. If there are none, read through the following steps to see how you would correct errors in the future. Otherwise, use these steps to correct your errors. (For the sake of example, assume that the second "a" in Salaries has been left out.)

1. Click on the entry to be corrected (A20 for Salaries).

2. Move the mouse pointer to the edit area, place the I-beam at or to the right of the error (between the "l" and "r" if the second "a" is missing in Salaries), and click to place the insertion point. Excel enters edit mode.

3. Correct the error. If you need to delete an incorrect character, press (DEL) to delete a character to the right of the insertion point, or use (BACKSPACE) to delete a character to the left. Then type the correction. In the case of Salaries, type the missing "a."

4. Press (ENTER). Excel returns to ready mode.

Correct all of the errors you see in the row labels this same way: move the active cell to the incorrect label, go into edit mode (you can press (F2) as well as click in the edit area), get to the incorrect character using the mouse or the arrow keys, use (BACKSPACE) or (DEL) to remove characters you do not want, type characters that need to be added, and press (ENTER) to complete the editing.

Spelling   The Spelling option on the Options menu provides an easier (and often more accurate!) way to edit misspelled words. You can choose to have your entire worksheet, a selected range, a word, or an embedded chart spell checked. The Spelling dialog box, shown here, offers suggested alternate spellings to words it does not find in the standard dictionary.

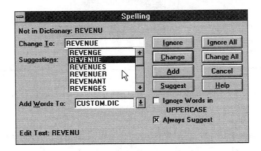

Spelling starts spell checking the worksheet from your selected cell. You can replace a misspelled word on your worksheet with the suggested word in the Change To box by clicking on the Change button. If you prefer one of the words in the Suggestions box, click on the word, and then click on the Change button. You can change the present use of the word or choose to change all instances throughout the worksheet. Additionally, you can add to the custom dictionary commonly used words, acronyms, or abbreviations unique to your work. Finally, after you have made your selections, Excel will ask you if you want to continue spell checking the worksheet from its beginning, or stop and return to the worksheet. Try the following instructions to get a feeling for the use of Spelling:

1. Click on cell A10 to move the active cell to A10.
2. Press (F2) to change to edit mode.

3. Press (BACKSPACE) once to delete the "E" and change REVENUE to REVENU.

4. Click on the Enter box in the editing area.

5. Press (DOWN ARROW) three times. Repeat steps 2 through 4 to change Total Revenue to Total Revenu.

6. Click on the Options menu and then choose the Spelling option.

7. Click on Revenue in the Suggestions box. Revenue becomes highlighted.

8. Click on the Change button. Excel substitutes the proper spelling of Revenue for the misspelled contents of cell A13; then it asks if you want to continue checking at the beginning of the worksheet.

9. Click on the Yes button since REVENU in cell A10 is still misspelled.

10. This time Excel provides the correct spelling of Revenue in the Change to box. Click on the Change button. Excel lets you know spell checking is finished. Since the Spelling dialog box did not reappear, there are no additional misspelled words.

Long Labels

As you look at the row labels, notice that many are longer than the width of column A. They hang over into the next column. This works fine while there is nothing in the next column. As you saw in Chapter 4, if you place a label or number in the cell to the right of the long label, the label will appear to be truncated. This worksheet was laid out with that in mind, providing a blank column B. In Chapter 6 you will see how columns can be widened to accommodate long labels and numbers, eliminating the need for a blank column beside them.

Centering a Title

The second step is to add a title to the worksheet: Third Quarter Budget. You want to center it across the width of the worksheet. Excel 4 has added the capability to center text across several columns. In this example, the title will fill columns D and E and part of F, leaving G and H on the right balanced against A and B on the left.

Follow these steps to add the title:

1. Click on cell A1 to move the active cell to A1.

2. Press (CAPS LOCK) for uppercase letters.

3. Type **THIRD QUARTER BUDGET**. Check your entry for mistakes. If you made any, either press (BACKSPACE) or click in the edit area to correct them.

4. Drag across row 1, from column A through column H. (Move the mouse pointer to A1, press and hold the mouse button while moving the mouse to H9, and then release the mouse button.) Row 1, cells A through H, is highlighted.

5. Click on the Format menu and the Alignment option.

6. The Alignment dialog box opens. Click on the Center across selection option button, and then on OK. (Alternately, you can click on the Center Across Columns tool, the eighth tool from the right on the Standard toolbar.)

7. Click on cell A1.

8. The upper-left corner of your screen should look like this:

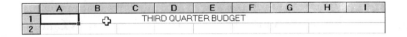

Entering a Row of Headings

Each column of data on this worksheet needs a heading. Two rows have been left for this purpose, plus one row for a double line under the headings. Enter these now.

1. Click on C7 to make that the active cell.

2. Type **Second** and press (DOWN ARROW).

3. Type **Quarter** and press (RIGHT ARROW).

4. Type **July** and press (RIGHT ARROW).

5. Type **August** and press (RIGHT ARROW).

Use Figure 5-3 as a guide to finish the remaining column headings.

Placing a Border

In this exercise you'll separate your row labels and column headings with a border. With Excel you can format a cell or range of cells to have a border on any or all of its four sides. This is different from using a string of hyphens, equal signs, or vertical lines to produce a border. It is actual formatting of a cell to include a line on one or more of its sides while keeping its text or number intact. The border is placed on the grid lines, so adjoining cells share a border.

To create a double line, it's easiest to make one of the borders on a cell a double line. The line will be on the edge of the cell, not centered within it. To center a double line, you need to place a top and bottom border on a row and then reduce the height of the row to the space you want between the lines. You would not be able to read anything else contained in the row.

Add a double-line border across row 9 using the second method and a single line between columns B and C with the following instructions:

1. Drag across row 9 from column A through column H. (Move the

Figure 5-3. *Completed column headings*

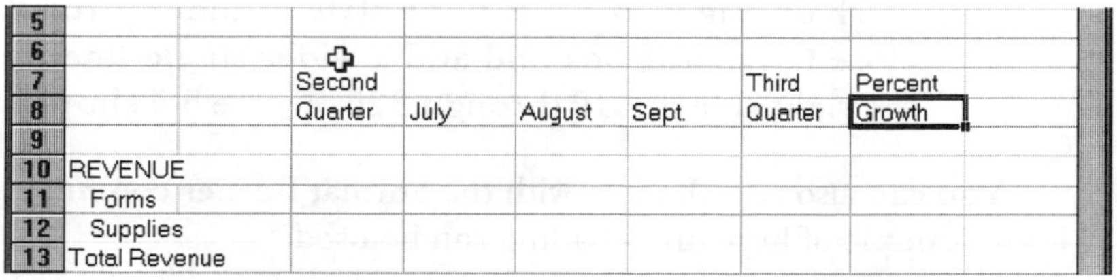

5							
6							
7		Second				Third	Percent
8		Quarter	July	August	Sept.	Quarter	Growth
9							
10	REVENUE						
11	Forms						
12	Supplies						
13	Total Revenue						

mouse pointer to A9, press and hold the mouse button while moving the mouse to H9, and then release the mouse button.) Row 9 cells A through H are highlighted.

2. Click on the Format menu and the Border option. The Border dialog box opens.

3. Click on Top and Bottom in the Border dialog box, as shown in Figure 5-4.

4. Click OK. The dialog box closes and a top and bottom border is placed across row 9.

5. Point on the row numbers on the left of the window at the intersection of rows 9 and 10. The mouse pointer becomes a two-headed arrow with a bar in the middle. This allows you to change the height of a row.

6. Press and hold the mouse button while dragging the mouse upward to reduce the height of row 9 to roughly 1/16 inch, as shown here:

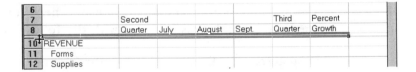

7. Drag down column B from row 10 through row 26. B10 through B26 are highlighted.

8. Click on the Format menu and the Border option to again open the Border dialog box.

9. Click on Right, the third line style in the top row, and OK to close the dialog box and add a wider single line border down the right side of B10 through B26. Figure 5-5 shows the results.

You can also add shading with the Format Border command. Figure 5-1 is an example of how such shading can be used.

Figure 5-4. *Creating a double-line border*

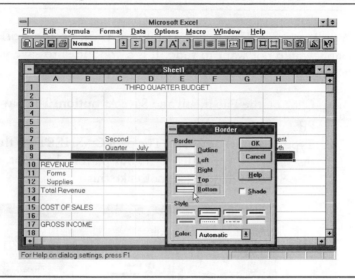

Figure 5-5. *Horizontal and vertical borders in place*

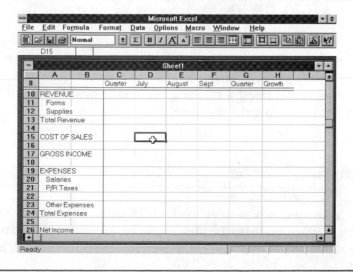

5

Saving the Worksheet

You have now done a fair amount of work on the worksheet that you probably would not want to redo. It is a good idea to save your worksheets early and often, so save this worksheet now.

1. Click on the File menu and Save As option. The Save As dialog box opens.

2. Type **c:\sheet\qtr3bud**. (The path C:\SHEET\ is the example path discussed in Appendix A. If your path is different, use your path.) The Save As dialog box looks like this:

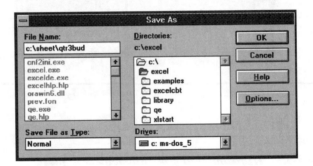

3. Click OK. The worksheet is saved on your hard disk, and Excel returns to ready mode.

Saving a file is simple and should be done often to prevent losing your work from a power failure or human error. As you will see later in this chapter, once you have saved a file, you can resave it with the File Save command without reentering the filename.

Entering Numbers and Formulas

Your next task is to enter the body of the worksheet—the numbers and formulas that make up the budget proper. Most budgets are projections based on actual sets of numbers. In this example you'll start with an actual second quarter to project the third quarter. In other words, the second quarter is an actual set of numbers, while each month of the third quarter contains a formula that calculates its value based on the second quarter. Start by entering the second quarter actuals.

Entering a Column of Numbers

You enter a column of numbers just as you entered the column of labels earlier: you type one number and press (DOWN ARROW) to move to the next one. Enter the numbers with commas and, with Excel 4, you will get automatic comma formatting. Follow these steps to enter the column of numbers:

1. Click on C11. The active cell moves to C11.

2. Type **87,000** and press (DOWN ARROW). If you make a mistake while typing, use (BACKSPACE) or (ESC) to correct it. If you see a mistake after completing an entry, wait until you finish the column to correct it.

   If you got 870 instead of 87000, you have the fixed decimal feature turned on (you will see the status indicator FIX in the right corner of the Status bar). Choose Workspace from the Options menu and click on Fixed Decimal to turn it off.

3. Type **147,300** and press (DOWN ARROW).

4. Type **234,300** and press (DOWN ARROW) twice.

In a similar manner, complete the column of numbers shown in Figure 5-6. When you reach Net Income, cell C26, press (ENTER) instead of (DOWN ARROW).

Editing and Completing the Column

When you finish entering the numbers, look back over them and compare what you see to Figure 5-6. It is important that the numbers be accurate because the rest of the worksheet is based on them. If you see an error, use the following instructions to correct it. (For the sake of example, assume that Other Expenses was entered as 14,660 instead of 14,760.)

1. Click on the cell in error (for example, C23 for Other Expenses).

2. Click or drag on the edit area to highlight the error. The mode indicator changes to EDIT. In this example you would drag across the left 6 in 14,660.

3. After dragging over any number(s) to be replaced, type the replacement numbers. For this example, type 7. In other cases use (BACKSPACE) or (DEL) to remove unwanted characters and type correct ones.

4. Press (ENTER). The correct number is placed on the worksheet, and Excel returns to ready mode.

Use this procedure to correct as many errors as you have, moving up the list as you go. In the next section you must be near the top of the list.

Building Formulas

The next three columns (D, E, and F) represent the projected amounts for July, August, and September. The amounts for each month are totally derived, using formulas based on the actual second quarter. There are 11 figures per month (including one for the blank after P/R Taxes) and three

Figure 5-6.   Completed column of numbers

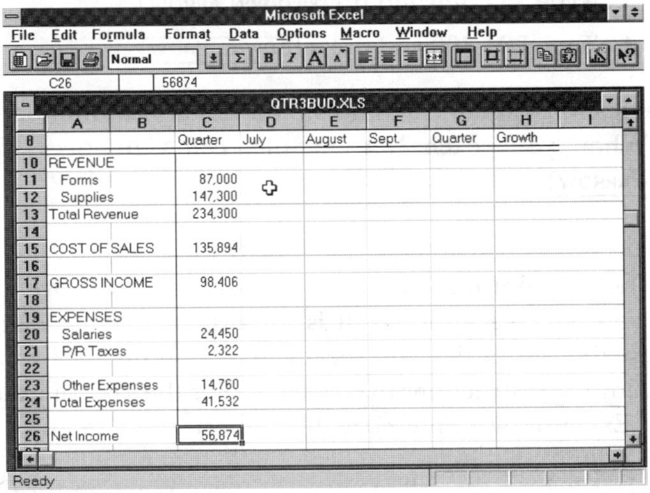

months. This means you have 33 formulas, which is a lot if you had to enter them all. Thankfully, the copying facility for formulas is very powerful in Excel, so most of the work will be done for you.

If you look ahead a month and think about the formulas, you will notice that four of the formulas are based on other numbers in the same column—summation formulas: Total Revenue, Gross Income, Total Expense, and Net Income. They are the same formula for all three months. It would be worthwhile doing them first in July so they can be copied to the other months.

In building the formulas, you can use ⊙ and ⊖ either above the typewriter keyboard or on the right of the numerical keypad, and you can use either upper- or lowercase letters. As you are building the formulas, check them carefully. It is easier to catch an error and correct it as formulas are being built rather than after the fact. The following steps build the first formula:

1. Click on D13, Total Revenue for July.

2. Type **=d11+d12** and the formula appears in the edit area and in D13. The formula adds Forms (D11) to Supplies (D12) to get Total Revenue.

3. Press ⒺⓃⓉⒺⓇ. Excel returns to ready mode.

On the worksheet you'll see only a 0 in D13, but in the edit area you'll see the formula. When numbers are available in D11 and D12, D13 will reflect them.

Pointing Versus Typing

When entering the first formula, you directly typed it as you would text or a number. This works fine when you can see on the screen the cell addresses that you want to use in the formula. Excel has another method of entering formulas that works even if the cell is not on the screen. The process is to start a formula with an equal sign (=), use the mouse or direction keys to point to the first cell in the formula, type one of the following arithmetic symbols,

+ - * / ^ % & : , ( )

and then point to the second cell, and so on to complete the formula. The following instructions demonstrate this.

1. Click on D17, Gross Income for July.

2. Type = and an = appears in the edit area. The mode indicator changes to ENTER.

3. Click on D13. A blinking dotted line appears around D13. D13 is displayed in the formula under construction in the edit area, and the mode indicator changes to POINT.

4. Type - and a - appears in the edit area after D13. The blinking dotted line disappears from D13.

5. Click on D15. A blinking dotted line appears around D15, and D15 goes into the formula in the edit area. Your screen looks like that shown in Figure 5-7.

6. Press (ENTER). The formula is completed, and Excel returns to ready mode.

Again you see only a 0 in the worksheet, but the formula appears in the edit area. The process of entering an arithmetic symbol and pointing at a cell

Figure 5-7.   *Formula under construction in the edit area*

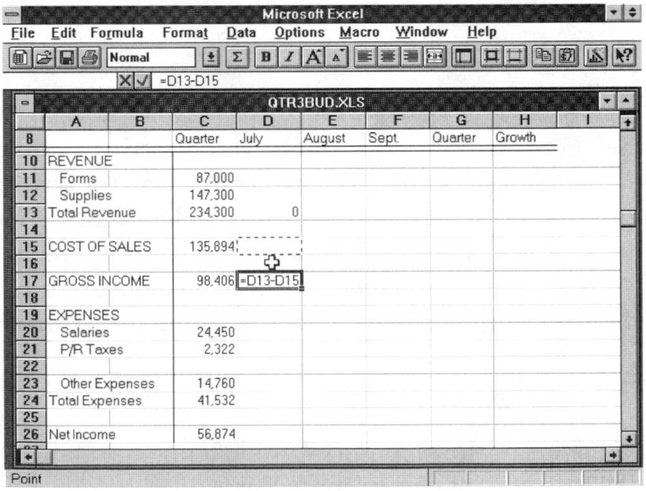

can go on as long as you want up to a maximum of 255 characters in a formula. Also, there are shortcuts for formulas, as you are about to see.

Functions Versus Formulas

The next formula is for total expenses in D24. This is the sum: D20+D21+D22+D23. You can type in such a formula; with an = in front it is 16 keystrokes. You also can point to the four cells and type + four times. Alternatively, you can use the SUM function that Excel uses for summing. Instead of identifying each cell, you identify (type or point to) the range encompassing the cells to be summed. Here is how it is done.

1. Click on D24. The active cell moves to D24, Total Expenses for July.

2. Type **=sum(** which appears in the edit area. The ENTER indicator comes on.

3. Click on D20. The blinking dotted line appears around D20. D20 is displayed in the formula under construction in the edit area, and the mode indicator changes to POINT.

4. Type : and the starting address of a range is anchored at D20. The EXT keyboard indicator comes on.

5. Click on D23. The blinking dotted line appears around the range D20:D23, and the formula in the edit area includes the range D20:D23, as shown in Figure 5-8.

6. Type) and press (ENTER). The completed formula is placed in D24, and you can see it in the edit area.

The SUM function is the most heavily used Excel function. You will find it very useful. A rule of thumb is to use SUM if you are summing three or more cells, and individually add two cells. Depending on how big the cell addresses are, you may not save keystrokes with SUM on three cells, but it provides another benefit—it is expandable.

When you insert a row or column in the middle of a normal summation, the summation adjusts so you are still summing the same cells you originally identified, but you do not add the new cell in between. For example, if your original formula is =C4+C5+C6 and you insert a new row between rows 4 and 5, the formula adjusts to become =C4+C6+C7. The formula is still the way you specified it—the old C5 has become C6 and is so recognized in the formula.

Figure 5-8.   *SUM formula under construction*

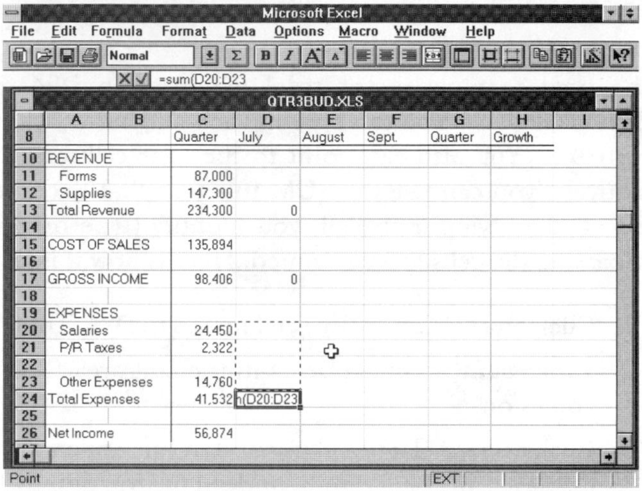

The problem is that the new C5 is not included. That may be the way you want it. Normally, however, when you insert a new cell in a range, you want that cell included in the summation. If you use SUM the new cell is included. In the previous example, the original formula is =SUM(C4:C6). After inserting the new row, the formula becomes =SUM(C4:C7) and includes the new C5.

Finishing Columnar Formulas

One columnar formula is left—Net Income in D26. Use these instructions to enter it:

1. Click on D26. The active cell moves to D26.

2. Type = and the mode indicator changes to ENTER. The = goes into the edit area.

3. Click on D17. The blinking dotted line appears around D17, Gross Income. D17 is reflected in the edit area, and the mode indicator changes to POINT.

4. Type - and the blinking dotted line disappears from D17.

5. Click on D24. The blinking dotted line appears around D24, Total Expense, and D24 is reflected in the edit area.

6. Press (ENTER). The formula is completed, and Excel returns to ready mode.

Copying Formulas

You have now completed the four columnar formulas and are ready to copy them to the columns for the other two months. You could copy the same formulas to the Third Quarter total in column G, but you will handle that differently. Also, you will be copying other formulas from August to September and you can include the totals in that copy. Therefore, the copying you do here is just from July to August, column D to E.

You might wonder how you can copy a formula from column D—for example, =D11+D12—to column E and have it work. It would need to be changed to =E11+E12. Excel knows that and, unless you tell it otherwise, it automatically changes the formula *relative* to the location to which it is copied. Follow these steps to copy one formula, and look at it for yourself (the active cell should be D26):

1. Click on the Edit menu and the Copy option. A blinking marquee appears around D26, indicating that it is the source of the copy.

2. Click on E26. The active cell moves to E26, indicating that E26 is the destination of the copy.

3. Press (ENTER). The copy finishes by placing the copied formula in E26.

Look now at the formula in E26. It is =E17-E24, as you can see in the edit area:

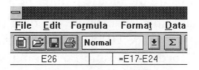

In the process of copying from D26 to E26, the formula automatically changed from =D17-D24 to =E17-E24.

Relative Addressing

This ability to adjust a formula from one location to another, as you just did, is called *relative addressing*. The formula is always adjusted relative to its location. This means that the net income formula within Excel is

= "the cell 9 cells up"-"the cell 2 cells up"

Such a formula will work anywhere on the worksheet. Of course, sometimes you want to fix one or more parts of an address. If the entire address is fixed—locked on to a particular cell no matter where you copy it—the addressing scheme is called *absolute addressing*. If some parts of the address are fixed and some are not, the addressing scheme is called *mixed addressing*. Mixed and absolute addressing will be discussed shortly.

Copying the Rest of the Columnar Formulas

You have seen how to copy formulas using the Edit Copy option, now you can use the Excel 4 drag and drop feature to copy the rest of the columnar formulas with the mouse, following these instructions (E26 should still be the active cell):

1. First you have to activate Cell Drag and Drop if it isn't already activated. Click on the Options menu and the Workspace option; then click on the Cell Drag and Drop check box. An X will fill the check box. Click on OK. The active cell, E26, will now contain a small box in its lower-right corner, called the *fill handle*.

2. Drag on D13 through D24 (point on D13, and then press and hold the mouse button while dragging down to D24). The range D13:D24 is highlighted.

3. Position the mouse pointer on the right border of the highlighted range. Ensure the mouse pointer becomes an arrow.

4. Press, and hold (CTRL) while you drag (by holding down the mouse button) the range D13:D24 to range E13:E24. When you have the shaded border in position over range E13:E24, release the mouse button and (CTRL). The contents of range D13:D24 are copied to E13:E24, as shown in Figure 5-9.

Figure 5-9. *Copying a column of formulas*

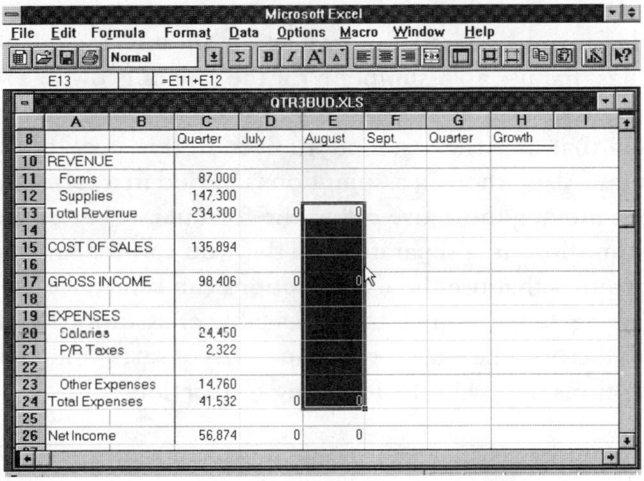

The three remaining columnar formulas are thus copied from column D to E and adjusted relative to their new location. You can now calculate all of the totals for July and August.

When you pressed (CTRL), you probably noticed the mouse pointer changed, as shown here:

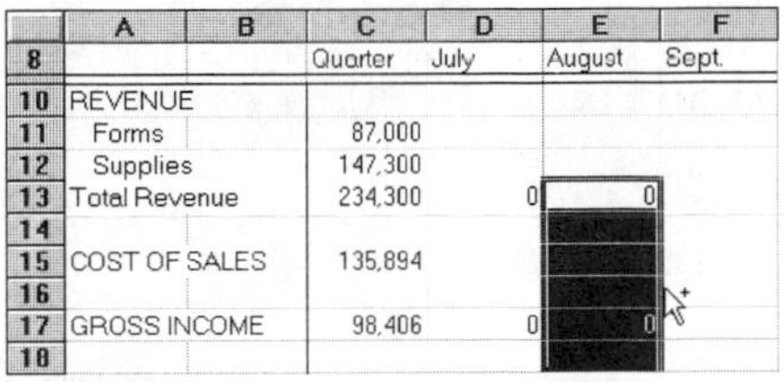

Pressing (CTRL) while using drag and drop *copies* the contents of a cell or range to a new location. Using drag and drop without pressing (CTRL) *moves* the contents to a new location and the original cell or range contents are cleared. Copy and move indicators are displayed in the message area of the Status bar.

Drag and drop is a powerful addition to Excel. In the remaining chapters of this book, it is assumed you are using drag and drop.

Using Assumptions

The formulas used for projection in this model are simple growth formulas that use an assumption for the rate of growth. This assumption can be built into the formula, but if you want to change it, you must edit each formula that uses the assumption. Even in this small budget, that is a lot of formulas. Also, when an assumption is buried in a formula, you cannot see it without moving the active cell to the formula. A better technique is to have all assumptions in a separate table that you can see and easily change. Then the formulas that use these assumptions can reference the table.

The next step, then, is to build a table of assumptions. It consists of three growth factors, one each for revenue, cost of sales, and expenses. Enter these assumptions now with the following instructions:

1. Press (CTRL)-(HOME) and (DOWN ARROW) twice. The active cell moves to A3.

2. Type **Revenue Growth/Mo.** and press (DOWN ARROW).

3. Type **C O S Growth/Mo.** and press (DOWN ARROW).

4. Type **Expense Growth/Mo.** and press (ENTER).

5. Click on C3. The active cell moves to C3.

6. Type **.012** and press (DOWN ARROW).

7. Type **.013** and press (DOWN ARROW).

8. Type **.01** and press (ENTER).

When you finish the last assumption, the upper-left corner of your screen should look like this:

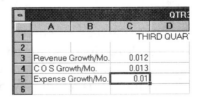

Absolute Addressing

The formula that you use to project July from the second quarter divides the quarter by 3 (to get months) and then multiplies by 1 plus the growth rate. It is the same formula for all accounts: revenue, cost of sales, and expense. The only difference is in the growth rate you use. For the two revenue accounts, the growth rate is the same. Therefore when you copy the formula from D11 to D12, if you do not use absolute addressing (which you'll learn more about in a moment) for the growth rate, it is changed by the copy and points to the growth rate for Cost of Sales. The growth rate in the formula, then, must use an absolute address. Use the following instructions to build a formula for projecting July's forms revenue with an absolute address for the growth rate and then copy it for use in projecting July supplies revenue.

1. Click on D11, Forms revenue for July.

2. Type = and press (LEFT ARROW). The mode indicator changes to POINT, and =C11 is placed in the edit area.

3. Type /3*(1+ which is added to the formula under construction in the edit area.

4. Click on C3. The blinking dotted line appears around C3, the revenue growth rate, and C3 is added to the formula in the edit area.

5. Press (F4) (Absolute). The address C3 in the edit area is changed to $C$3, an absolute address. The upper-left corner of your screen should look like this:

6. Type) and press (ENTER). The formula is completed and placed in D11, which becomes the active cell. Note that the totals immediately reflect the number.

7. Press (CTRL) to start drag and drop and place the mouse pointer on the lower border of D11.

8. While holding down (CTRL), drag D11 to D12.

9. Release (CTRL) and the mouse button to complete drag and drop. The copy operation is completed; the formula in D11 is copied to D12 and the active cell moves to D12 so you can see the resulting formula in the edit area. It should look like this:

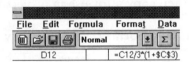

In the formula in D12, the reference to the second quarter has changed from C11 to C12 but the reference to the growth rate has remained C3. The $ in front of each part of the growth rate address means that it is an absolute reference and it remains the same no matter where it is copied.

Types of Mixed Addresses

When you make an address absolute, each part of the address—the column and the row—is fixed. You also can have various combinations of fixed and relative. These are called mixed addresses. To get a mixed address you must keep pressing (F4) (Absolute), which cycles through all four possible combinations as follows:

If you have	Pressing (F4) will give you	Type of address
C3	$C$3	Absolute address
$C$3	C$3	Mixed (fixed row)
C$3	$C3	Mixed (fixed column)
$C3	C3	Relative

(F4) (Absolute) always cycles through the alternatives in the same order independent of where you start.

Editing Formulas

The formulas for projecting cost of sales and expenses are relatively the same as the formulas for projecting revenue, except for the growth rate. You can easily copy the revenue formula to cost of sales and expense and then edit the formula. Once the first expense account is corrected, it can be copied to the other expense accounts. Use these steps to do the copying and editing of July's formulas. Your active cell should be D12.

1. Press (CTRL) and drag and drop D12 to D15. The active cell moves to D15 along with a copy of the contents of D12.

2. Press (CTRL) and drag and drop D15 to D20. D15 is copied to D20 and the active cell moves to D20.

3. Drag across the rightmost 3 in the formula in the edit area. Excel goes into edit mode, and the row reference to the growth rate is highlighted.

4. Type **5**. The formula reference, previously referring to the growth rate in C3, is changed to C5, as shown here:

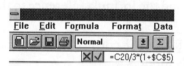

5. Press (ENTER). The correct formula is placed in D20, and Excel returns to ready mode.

6. Drag D20 through D23. The range D20:D23 is highlighted.

7. Click on the Edit menu and then click on Fill Down. The formula in D20 is copied to D21, D22, and D23, as shown in Figure 5-10.

As you can see, Fill Down and its partner Fill Right are fast ways to copy when you have a range immediately above or to the left of the area to which you want to copy. By pressing (SHIFT) when you select the Edit menu, you get Fill Up and Fill Left, which do the same thing in those directions.

8. Click on D15 and drag across the rightmost 3 in the formula in the edit area.

Figure 5-10. *Copying expense formulas*

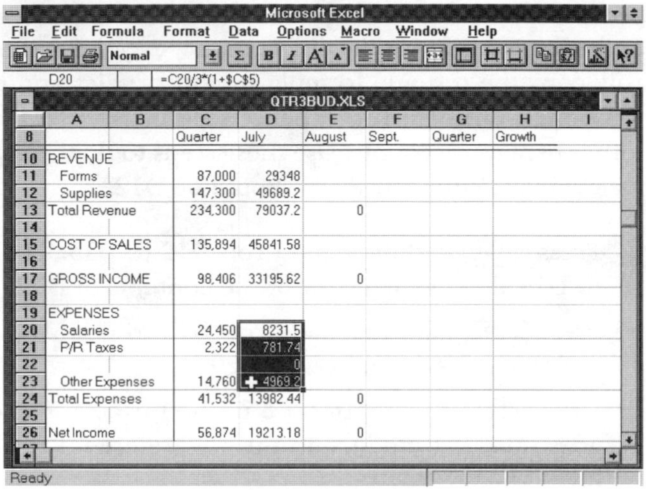

9. Type **4** and the formula reference to the growth rate in C3 is changed to C4.

10. Press (ENTER). The correct formula is placed in D15, and Excel returns to ready mode.

A similar situation exists between the formulas that project July and those that project August. In the formulas used in July, the second-quarter amounts (in the cell to the left) were divided by 3 to get a monthly amount and then multiplied by the growth factor. In the formulas for August, you will multiply the July amounts (in the cell to the left) by the same growth factor. The only difference is that in July you divided the cell to the left by 3 and in August you will not. You can copy the July formulas to August and edit out the /3. Follow these steps to build the projection formulas for August:

1. Click on D11.

2. Press (CTRL) and drag and drop D11 to E11. D11 is copied to E11.

3. Drag across /3 in the formula in the edit area, press (DEL), and press (ENTER). The formula for projecting August Forms revenue in E11 is modified to remove the division by 3, as shown here:

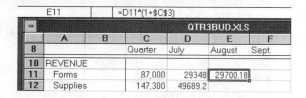

E11		=D11*(1+$C$3)			

				QTR3BUD.XLS		
	A	**B**	**C**	**D**	**E**	**F**
8			Quarter	July	August	Sept.
10	REVENUE					
11	Forms		87,000	29348	29700.18	
12	Supplies		147,300	49689.2		

4. Press (CTRL) and drag and drop E11 to E12. E11 is copied to E12.

5. Click on D15.

6. Press (CTRL) and drag and drop D15 to E15. D15 is copied to E15.

7. Drag across /3 in the formula in the edit area, press (DEL), and press (ENTER). August Cost of Sales in E15 is modified to remove the division by 3.

8. Click on D20.

9. Press (CTRL) and drag and drop D20 to E20. D20 is copied to E20.

10. Drag across/3 in the formula in the edit area, press (DEL), and press (ENTER). E20 is modified to remove the division by 3.

11. Drag E20 through E23. The range E20:E23 is highlighted.

12. Click on the Edit menu and then click on Fill Down. E20 is copied to E21, E22, and E23.

Your screen should look like the one shown in Figure 5-11.

Copying a Column of Formulas

Once the August projection is completed, you can copy it to September. There are no differences between the relative formulas as they are now constructed in August and what is needed for September. Use the following instructions to produce September's projection.

Figure 5-11.   *Completed August projection*

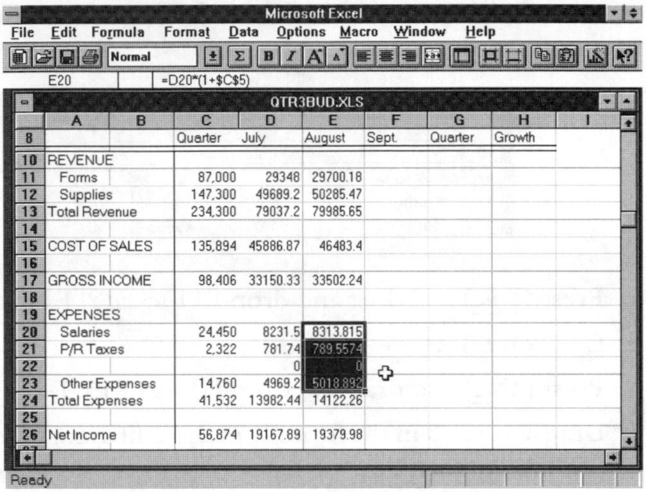

1. Drag from E11 through E26. The entire range of Revenue, Cost of Sales, and Expense (E11:E26) is highlighted.

2. Press (CTRL) and drag and drop E11:E26 to F11:F26. E11:E26 is copied to F11:F26, as shown in Figure 5-12.

Here again you see the power of the Copy command. If you want to build an annual budget by month, all you have to do is build one month and copy it to the other eleven.

Copying

The copying capability is extremely valuable and quite simple. As you have seen, there are three types of copying. With the Copy option, you identify a range you want to copy from—the source range—choose the Copy option from the Edit menu, and then specify the range you want to copy to—the destination range. With the Fill Down or Fill Right option (or Fill Up or Fill Left, which

Figure 5-12. *September projection, as a result of copying August projection*

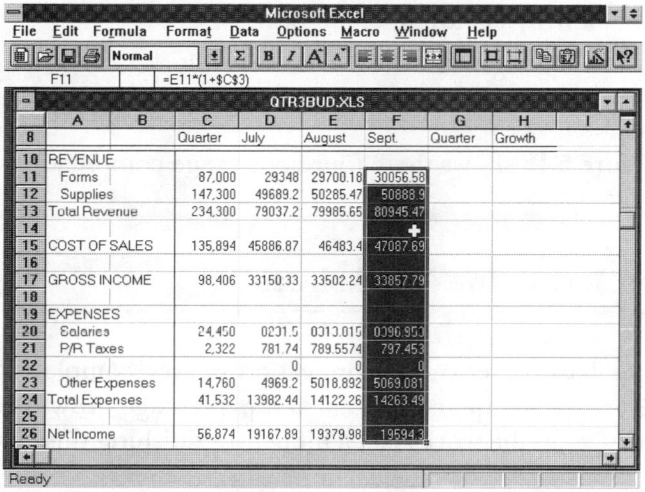

you get by pressing (SHIFT) when you select the Edit menu), you identify both the source and destination ranges and then choose the command from the Edit menu. The Copy option can do the same type of copying as the Fill options, but the Fill options do it faster with fewer steps. Finally, with Excel 4, you can use drag and drop for both copying and filling.

For all types of copying, the mouse is by far the easiest means of identifying both the source and destination ranges. The keyboard can also be used, however. Using the direction keys, you first move the active cell to one of the corners of the range, and then press and hold (SHIFT) while using the direction keys to expand the highlight to the other cells in the range.

There are four copy range combinations that work:

- Copying a single column to a range spanning several columns. The destination is a single row—the top row of the receiving columns.

- Copying a single row to a range spanning several rows. The destination is a single column—the left column of the receiving rows.

- Copying a single cell to another single cell, to a row of cells, to a column of cells, or to a block of cells. The destination is another cell, a row, a column, or a block.

- Copying a block to a second block. The destination is a single cell—the upper-left corner of the receiving range.

Figure 5-13 shows these four copy range combinations.

Completing the Worksheet

The basic three-month projection is now complete. Still to be added, however, are the quarterly total and percentage growth columns. Also, you will spruce up the worksheet a bit before finishing this chapter.

Producing a Total

The quarterly total is just the sum of the three months. Use the SUM function again to produce a quarterly total:

1. Click on G11. The active cell moves to G11.

2. Click on the AutoSum tool in the toolbar. The edit area contains =SUM(C11:F11), as shown here:

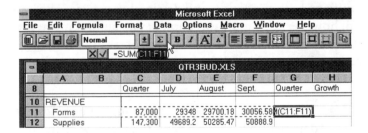

The AutoSum tool automatically builds a SUM formula in the active cell based on a contiguous range of numbers, either above or to the left of the active cell. In this case the contiguous range of numbers is to the left and includes the second quarter, which you don't want. You therefore need to revise the range to be summed.

3. Press (RIGHT ARROW). The range in the SUM formula changes to just D11.

Figure 5-13.   *Four copy range combinations*

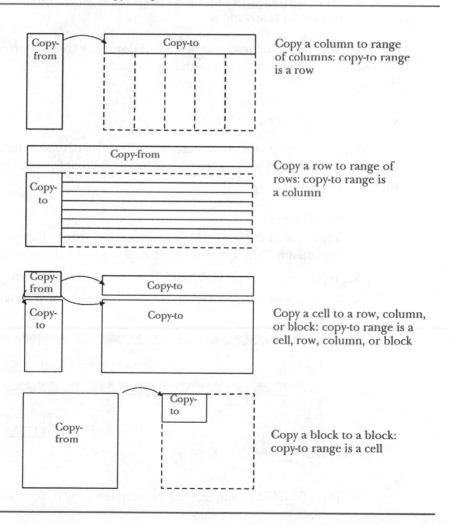

Copy a column to range of columns: copy-to range is a row

Copy a row to range of rows: copy-to range is a column

Copy a cell to a row, column, or block: copy-to range is a cell, row, column, or block

Copy a block to a block: copy-to range is a cell

4. Press (SHIFT)-(RIGHT ARROW) twice. The range in the SUM formula becomes D11:F11, which is what you want to sum in the third quarter.

   Pressing (SHIFT) and any arrow key extends the selection of cells in the direction of the arrow key. This is also true with (HOME), (END), (PGDN), and (PGUP). Unless you press (SHIFT), you will replace D11 with the new active cell instead of creating a range as you intended.

5. Press (ENTER). The summation formula is completed, and Excel returns to ready mode.

The summation formula will be copied down the third-quarter summary column with the percentage growth in a moment.

Calculating a Percentage

The percentage growth formula is the difference between the second and third quarters divided by the second quarter. Build that formula by following these instructions:

1. Click on H11.

2. Type =(and click on G11. The mode indicator changes to ENTER and then to POINT, and =(G11 is placed into the edit area.

3. Type - and click on C11. -C11 is added to the edit area.

4. Type)/ and click on C11 again. The edit area now looks like this:

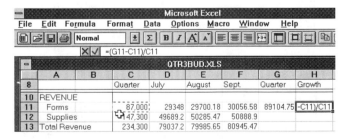

5. Press (ENTER) to complete the percentage growth formula.

Copying a Row of Formulas

The quarterly summation and percentage growth formulas now must be copied down their columns. There are three ways to do this. One way is to copy the formulas in five operations to the five segments that need it (Revenue accounts, Cost of Sales, Gross Income, Expense accounts, and Net Income). The second method is to copy the formulas to the entire column at one time and then erase the four blank lines that divide the segments. Finally, you can use *AutoFill* to copy the quarterly summation and percentage growth formulas to the entire column. AutoFill allows you to create a filled range of fixed values (as in this case) or extend a *series* by incrementing numbers or dates. Series will be discussed in Chapter 7. In this example, you will still need to erase the four blank lines that divide the segments, but now the copy operation can be done in one mouse operation. Use AutoFill in the following exercise:

1. Drag across G11 and H11 and point on the fill handle in the lower-right corner of the highlighted range G11:H11. The mouse pointer will change as shown in Figure 5-14.

2. Drag the mouse pointer down the right border of range G11:H26. Release the mouse button when the shaded border covers the range. Columns G and H are filled with figures, as shown in Figure 5-15.

On the unused rows, like 14, you get the message #DIV/0!. This is an error message stating you are dividing by zero. Don't let it bother you. You are going to erase or clear these next.

Clearing a Range of Cells

Clearing a range (which, you remember, can be a cell, a column, a row, or a block) is very easy: highlight the range, press (DEL), and click on OK. Do that next for row 14:

1. Drag across G14 and H14. The range G14:H14 is highlighted.

2. Press (DEL) or choose Clear from the Edit menu. The Clear dialog box opens.

Figure 5-14.   *Mouse pointer changed to a fill handle*

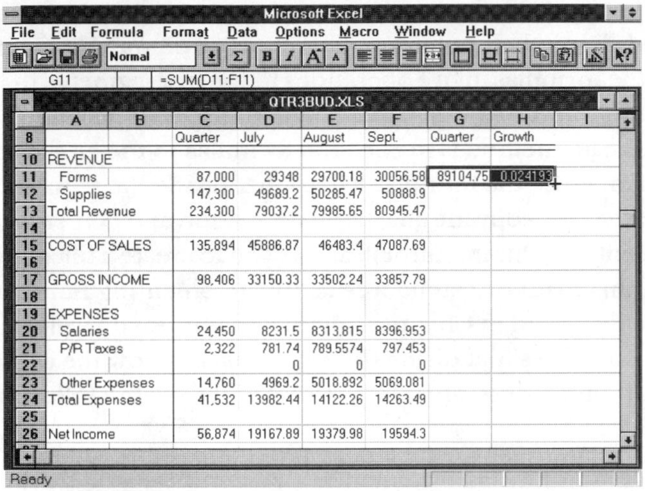

Figure 5-15.   *Completed totals and percentages*

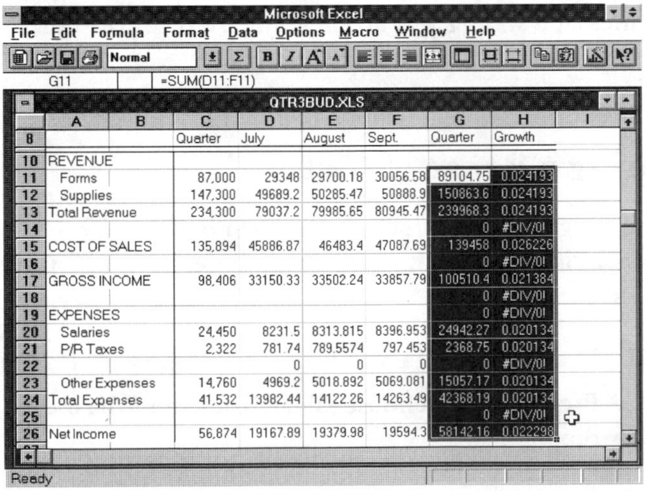

The options that are available in the Clear dialog box and their results are as follows:

Option	Result
All	Erases everything (contents, formats, and notes) from the cell and returns it to the General format.
Formats	Erases only the formats, leaving the contents and notes. The cell is returned to the General format.
Formulas	Erases only the contents, leaving the formats and notes.
Notes	Erases only the notes, leaving the contents and formats.

The Formulas option is the default and the one most generally used. Since your Third Quarter Budget worksheet does not have any formatting or notes, Formulas is just fine here. (Notes, which are discussed in Chapter 6, are blocks of text that you can attach to a cell.)

3. Click on OK to accept clearing only the contents of the cells G14 and H14, as shown here:

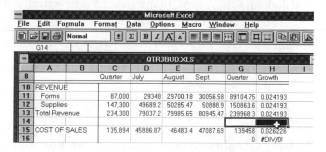

4. Drag across G16 and H16.

5. Press (DEL) and click on OK to clear G16 and H16.

Use similar steps to erase rows 18, 19 (which can be done together), and 25. Leave row 22 for the moment.

Inserting a Row

To make the worksheet easier to read, you will now insert a line between the expense and revenue totals and the detail accounts above them. To do this, you must insert a blank row and then copy a line across it.

1. Drag across A13 through H13.

2. Click on the Edit menu and on the Insert option. The Insert dialog box opens, as shown here:

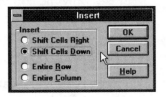

The Insert dialog box gives you four options: Shift Cells Right, Shift Cells Down—which is what you want here—Entire Row, or Entire Column. Since Shift Cells Down is the default, you only need to click on OK.

3. Click on OK. A new, blank row 13 is inserted, and all the cells below A13:H13 are shifted down.

4. Click on C13, type - and press (ENTER). C13 contains a single hyphen.

5. Click on the Format menu and the Alignment option. The Alignment dialog box opens.

6. Click on Fill and OK. The dialog box closes, and C13 fills with hyphens.

7. Drag C13 through H13. Click on the Edit menu and the Fill Right option. The line in C13 is copied across the range D13:H13, as shown here:

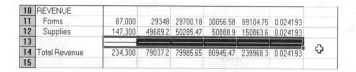

10	REVENUE						
11	Forms	87,000	29348	29700.18	30056.58	89104.75	0.024193
12	Supplies	147,300	49689.2	50285.47	50888.9	150863.6	0.024193
13							
14	Total Revenue	234,300	79037.2	79985.65	80945.47	239968.3	0.024193
15							

Go down to A25 and, following the previous instructions, insert a new row and copy a line across columns C through H. Note that in both cases the total formulas remain unaffected by the new rows.

Deleting a Row

You have been hanging on to what is now row 23 with the idea that you will do something with it. You will, you'll delete it. Row 23 was added to demonstrate deleting a row in a SUM range. Do that now by following these instructions:

1. Drag across A23 through H23.

2. Click the right mouse button (Shortcut menu) and the Delete option. The Delete dialog box opens with the options Shift Cells Left (to delete columns) or Shift Cells Up (to delete rows), as shown in Figure 5-16. The default, Shift Cells Up, is what you want. Therefore, you need only click on OK.

3. Click on OK. The range A23:H23 is deleted and all the cells below that row shift up. Note that the row deletion did not change the Total Expenses or Net Income amounts.

Inserting and Deleting

Inserting and deleting rows and columns are simultaneously very powerful and potentially dangerous operations. They are powerful because they allow you to easily change the structure of a worksheet after it is built; for example, adding new or forgotten accounts or deleting unwanted elements. Inserting and especially deleting can also be dangerous because, under certain circumstances, you can cause a formula to become incorrect.

Figure 5-16.   *Row deletion in progress*

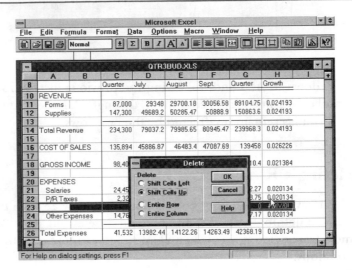

Excel has many safeguards against causing a formula error with an insertion or a deletion. You have seen how both cell-by-cell addition and SUM formulas are not affected by inserting rows. Even an absolute range is correctly adjusted if an inserted row changes its position. For example, if a row is inserted between rows 2 and 3, pushing the assumptions in C3 through C5 down a row, the absolute references to those cells are corrected automatically.

One safeguard is that both inserts and deletes can be undone if you choose Undo from the Edit menu or press (ALT)-(BACKSPACE) before you carry out another operation that takes Excel out of ready mode. You can look at a formula, but do not try to edit it. Get into the habit of pausing after doing an insert or delete and looking around the worksheet. Highlight several formulas to see if they have been correctly changed, thereby giving yourself a chance to use Undo if necessary.

Excel's formulas are extremely flexible, especially SUM. Not only can you insert or delete cells in the middle of a summation range, but you can also delete the named first and last cells in a summation and the formula will be correctly adjusted.

When you do an insert or delete, it is handy to think of it as inserting or deleting rows or columns. However, there is good reason for Excel's not using this terminology in their dialog boxes: you insert or delete only the specific cells you previously highlighted. You do not insert or delete a row or column across or down the entire worksheet.

While it may be obvious that to delete three rows, you need to highlight three rows, it is not so obvious that to insert three rows, you need to highlight three rows. The number of rows highlighted are inserted immediately above the top row highlighted. For columns, the number of columns highlighted are inserted immediately to the left of the leftmost column highlighted.

Making Corrections

This completes the work you will do on the worksheet in this chapter. Your screen should now look like the one shown in Figure 5-17. If your numbers are different, you may have an error in one of your formulas. Although it is a bit of a pain, you might want to look for it just to scc how a search is done. Go down columns D and E, highlighting each cell. Also, look at cells G11 and H11. Compare the cell contents in the edit area with various figures and descriptions in this chapter. It should not take long to find it. A good rule is to thoroughly check formulas as you are building them to prevent having to go back and correct them later.

Saving and Quitting Excel

The only task remaining is to save the worksheet and leave Excel. Use the following instructions for that purpose.

Figure 5-17. ***Finished worksheet***

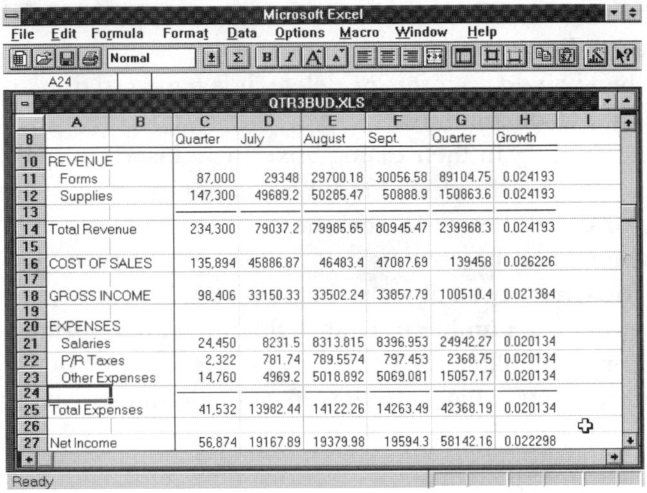

	A	B	C	D	E	F	G	H
8			Quarter	July	August	Sept.	Quarter	Growth
10	REVENUE							
11	Forms		87,000	29348	29700.18	30056.58	89104.75	0.024193
12	Supplies		147,300	49689.2	50285.47	50888.9	150863.6	0.024193
13								
14	Total Revenue		234,300	79037.2	79985.65	80945.47	239968.3	0.024193
15								
16	COST OF SALES		135,894	45886.87	46483.4	47087.69	139458	0.026226
17								
18	GROSS INCOME		98,406	33150.33	33502.24	33857.79	100510.4	0.021384
19								
20	EXPENSES							
21	Salaries		24,450	8231.5	8313.815	8396.953	24942.27	0.020134
22	P/R Taxes		2,322	781.74	789.5574	797.453	2368.75	0.020134
23	Other Expenses		14,760	4969.2	5018.892	5069.081	15057.17	0.020134
24								
25	Total Expenses		41,532	13982.44	14122.26	14263.49	42368.19	0.020134
26								
27	Net Income		56,874	19167.89	19379.98	19594.3	58142.16	0.022298

1. Click on the Save tool (the third tool from the left in the Standard toolbar). The file is saved under the name you originally gave it: QTR3BUD.

As a default, when Excel saves a file it simply copies over the last copy of the same file on disk. The save you just completed copied over the file that you created by saving the worksheet early in the chapter. You can have Excel make a new file each time you save a file. Since you can have only one file with a given name, Excel automatically renames the old file by changing its extension to .BAK. The third time you save a file, the first copy is deleted and the second copy is given the .BAK extension. This is called making a *backup.*

To have Excel make a backup, use the Options button in the File Save As dialog box, as shown in the following steps:

2. Click on the File menu and click on Save As. The File Save As dialog box opens.

3. Click on the Options button in the File Save As dialog box. A new dialog box opens, as shown here:

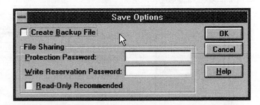

4. Click on the Create Backup File check box, and then click on OK twice. The Options and the File Save As dialog boxes close, and another dialog box opens asking if you want to replace the existing QTR3BUD.XLS file.

5. Click on OK.

   The previous file, which was called QTR3BUD.XLS, is now renamed QTR3BUD.BAK, and a new file named QTR3BUD.XLS will be created. You now have two files on disk. The file backup capability is handy should you need to reuse the earlier file for any reason.

You are done with Excel and Windows for this chapter. Therefore shut them both down now.

6. Double-click on Excel's Control-menu box and then on Windows' Control-menu box. Click OK to end your Windows session.

At this point, the worksheet in printed form is not particularly pretty, as shown in Figure 5-18 with the grid and in Figure 5-19 without the grid. The formatting of the numbers is messy and the columns seem to run together. Making it look better in a number of ways, as well as printing it, are the subjects of Chapter 6.

Figure 5-18.   *Printed worksheet with grid*

	A	B	C	D	E	F	G	H
1			THIRD QUARTER BUDGET					
2								
3	Revenue Growth/Mo.		0.012					
4	C O S Growth/Mo.		0.013					
5	Expense Growth/Mo.		0.01					
6								
7			Second				Third	Percent
8			Quarter	July	August	Sept.	Quarter	Growth
10	REVENUE							
11	Forms		87000	29348	29700.18	30056.58	89104.75	0.024193
12	Supplies		147300	49689.2	50285.47	50888.9	150863.6	0.024193
13								
14	Total Revenue		234300	79037.2	79985.65	80945.47	239968.3	0.024193
15								
16	COST OF SALES		135894	45886.87	46483.4	47087.69	139458	0.026226
17								
18	GROSS INCOME		98406	33150.33	33502.24	33857.79	100510.4	0.021384
19								
20	EXPENSES							
21	Salaries		24450	8231.5	8313.815	8396.953	24942.27	0.020134
22	P/R Taxes		2322	781.74	789.5574	797.453	2368.75	0.020134
23	Other Expenses		14760	4969.2	5018.892	5069.081	15057.17	0.020134
24								
25	Total Expenses		41532	13982.44	14122.26	14263.49	42368.19	0.020134
26								
27	Net Income		56874	19167.89	19379.98	19594.3	58142.16	0.022298

Figure 5-19.   *Printed worksheet without grid*

	Second				Third	Percent
THIRD QUARTER BUDGET						
Revenue Growth/Mo.	0.012					
C O S Growth/Mo.	0.013					
Expense Growth/Mo.	0.01					
	Second	July	August	Sept.	Third	Percent
	Quarter				Quarter	Growth
REVENUE						
Forms	87000	29348	29700.18	30056.58	89104.75	0.024193
Supplies	147300	49689.2	50285.47	50888.9	150863.6	0.024193
Total Revenue	234300	79037.2	79985.65	80945.47	239968.3	0.024193
COST OF SALES	135894	45886.87	46483.4	47087.69	139458	0.026226
GROSS INCOME	98406	33150.33	33502.24	33857.79	100510.4	0.021384
EXPENSES						
Salaries	24450	8231.5	8313.815	8396.953	24942.27	0.020134
P/R Taxes	2322	781.74	789.5574	797.453	2368.75	0.020134
Other Expenses	14760	4969.2	5018.892	5069.081	15057.17	0.020134
Total Expenses	41532	13982.44	14122.26	14263.49	42368.19	0.020134
Net Income	56874	19167.89	19379.98	19594.3	58142.16	0.022298

6

Enhancing a Worksheet

In Chapter 5 you created a worksheet for preparing a third quarter budget. The results were usable, but they were difficult to read and not particularly attractive. In this chapter you'll use a number of techniques to make the budget easier to read and more attractive. This includes changing the formatting of numbers and headings, and moving, deleting, and erasing sections of the worksheet. You will also set the parameters for and print the worksheet. Finally, you'll change the Third Quarter Budget worksheet into a template that can be used to set up any quarterly budget.

Loading a Worksheet

To begin working on the budget worksheet, you must load the file that holds it on the disk. Remember that the last thing you did in Chapter 5 before leaving Excel was to save the file. You must now load that file back into memory so you can work on it. If necessary, load Windows and Excel, and use the following instructions:

1. Click on the File menu and the Open option. The File menu opens, followed by the Open dialog box, which asks for the name of the file to open. A list of files is shown in the list box, similar to what is seen here:

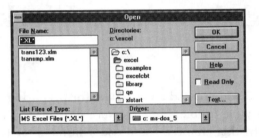

If you came directly here from Chapter 5 without leaving Excel, you are probably looking at the correct directory and can skip the next two steps. However, if you closed Excel and Windows as suggested in Chapter 5 and restarted both here, the directory you are looking at in the Open dialog box is the Excel program directory, not the \SHEET directory where you stored QTR3BUD. Your first task, then, is to change directories. Make the necessary changes with the following steps:

2. Double-click on c:\ in the Directories list box. A new Directories list box is shown. (If you need to use the keyboard, press (ALT)-(D) and, if necessary, an arrow key to highlight c:\, and then press (ENTER).)

3. Double-click on [sheet] in the Directories list box. If you do not see [sheet], use the vertical scroll bar (click on the down arrow scroll box) to find it. In the list of files, QTR3BUD.XLS should appear, as shown here:

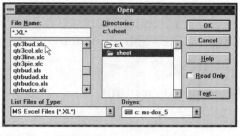

4. Double-click on QTR3BUD.XLS in the list box.

The third quarter budget opens on your screen, as shown in Figure 6-1. You can now begin working on it.

Formatting

Excel lets you *format* (change the appearance of) individual cells as well as groups or ranges of cells. After formatting a range with the most common format in that range, you can come back and change specific cells that you

Figure 6-1.   *Third quarter budget as initially loaded*

	A	B	C	D	E	F	G	H	I
8			Quarter	July	August	Sept.	Quarter	Growth	
10	REVENUE								
11	Forms		87,000	29348	29700.18	30056.58	89104.75	0.024193	
12	Supplies		147,300	49689.2	50285.47	50888.9	150863.6	0.024193	
13									
14	Total Revenue		234,300	79037.2	79985.65	80945.47	239968.3	0.024193	
15									
16	COST OF SALES		135,894	45886.87	46483.4	47087.69	139458	0.026226	
17									
18	GROSS INCOME		98,406	33150.33	33502.24	33857.79	100510.4	0.021384	
19									
20	EXPENSES								
21	Salaries		24,450	8231.5	8313.815	8396.953	24942.27	0.020134	
22	P/R Taxes		2,322	781.74	789.5574	797.453	2368.75	0.020134	
23	Other Expenses		14,760	4969.2	5018.892	5069.081	15057.17	0.020134	
24									
25	Total Expenses		41,532	13982.44	14122.26	14263.49	42368.19	0.020134	
26									
27	Net Income		56,874	19167.89	19379.98	19594.3	58142.16	0.022298	

want to be different from the overall format. You can set overall formats for several aspects of the worksheet, but here you will set the overall format just for numbers and for the width of columns.

Overall Number Format

The overall number format determines how numbers appear on a worksheet, both on the screen and when printed. Most of the numbers in Figure 6-1 are formatted with the General format, which is the format Excel starts with. It is the most versatile format in terms of the variety of numbers it can display, but it looks the least appealing. Let's first see how to change the number format and then look at some of the formatting alternatives. Start out by highlighting the area to be formatted.

1. Drag the mouse from C10 through H27 to highlight that area, as shown in Figure 6-2.

2. Click on the Format menu and the Number option. The Number Format dialog box opens, as shown here:

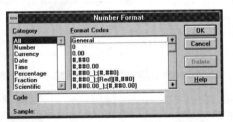

3. Double-click on the fourth alternative (#,##0) in the Format Codes list box. The Format command finishes, and the worksheet is redisplayed in the new format.

Your screen should now look like the one in Figure 6-3. Don't be concerned that all of the percentages disappeared. When you selected #,##0 from the Number Format dialog box, you told Excel to format the numbers without decimal places (you'll see how this works in a moment). Excel took you literally and displayed no decimal places even when decimals were all you had. You will come back soon to override the overall format with a specific percentage format for column H.

Figure 6-2. *Highlighting the range to be formatted*

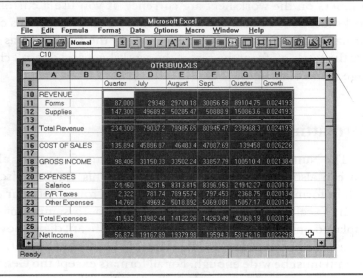

Figure 6-3. *Third quarter budget after setting the overall format*

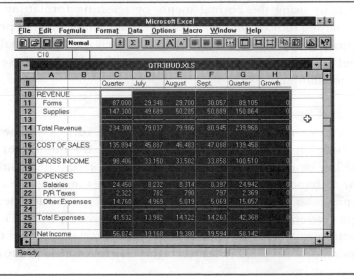

You might wonder why you use the format chosen, when the majority of numbers on the worksheet are currency. If you use a currency format, the worksheet becomes cluttered with dollar signs. Later in this chapter you will format just the total lines at the bottom of the worksheet as currency. That sets the totals off from the rest of the worksheet and doesn't clutter the entire page with dollar signs.

Formatting Alternatives

The Number Format dialog box offers many formatting alternatives, and you can also construct your own format. This chapter discusses both the built-in formats and how you can construct a format of your own.

In Excel, numbers are stored with up to 15 significant digits and also displayed on the worksheet with up to 15 significant digits; however, only nine places can be displayed to the right of the decimal point. Of course, the column must be wide enough. For all formats except the General format, the column must be wide enough to display all of the whole digits to the left of the decimal point, the number of decimal digits specified, and any other characters such as dollar signs, commas, or periods that are part of the format. If the column is not wide enough, it is filled with # symbols.

There are three ways Excel allows you to add formatting to your worksheet: by using the Format menu, by selecting formatting tools from the Formatting toolbar, and by choosing the automatic formats provided by Excel (AutoFormat). There are advantages to each method in making your worksheet more attractive. You will learn more about each of these in the exercises in this chapter.

Format Symbols

You communicate to Excel the type of format you want to use with symbols. The symbols describe such things as the number of decimal places; whether or not a dollar sign, percent sign, or comma should be used; and how to handle negative numbers, zero values, and text. Excel provides 23 format *codes*, including the General format. Excel divides these 23 codes into eight *categories*, as follows: All, Number, Currency, Date, Time, Percentage, Fraction, and Scientific. Each category has a certain number of the 23 format codes. For example, the Date category has five codes, as shown here:

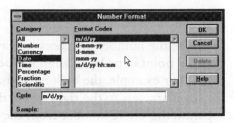

Each of these built-in format codes, plus any that you build, use the following symbols to communicate their formats:

Symbol	Usage
0	Specifies the number of decimal places to the right of the decimal point and the minimum digits to the left of the decimal point. For example, with the built-in format 0.00 you always have two decimal places to the right of the decimal point and at least one digit to the left of the decimal point. With the 0.00 format, the following numbers are formatted as shown:

Entry	Display
.456	0.46
45	45.00

| # | Specifies the number of optional digits on either side of the decimal point. For example, in the built-in format #,##0 the # provides the optional digits surrounding the comma, which is used as a thousands separator. If there are not enough digits to fill the number of places, these will be blank and space will not be left. You want the first place to be a 0 and not a #, so you will get at least a 0 printed if you have a decimal too small to round to 1. With the #,##0 format, the following entries are formatted as shown: |

Entry	Display
46.67	47
12345	12,345

Symbol	Usage
?	Specifies the number of spaces to leave on either side of the decimal point in order to align the decimal point with fewer digits. For example, the built-in format # ??/?? provides space for six characters to the right of the decimal place (one to separate the whole number from the fraction, two for the denominator, two for the numerator, and one for /). Space is always left for each ?. With the # ??/?? format, the following entries are formatted as shown:

Entry	Display
5.8125	5 13/16
5.25	5 1/4

Note that the three symbols, 0, #, and ? are placeholders that may be filled with numbers if there are numbers available for that place. If there is no number to fill 0, a 0 will take the place; if there is no number to fill #, nothing takes its place and no space is left; if there is no number to fill ?, a blank space takes its place.

Symbol	Usage
. (period)	Specifies where the decimal point is.
, (comma)	Specifies that the thousands separator is a comma if a comma is surrounded by zeros or # symbols, for example, #,##0. One or more commas on the right of a format will scale the resulting number by a thousand for each comma. For example, formatting 5,650,000 by typing, **0.00,,** in the Code text box would produce the number 5.65.
;	Separates sections of a format. You can have up to four sections. The first, or leftmost, specifies how to format positive numbers, the second section specifies how to format negative numbers, the third specifies how to format zero, and the fourth section specifies how to handle text. All numbers are handled the same if there is

Symbol	Usage

only one section. With two sections, positive and zero values are formatted with the first, and negative numbers are formatted with the second. Text is not given special treatment with only three sections. An example of using a semicolon is shown with the next set of symbols.

$ + - ( ) / : space Specifies a literal character to be displayed. For example, the built-in format $#,##0_);($#,##0) places a $ to the left of the leftmost number and ( ) around negative numbers. With the $#,##0_);($#,##0) format, the following numbers are formatted as shown:

Entry	Display
-45.67	($46)
1234	$1,234

If you want to enter a literal character other than

$ + - ( ) / : or space

precede the character with a backslash (\) or enclose one or more of the characters in double quotation marks (" "). These are explained shortly.

_ (underline) Specifies that a space be left that is equal in width to the character immediately following the underline. For example, the built-in format $#,##0_);($#,##0), the _) shifts positive numbers to the left an amount equal to the width of a). This aligns positive and negative numbers by leaving room for the).

"text" Specifies that whatever is between the " " is displayed. As an example, $#,##0"DB" ;$#15##0"CR";0 places DB after positive numbers, CR after negative numbers, and 0 for zero values.

Symbol	Usage

**** Specifies that the character following the \ is displayed. This is the same as enclosing a single character in " ". For some characters, you do not have to enter the \ because Excel will automatically do it for you. These characters are

~ ! ^ & ' ' = { } < >.

For example, you can enter the format '#,##0'! and Excel will in effect (but not on the screen) change it to \'#,##0\'\!. If you format the number 45 with this format you will get '45'!.

@ Specifies where any text in a cell is placed in a format. For example, 0.00 ;@ formats all numbers with 0.00 and displays any text appearing in the cell. (0.00 by itself does the same thing.)

* Specifies that the character following the * is repeated to fill any unused space in the cell. For example, $**#,##0 places a $ in the leftmost position in a cell, fills any intervening space with *, and right aligns the number in the cell as usual. With the $**#,##0 format, the following numbers are formatted as shown:

Entry	Display
45	$******45
1234	$****1,234

You cannot have more than one sequence beginning with an asterisk in one section of a format.

% Specifies that a number is multiplied by 100 and a % placed to the right. For example, the built-in format 0.00% multiplies the number by 100 and places a % after it. With the 0.00% format, the following numbers are formatted as shown:

Symbol	Usage	
	Entry	**Display**
	.07	7.00%
	.4575	45.75%
	-0.067	-6.7%
E+ E- e+ e-	Specifies that the scientific format is used with either E or e. If a - is specified, only negative numbers have a sign. With + both positive and negative numbers have a sign. For example, the built-in format 0.00E+00 uses a capital E and both plus and minus signs for the scientific format. With the 0.00E+00 format, the following numbers are formatted as shown:	
	Entry	**Display**
	4567	4.57E+03
	-12345	-1.23E+04
	.0045	4.50E-03
m mm mmm mmmm	Specifies that a month is displayed as a number without a leading zero (m) or with a leading zero (mm), as a three-letter abbreviation (Apr or Sep), or as a full name. If m or mm follows h or hh it specifies minutes rather than a month.	
d dd ddd dddd	Specifies that a day is displayed as a number without a leading zero (d) or with a leading zero (dd), as a three-letter abbreviation (Tue or Thu), or as a full name.	
yy yyyy	Specifies that a year is displayed as either a two- (92) or four-digit number (1992).	
h hh	Specifies that an hour is displayed as a number either without a leading zero (4) or with a leading zero (04).	

6

Symbol	Usage
m mm	Specifies that a minute is displayed as a number either without a leading zero (5) or with a leading zero (05). If the m or mm does not appear after an h or hh, the month is displayed.
s ss	Specifies that a second is displayed as a number either without a leading zero (6) or with a leading zero (06).
AM/PM am/pm A/P a/p	Specifies that time is displayed using a 12-hour clock with AM, am, A, or a with times before noon and PM, pm, P, or p from noon to midnight.
[color]	Specifies that the characters in the cell should be displayed in a color. The colors available are black, white, red, green, blue, yellow, magenta, and cyan or [color *n*] where *n* is a number from 1 through 16 indicating one of the 16 colors in the custom color palette.

When you have a fixed number of decimal places, the decimal digits are rounded to fit the format. Also, if you have blank format sections (semicolons with nothing between them), that type of number is not displayed. For example, 0.00;;;@ displays and formats positive numbers and text, but does not display negative numbers and zero values.

General Format

Every time you create a new worksheet, all cells are automatically formatted with the General format. The General format displays numbers with a variable number of decimal places, no thousands separators, a minus sign if the number is negative, and a leading zero if the number is less than 1. If the column is not wide enough to display all of the decimal digits, they are rounded to the nearest digit that can be displayed. If the column is not wide enough to display all of the whole digits to the left of the decimal point, the number is converted to scientific notation.

Here are some examples of General formatting with the standard column width of 8.43 characters:

Entry	Display
1234567.89	1234568
1234567890	1.23E+09
-4567.89	-4567.89
.8956	0.8956

Setting Overall Column Width

Excel starts with a standard column width of 8.43 characters. This allows you to display eight or nine text characters or a number with eight characters in it (a blank character always remains on the left of a right-aligned number). A column's width can be set from 0 to 255 characters.

To change the width of a column in a worksheet, you can either drag the intersection between two column headings to the right of the column whose width you want to change, or you can use the Column Width dialog box. You can change single or multiple columns with either method. Try the dialog box next with the following steps:

1. If columns C through H are not currently highlighted (it doesn't matter what rows), drag across C11 through H11.

2. Click on the Format menu and the Column Width option. The Column Width dialog box opens, as shown here:

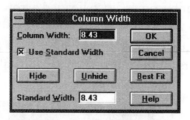

3. Type **10** and press (ENTER). All columns in the C through H range are widened to ten characters, as shown in Figure 6-4.

Now compare this dialog box method with dragging the width of multiple columns.

Figure 6-4.   *Effect of widening columns C through H to ten characters*

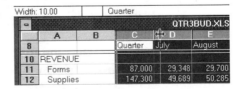

1. Click on the Edit menu and the Undo Column Width **option to** restore the original width to columns C through H.

2. Drag across the column *headings* (not the worksheet **cells) for** columns C through H. Six entire columns will be highlighted.

3. Point on the line between the column headings C and D. The mouse pointer becomes a two-headed arrow with a bar in the middle. This allows you to change the column width.

4. Drag the right edge of column C's heading until "Width: 10.00" appears on the left side of the formula bar, as shown here:

Columns D through H will be widened to ten characters.

The dragging method is not only slightly easier, but, with Excel 4, you can also now see exactly how wide the column will be.

Detail Formatting

You have now set the overall format and column width. Now you can tailor specific areas with the formatting that makes them look best. In the following sections your formatting tasks include recovering the percentages that disappeared, formatting the summary lines in the budget as currency, and centering the column headings in their columns.

Creating a Percentage Format

The percentages disappeared when the overall format was set with no decimal places. With the General format the percentages were not easy to read. A format with the % symbol, which multiplies a number by 100 and adds a percent sign, is a better way to display percentages. Two areas or ranges on the worksheet require this kind of format: the percent growth in column H and the assumptions in the upper part of column C. First you will create your own custom format.

Excel comes with two built-in formats for percentages: one with zero decimals and one with two decimals. If you want a percentage format with one decimal place, you must create it. The easiest way to create a format that is only slightly different from a built-in format is to start with the built-in format. Do that now.

1. Drag down column H from H11 through H27 to highlight the first area to be formatted.

2. Press the right mouse button to display the Shortcut menu and click on the Number option.

3. Click on the Percentage category, and then click on the 0.00% format code.

    Your Number Format dialog box should look like this:

6

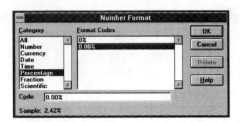

4. Drag across one of the decimal zeros in the lower Code text box and press (DEL). You have created a new format, as shown here:

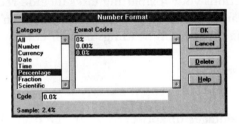

5. Click on OK. The Number Format dialog box closes, and the percentage growth numbers in column H are formatted as shown in Figure 6-5. (You may have to scroll the worksheet to display columns A through H.)

   The new percent format you created is an additional format now available on this worksheet. It does not replace the original format you used to create the new one.

6. Scroll your worksheet up and to the left and then select C3 through C5. The upper-left corner of your screen should look like this:

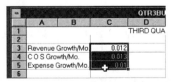

7. Click on the Format menu and the Number option. The Number Format dialog box opens.

8. Click on the Percentage category.

Figure 6-5. *Growth percentages formatted with a single decimal place*

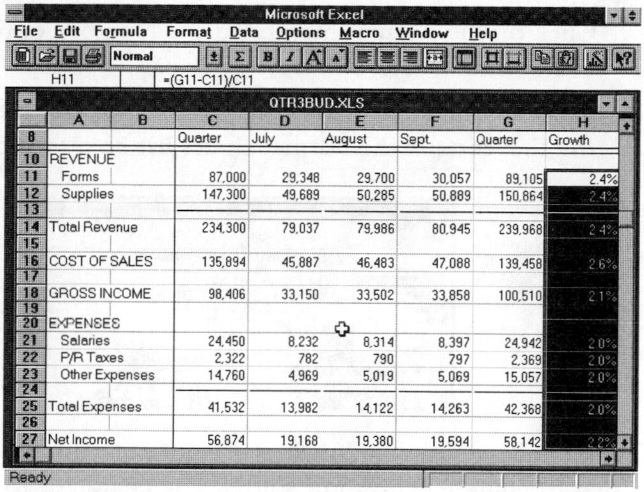

Microsoft Excel
File Edit Formula Format Data Options Macro Window Help
Normal
H11 =(G11-C11)/C11
QTR3BUD.XLS
A B C D E F G H
8 Quarter July August Sept. Quarter Growth
10 REVENUE
11 Forms 87,000 29,348 29,700 30,057 89,105 2.4%
12 Supplies 147,300 49,689 50,285 50,889 150,864 2.4%
13
14 Total Revenue 234,300 79,037 79,986 80,945 239,968 2.4%
15
16 COST OF SALES 135,894 45,887 46,483 47,088 139,458 2.6%
17
18 GROSS INCOME 98,406 33,150 33,502 33,858 100,510 2.1%
19
20 EXPENSES
21 Salaries 24,450 8,232 8,314 8,397 24,942 2.0%
22 P/R Taxes 2,322 782 790 797 2,369 2.0%
23 Other Expenses 14,760 4,969 5,019 5,069 15,057 2.0%
24
25 Total Expenses 41,532 13,982 14,122 14,263 42,368 2.0%
26
27 Net Income 56,874 19,168 19,380 19,594 58,142 2.2%
Ready

6

9. Double-click on the new format. The three growth assumptions are formatted into percentages, as shown here:

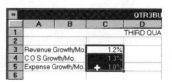

QTR3BU
A B C D
1 THIRD QUA
2
3 Revenue Growth/Mo. 1.2%
4 C O S Growth/Mo. 1.3%
5 Expense Growth/Mo. 1.0%
6

Adding Dollar Signs

To set off the total lines from the rest of the budget, you can format them as currency, which places a dollar sign in front of each number. There are four total lines: Total Revenue, GROSS INCOME, Total Expenses, and Net Income. Use these instructions to format the first of the lines:

1. Drag across C14 through G14. The two quarterly and three monthly totals are highlighted.

2. Click on the Format menu and the Number option. The Number Format dialog box opens.

3. Click on Currency in the Category list box, and then double-click on the first code in the Format Codes list box, as shown here:

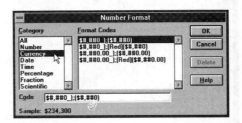

The Total Revenue amounts are now formatted with dollar signs. Also, notice that the numbers are now shifted one character to the left, leaving a blank space on the right. This is because the formats contain a _) on the right of the positive number section so positive numbers will align with negative numbers that have parentheses around them. Since you don't have any negative numbers in this budget, let's get rid of the space on the right to improve the worksheet's appearance. Do that with another custom format by removing the _) in the dollar format you used earlier. (C14 through G14 should still be selected.)

4. Click on the Format menu and the Number option to again open the Number Format dialog box. The first dollar format should still be selected.

5. Drag across the _) in the Code text box at the bottom of the dialog box, press (DEL), and then click on OK. When you return to the worksheet you will see that the numbers in row 14 are shifted back one character to the right.

Use your new dollar format without the _) (it will be at the bottom of the Currency category) to format the GROSS INCOME amounts in row 18, Total Expenses amounts in row 25, and Net Income amounts in row 27 (rows 25 and 27 can be done together by dragging C25:G27, since row 26 is blank).

Figure 6-6.   *Formatting the totals as currency*

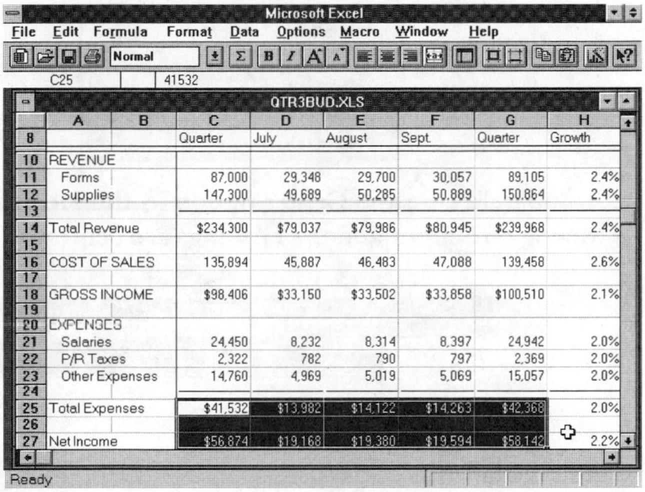

Alternate between the Format and Shortcut menus as you use the new dollar format. When you are done your screen should look like the one shown in Figure 6-6.

Centering Headings

The final item of detail formatting that you need to do is to center each of the column headings within their columns. Remember from Chapter 4 that Excel automatically left aligns text. Unless you or someone else changed your third quarter budget, all of the headings are left aligned.

Centering the column headings makes them look better and is easy to do with the Format Alignment option. Use it now to center the column headings:

1. Drag across C7 through H8.

2. Click on the Format menu and the Alignment option. The Alignment dialog box opens, as shown here:

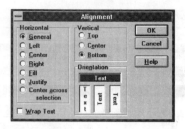

3. Double-click on the Center option in the Horizontal list box. The dialog box closes and the headings are centered, as shown here:

The Formatting Toolbar

The Formatting toolbar provides convenient access to many of the common formatting techniques you will use. The following instructions show how to add the Formatting toolbar to your display.

1. Click on the Options menu and choose the Toolbars option.

2. Double-click on Formatting in the Show Toolbars list box. The Formatting toolbar window opens, as shown here:

3. Drag the Title bar of the Formatting toolbar window up until it is beneath the Standard toolbar.

To regain more rows of your worksheet and make the area above the worksheet less "busy," you may want to display only the Formatting toolbar. Try the following instructions to remove the Standard toolbar from the screen.

1. Click on the Options menu and choose Toolbars. The Standard toolbar is highlighted.

2. Click on the Hide button. The Standard toolbar is removed from the screen, and your screen looks much like it always has except the toolbar is the Formatting toolbar instead of the Standard toolbar.

Appendix B describes each of the tools on the toolbar and provides instructions on how to customize the toolbar by adding or deleting individual tools.

AutoFormat

AutoFormat is a feature new to Excel 4, which allows you to automatically format your worksheet. From a list of five formatting styles and a total of 14 formats, you can change the appearance of any selected range, or even an entire worksheet, to give your work a professionally designed look.

In the previous formatting exercises, you learned how to use and customize built-in formats to give the third quarter budget a more personalized appearance. Through this process, you were offered a number of different options in which to format the worksheet. This greater flexibility carries with it the extra burden of time it takes to design and construct the final appearance of the worksheet. AutoFormat provides an already proven combination of number formats, fonts, alignment, borders, patterns, column widths, and row heights from which to choose. Additionally, AutoFormat displays a sample of each of the 14 formats and allows you to see the immediate effect of changing the formatting combinations.

The best way to appreciate AutoFormat is to use it. In the following instructions you will change your worksheet a number of times. In order to restore the worksheet to the way it looked before you applied the AutoFormat changes, you will use the Undo feature. Undo is a lifesaver, as you will see. The key is to use it *immediately* after making the change (or mistake). If you do anything that causes Excel to leave ready mode, Undo undoes only to that point. Note that you can choose Undo from the Edit menu as well as use the shortcut (ALT)-(BACKSPACE). Try AutoFormat now:

1. Click on the Format menu and choose AutoFormat.

2. The AutoFormat dialog box appears, as shown below:

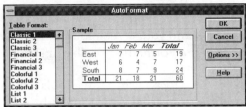

3. Take a moment to click on each format in the Table Format list box and see the different appearances you can choose.

4. Click on the Classic 3 format.

5. Click on the Options button.

   Six formats are displayed in the Formats to Apply section, with a check box next to each one, as shown here:

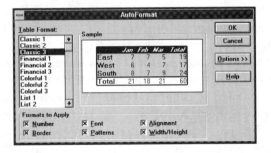

   Initially, all formats are selected.

6. Click on the Border check box. Notice how the borders are removed from the sample.

7. Click on the Width/Height check box; the column widths are expanded.

   When you clear formats from the Formats to Apply box, AutoFormat deletes the effect of those formats on the Table format, and retains any previous formatting you may have applied to the selected range or worksheet.

8. Click on Cancel to return to the worksheet.

Let's see how AutoFormat can change the third quarter budget. Since experimentation with AutoFormat is part of the exercise, your worksheet will need to be restored to its present appearance so you can continue the remainder of the chapter. This is easily done by saving the file now.

1. Click on the File menu and choose Save. The file **QTR3BUD.XLS** is saved to disk. You can now use AutoFormat freely, without worrying about making unrestorable changes.

2. Columns C7 through H8 should still be highlighted; if they are not, highlight them now.

3. Click on the Format menu and AutoFormat.

4. Click on Classic 3; then click on the Options button, the Width/Height box, and OK. Clicking on Width/Height preserves the column widths applied earlier in the chapter.

AutoFormat looked at row 7, took it to be the only title row, and italicized it as shown in the sample. In your worksheet, there are two title rows, so you will have to modify your highlighted area accordingly.

5. Click on the Edit menu and Undo to clear the AutoFormat.

6. Drag across D8:F8. Click on Format, AutoFormat, Classic 3, Options, Width/Height, and OK. Just the highlighted month columns are italicized.

In your worksheet the column headings were centered but are now right justified. To return them to the center of the column:

7. Click on Format, AutoFormat, Classic 3, Options, Alignment, Width/Height, and OK. By clearing the Alignment check box, your previous center alignment is restored.

Continue to experiment with different title formats, applied formats, and ranges to get a sense of what AutoFormat can and cannot do. Also, you can use the Formatting toolbar to quickly apply some formatting. As you will discover, AutoFormat works best on a simple table, as in the samples. Depending on the structure of your worksheet, it may be easier to set the formats individually, by using AutoFormat, or by using a combination of individual and automatic formats. Now, to return to the third quarter budget worksheet without AutoFormat changes:

8. Click on the File menu and Close. Excel will ask if you want to save changes to QTR3BUD.XLS. Click on No.

9. You will return to a blank SHEET1.XLS. Click on the File menu and then click on the first file in the list of four files at the bottom of the menu. This is the last saved file of QTR3BUD.XLS. Your screen should look like Figure 6-6, but with the column headings centered.

Changing the Layout

Now you can make some changes to the worksheet. The largest change is deleting column B. To facilitate that, you'll move the assumptions over one column. Then you'll widen column A, narrow column H, and recenter the title. To make the formulas more understandable, you'll add some notes to them. Finally, you'll erase the previous month in preparation for the next quarter, and then, remembering that you have not printed the worksheet yet, you'll undo the erasure.

Moving Formulas

You need to move the growth assumptions from column C to column D so the assumption labels still have enough room when column B is deleted. When the contents of a cell are moved, any formula that refers to that cell is changed to reflect the move, even if it has an absolute reference. This gives you significant flexibility.

1. Drag down C3 through C5. The assumptions are highlighted.

2. Point on the right border of range C3:C5. Drag and drop the range to its new position, D3:D5. The assumptions are moved.

3. Click on D11 to look at the formula.

The reference to the assumption in the formula in D11 used to be $C$3. It has now changed to $D$3, as shown here:

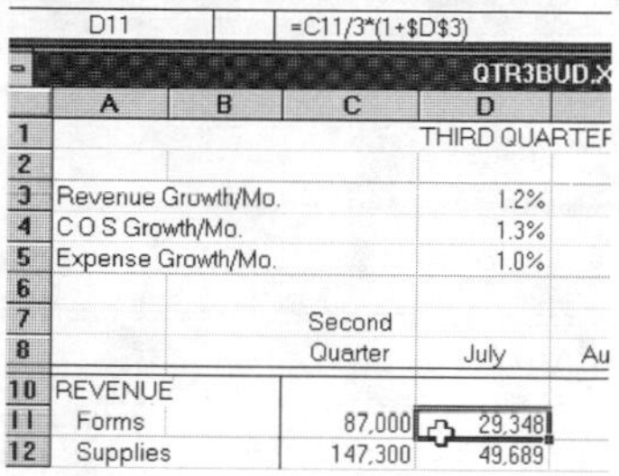

Deleting a Column

Column B of the third quarter budget was used to provide room for the row labels without changing the column width. Now that you can change the column width, there is no longer a reason to keep column B. Using these instructions, delete column B:

1. Click on the column heading for column B.
2. Click on the right mouse button to display the Shortcut menu and click on Delete.

When column B is deleted, the remaining columns to the right are relettered, as shown in Figure 6-7. Also, all formulas are revised accordingly. Look at several formulas that used to refer to the old column C, and you'll see they now refer to column B.

Adjusting Individual Column Width

Now that column B is gone, you need to widen column A so you can read the row labels. Do that by following these steps:

6

Figure 6-7.   *Effects of deleting the original column B*

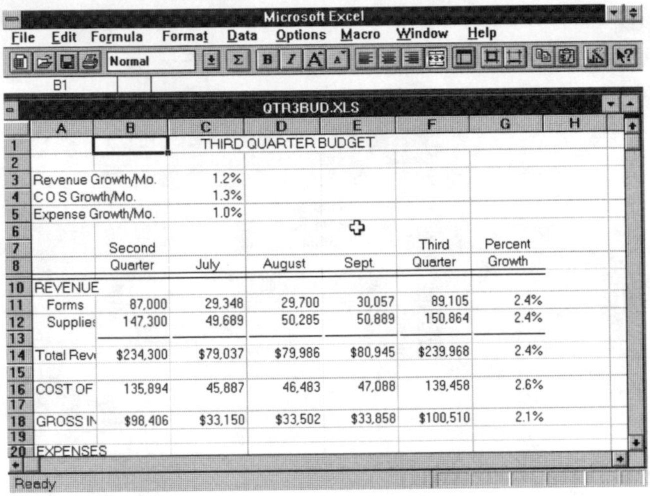

Microsoft Excel
File Edit Formula Format Data Options Macro Window Help

B1

QTR3BUD.XLS

	A	B	C	D	E	F	G	H
1			THIRD QUARTER BUDGET					
2								
3	Revenue Growth/Mo.		1.2%					
4	C O S Growth/Mo.		1.3%					
5	Expense Growth/Mo.		1.0%					
6								
7		Second				Third	Percent	
8		Quarter	July	August	Sept.	Quarter	Growth	
10	REVENUE							
11	Forms	87,000	29,348	29,700	30,057	89,105	2.4%	
12	Supplie	147,300	49,689	50,285	50,889	150,864	2.4%	
13								
14	Total Rev	$234,300	$79,037	$79,986	$80,945	$239,968	2.4%	
15								
16	COST OF	135,894	45,887	46,483	47,088	139,458	2.6%	
17								
18	GROSS IN	$98,406	$33,150	$33,502	$33,858	$100,510	2.1%	
19								
20	EXPENSES							

Ready

1. Place the mouse pointer in the column heading, at the intersection of columns A and B. The mouse pointer turns into a two-headed arrow with a line in the middle, as shown here:

2. Drag the column intersection to the right until you are almost over the intersection of columns B and C: you are making column A about equal to the sum of the old columns A and B. Notice in the Formula bar how the column width is increasing. Size the column to 17.57.

The second column sizing you want to do narrows the percentage growth column to about seven and a half characters.

Figure 6-8. *After column resizing is completed*

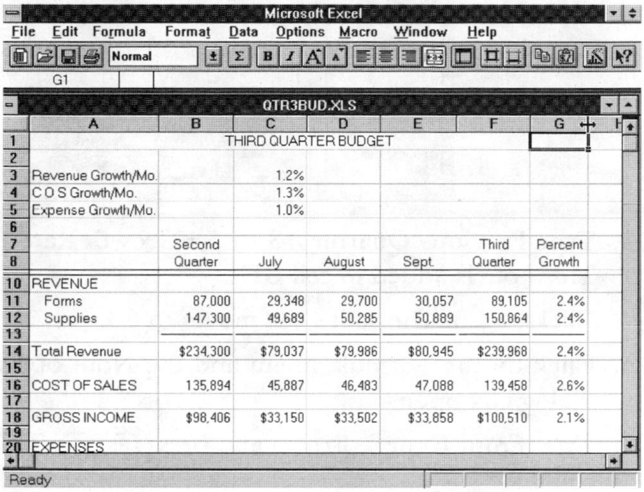

3. Place the mouse pointer in the column heading at the intersection of columns G and H.

4. Drag the column intersection to the left until the width in the Formula bar reads 7.57. Your worksheet should look like the one shown in Figure 6-8.

Adding Notes to Cells

After a period of time, it is sometimes difficult to remember why you built a formula the way you did or who gave you a certain figure. This problem becomes more important if you give your worksheet to someone else to use. Excel has a feature that allows you to add notes to cells to explain their contents. Use this feature with the following steps to add a couple of notes to your worksheet:

1. Click on C11. The active cell moves to C11.

2. Click on the Formula menu and the Note option. The Cell Note dialog box opens, as shown here:

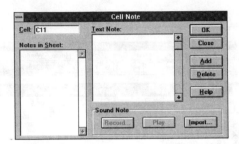

3. Type **Previous Quarter / 3 * (1 + Growth Rate)** and press (ENTER). This note is added to cell C11.

4. Click on C3. The active cell moves to C3.

5. Click on the Formula menu and the Note option. **The Cell Note dialog box opens.**

6. Type **From George Brown** and press (ENTER). This note is added to cell C3.

You can tell a note is in a cell by the small black (or red on color monitors) mark in the upper-right corner of the cell. To read a note, move the active cell to a cell with a note and double-click, opening the Cell Note dialog box from the Formula menu, or opening the Information window from the Window menu. You can also print notes by selecting the appropriate option in the Page Setup dialog box from the File menu.

Excel 4 allows you to record and play back a sound note and add it to the active cell. To use this feature, you need to be using Microsoft Windows version 3.0 with Multimedia Extensions version 1.0 or later, or Microsoft Windows version 3.1 or later, and have the appropriate hardware installed in your computer. From the Cell Note dialog box, you can choose to record a new sound note, play back an existing note, or import a prerecorded sound.

Erasing a Range

The third quarter budget is now complete. You can turn it into another quarter's budget by changing the previous quarter's actuals and growth rates. All the formulas are based on those two sets of numbers. A simple way to change the actuals is to erase them and enter new ones. Use the following steps to save the worksheet twice, once under its current name and once under a name for the new quarter. Then in the new quarter's worksheet erase the second quarter actuals. But first, remove the Formatting toolbar from the screen and return the Standard toolbar as the only toolbar. If you need help, return to the "The Formatting Toolbar" section.

1. Click on the File menu and the Save option. The worksheet is saved under its current name, QTR3BUD.XLS.

2. Click on the File menu and the Save As option, type **\sheet\qtrbud**, and press (ENTER). The worksheet is saved again under the name QTRBUD.XLS.

3. Drag down column B from B11 through B27. The second quarter actuals are highlighted.

4. Press (DEL). The Edit Clear dialog box opens and the Formulas option is selected. This, remember, is synonymous with the cell contents, which is what you want to erase or clear.

5. Click on OK. The second quarter actuals disappear, as shown in Figure 6-9.

6

Figure 6-9. *Erasing the second quarter actuals*

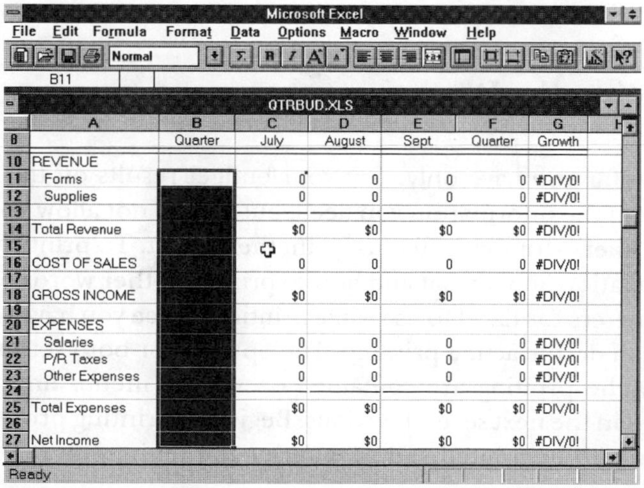

Notice that most of the formulas that depended on the second quarter actuals have changed to 0. The exception is the percentage growth amounts, which changed to #DIV/0!, indicating you are trying to divide by zero. All of the formulas, including the percentages, will change back to legitimate values as soon as you enter a new set of actuals. However, don't do that yet.

Using Undo

We forgot to print the worksheet before erasing column B. Luckily, Excel has a feature that can restore the column, as long as you have done nothing since you erased it.

1. Press (ALT)-(BACKSPACE) (Undo) now. Your worksheet should be restored to the way it was before you erased column B.

Undo even restores a full worksheet erase. (Remember, the key is to use it *immediately* after making a mistake.)

If, for some reason, your worksheet is not restored, restore it from disk by doing the following:

2. Click on the File menu and the Open option, type **qtr3bud**, and press (ENTER). Your worksheet is restored to its original condition.

Printing the Worksheet

So far you have only seen your budget results on the screen. That may give you the information you need, but it does not allow you to share it easily with others—for that you must print the budget. To print you must give Excel information about what and how to print. In other words, you must set some parameters for Excel to use while printing. Once you have set the parameters, you can do the actual printing. The options for both setting parameters and doing the printing are contained on several menus and dialog boxes, discussed in the next several sections. Begin the printing process by determining the area to be printed and by entering the settings on the Page Setup dialog box.

Setting the Parameters

If you specified your printer correctly when you installed Windows, the only required parameter for printing is the range on the worksheet that you want to print. To give the printed output the same polish you did to the screen image you can add a heading and check the page margins and length. Excel has a number of other parameters that can be set, but these are the ones most people use.

Identifying the Print Range

For this example you'll want to print the entire worksheet—everything you have done on the third quarter budget. Excel's default is just that—to print everything that has been entered on the worksheet. You do not need to identify what to print here; it's done for you in this case. In other circumstances you might want to print only a section of a worksheet. In that case you'll need to specify that specific cells be printed. See how that is done in the following example.

1. Click on the vertical scroll bar to see the top of the worksheet.
2. Drag from A1 through G27 to highlight the entire worksheet.
3. Drag on the Options menu to highlight Set Print Area option. Your screen should look like Figure 6-10 while the Options menu is open.

Whenever possible, print using the default of the entire worksheet instead of specifying the print area. The reason for this is that if you modify your worksheet by adding columns or rows and you have specified a print area, you will have to modify the print area to incorporate the new columns or rows. Also, once defined, getting rid of a print area is a very obscure procedure: choose Define Name from the Formula menu, select Print_Area from the Names in Sheet list box, click on Delete, and then click on OK.

Setting Up a Printed Page

Use the Page Setup dialog box to specify the major facets of the page to be printed. Through this dialog box you can enter a header and/or footer to be printed on the page, set the page margins, and turn the row and column headings and gridlines on or off. Open that dialog box now by clicking on the File menu and the Page Setup option. The Page Setup dialog box opens, as shown here:

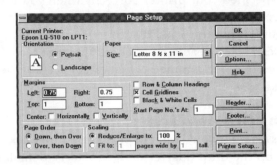

The next two sections examine the areas of this dialog box.

A *header* or heading is a line of text that is added to the top of every printed page. It often contains a page number, the date of printing, and a descriptive line of text (like a company name). A *footer* is a line of text added to the bottom of every printed page. Excel provides several codes that you can include in either a header or footer to specify the

Figure 6-10.   *Highlighting the print range*

alignment, use of bold or italic fonts, and inclusion of such things as the date and page number. These codes and their functions are listed here:

Code	Function
&b	Prints the following header or footer segment in bold.
&c	Centers the following header or footer segment.
&d	Prints the date maintained in your computer.
&f	Prints the filename of the currently active worksheet, chart, or macro sheet.
&"*typeface*"	Prints the following header or footer segment in the typeface specified by typeface. For example, &"tmsrmn" prints the following segment in the TMSRMN (Times Roman) typeface.
&i	Prints the following header or footer segment in italic.
&l	Left aligns the following header or footer segment.
&n	Prints the total number of pages to be printed. For example, Page &p of &n prints the word "Page" followed by the current page number, the word "of," and the total number of pages to be printed.
&*nn*	Prints the following header or footer segment in the typesize, measured in points, specified by the two-digit number *nn*. For example, &14 prints the following segment in 14-point type.
&p	Prints the current page number.
&p+*number*	Prints the page number after adding *number* to it.
&p-*number*	Prints the page number after subtracting *number* from it.
&r	Right aligns the following header or footer segment.
&s	Prints the following header or footer segment with a strike through the characters.
&t	Prints the time maintained in your computer.
&u	Prints the following header or footer segment with an underline.
&&	Prints a single &.

6

A header or footer can have up to three segments: a left-aligned segment, a centered segment, and a right-aligned segment. Prior to Excel 4, each of these segments was identified by the codes to the left of the segment, and any formatting (bold or italic) applied only to that segment. In Excel 4, there are three separate text boxes for entering each of the segments.

A header always prints on the first line of a page, approximately a half inch from the top, independent of the top margin. A footer always prints on the last line of a page, approximately a half inch above the bottom, independent of the bottom margin. Headers and footers also have fixed 0.75-inch margins on the left and right, independent of the left and right margins you set in the Page Setup dialog box.

Add a header containing the date, company name, and page number to the printout of the Third Quarter Budget worksheet with the following steps:

1. Click on the Header button to display the Header dialog box, as shown here:

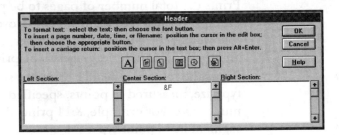

Each of the three segments has its own text box. All left-aligned text is typed in the leftmost text box, center-aligned text in the center text box, and so forth.

The six buttons in the middle of the dialog box insert the following codes in the alignment boxes. From left to right: fonts, page number (&p), page number of total pages (&n), date (&d), time (&t), and filename (f).

2. Click on the date button (the third from the right).

3. Press (TAB) to move the insertion point to the center-alignment box. Press (DEL) to erase the filename code. Type **&bMORNINGSIDE SPECIALTIES**. This enters the company name and makes it bold.

4. Press (TAB) one more time to move to the right-alignment box. Type **Page**, press (SPACEBAR) once, and click on the page number button. Click on OK.

5. You are returned to the Page Setup dialog box. Click on the Footer button.

6. Press (TAB), (DEL), and then click on OK to remove the standard footer, which contains the page number.

Setting the Margins   Margins are the distances in inches from the edge of the page to the printed data or graph on four sides: top, bottom, left, and right. Figure 6-11 shows the four margins and their relationship to the header, footer, and page length.

The maximum width of a printed line or a graph is determined by subtracting the left margin and right margin from the page width. For example, using the default margins of 0.75-inch for the left margin and 0.75-inch for the right margin, you can print a line or graph that is 7 inches wide on a normal 8.5-by-11-inch page.

Set the margins now for the third quarter budget with the following steps:

1. If it isn't already selected, drag across the number in the Left margin text box. Press (DEL) to delete the default margin.

2. Type **1** and press (TAB). The left margin is set to 1 inch, and the highlight moves to the Right margin text box.

3. Type **1** and press (TAB). The right margin is set to 1 inch, and the highlight moves to the Top margin text box.

4. Type **2.5** and press (TAB). The top margin is set to 2.5 inches, and the highlight moves to the Bottom margin text box.

5. Type **2.5**. The bottom margin is set to 2.5 inches. Your Page Setup dialog box should look like this:

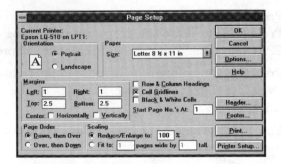

Under the margin text boxes there are two check boxes that allow you to horizontally and vertically center the worksheet or chart you are printing. This saves a lot of time by letting Excel calculate the width and height of whatever you are printing and subtract it from the page width and height.

Next in the dialog box are three check boxes, one currently checked, that control whether the row and column headings (A, B, C, and so on across the columns and 1, 2, 3, and so on down the rows) or the gridlines are printed. Click on the check boxes as necessary to tell Excel whether or not you want headings and gridlines on your output.

Also in the dialog box you can change the paper size and orientation of what you are printing. There are two orientations: portrait, in which the long side of an 8.5-by-11-inch page is vertical (the normal way a page is held), and landscape, in which the long side is horizontal. Not all printers can support various paper sizes and/or landscape printing. If yours doesn't, these options will be dimmed or light gray.

Additionally, you can determine how you print a multipage worksheet—*down* the worksheet, one page wide until the end and then over to the next range of columns, or *across* the worksheet, one page long to the end and then down.

Finally, you can scale your worksheet to different horizontal and vertical page dimensions. For example, a worksheet two pages wide by three pages long can be condensed to print in an area one page by one page. The Fit to option button and adjacent text boxes in the Scaling section allow you to adjust the printed page from the default—one page by one page—to a different size. You can change either or both dimensions when you use the Fit to options.

6. Press (ENTER) to close the dialog box and return to the worksheet.

Figure 6-11. *Margins on a printed page*

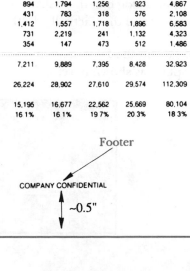

~0.5"

Header

5 8 90

Top Margin

ANNUAL BUDGET

0.75"

Page 1

0.75"

SUPERIOR OFFICE SUPPLIES

Left
Margin

1991 BUDGET

Right
Margin

6

ACCOUNT	1st QTR	2nd QTR	3rd QTR	4th QTR	TOTAL YR	% GTH
REVENUE						
PAPER SUPPLIES	42,361	47,021	52,193	57,934	199,509	36 8%
WRITING INSTRUMENTS	32,947	35,912	39,144	42,667	150,671	29 5%
CARDS AND BOOKS	14,120	15,814	17,712	19,838	67,484	40 5%
OTHER ITEMS	4,707	5,084	5,490	5,929	21,210	26 0%
TOTAL REVENUE	94,135	103,831	114,540	126,369	438,874	34 2%
COST OF SALES	52,716	58,251	64,368	71,126	246,461	34 9%
GROSS INCOME	41,419	45,580	50,172	55,242	192,413	33 4%
GROSS MARGIN %	78 6%	78 2%	77 9%	77.7%	78 1%	
EXPENSES						
SALARIES	16,944	16,944	18,015	18,845	70,748	11 2%
TAXES & BENEFITS	1,864	1,864	1,982	2,073	7,782	11 2%
OTHER LABOR	205	205	218	228	856	11 2%
TOTAL LABOR EXPENSE	19,013	19,013	20,215	21,146	79,386	11 2%
BUILDING RENTAL	2,824	2,824	2,824	2,824	11,296	0 0%
UTILITIES	565	565	565	565	2,260	0 0%
PROF SERVICES	894	1,794	1,256	923	4,867	3 2%
SUPPLIES	431	783	318	576	2,108	33 6%
TAXES	1,412	1,557	1,718	1,896	6,583	34 2%
MEETINGS AND TRAVEL	731	2,219	241	1,132	4,323	54 9%
MISCELLANEOUS	354	147	473	512	1,486	44 6%
TOTAL NONLABOR EXPEN	7,211	9,889	7,395	8,428	32,923	16 9%
TOTAL EXPENSE	26,224	28,902	27,610	29,574	112,309	12 8%
NET INCOME	15,195	16,677	22,562	25,669	80,104	68 9%
NET MARGIN %	16 1%	16 1%	19 7%	20 3%	18 3%	

Footer

Bottom
Margin

COMPANY CONFIDENTIAL

~0.5"

Determining where to set the margins is almost always a guess the first time you print a worksheet. As soon as you print the worksheet you can tell how to correct them, so it is not worth much effort on the first pass. Just make a quick guess and then come back and correct the margins after seeing the results. Better yet, tell Excel to center for you by clicking the appropriate check boxes.

Doing the Printing

The actual printing is anticlimactic after setting up the page, but you still must perform several steps, such as readying your printer, setting some final printing parameters, and, finally, telling Excel to print.

The steps to prepare your printer depend on the printer you are using. All printers must be turned on and placed online. In most printers the paper must be aligned so the upper-left corner is correctly positioned. Also, your printer must be correctly cabled to your computer. Finally, you should have installed your printer with the Windows Setup program or by using the Windows Control Panel. (If you do not know whether your printer is installed correctly, try printing. If it works, you have an affirmative answer.) If your printer is not installed in Windows, see the section on installing it in Appendix A. Take any other steps necessary to ensure that your printer is ready to print.

Once your printer is ready, start printing with the Print option from the File menu. The Print option does not begin the printing directly but rather opens another dialog box that asks you several more questions. Look at that dialog box next and then actually do the printing.

1. Click on the File menu and the Print option. The Print dialog box opens, as shown here:

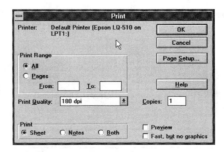

This Print dialog box is for the Epson LQ-510 printer. If you are using a different printer, your dialog box may be slightly different but should have most of the options shown. Among these are the ability to specify the number of copies you want, to print all or only selected pages, to preview the output on your screen, and to print just the worksheet, just notes, or both. Look at the last two of these options.

2. Click on the Preview check box, click on the Print Both option button, and click on OK. The worksheet and dialog box clear from your screen and a small representation of the printed worksheet appears, as shown in Figure 6-12.

On most displays you cannot easily read the image on the preview screen, but you can tell a lot about placement on the page and how good a guess you made on the margins. You can also zoom in and see a particular area. Do that next.

3. Move the mouse pointer, which you notice has become a magnifying glass, to the approximate center of the worksheet and click. The

6

Figure 6-12.   *Preview of the printed worksheet*

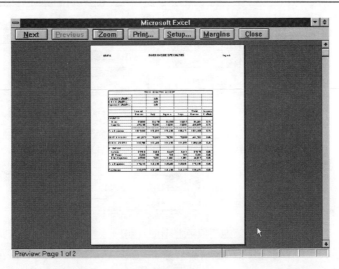

image expands to clearly show the center of the worksheet, as you can see in Figure 6-13.

4. Use the horizontal and vertical scroll bars to look around the worksheet and the header.

5. Click on the Next command button at the top of the window. The two notes you entered appear, as shown here:

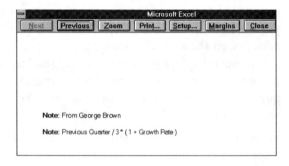

Figure 6-13.   *Preview zoomed in on the center*

	Second Quarter	July	August	Sept.	Third Quarter	Percent Growth
Revenue Growth/Mo.	1.2%					
C O S Growth/Mo.	1.3%					
Expense Growth/Mo.	1.0%					
REVENUE						
Forms	87,000	29,348	29,700	30,057	89,105	2.4%
Supplies	147,300	49,689	50,285	50,889	150,864	2.4%
Total Revenue	$234,300	$79,037	$79,986	$80,945	$239,968	2.4%
COST OF SALES	135,894	45,887	46,483	47,088	139,458	2.6%
GROSS INCOME	$98,406	$33,150	$33,502	$33,858	$100,510	2.1%
EXPENSES						
Salaries	24,450	8,232	8,314	8,397	24,942	2.0%
P/R Taxes	2,322	782	790	797	2,369	2.0%
Other Expenses	14,760	4,969	5,019	5,069	15,057	2.0%
Total Expenses	$41,532	$13,982	$14,122	$14,263	$42,368	2.0%
Net Income	$56,874	$19,168	$19,380	$19,594	$58,142	2.2%

Preview: Page 1 of 2

6. Finally, click on the Print command button to actually print. Your final printed output should look like Figure 6-14.

7. If you want to stop printing once you have started, click on the Cancel button in the Printing information box, as shown here:

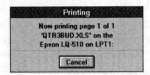

When you tell Excel to print, it creates a print job in memory, containing all of the information to be printed, and sends it to the Windows Print Manager. You can then go back to work while, in the background, the Print Manager is actually doing the printing. You can have several print jobs in memory waiting to be printed. The Print Manager gives you the ability to cancel a job after it has left Excel and to rearrange the priority of the jobs waiting to be printed. For a small worksheet like the one you built here, the advantage of the Print Manager is not very evident, but with a large multipage print job it offers a significant benefit.

6

Figure 6-14.   *Printed worksheet*

	A	B	C	D	E	F	G
1			THIRD QUARTER BUDGET				
2							
3	Revenue Growth/Mo.		1.2%				
4	C O S Growth/Mo.		1.3%				
5	Expense Growth/Mo.		1.0%				
6							
7		Second				Third	Percent
8		Quarter	July	August	Sept.	Quarter	Growth
10	REVENUE						
11	Forms	87,000	29,348	29,700	30,057	89,105	2.4%
12	Supplies	147,300	49,689	50,285	50,889	150,864	2.4%
13		-------	-------	-------	-------	-------	-------
14	Total Revenue	$234,300	$79,037	$79,986	$80,945	$239,968	2.4%
15							
16	COST OF SALES	135,894	45,887	46,483	47,088	139,458	2.6%
17							
18	GROSS INCOME	$98,406	$33,150	$33,502	$33,858	$100,510	2.1%
19							
20	EXPENSES						
21	Salaries	24,450	8,232	8,314	8,397	24,942	2.0%
22	P/R Taxes	2,322	782	790	797	2,369	2.0%
23	Other Expenses	14,760	4,989	5,019	5,069	15,057	2.0%
24		-------	-------	-------	-------	-------	-------
25	Total Expenses	$41,532	$13,982	$14,122	$14,263	$42,368	2.0%
26							
27	Net Income	$56,874	$19,168	$19,380	$19,594	$58,142	2.2%

Trial and Error

Your printout probably did not come out exactly the way you wanted it—or maybe it did not come out at all. Using a printer is almost always a trial-and-error process. Be persistent, and you should get it to work. To cure several types of problems, try the following ideas. (If you leave Excel, choose Save from the File menu to save the worksheet on disk before leaving.)

If you could not print at all, try these steps:

1. Start at the printer end. Is the printer plugged in, turned on, and set online? Does it have adequate paper and a ribbon? Is there a cable connecting the printer to the computer?

2. Look at the computer. To which port is the printer connected (LPT1, COM1, COM2)? Do you need a MODE command in your AUTOEXEC.BAT file? (If so, see your operating system manuals.) Are any other devices interfering with the printer port (for example, are both a printer and a modem connected to the same port)?

3. Open the Windows Control Panel in the Main group. Double-click on Printers, and make sure your printer name is correctly specified and that the port to which it is connected is also correct.

4. Look at the print settings you have specified. Go through the steps of setting the parameters again, checking each against the figures and illustrations in this book.

If the budget printed but it is not the way you want it, try these steps:

5. Adjust the print settings to fit your particular situation. For example, if the margins are not right, change them until the worksheet is located on the page as shown in Figure 6-14.

6. Make sure your printer is not set through its console for some particular type of printing (for example, compressed printing when you want to print at full size).

Saving the Worksheet

When you are satisfied with your printout, you need to resave the worksheet to capture the print settings you entered. Click on the File menu and the Save option.

Making a Template

After building the third quarter budget, you can use it for the fourth quarter and other future quarters. None of the formulas needs to be changed. You must change only the titles and the previous quarter actuals. When you make this worksheet more general purpose, it becomes a template for use in any quarter. The remainder of the chapter discusses how this is done.

Changing Titles

To make the titles general purpose, you need to remove the references to the third quarter. With the following instructions, edit the titles to make them generic:

1. Drag across columns A1 through G1. The active range moves to the worksheet title.
2. Drag across the word "Third" in the edit area and press (DEL). The word "Third" is removed.
3. Click immediately after the word "Quarter."
4. Type **ly**, press (SPACEBAR), and press (ENTER).
5. Click on B7. The active cell moves to the first column heading.
6. Type **Previous** and press (ENTER). "Second" is changed to "Previous," which is centered in the column.

6

7. Press (DOWN ARROW) and (RIGHT ARROW.) The active cell moves to the July column heading.

8. Type **Month 1** and press (ENTER). "July" is changed to "Month 1" and centered in the column.

In a similar manner, change the second and third months and the third quarter total, so the column headings are as shown here:

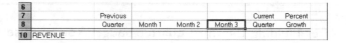

Copying Values—Paste Special

There are several ways to change the previous quarter's actual values. One way is to erase the column and reenter the new numbers. Another way is either to edit or type over the current numbers. A third way is to copy the current quarter's numbers to the previous quarter. These are not actuals *per se*. If you literally copy column F to column B, you would get a set of formulas that did not have meaning. What you want to do is to copy the *values* produced by the formulas in F, but not the formulas themselves. To do this, use Excel's Paste Special command. Follow these steps to see how Paste Special works.

1. Drag on F11 through F27.

2. Press the right mouse button for the Shortcut menu and click on Copy. A blinking marquee appears around the highlighted cells in column F.

3. Scroll your worksheet up, and then click on B11, which you want to be the recipient of the copy.

4. Click on the Edit menu and the Paste Special option. The Paste Special dialog box opens, as shown here:

5. Click on Values and OK in the Paste Special dialog box. The dialog box closes. Now only the values in column F are copied to column B. See Figure 6-15 for the result. Note the number in the Formula bar for B11.

Other Modifications

You could make many other changes to this worksheet. You could add an assumption for every account by inserting a new column to the left of column A with the assumptions in it. You could also add more accounts and

Figure 6-15. *Results of copying values*

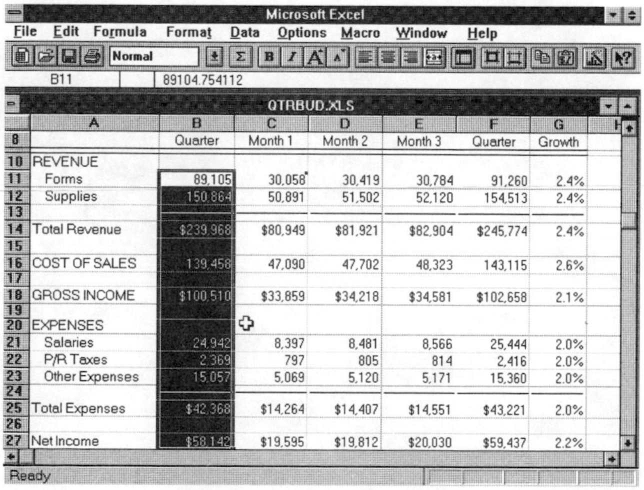

	Quarter	Month 1	Month 2	Month 3	Quarter	Growth
10 REVENUE						
11 Forms	89,105	30,058	30,419	30,784	91,260	2.4%
12 Supplies	150,864	50,891	51,502	52,120	154,513	2.4%
13						
14 Total Revenue	$239,968	$80,949	$81,921	$82,904	$245,774	2.4%
15						
16 COST OF SALES	139,458	47,090	47,702	48,323	143,115	2.6%
17						
18 GROSS INCOME	$100,510	$33,859	$34,218	$34,581	$102,658	2.1%
19						
20 EXPENSES						
21 Salaries	24,942	8,397	8,481	8,566	25,444	2.0%
22 P/R Taxes	2,369	797	805	814	2,416	2.0%
23 Other Expenses	15,057	5,069	5,120	5,171	15,360	2.0%
24						
25 Total Expenses	$42,368	$14,264	$14,407	$14,551	$43,221	2.0%
26						
27 Net Income	$58,142	$19,595	$19,812	$20,030	$59,437	2.2%

B11   89104.754112

QTRBUD.XLS

6

subtotals of accounts, or you could add more months and quarterly totals for a year. Try these on your own if you like.

Saving and Quitting

The last step prior to leaving Excel is to save your work, even if you just did it a few moments earlier. In this case you want to save the generalized version of the budget. Use these instructions to do that and then leave Excel:

1. Click on the File menu and the Save As option. The Save As dialog box opens and asks you for a filename.

2. If not already shown, type **\sheet\qtrbud**, press (ENTER), and click on OK. Click on OK again to replace the existing QTRBUD.XLS. The current worksheet is saved under the name QTRBUD.XLS, replacing the worksheet you saved under that name earlier.

3. Double-click on the Excel and Windows Control-menu boxes and click on OK to leave Excel and Windows and return to the operating system.

7

Producing Charts

In this chapter you'll work with the second of Excel's three components: charts. First you'll look at creating charts in Excel. Then you'll go over the types of charts that are available and their variations and peculiarities. Finally, you'll build three types of charts using the data from Chapter 6.

Many people find information in a pictorial form easier to understand than the numbers that generated the picture. Excel charts are pictorial representations of data on the worksheet. They are another way of displaying the results a worksheet produces.

How a Chart Is Built

Producing charts in Excel is very simple: you create a range on a worksheet, highlight that range, and tell Excel to create a new chart. This produces a standard chart based on the defaults built into Excel. You can then change any of these defaults and add many special features to customize the chart. You can create charts by *embedding* them in your worksheet so that they become a part of the worksheet, or as *chart documents* that can be printed, viewed, or edited separately. Both embedded charts and chart documents are updated as you change the data on the worksheet.

There are three ways to create charts:

- The new ChartWizard is the easiest way to create an embedded chart. By clicking on the ChartWizard tool in the Standard toolbar you can quickly see a chart displayed on the screen.

- The Chart toolbar provides 17 charting tools that allow you to easily switch between chart types and alternates as you create an embedded chart on the worksheet.

- The New command from the File menu followed by selecting the Chart option creates a chart as a separate document.

Let's look first at a standard chart and then learn how to customize it.

Standard Charts

A standard chart lets you see quickly how data looks when it is plotted and provides a starting point for a customized chart. It is not meant to be a final, presentation-quality chart.

A standard chart is based on a range of data on the worksheet. For Excel to turn this data into a chart, the range must adhere to the following guidelines:

- The highlighted range must be a rectangle or a multiple selection, with text labels on the topmost row and/or leftmost column. Otherwise, the range may contain numbers or text, but text is interpreted as zeros.

- Excel defines the first *data series*—a range of numbers on the worksheet that are related *data points* to be plotted (points that would form, for example, a single line on a chart)—as beginning with the first cell in the upper-left corner of the highlighted range containing a number not formatted as a date and continuing across the rows and columns that are highlighted.

- Excel determines whether more rows or more columns are high-lighted and, with the assumption that there will be more data points than data series, makes the larger of the two the data points. So if you highlight six columns and three rows, each column will be a data point (a single number to be plotted) and each row a data series.

- Additional data series can be included in the range by highlighting additional rows or columns, depending on whether you are building a columnwise or rowwise chart. You can have ten or more data series, but the resulting chart may not be readable.

- If the first column or row of the highlighted range contains labels or date-formatted numbers and/or the cell in the upper-left corner is blank, the first column or row—depending on whether data series are down columns (columnwise) or across rows (rowwise)—is used for the X- or *category axis.*

- The numbers on the Y- or *value axis* are formatted with the same format that has been used with the data points on the worksheet.

- The initial default is to produce a Column or vertical Bar chart. This and other options can be easily changed.

Figure 7-1 contains a range of rowwise data series that fit the guidelines for a standard chart. The topmost row contains date-formatted numbers that are used for the X- (category) axis; the next two rows are two data series, each containing four numeric data points used to produce the Column chart shown in the lower part of the figure.

Customizing Charts

Once you have a standard chart, you can customize it using three special chart menus: Gallery, Chart, and Format, as shown in the Menu bar in Figure 7-1. Using these menus you can change the type of chart by choosing from among 14 chart types in the Gallery menu; adding titles, arrows, legends, and gridlines from the Chart menu; and applying many formatting features from the Format menu. Almost all charts, both "quick and dirty" charts and

Figure 7-1.   *A data range and its resulting chart*

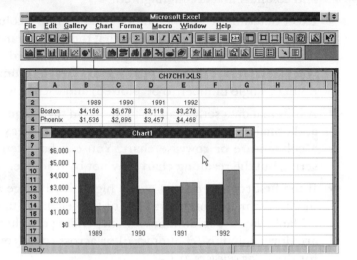

presentation-quality charts, require some amount of customization. **The rest of this chapter is devoted to the topic of customizing charts.**

The Chart Menus

When you create a new chart or load an existing chart from disk, you get a set of chart menus in the Menu bar. Of the eight menus, five—File, Edit, Macro, Window, and Help—are virtually the same as the worksheet menus. The other three—Gallery, Chart, and Format—are either unique or considerably different from the worksheet menus. Let's briefly look at each of the three different chart menus.

Gallery Menu   **The Gallery menu, shown in the following illustration, allows you to choose from among 14 types of charts (eight two-dimensional and six three-dimensional) and then from four to eight alternatives of each type.**

```
Gallery
 Area...
 Bar...
√Column...
 Line...
 Pie...
 Radar...
 XY (Scatter)...
 Combination...

 3-D Area...
 3-D Bar...
 3-D Column...
 3-D Line...
 3-D Pie...
 3-D Surface...

 Preferred
 Set Preferred
```

The 14 chart types—Area, Bar, Column, Line, Pie, Radar, Scatter, Combination, 3-D Area, 3-D Bar, 3-D Column, 3-D Line, 3-D Pie, and 3-D Surface—are discussed in the sections that follow. When you select a chart type from the Gallery menu, you get a pictorial dialog box, or gallery, that offers up to ten alternatives of the chart type you picked, as shown here:

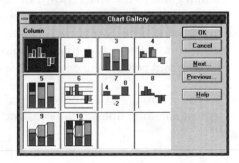

One of the alternatives in the gallery (chart type dialog box) is highlighted (the first alternative in the illustration). This is known as the *preferred alternative,* and the column type of chart is the *preferred type.* From the Gallery menu you can return to the preferred type and alternative with the Preferred option. Also, you can set the preferred type and alternative. This setting, however, is lost when you leave Excel.

Chart Menu   The Chart menu, shown in the next illustration, allows you to make a number of changes and additions to a chart you have created.

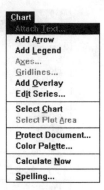

The additions include adding text and titles to many chart elements, adding arrows and gridlines, and adding legends. The changes include turning one or both of the axes on or off, changing the type of gridlines used, changing the chart into a combination chart by placing half of the data series in an overlay that can be a different chart type, and editing the formulas that create the chart. Figure 7-2 shows the addition of a title, arrow, unattached text, gridlines, and legend to the chart shown in Figure 7-1.

From the Chart menu you can also select the active chart or the plot area on the active chart for various formatting functions. In addition, you can protect the chart with a password, define the color palette, recalculate the underlying worksheet and redraw the chart, and spell check the chart.

Format Menu   The Format menu, shown here, allows you to change the patterns, font, color, shading, line width, size, and position of many of the chart elements.

Figure 7-2.   *Enhanced chart*

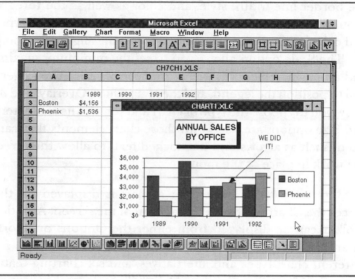

Before using the Format menu, you need to select a chart element that you want to format. Elements include the various titles and text, either of the two scales, any of the data series, legends, the whole chart, and just the plot area. You can select most elements by simply clicking on them (with the keyboard press a direction key and cycle through the elements). To select the whole chart or the plot area, you must use the Chart menu or cycle through the elements using a direction key.

When you select a chart element, selection boxes appear around or on either end of the element. For most elements, such as titles, gridlines, and axes, the selection boxes are white or empty. For other elements, such as arrows and unattached text, the selection boxes are black and indicate that the element can be moved and sized with the mouse or the keyboard.

When you select a chart element and open the Format menu, certain options become available, but others do not. Which options are available depends on the element. For example, the Patterns, Font, and Text options are available for text elements such as titles. Patterns allows you to change the border line width, style, and color as well as the foreground and background pattern and color. Font allows you to select the typeface, size, style, and color, while Text allows you to adjust the alignment and position of text.

The Scale option allows you to set the minimum, maximum, and major and minor increments as well as the type of scale. The Legend option allows you to position the legend, and the Main Chart, Overlay, and 3-D View options allow you to choose the type of chart and some of its characteristics. The Move and Size options are used with those chart elements that can be moved and sized, such as arrows and unattached text, to allow the direction keys to do the work in place of the mouse.

The Chart Toolbar   Whenever a chart is displayed on the screen, Excel places the Chart toolbar at the bottom of the screen. Additionally, the Chart toolbar can be displayed from either the Options or Shortcut menu. The Chart toolbar provides 23 charting tools. These include a selection of 17 different chart types and alternatives, and six charting features: embedded chart, the ChartWizard, horizontal gridlines, legend, arrow, and the text box. You can create a different chart easily if your current chart is not the type or format you want, simply by clicking on another tool. The name of an individual tool can be seen on the Status bar (below the Chart toolbar) when you point on the tool and hold the mouse button down. Appendix B provides a complete listing of the individual tools and their descriptions. The Chart toolbar is shown here:

ChartWizard   The ChartWizard, located on both the Standard and Chart toolbars, guides you through the steps necessary to create a chart. The Chart-Wizard allows you to size a chart it creates, displays your selected range on that chart, offers a menu of chart types and alternates, and then prompts you to add descriptive text to the chart. A ChartWizard chart in the process of being developed is shown here:

Deciding What to Chart

The first step in creating a chart is deciding what to chart; this step may be one of the hardest. It is easy to pick a range of numbers to put on a chart, but does that range or comparison of several ranges tell the story that you believe is in the numbers? Consider the third quarter budget from Chapter 6, shown in Figure 7-3. It has lots of numbers, but which are the most important and which best lend themselves to a chart?

These questions are not easy to answer, and there are probably several substantially different opinions. The best answer comes from asking yourself if the chart tells the story you are trying to tell. In later sections of this chapter, you will build charts based on the third quarter budget. For each, you can decide how well the chart tells the story that is in the numbers.

Selecting the Type of Chart

The type of chart to use is as much a subjective decision as what to chart. The choice depends primarily on what you like, but there are some rules of thumb. The next several sections discuss each of Excel's chart types and when to use them. You also learn what variations are available for each type of chart and how each uses particular options in the chart menus.

Figure 7-3.   *Third quarter budget from Chapter 6*

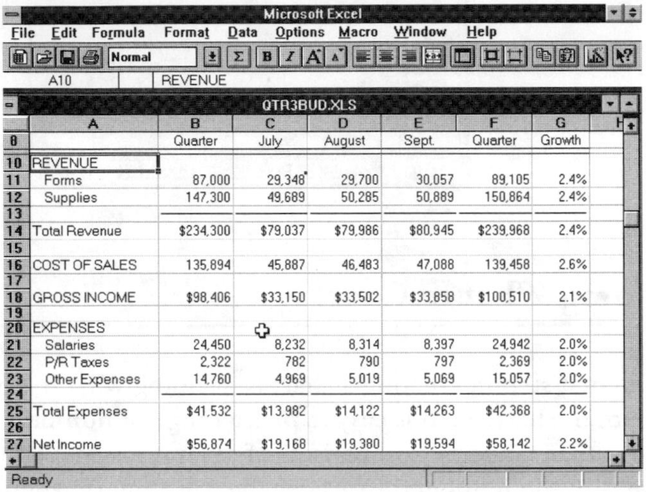

	A	B	C	D	E	F	G
8		Quarter	July	August	Sept.	Quarter	Growth
10	REVENUE						
11	Forms	87,000	29,348	29,700	30,057	89,105	2.4%
12	Supplies	147,300	49,689	50,285	50,889	150,864	2.4%
14	Total Revenue	$234,300	$79,037	$79,986	$80,945	$239,968	2.4%
16	COST OF SALES	135,894	45,887	46,483	47,088	139,458	2.6%
18	GROSS INCOME	$98,406	$33,150	$33,502	$33,858	$100,510	2.1%
20	EXPENSES						
21	Salaries	24,450	8,232	8,314	8,397	24,942	2.0%
22	P/R Taxes	2,322	782	790	797	2,369	2.0%
23	Other Expenses	14,760	4,969	5,019	5,069	15,057	2.0%
25	Total Expenses	$41,532	$13,982	$14,122	$14,263	$42,368	2.0%
27	Net Income	$56,874	$19,168	$19,380	$19,594	$58,142	2.2%

Area Charts

An Area chart shows the magnitude of change over time. It is particularly useful when several components are changing and you are interested in the sum of those components. You can see the change in the individual components as well as the change in the total. For example, in the Area chart shown in Figure 7-4, you can see the change in the sales of three products as well as the change in total sales, which is the sum of the three products.

An Area chart is a *Stacked Line chart,* with the area between the lines filled in with color or shading. An Area chart plots one data series above another. Assume, for example, that you have two data series in an Area chart. If the first data point of the first series is 50 and the first data point of the second series is 60, the data points would be plotted at 50 and 110. In a normal Line chart, the points would be plotted at 50 and 60. In Figure 7-4, floor units are added to desktop units and laptop units are added to the sum of the first two.

Figure 7-4.   *Area chart showing product sales*

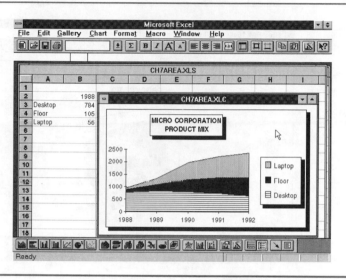

The top line on the chart represents total sales, and each layer is that product's share of those sales.

Another variation of the Area chart is the 3-D Area chart shown in Figure 7-5. While this chart has a certain "gee whiz" factor, it does not have one of the major features of an Area chart—the ability to show the total as well as the individual components.

Bar Charts

A Bar chart consists of a series of horizontal bars that allow comparison of the relative size of two or more items at one point in time. For example, the Bar chart shown in Figure 7-6 compares sales among offices for one year by presenting a bar for each office's sales. Each bar in a Bar chart is a single data point or number on the worksheet. The set of numbers for a single set of bars is a data series. For example, the Bar chart in Figure 7-6 contains a single data series representing the sales figures for six offices.

7

Figure 7-5.   *3-D Area chart showing product sales*

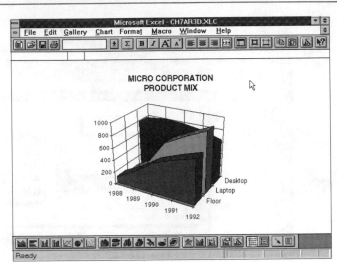

Figure 7-6.   *Bar chart showing sales by sales office*

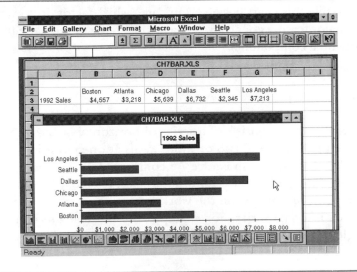

Bar Chart Variations

The Bar chart has three primary variations: the Stacked Bar chart, the Clustered Bar chart, and the 100% Bar chart. The Stacked and Clustered Bar charts are similar: in both you use additional data series for either the multiple bars or multiple segments. With three data series and the first or preferred alternative in the Bar chart gallery, you get the Clustered Bar chart shown in Figure 7-7. The same multiple ranges with the third gallery alternative produce the Stacked Bar chart shown in Figure 7-8. In both cases each of the three regions or offices is contained in a separate data series.

In the Stacked Bar chart, the total length of the bar is the sum of the segments (total company sales, in the example). Therefore, the size of each segment is relative to both the total and to the other segments. In a Clustered Bar chart you can only visually compare the bars; you do not see the total of the bars added together. There are places for both types of charts, but for our example the Stacked Bar chart is more informative.

In the 100% Bar chart, all bars become the same height, representing 100 percent. The segments then become their percentage of the total instead of their numerical number, as shown in Figure 7-9. An additional Bar chart

Figure 7-7.   *Clustered Bar chart showing regional sales*

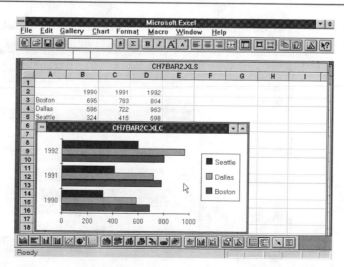

7

Figure 7-8.   Stacked Bar chart showing regional sales

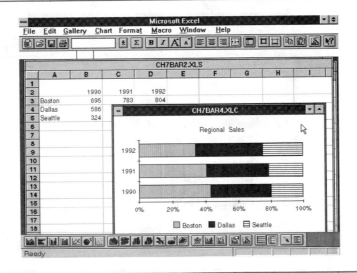

Figure 7-9.   100% Bar chart showing regional sales

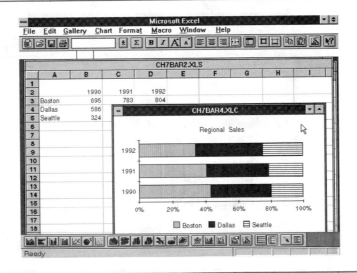

variation is the 3-D Bar chart. The 3-D Bar chart provides 3-D markers in place of 2-D horizontal bars.

Column Charts

A Column chart consists of a series of vertical columns that allow comparison of the relative size of two or more items, often over time. For example, the Column chart shown in Figure 7-10 compares quarterly sales by presenting a column for each quarter's sales. Each column in a Column chart is a single data point or number on the worksheet. The set of numbers for a single set of columns is a data series. For example, the Column chart in Figure 7-10 contains three data series, each showing the quarterly sales for one office.

Column charts have the same variations as Bar charts, including the 3-D Column chart, as shown in Figure 7-11.

Figure 7-10. *Column chart showing quarterly sales*

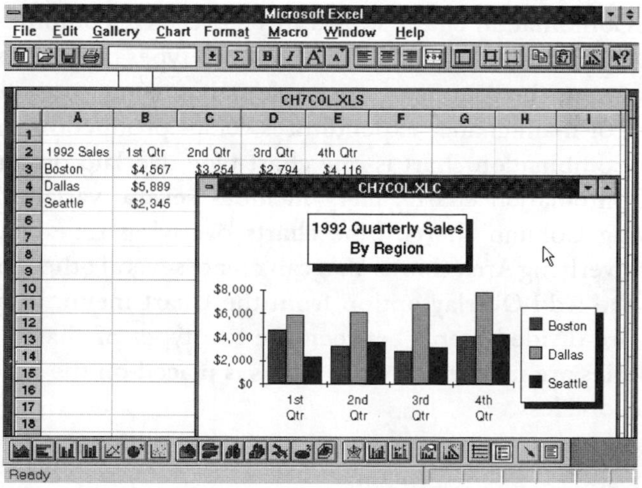

Figure 7-11.   *3-D Column chart showing quarterly sales*

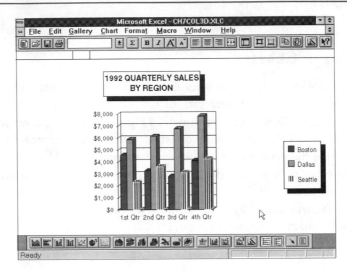

Combination Charts

A Combination chart, shown in Figure 7-12, combines a Column chart with a Line chart. It is used to compare two types of data. Examples are stock prices versus the volume of stock sold, advertising expenditures versus sales dollars, or maintenance expenditures versus production volume.

A Combination chart is one chart type overlaid on another chart type. The Combination chart gallery includes several variations of Line charts overlying Column charts, Line charts overlying Line charts, and Column charts overlying Area charts. You can create several other combination charts using the Add Overlay option from the Chart menu. In all cases, the data series are divided evenly between the two types of charts. If the number of data series are uneven, an extra series is placed on the base chart giving the overlay one less.

Figure 7-12.   *Combination chart showing advertising versus sales*

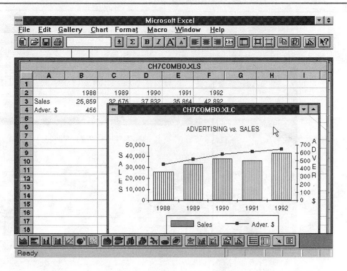

Line Charts

A Line chart is used to show trends over time. For example, the Line chart in Figure 7-13 shows that sales are trending upward while expenses remain fairly flat, allowing earnings to follow revenue. With Line charts, the reader can make a projection into the future.

In a Line chart, each of the data series is used to produce a line on the chart, with each number in the range producing a data point. There are three data series in Figure 7-13—Sales, Expenses, and Earnings—with 12 data points in each series.

Other than the 3-D Line chart shown in Figure 7-14, only one of the Line chart gallery alternatives deserves further discussion. This is the Stock Market or High-Low-Close chart.

Stock Market Charts

A Stock Market or High-Low-Close chart is a Line chart with three data series used to display a stock's high, low, and closing prices for a given time

Figure 7-13.   Line chart showing sales

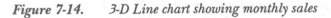

Figure 7-14.   3-D Line chart showing monthly sales

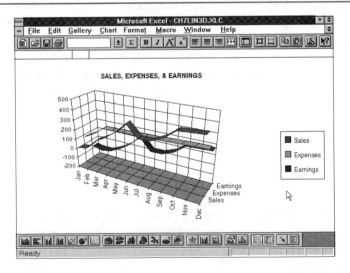

period. High-Low-Close charts also work well for commodity prices, currency exchange rates, and temperature and pressure measurements.

Figure 7-15 shows a High-Low-Close chart for stock prices. It contains three data series for the high, low, and closing prices of a stock issue on a given day. The vertical lines are formed by drawing a line between the high and the low data points while the tick mark is the closing price.

Pie Charts

A Pie chart is best used for comparing the percentages of a sum that several numbers represent. The full pie is the sum, and each number is represented by a wedge or slice. Figure 7-16 shows an example of a Pie chart. Each slice represents the percentage of total sales for a given product category. There is only one data series in a Pie chart. If more than one series is selected, Excel plots the first one. In the example in Figure 7-16, five numbers are in the data series, one for each product category, that represent the sales of each category. Excel automatically adds the numbers together and calculates the percentages to produce the chart.

Figure 7-15.   *Stock Market or High-Low-Close chart*

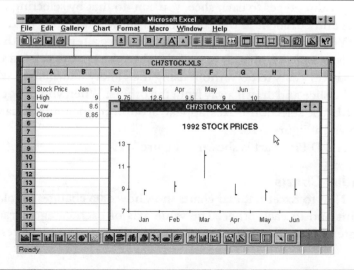

Figure 7-16.   *Pie chart for product comparison*

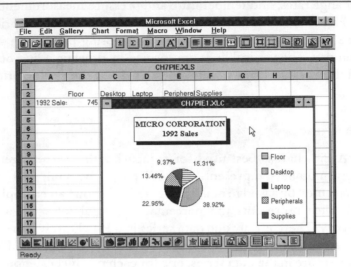

Figure 7-16 was created by selecting alternative 6 from the **Pie chart** gallery, which provided the percentages for each slice. This saves you from calculating the percentages. If you want to do away with the legend and add the product types to each slice, you can do that by selecting each percentage label and editing it in the edit area, as shown in Figure 7-17.

You may notice that the Pie chart gallery alternative with the percentage labels is *exploded*—that is, one of the slices is separated from the other slices. This is very easy to do without using the gallery alternatives. You simply click on the slice and drag it away from the others. When you click on a slice, notice that black selection boxes appear around it, meaning it can be moved, as shown in Figure 7-18.

A 3-D Pie chart is shown in Figure 7-19.

Radar Charts

New to Excel 4, Radar charts show how data changes in relation to a center point and to each other. The value axis of each category radiates from the center point. Data from the same series is connected by lines.

Figure 7-17. *Editing Pie chart labels*

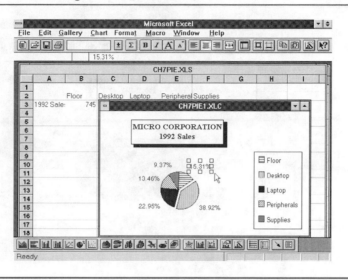

Figure 7-18. *Pie chart with a selected slice*

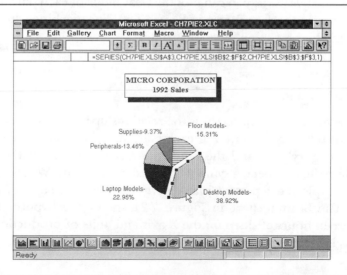

Figure 7-19.   *3-D Pie chart for product comparison*

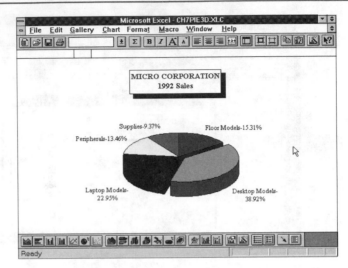

You can use the Radar chart to plot several interrelated series and easily make visual comparisons. For example, if you have three machines containing the same five parts, you can plot the wear index of each part on each machine on a Radar chart, as shown in Figure 7-20. The machine with the largest area has the highest cumulative wear index.

Scatter Charts

Scatter or XY charts show the relationship between pairs of numbers and the trends they present. For each pair, one of the numbers is plotted on the X- (category) axis and the other number is plotted on the Y- (value) axis. Where the two meet, a symbol is placed on the chart. When a number of such pairs is plotted, a pattern may emerge, as shown in Figure 7-21.

The Scatter chart in Figure 7-21 shows the hypothetical correlation between hours of sleep on the X-axis and units of production on the Y-axis. This is typical of how a Scatter chart is used.

Figure 7-20. *Radar chart comparing part wear on several machines*

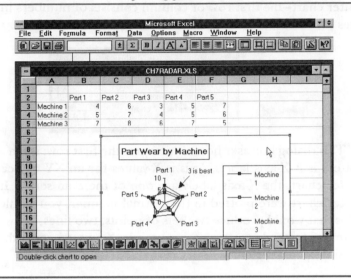

Figure 7-21. *Scatter or XY chart*

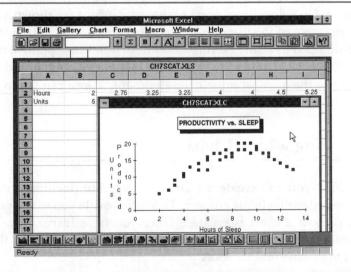

When you begin to produce a chart that Excel might consider to be a Scatter chart—the first row or column consists of numbers instead of text or dates for X-axis labels—you get the dialog box shown here:

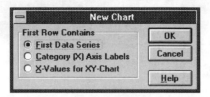

This dialog box asks how to interpret the first row: is it a data series to be plotted, is it X-axis labels, or is it X-values for an XY or Scatter chart? In a Scatter chart, the X-axis labels are one of the data series. If the data for a Scatter chart were plotted in the normal manner, you would have two data series that would produce two sets of points, two lines, or two sets of bars or columns. Instead, you want a numeric X-axis against which to plot the remaining data series.

3-D Surface Charts

3-D Surface charts are new to Excel 4. There are two types of 3-D Surface charts: color charts that look like a flexible sheet draped over a 3-D Column chart, and charts without color that look like a wireframe chart.

Both types are useful for showing the optimum combinations of two sets of data. On color charts, areas of the same height are shown as the same color. An example of the use of 3-D Surface charts would be bodybuilding: muscle is developed by lifting varying amounts of weight a repetitive number of times. A 3-D Surface chart shows the combinations of weight and repetitions that produce the greatest muscle development, as you can see in Figure 7-22.

Creating a Line Chart

First you will create a chart as a separate document using the menus discussed earlier in the chapter. This will provide you with a good understanding of how a chart is created. Once you have learned the basics of chart development, you can better appreciate the ease added by the ChartWizard and the Chart toolbar tools.

Figure 7-22. *3-D Surface chart of muscle development*

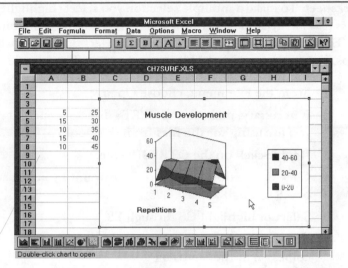

Remember that a Line chart is best at showing trends. In the third quarter budget completed in Chapter 6, Total Revenue, Cost of Sales (COS), and Total Expenses are among the items whose trends are important. Therefore, for your first chart, build a Line chart of Total Revenue, COS, and Total Expenses data from the third quarter budget.

Selecting the Ranges to Plot

Your first step in building a chart is to select the ranges on the worksheet that you want to plot. Load the third quarter budget, position the screen, and select the ranges. For this Line chart you want to identify four data series. The data series for the X-axis or category labels is the three months of July, August, and September in C8 through E8. The other three data series are Total Revenue, COS, and Total Expenses, respectively, in rows 14, 16, and 25.

Unlike the other charts you have seen so far in this chapter, the data series ranges on the worksheet are not a contiguous rectangular range, they are separated from one another by several intervening rows. This is called a multiple selection—you must select multiple independent ranges on the worksheet. To make a multiple selection you select (highlight) the first range, press (SHIFT)-(F8) (Add Selection), and then select the remaining ranges. Open the Third Quarter Budget worksheet and select the ranges with the following steps. Your computer should be turned on and Excel loaded.

1. From the File menu, choose Open.

2. If necessary, make the \SHEET\ directory current (or the directory you are using for the files from this book).

3. Double-click on the QTR3BUD file.

4. Click on the downward scroll arrow until you can see the range A7 or A8 through at least G25.

5. Select or highlight C8 through E8.

6. Press and release (SHIFT)-(F8) (Add Selection). The ADD indicator comes on in the Status bar.

7. Select C14 through E14, C16 through E16, and C25 through E25.

When you are done selecting the four ranges, your screen should look like Figure 7-23.

Creating a New Chart

The second step is to create a new chart that you can then modify. Use the following instructions to create a chart:

1. From the File menu, choose New. The New dialog box opens.

2. Click on Chart and on OK. A new Column chart is created, as shown in Figure 7-24.

Your bars may be colored if you have a color display, or they may have a different shading if you have a monochrome display. The color or shading does not matter at this point.

Figure 7-23.   *Ranges selected for the Line chart*

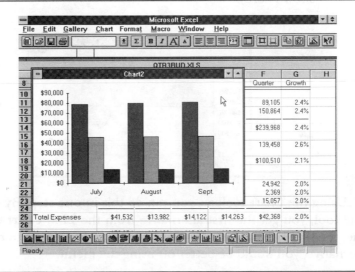

Figure 7-24.   *Initial Column chart of third quarter data*

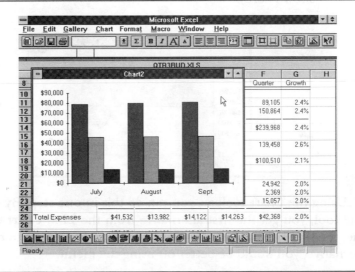

7

Changing the Chart Type

You now have the standard Column chart—one that appears every time you create a new chart—so your next task is to change it to a Line chart. The Gallery menu serves that purpose. Use it with these instructions and see the results on your screen:

1. From the Gallery menu, choose Line. The Line Chart Gallery opens, as shown here:

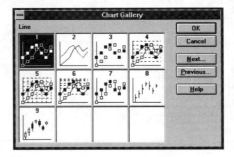

2. You want the first alternative, which is already selected, so just click on OK. The following Line chart appears on your screen (the markers or symbols on your screen may be different than what is shown here):

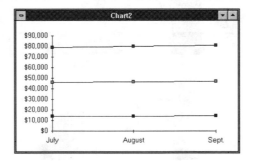

Using the Chart toolbar, you can do this in one step. By clicking on the Line tool, you get the first alternative from the Line Chart Gallery. In this case, the first alternative is the one you want. If you want to choose another alternative, you would be better off using the menu.

What you see on your screen is the barest rudiments of a chart. You can see the three month labels along the X-axis at the bottom and three lines across the chart representing Total Revenue, Cost of Sales, and Total Expenses. Only by knowing that Total Revenue is greater than Cost of Sales, which is greater than Total Expenses, do you know which line is which. Also, from looking at the chart there is no way of knowing that the chart has anything to do with Morningside Specialties' Third Quarter Budget.

Adding Annotation

The next step in building the Line chart is to add annotation. This includes titles in several locations, legends for the lines on the chart, and possibly some notes. All of these items are handled with options on the Chart menu.

Excel allows you to add a number of titles, legends, and notes to a chart, as shown in Figure 7-25. At the top of the chart is the first title with the second title below it. On the left side is the Y-axis or value text. At the bottom of the

Figure 7-25. *Titles, legends, and notes*

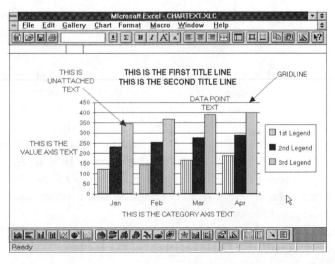

chart is the X-axis or category text, to the right are the legends, and in the upper-left and upper-right corners are two notes, called *unattached text*. For your Line chart, you want to add a legend to identify the three lines and add text in several places.

Building a Legend

A legend is a set of labels or short descriptions, one for each data series or range that is plotted. These descriptions are attached to a symbol, to a color, or to crosshatching that is associated with the plotted data series and placed on the chart (initially to the right, but you can move it). For your Line chart, you need a legend consisting of three descriptions, one each for the Total Revenue, Cost of Sales, and Total Expense data series.

To add a legend to the chart from the Chart menu, choose Add Legend. A legend box is created on the Line chart, as you can see here:

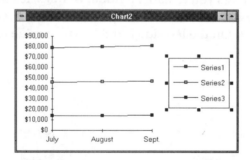

The legend box that appears on the Line chart gives you a reference to each line, but it does not tell you what they are, because in highlighting the data series you did not highlight a name for each. The names are the row labels in column A and are therefore not contiguous to the data series in columns C through E. Without including column B there was no way to connect the series name with the data series. In a neat, contiguous set of ranges, the series name is immediately above or to the left of the data series. Excel can then create a legend containing the series names using only the steps you just followed.

In this case you must go to more effort to get the series names, but in the process you will learn how Excel does its plotting.

Editing the Series Formula

Each line, bar, column, or pie wedge on an Excel chart is created with a *series formula*. A series formula contains the SERIES function as well as up to four elements or arguments needed to plot a line, bar, column, or wedge. The four arguments are the series name or a reference to it, a reference to the categories (X-axis) against which you are plotting, a reference to the values that are to be plotted, and the order in which you want a line, bar, column, or wedge plotted.

When Excel builds a new chart with File New Chart, a set of series formulas are automatically built based on the ranges that have been selected on the worksheet. The Line chart currently on your screen has three such formulas, one for each line. Use the following instructions to first look at the series formulas and then edit them:

1. Click on the center marker on the top line of your Line chart. (If you are using the keyboard, press (DOWN ARROW) several times. You cycle through several chart elements and eventually get to the top line.) The series formula appears in the edit area of the Formula bar, as shown here:

```
=SERIES(,QTR3BUD.XLS!$C$8:$E$8,QTR3BUD.XLS!$C$14:$E$14,1)
```

The series formula always starts out with =SERIES(. It then contains up to four arguments separated by commas and a closing parenthesis. In the series formula just shown, the first argument, for the series name, is missing. The other three arguments are

Category range:	QTR3BUD.XLS!$C$8:$E$8
Values range:	QTR3BUD.XLS!$C$14:$E$14
Plot order:	1

Both the category argument and the values argument are references to absolute ranges on the worksheet QTR3BUD. When you refer to a range on another worksheet, whether from a chart or a second worksheet, you use the complete worksheet name and extension (and path if it is stored in another directory), followed by an exclamation mark (!) and the absolute reference

7

or range name. So the category range is the set of three column headings—
July, August, and September—contained in C8:E8 of the QTR3BUD worksheet. The values range is the Total Revenue dollars in C14:E14 of the same
worksheet.

In the current series formulas for the lines on your Line chart, there is a
comma immediately after the opening parenthesis. This tells you that the first
argument for the series name is missing. The series name can be either its
name in quotation marks or a reference to a worksheet cell. You could edit
the formula in the Formula bar, adding the name or reference to the left of
the leftmost comma. Excel, though, has an even easier way—a dialog box for
this purpose. Try that next:

2. From the Chart menu, choose Edit Series. The Edit Series dialog
   box opens as shown here:

The Edit Series dialog box shows you the four elements of the series
formula: the series name (Name) which is blank, the Category range (X
Labels), the Values range (Y Values), and the Plot Order. In the list box to
the left are all of the data series, as well as an entry for a new series if you wish
to create one.

3. Click in the Name text box and type **=qtr3bud.xls!a14**. This is the
   reference to "Total Revenue," the label for the first series.

4. Click on Series2 in the list box and then click on Yes in answer to
   the question "Save changes to current series?".

5. Click in the Name text box for the second series and type **="Cost of
   Sales"**. The Name can be either a literal name in quotation marks
   or a reference to a name on the worksheet.

6. Click on Series3, on Yes, and in the Name text box. Then double-click on cell A25 in the worksheet. The reference to "Total Expenses" is entered in the Name text box as shown here:

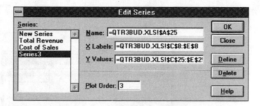

7. Click on OK to close the dialog box. You are returned to the chart you are building.

The legend now contains meaningful names for each of the lines, as shown in Figure 7-26. Notice also how the series formula in the Formula bar has changed to include the location of the series name.

Figure 7-26.   *Completed legend*

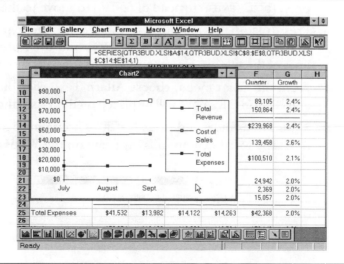

Placing Titles and Text

The next step is to add two title lines to the top of the chart and some text on the Y-axis. Type each piece of text directly with these instructions:

1. From the Chart menu, choose Attach Text. The Attach Text dialog box opens, as shown here:

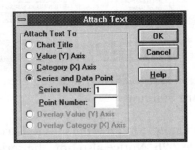

2. Click on Chart Title and on OK to prepare to enter the chart title.

3. Type **MORNINGSIDE SPECIALTIES**. Since this is just the first line of the title, do not press (ENTER).

   A two-line title is one field, not two. At the end of the first line press (CTRL)-(ENTER) instead of (ENTER) to move to the second line.

4. Press (CTRL)-(ENTER) to move to the second line, type the rest of the title, **THIRD QUARTER BUDGET**, and then press (ENTER). Both lines of the title are placed on the worksheet, as shown in Figure 7-27.

5. From the Chart menu, choose Attach Text, click on the Value Axis, and click on OK. A "Y" will be placed on the Y-axis and in the edit area.

6. Type **Thousands**, and press (ENTER). Thousands becomes the Y-axis title. The word "Thousands" appears on the Y-axis as shown here:

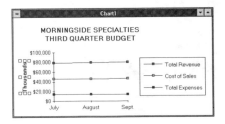

Figure 7-27. *Title placed on the worksheet*

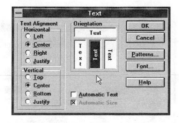

Text on the Y-axis can be rotated to four orientations. Choose Text from the Format menu to open the Text dialog box displayed here:

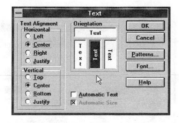

In most instances, though, the default just shown is acceptable.

Formatting Text

Text, as you enter it, is given a default format by Excel. The title is formatted as 12-point bold Microsoft Sans Serif. The Y-axis text is formatted as 10-point bold Microsoft Sans Serif. You can change this formatting as you desire. Try that next. The Y-axis text should still be selected.

1. From the Format menu, choose Font. The Font dialog box opens, as shown here:

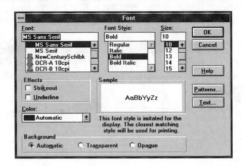

2. Scroll the Size list until you see 8 and click on it for the text size (press (ALT)-(S) and type 8 from the keyboard). Click on Regular in the Font Style list box, and click on OK.

3. Click on the legend in the chart, choose Font from the Format menu, again click on 8 for the text size, and click on OK. The legend text becomes smaller.

4. Click on the chart title, and choose Patterns from the Format menu. The Patterns dialog box opens, as shown here:

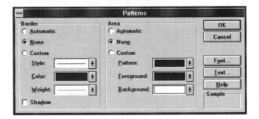

   The Patterns dialog box for the chart title lets you place a border around the title, select among a number of alternatives for that border, and select from among a number of colors and patterns for the area behind the title. What you want to do with the Line chart is place a shadow border around the title. Do that next and you will see its effect.

5. Click on Shadow in the Border area of the dialog box, and then click on OK.

6. Click somewhere else on the chart to remove the selection boxes from the title. The results are shown here:

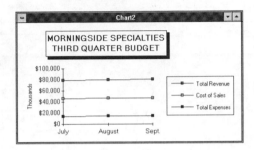

In a similar manner you could place a shadow border behind the legend and the chart itself. Now you simply save and print the chart.

Saving and Printing the Chart

You are now done with the Line chart, so you need to save it and then print it. Follow these instructions:

1. From the File menu choose Save As. The Save As dialog box opens.

2. Type **qtr3line** and click on OK. The chart is saved with the name QTR3LINE.XLC.

3. Choose Print from the File menu and click on OK. The Line chart is printed, as shown in Figure 7-28.

Closing a Chart

You are now done with the Line chart. While you can leave it open on the desktop, it serves no real purpose to do so. Close it by double-clicking on the Line chart's Control-menu box. When the Line chart closes, the chart Menu bar is replaced with the worksheet Menu bar.

7

Figure 7-28.   Printed Line chart

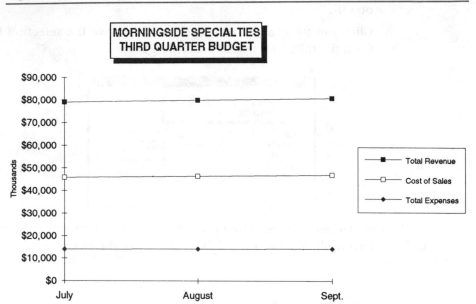

Creating a New Chart Using ChartWizard

In the previous section you learned how to create a Line chart using the chart menus. The menus and their associated options and dialog boxes provide you with the most flexibility in creating a chart. The ChartWizard does not offer the same flexibility, but it can allow you to quickly see different chart types and create a standard chart which you can customize later using the chart menus or Chart toolbar. The following instructions show you how quickly you can create a basic chart.

1. The ranges C8:E8, C14:E14, C16:E16, and C25:E25 should still be highlighed in the QTR3BUD.XLS worksheet. If not, highlight them by using the ADD key ((SHIFT)-(F8)).

2. Click on the ChartWizard tool on the Standard toolbar. The borders of the highlighted ranges start blinking, and the mouse pointer turns into a crosshair when you move the mouse back onto the spreadsheet.

3. On the worksheet, drag the crosshair from the upper-left corner of A11 to the lower-right corner of G24. This defines the size of the embedded chart. It can be anywhere on your worksheet. By pressing (SHIFT) as you drag, the chart can be forced into a square.

4. The ChartWizard now asks if you want to change the highlighted range on the worksheet. In this example, the ranges are listed correctly in the range text box. Click on the Next button.

   The explanation of the ChartWizard buttons is:

Button	ChartWizard Action
Help	Provides access to help menus
Cancel	Cancels ChartWizard actions and returns to the worksheet
<<	Returns to the beginning of ChartWizard
Next	Continues on to the next step
Back	Returns to the previous step
>>	Creates a chart with the options chosen to that point and exits ChartWizard

5. ChartWizard displays the 14 chart types. Double-click on the Line chart to choose it.

6. Nine alternate line formats are offered. Double-click on number 2.

A familiar chart appears in the ChartWizard dialog box, as shown here:

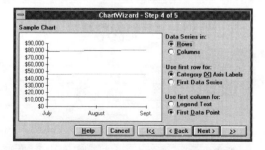

The option buttons on the right of the chart allow you to change the appearance of the chart, but the defaults are fine in this example. If you have any questions on the actions performed by the different options, click on them to immediately see the change to the chart or click on Help for further explanation.

7. Click on Next. The final ChartWizard step appears.

8. To the question, "Add a legend?", click on Yes. A legend box appears.

9. Click on the Chart Title box. Type **MORNINGSIDE SPECIALTIES THIRD QUARTER BUDGET**; the title is displayed on the worksheet.

10. Click on the Value axis title. Type **Thousands**. The Y-axis title is displayed.

11. Click on OK. The embedded chart is displayed in the range A11:G24 you chose earlier, as shown in Figure 7-29.

12. The chart can now be sized by pointing on and dragging a corner, or moved by pointing on and dragging a border. Experiment with

Figure 7-29.   *Chart created with the ChartWizard*

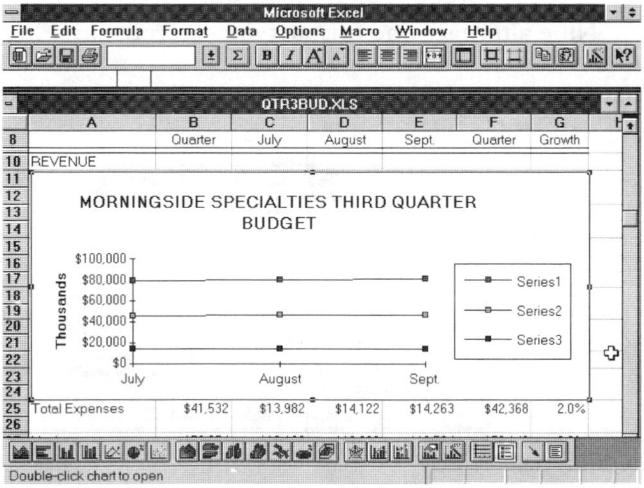

different sizing and location ideas. Notice how as you make the chart smaller, the letters in the months begin to wrap to a second line, the title wraps, and the Y-axis scale changes.

Compare the chart created by ChartWizard with the one you printed at the end of the previous section (Figure 7-27). They are not quite the same, but with the exception of the legends, the chart created by ChartWizard is acceptable, and certainly faster to develop. As mentioned earlier, if the row labels in column A were contiguous to the data series in columns C through E, ChartWizard would have created the legend titles.

If you want to embed the chart in the worksheet, you just save the worksheet and the chart is saved with it. To edit or format the embedded chart, you double-click on the chart to open it in a chart window. The Chart menu replaces the Worksheet menu and allows you to edit and format. Finally, you can save the chart as a separate document by double-clicking on the chart, and then selecting the File menu and Save As option. In this example, leave the chart as is, and continue with the next section to see how the Chart toolbar can assist you in your charting choices.

Using the Chart Toolbar

Using the Chart toolbar, you can quickly change the type of chart displayed on the screen. Try the following instructions to see how easy it is to use the Chart toolbar.

1. Return the embedded chart to its original size, A11:G24.

2. From the left of the Chart toolbar, click on each tool in turn and see how the appearance of the chart can quickly change. The Status bar displays the name of each chart as you click on it.

    At this point, you will leave the embedded chart created by ChartWizard and create two more charts using the chart menus. This will give you more practice learning how Excel formats, and will let you modify your charts created with ChartWizard faster and with more confidence.

3. Click on File menu and Close. When asked if you want to save the change, click on No. Excel returns you to a blank worksheet.

7

4. Open the QTR3BUD.XLS worksheet without the embedded chart by clicking on File and QTR3BUD.XLS at the bottom of the menu.

Building a 3-D Pie Chart

The 3-D Pie chart you will build displays the percentage of contribution to third quarter expense from each of the expense accounts (the Salaries, P/R Taxes, and Other Expenses fields). The first steps are to select or highlight the third quarter expenses and create a new chart.

1. Select F21 through F23.

2. From the File menu, choose New, click on Chart, and then on OK. A standard Column chart is produced, as shown here:

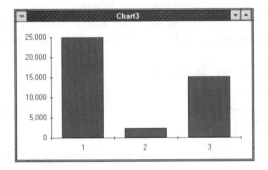

Selecting a Pie Chart

The 3-D Pie chart to be created is an exploded Pie chart (one of the wedges separated from the rest) with both a description and a percentage on each wedge. The 3-D Pie chart gallery provides seven alternatives, but none of them provides all of the features you want. From the gallery you can choose a Pie chart with any one of the three features (exploded, description, or percentage), but not all three. Remember from the earlier Pie chart discussion, moving a wedge to explode it is very easy, as is adding a description to a percentage. Adding a percentage, however, requires manual calculation.

Though alternative 7 allows for both percentages and descriptions, for the purposes of learning how it's done, you want alternative 6 with the percentages, and you can add the other two features after creating the chart. Change the chart type to a Pie with percentages with these instructions:

1. From the Gallery menu choose 3-D Pie. The 3-D Pie Chart Gallery opens, as shown here:

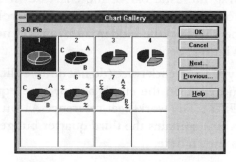

2. Click on alternative 6 and click on OK. The following Pie chart appears:

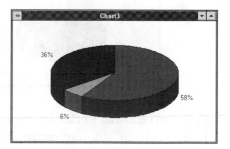

Adding a Title from the Worksheet

Text on a chart can be typed in as you did for the Line chart, or you can pick up text already on the worksheet by entering a formula instead of the text. For the Pie chart, pick up the third quarter budget title from the QTR3BUD worksheet instead of typing the title. Use these instructions:

1. From the Chart menu, choose Attach Text. The Attach Text dialog box opens with Chart Title, the option you want, already selected. You need only click on OK.

2. When you click on OK, the word "Title" appears at the top of the chart with selection boxes around it. You can enter a new title by simply typing.

3. Drag the Title bar of the chart down so you can see A1 on the worksheet. You may need to use the scroll bar to see A1. In that case the chart will be hidden and you will need to reselect it from the Window menu.

4. Type = and click twice (do not double-click) on A1 on the worksheet, and click on the check box or type **=qtr3bud.xls!a1** and press (ENTER). The worksheet reference A1 on the QTR3BUD worksheet (which contains the third quarter budget title) is used for the title, as shown here:

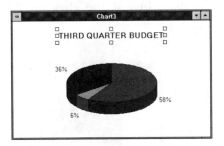

To pick up text off a worksheet for any text field on a chart, enter a formula with an absolute external reference to the worksheet filename and cell.

Adding Refinements

Now you can make several refinements to improve the appearance of the 3-D Pie chart. First, change the labels on the slices to include the expense title. Second, change the color or pattern of the slices. Finally, separate the slice that represents salaries since it is the largest.

Adding Titles to Wedges

The wedges currently have the percentages they represent. To these percentages you want to add the expense title. You do this simply by editing the percentages and typing in the title. Follow these steps:

1. Click on the 58% (or press (RIGHT ARROW) and cycle through the chart elements until you get to 58%).

2. Click the insertion point to the left of the 58% in the edit area.

3. Type **Salaries-** and press (ENTER). The expense title "Salaries" is added to the right-hand wedge of the Pie chart.

4. In a similar manner type **P/R Taxes-** to the left of 6% and type **Other Expenses-** to the left of 36%. The completed wedge titles look like this:

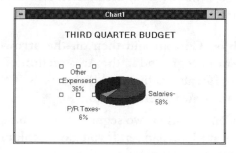

Changing the Color or Pattern of a Wedge

If you have a color display, each wedge in the Pie chart is in a different color. If you have a monochrome display, each wedge has a different pattern. You may or may not like the colors or patterns that you automatically get, so Excel provides a way to change them. Use the following instructions to see how that is done:

1. Click on the Salaries wedge. Selection boxes appear around the wedge.

2. From the Format menu, choose Patterns. The Patterns dialog box opens, as shown here:

This Patterns dialog box is slightly different from the one you got for the Line chart title. Like the title Patterns dialog box, this one has two major areas: one for the border around the wedge, and one for the area within the wedge. Both of these should have the Automatic option button selected. The wedge Patterns dialog box does not have the Shadow option that is on the title Patterns, and some of the other options and command buttons are different. You can change either or both the pattern and color of the area within the wedge with these steps:

3. Click on Custom and then on the arrow to the right of Pattern and/or Foreground in the Area section of the Patterns dialog box. Choose an alternative, and click on OK. The Pie chart is redisplayed with the new pattern or color.

4. Click on the other two segments, and change their patterns and/or colors in a like manner. If you have a color display, experiment with combinations of color and pattern.

Exploding a Wedge

The final bit of refinement is to explode or move the Salaries wedge away from the other wedges. See how easy that is with these steps:

1. Click on the Salaries wedge. Selection boxes appear around the wedge.

2. Drag the Salaries wedge about 1/16 of an inch away from the other wedges.

3. Press (ESC) to remove the selection boxes from the Salaries wedge. Your Pie chart should look like the one shown here:

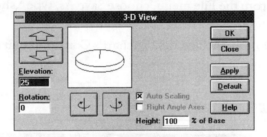

3-D Rotator On 3-D charts, you can modify the elevation, rotation, perspective, height, and axis angles to change the appearance of the chart. Try the following example to change the appearance of the THIRD QUARTER BUDGET 3-D Pie chart:

1. Click on the Format menu and choose 3-D View. This dialog box appears:

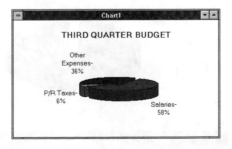

2. Change the elevation to 10 by clicking on the large down arrow. Increase the rotation to 30 by clicking on the left rotational box.

3. Click on OK. The chart changes orientation, as shown below:

7

Continue to experiment with the elevation, rotation, and other orientation features.

Saving, Printing, and Closing

You have now completed the Pie chart. Print it, and then save and close it with the following steps:

1. From the File menu, choose Print and then click on OK in the Print dialog box. (If you want to change the standard header or footer, do so in the Page Setup dialog box first.)

   When your Pie chart is printed it should look something like Figure 7-30. If you used different crosshatch patterns, orientation, or color, your chart will differ.

2. From the File menu, choose Save As, type **\sheet\qtr3pie**, and click on OK.

3. Double-click on the Pie chart's Control-menu box to close the chart.

Figure 7-30.   *Final 3-D Pie chart*

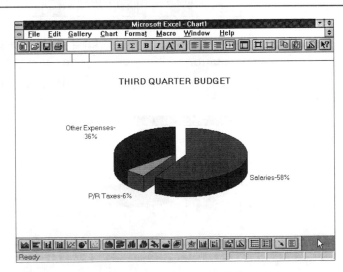

Generating a Stacked Column Chart

The third chart to be created is a Stacked Column chart in which each of the three columns is one month's total expenses, and each layer is one type of expense (salaries, payroll taxes, and other expenses). The layers, therefore, show a type of expense in proportion to the total expense for a given month. Since you have done two charts already, this chart can be done quickly.

Building the Chart

The now familiar steps to building a chart are: highlight the appropriate ranges on the worksheet, create a new chart, change its type as necessary from the Gallery menu, and add titles, text, and formatting as desired. Use these instructions to do that:

1. Select the range C8:E8, press (SHIFT)-(F8) (Add Selection), and select the range C21:E23.

2. From the File menu, choose New, click on Chart, and click on OK to create a new chart.

3. From the Gallery menu, choose Column, click on alternative 3, and click on OK to change the chart type to a Stacked Column chart.

4. From the Chart menu, choose Attach Text, and click on OK to select Chart Title.

5. Type **THIRD QUARTER EXPENSES** and press (ENTER) for the title.

6. From the Chart menu, choose Edit Series, click on Series1, click on the Name text box, and type **Salaries**. Excel will change this into the formula ="Salaries" for you.

7. Click on Series2 and 3 and, following the procedure in step 6, enter the series names **P/R Taxes** and **Other Expenses**, respectively.

8. From the Chart menu, choose Add Legend.

9. Click on the legend to select it, and then choose Legend from the Format menu. The Legend dialog box opens, as shown here:

7

10. Click on Bottom and OK to move the legend to the bottom of the chart. Your Stacked Column chart should look like this:

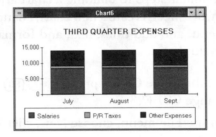

Saving, Printing, and Closing

You have completed the Stacked Column chart. Print, save, and close it now.

1. From the File menu choose Print, and then click on OK in the Print dialog box. When the chart is printed it should look something like Figure 7-31. Again, different crosshatch patterns or colors may make your chart look slightly different than the one shown here.

2. From the File menu, choose Save As, type **qtr3col**, and click on OK.

3. Double-click on the chart's Control-menu box to close the chart.

Figure 7-31.   *Printed Stacked Column chart*

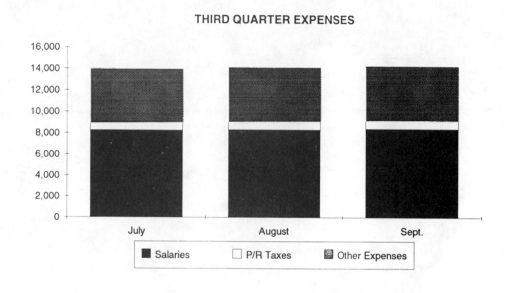

Leaving Excel

Since you have not made any changes to the QTR3BUD worksheet in this chapter, it does not need to be resaved. You need only leave **Excel and Windows**. Do that now with these steps:

1. Double-click on Excel's Control-menu box to close **Excel**.
2. Double-click on the Program Manager's Control-menu box and click on **OK** to close Windows.

8

Working with a Database

A database is a list—a phone list, a list of products, a list of parts, a list of cities—a set of related information organized into the row-and-column structure of Excel. In this chapter you build two databases. You then sort the tables, extract information from them, and analyze the information.

Databases are the third of Excel's three components (worksheets and charts are the other two). A database is a natural adjunct to Excel because Excel's row-and-column structure lends itself to containing information in a database. One entry in the database, called a *record*, is placed across a row. For example, in a phone list containing names and phone numbers, a record is a single name and phone number combination. Each part of a record (for example, the name or the phone number) is called a *field* and is entered in a column. Thus, a direct relationship exists between rows and columns on a worksheet, and records and fields in a database.

A database must be contained on a single worksheet. A single worksheet can contain many databases, but only one of them may be designated "the database" that allows you to do several predefined operations on that database. The first row of a database must contain *field names*—the labels in each column of a database that name the field in that column. The maximum size of a database in Excel is 256 fields in 16,383 records (the maximum number of columns in a worksheet, and one less than the maximum number of rows to accommodate the field names).

A database can contain any information you want to organize into fields and records. However, it is a good idea to have *at least one blank row at the bottom* of the database to allow for expansion. (You can insert a new record above the last record, and the database range will automatically expand to include the new record.) All of the field names in a database must be unique—they cannot be duplicated—and field names cannot be numbers, logical values, error values, blank cells, or formulas.

Building a Database

Building a database involves little more than typing. You enter a set of field names and then enter the records, and that's all there is to it. Later you will learn some tricks to speed up the entry, but otherwise the process is simply typing.

Entering Field Names

The first database for you to build is a list of six sales offices. The record for each office contains an office number, a location, a manager's name, a quota, and a commission rate. The first step in building the database is entering the field names. Your computer should be on and Excel loaded, and you should have a blank worksheet on your screen with A1 as the active cell.

1. Type **Number** and press (RIGHT ARROW). "Number" is entered in A1, and the active cell moves to B1.

2. Type **Office** and press (RIGHT ARROW). "Office" is entered in B1, and the active cell moves to C1.

Complete the remaining field names as shown in the following illustration, using a similar procedure. In column E press (ENTER) instead of (RIGHT ARROW).

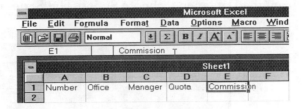

Numbering with a Data Series

When you have to enter almost any sort of consecutive numbers or dates, you can get help from Excel's Data Series option. To use this option you must specify the range you want to fill and then enter a start number, an increment or step number, and, optionally, a stop number. For example, if you want a list of numbers from 1 to 10 in column A, beginning in A1, you enter **1** as the start number, highlight the range, and enter (or accept the default of) **1** as the step number. You get 1 in A1, 2 in A2, 3 in A3, and so on to 10 in cell A10.

The start number must be entered on the worksheet in the first cell of the row or column you want to fill. Excel uses 1 and the remaining rows or columns selected as the defaults for the step and stop numbers if you do not enter them. You can enter any number as the start number, including dates (in a recognizable format), negative numbers, or formulas that evaluate to one of those. The step or stop value must be a recognizable number, not a formula or range name. You can use fractional numbers for the step and stop values, and the stop number may be a date (in a recognizable format).

Either the stop number or the end of the range can stop the series operation. If the stop number stops the series, it does so before the stop number is exceeded. There are special considerations for series with dates. These are discussed later in this chapter.

Even though you have only six numbers to enter, the Data Series option makes short work of it. Try it with these steps:

1. Click on A2. The active cell moves to A2.

2. Type **250** and press (ENTER). The start value of 250 is entered in A2.

3. Highlight the range A2 through A7.

4. From the Data menu, choose Series. The Series dialog box opens, as shown here:

You can see in the Series dialog box that Excel has detected you want the series to go down a column. The default Type setting is Linear, which is what you want. The other Type options are Growth, which multiplies the last cell times the step value, Date, which produces a series of date values, and AutoFill, which will be discussed in the next section. If you choose Date, the Date Unit option becomes available (in the illustrated dialog box this option is grayed) and allows you to choose whether the date increment is Day, Weekday, Month, or Year.

5. Type **5** for the step value and press (ENTER). The dialog box closes and the series of numbers appears in column A, as shown in Figure 8-1. Notice that the range size was used to stop the fill operation.

Numbering with AutoFill

AutoFill looks at the values in the highlighted cells and makes an intelligent decision on how to extend those values in a series that fill the remainder of the highlighted cells. As you saw in Chapter 5, AutoFill allows you to create or extend a series by either dragging the fill handle across the worksheet in any direction or by selecting an option from the Data Series dialog box. Creating a series by dragging provides a faster, real-time display of the results, while using the Data Series option offers greater flexibility in defining the range and incremental values.

To start a series, enter the first two values in two adjacent cells or choose a value with a known increment, such as a date. For example, if you highlight the range C2:D2 and enter **50** in C2 and **100** in D2, you could then simply drag the fill handle of C2:D2 to the right to extend the series. The value 150

Figure 8-1. *Numbers produced with the Data Series option*

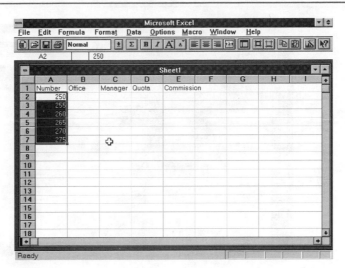

would automatically be placed in E2, 200 in F2, and so on. Unlike the Data Series menu option, there is no way to set a stop value; the series is extended as long as you continue dragging. The Formula bar Reference area displays the prospective values of the active cells as they are dragged. Try the following instructions to see how AutoFill works by dragging the fill handle:

1. Highlight A2:A7, press (DEL), and click on OK in the dialog box. The series you previously made is deleted.

2. Make sure that Cell Drag and Drop is turned on in the Options Workspace dialog box, and then highlight A2:A3. Type **250** in the active cell, A2, and press (ENTER).

3. Type **255**, and press (ENTER) to establish the series increment in cell A3.

4. Drag the A2:A3 fill handle down column A to A7. Notice how the numbers increase in the Formula bar as you drag.

Continue to experiment with AutoFill by dragging the fill handle up and down column A. Click on a single cell in column A. Drag its fill handle to the

8

Figure 8-2.   *Completed sales office database*

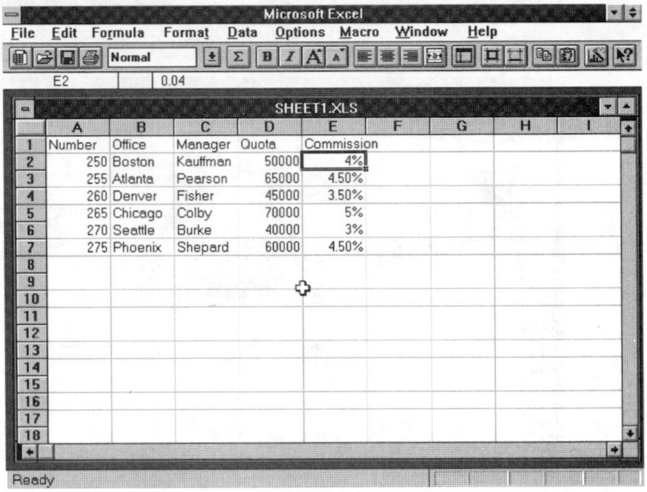

right. The adjacent cells are filled in with the same values since there is no incrementing detected by AutoFill. When you are through experimenting with AutoFill, make sure your screen looks like Figure 8-1.

Entering Records

Entering the remaining parts of the records is just rote typing. You can either type down a column or across a row, whichever is easier for you. Do that now, entering all of the information shown in Figure 8-2. If it is easier for you, you may enter the commissions as decimals instead of percentages, for example, entering **.04** instead of 4%. If you do enter decimal percentages, they will appear that way on the screen.

Making the Database Easier to Read

The rightmost pair of columns could benefit from formatting, so do that now with these steps:

1. Drag on D2 through D7.

2. Choose Number from the Format menu. The Number Format dialog box opens.

3. Click on #,##0 and on OK. The quotas in column D are formatted with a comma.

4. Drag on E2 through E7 and choose Number from the Shortcut menu.

5. Click on the Code text box at the bottom of the Number Format dialog box, type **0.0%** to create a single decimal percentage, and press (ENTER). The percentages in column E are formatted with a single decimal.

The result of formatting the right pair of columns is shown in Figure 8-3.

Sorting a Database

Sorting a database rearranges the records in the database to produce a specific order to the records. You must identify the range or database you

Figure 8-3.   *Columns D and E formatted*

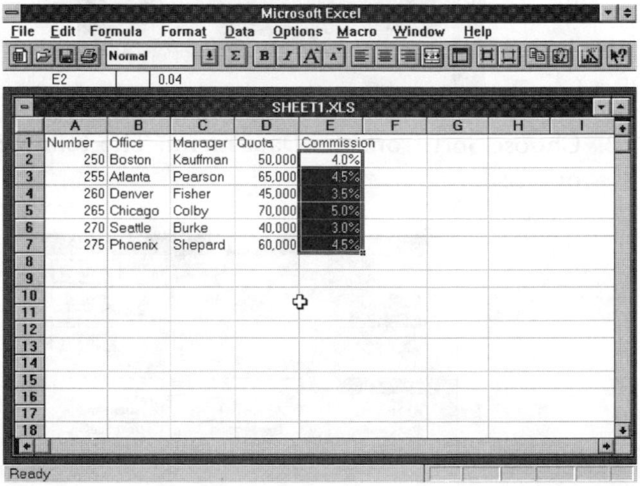

8

want sorted and then specify the key or keys you want to sort on. The keys are one or more fields that you want ordered. Unlike many of the other Data commands, Data Sort does not require the field names, and they should *not* be included in the data range. That means you can sort anything on an Excel worksheet, not just a database. When you use Data Sort, each record (which can be a row or a column) within the range you specify is reordered along with the key fields in that record.

Selecting the Sort Range

There are several ways to sort the database you just built; alphabetically by either office or manager are two ways you consider here. Start by sorting the table by office. The basic procedure is to highlight a range of records to be sorted, choose Sort from the Data menu, enter the keys on which to sort, and start the sort by clicking on OK. Begin that procedure with these instructions:

1. Select the range A2 through E7, as shown here:

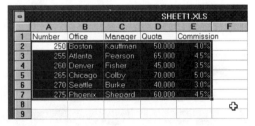

2. Choose Sort from the Data menu. The following Sort dialog box opens:

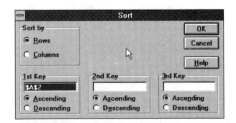

The Sort dialog box shows that Excel has guessed correctly that you want to sort by rows. This means that all the cells in one row within the highlight are moved together as the sort is carried out. This makes sense in terms of the database because one row is a single record and, while you want to rearrange the records, you want any given record to remain intact. You can also sort by columns, which has the opposite implication.

Identifying a Sort Key

The sort key, when sorting by rows, is the column containing the field you want sorted. In this example, you want the records sorted by offices, so column B is the sort key. It does not matter what row you specify. You can type in the cell address or you can click on the worksheet. If necessary, you can move the dialog box to see the worksheet.

Click on B2 to select the column you want to sort on. A blinking marquee appears around B2, and $B$2 appears in the 1st Key text box. Figure 8-4 shows how your screen should look.

Figure 8-4. *Sort key selected for sorting by office*

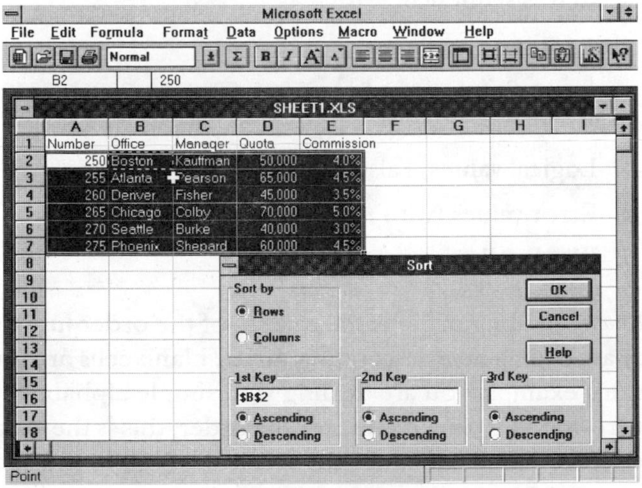

8

You have entered the first sort key, which is all you want to sort on in this example. You might wonder what happens in a larger database when you have duplicates in the key you are sorting on. If you specify only one key, duplicates are left in the same order in which they started. But you can specify a second key to sort records with duplicate first keys, and even a third key to sort duplicate second keys. You even can sort on more than three keys by doing more than one sort, using the lowest priority keys first and the highest priority keys last.

Ascending Versus Descending

Once you have specified the sort key, you can specify the sort order—ascending or descending. You indicate whether you want to sort in normal *ascending* alphabetical order (A first, Z last) or the reverse of that, *descending* order.

The normal alphabetic sequence (A,B,C,...Z) has been extended to include numbers, blanks, symbols, and logical and error values. Microsoft has established a specific sort order that is followed in all cases. The ascending sequence of this sort order is as follows:

1. Numbers entered as values from the largest negative number to the largest positive number

2. Text, ignoring capitalization and including numbers entered as text, in this sequence:

   ```
   Space ! " # $ % & ' ( ) * + , - . / : ; < = > ? @ [ \ ] ^ _ ` {
   | } ~ ¢ ¥ ± (and all other special characters) 0 1 2 3 4 5 6
   7 8 9 a b c d e f g h i j k l m n o p q r s t u v w x y z
   ```

3. Logical values, False first and then True

4. Error values (with no particular sort order)

5. Blank cells

The descending order is the reverse of the order just shown, except that, in both ascending and descending order, blank cells are always sorted last.

In this example you are dealing with simple alphabetic letters. You want to sort from A to Z, which is ascending order; this is the default and is already selected. If you want to change the sort order, you would click on Descending.

Doing the Sort

The actual sorting is anticlimactic, just click on OK. The dialog box closes, and the database is sorted alphabetically by office, as shown in Figure 8-5. Excel is returned to ready mode.

Changing and Re-sorting

Once sorted, the database can be re-sorted on a different sort key in a few quick steps. One reason to have a numbered column in the database is you can re-sort the list on the numbers and return the database to the original order in which it was entered. You could do that with this database, but instead follow these steps to change the sort key to carry out the sort on the office manager. You should be in ready mode with the database still selected.

Figure 8-5. *Database sorted by office*

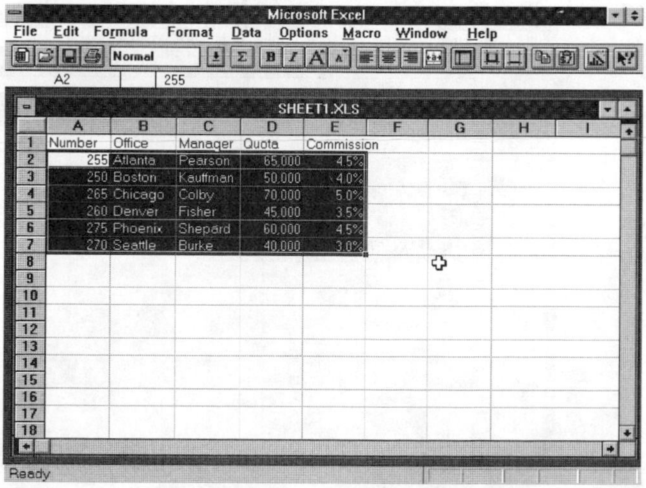

1. Choose Sort from the Data menu. The Sort dialog box opens.

   If the Sort dialog box is covering C1, drag on the dialog box's Title bar to uncover C1.

2. Click on C1 as the sort key, and click on OK to close the dialog box and do the sort.

The database is sorted alphabetically by manager, as shown in **Figure 8-6.**

Selecting Information from a Database

A database is primarily an ordered storage place for information. You place information in a database so you can get to it more easily, either to select particular records or to analyze it. After building a second database, you will spend the remainder of this chapter selecting or analyzing information in one or both of the databases.

Figure 8-6.   *Database sorted by manager*

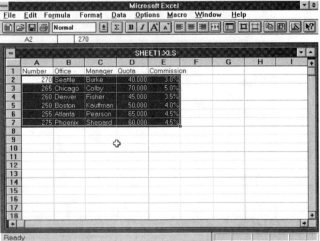

Building a Second Database

The second database contains the weekly sales amounts for three of the offices for the month of April. The fields will be the office number and name, the week the figures are for, the number of sales, and the total dollar amount of sales. Enter the field names for this table with these instructions:

1. Click on the vertical scroll bar below the scroll box, and click on A21 to move your active cell to A21.

2. Type the five field names shown here:

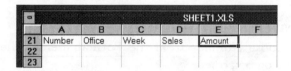

Entering Dates as a Data Series

One of the fields is an identifier for the week of the month for each record. Instead of typing this sequence of dates, you can use the Data Series option to enter them automatically. For the start number you enter the starting date, for the step number you enter a calendar increment (day, weekday, month, or year), and for the stop number you enter the ending date. The starting and ending dates can be in any recognizable Excel date format. The step number can be a decimal—1.5, for instance. Its units depend on the date units you select: days, weekdays, months, or years. Since you cannot display fractional days without also displaying the time (which you can do), the entries for this database are rounded to the closest whole day.

For the April sales database, you want to enter the weeks in column C, beginning with April 1, 1992, and ending May 1, 1992. Do that with these steps:

1. Click on C22, type **4/1/92** and press (ENTER).

2. Choose Series from the Data menu, type **7** for a step value of seven days, press (TAB) to move to the Stop Value field, type **5/1/92,** and click on Columns for the direction of the series. The Series dialog box looks like this when you are done:

8

3. Click on OK. The dialog box closes and the dates appear on your worksheet as shown in Figure 8-7.

The dates could use a little formatting, so do that next.

4. Select the range C22 through C26.

5. Choose Number from the Format menu. The Number Format dialog box opens.

6. Press (TAB) to highlight the contents of the Code text box, and type **mmm dd**. Your dialog box should look like this:

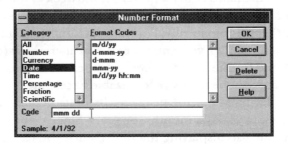

7. Click on OK. The date sequence is formatted as demonstrated in Figure 8-8.

Completing Data Entry

The table of sales amounts that you must enter is for five weeks and three sales offices—a total of fifteen entries. The dates that you just entered are for one sales office and therefore need to be copied twice more down column C. Each sales office (Boston, Denver, and Seattle) and its corresponding number must be entered five times, once for each week in the month. Finally, you must enter the sales quantities and amounts. Perform these tasks with the

Figure 8-7.   *Data series displayed*

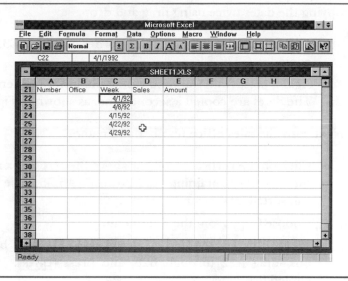

Figure 8-8.   *Dates reformatted*

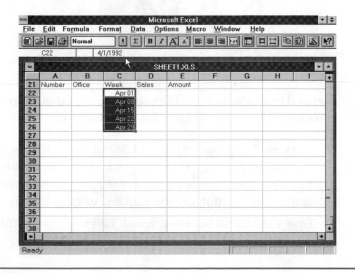

following steps. The week beginning dates still should be highlighted. **Begin by copying the dates twice using drag and drop.**

1. Press (CTRL) and drag the lower border of C26 to C31. The dates are copied to C27:C31.

2. Again, press (CTRL), and now drag the lower border of C31 to C36. The dates are copied a second time, as shown in Figure 8-9.

Next copy the sales office number and name.

3. Click on the vertical scroll bar above the scroll box and drag across the two cells containing "250 Boston" (A5:B5 if the first database is still sorted by manager).

4. Choose Copy from the Edit menu.

5. Again click on the vertical scroll bar—this time below the scroll box—drag A22 through B26, and press (ENTER). "250 Boston" is copied five times, as shown here:

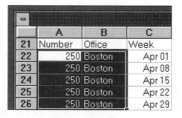

6. Repeat steps 3 through 5 to copy "260 Denver" to A27:B31 and "270 Seattle" to A32:B36.

Enter and copy a formula to calculate the sales amount from the sale units, and then enter those units to complete the database.

7. Click on E22, type **=D22*145.95**, press (ENTER), and with Number Format, format E22 with a comma and no decimals (#,##0). (Since 145.95 is the average value of a sale, you can derive the total sales amount by multiplying the number of sales by this average.)

8. Drag the E22 fill handle through E36 to copy the formula down the column.

Figure 8-9. *Dates as copied*

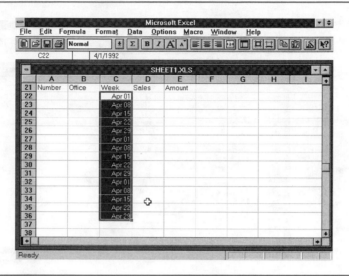

9. Type the sales figures in D22 through D36 as shown in Figure 8-10, which shows the finished database.

Carefully check your work against Figure 8-10. This April sales database is used for the remainder of the chapter. Entry errors could cause considerable confusion in subsequent sections.

Using the Database

The selection or modification of data within an Excel database requires that you identify two or three ranges for use in these operations. The first range is the database itself and is required by all operations other than sorting. The *database range* is the source for selecting records on which you will operate. The second range, the *criteria range*, also is required by all operations other than sorting. The criteria range contains the criteria by which the selections are made. The third range, the *extract range*, is required only by the

8

Figure 8-10. *Completed April Sales database*

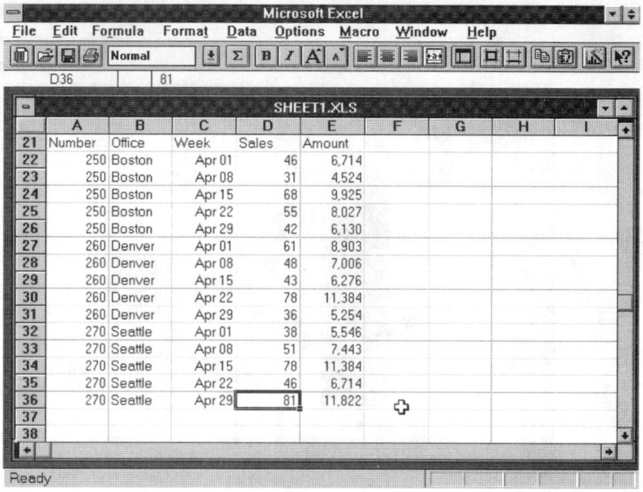

	A	B	C	D	E
21	Number	Office	Week	Sales	Amount
22	250	Boston	Apr 01	46	6,714
23	250	Boston	Apr 08	31	4,524
24	250	Boston	Apr 15	68	9,925
25	250	Boston	Apr 22	55	8,027
26	250	Boston	Apr 29	42	6,130
27	260	Denver	Apr 01	61	8,903
28	260	Denver	Apr 08	48	7,006
29	260	Denver	Apr 15	43	6,276
30	260	Denver	Apr 22	78	11,384
31	260	Denver	Apr 29	36	5,254
32	270	Seattle	Apr 01	38	5,546
33	270	Seattle	Apr 08	51	7,443
34	270	Seattle	Apr 15	78	11,384
35	270	Seattle	Apr 22	46	6,714
36	270	Seattle	Apr 29	81	11,822

Extract option. The extract range is a separate database that is filled by the Extract option.

Defining the Database

To define the database from which you want to select records, you must select or highlight it and choose the Data Set Database option. The database range must contain the full set of records from which you want to select, as well as the field names for those records. When you choose the Set Database option, Excel attaches the name Database to the range you have highlighted. This range name is the same as range names you can create yourself with the Formula Define Name option. Define the database range for the April sales database with these steps:

1. Drag from A21 through E36. The database is highlighted as shown in Figure 8-11.
2. Choose Set Database from the Data menu.

Figure 8-11. *April Sales database highlighted*

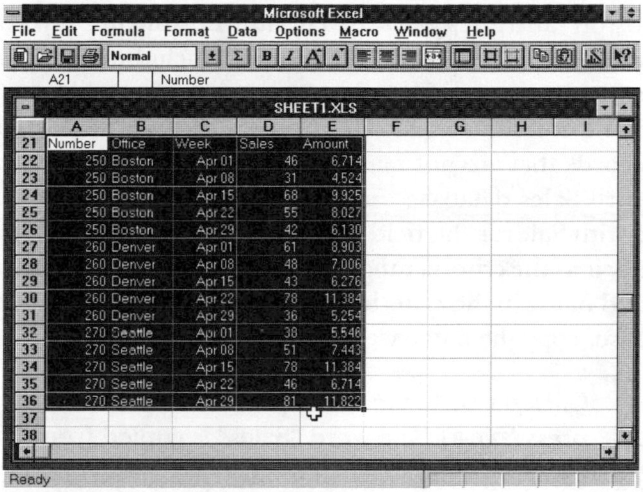

The highlighted range is accepted as the database, and you are returned to ready mode.

Establishing the Selection Criteria

Establishing the selection criteria requires that you identify a criteria range with the Set Criteria option. The criteria range is a small database. The first row of the criteria range must contain some or all of the field names from the database you just defined. The rest of the criteria range contains the criteria that will be the basis of your selection.

You can build the criteria range in any blank area of the worksheet, but it is usually best not to build it directly below the database so there is room for expansion. The field names in the criteria range must be exact copies of the field names in the input range. Frequently the full set of field names is copied from the input range with the Copy option.

The criteria directly relate to the field name under which they are entered. For example, if you want to select all of the records for the Boston sales office in the April sales database, you'll build a two-cell criteria range. The top cell has the field name Office; the bottom cell contains "Boston." The selection process searches for "Boston" in the Office field. This process gives you the matches between the criterion and the records in the input range. A criterion of "Boston" also gives you a match with "Bostonian." If you want just "Boston" you must enter the formula **="=Boston"**, including the quote marks. You can use text, numbers, or formulas as criteria for matching.

You can also use text, numbers, or formulas that cause Excel to search for records that are not matches. For example, if you want all records from the April Sales database that have more than 60 sales, you build a criteria range with Sales as the field name and >60 as the criterion. Do that now, and identify it as the criteria range with the following instructions. Since you want the field name in the criterion to be exactly the same as the field name in the database, copy the database field name.

1. Click on D21, choose Copy from the Edit menu, click on G21, and press (ENTER). The word "Sales" is copied from D21 to G21.

2. Click on G22, type **>60**, and press (ENTER). The field name and criterion are entered as shown here:

F	G	H
	Sales	
	>60	

3. Drag on G21 through G22 and choose Set Criteria from the Data menu. The criterion is identified.

The >60 criterion entered in the example is just one of many ways to specify criteria. Some rules on specifying criteria follow:

- Use relational operators (< for less than, > for greater than, = for equal to, < > for not equal to, < = for less than or equal to, and > = for greater than or equal to) with both text and numbers, either alone or in a formula.

- Use wildcard characters (? for any single character and * for any group of characters) in text that may not exactly match. For example, entering **pea**? as the criterion selects "peak", "peal", and "pear", while entering **for*** selects "for", "foray", "forecast", and "forest". You can combine wildcard characters. For example, AM??DC* might be used with part numbers in an inventory system to select all parts from a given manufacturer (the AM) for a particular machine (the DC).

- Numbers are matched without regard to their format. For example, the number 54 matches $54, 5400%, 5.40E+01, and 54.00.

- Formulas that refer to fields in the database range should use relative addresses. Formulas that refer to fields outside the database range should use absolute addresses. For example, the formula =SALES>=AMOUNT/150 is the same as =D22>=E22/150 and uses relative addressing to refer to fields within the database range of the April sales database. On the other hand, =SALES>=$H$23 uses absolute addressing to refer to an address outside the database range.

- Usually a criterion refers to the field name under which it has been entered. If the criterion is a formula that relates to the total record instead of a specific field (as =SALES>= AMOUNT/150), then you need to use a field name in the criteria not used in the database. For example, Formula might be such a field name.

- You can use the database field names in a criterion formula (for example, =SALES>=AMOUNT/150) without defining them with the Formula Define Names option. You will get the error message #NAME? in the criterion cell, but the formula is utilized correctly for database selection. An example of an erroneous message resulting from a field name formula is shown here:

F	G	H	I
	Formula		
	#NAME?		

- If you put criteria in multiple columns but only one row of a criteria range, *all* of the criteria must be satisfied for a record in the database range to be selected. It is as if you had put a logical AND between the fields. For example, if you create a criteria range with field names of Sales and Amount and enter **>60** under Sales and **>8000** under Amount, only records that have both greater than 60 sales and greater than $8,000 in the amount are selected. If either of those conditions is not met, the record is not selected. This is an AND criteria range:

F	G	H	I
	Sales	Amount	
	>60	>8000	

- If you put criteria in multiple rows of a criteria range, satisfying *either* of the criterion causes a record in the database range to be selected. It is as if you had put a logical OR between the fields. For example, if you enter **>60** under Sales in row 1 and **>8000** under Amount in row 2, records that satisfy either criterion are selected. This is an OR criteria range:

F	G	H	I
	Sales	Amount	
	>60		
		>8000	

- If you have a blank row in a criteria range, you select all of the records in the database. You can combine as many rows and as many columns as necessary to specify the criteria you need, but do not include a blank row unless you want to select all records.

- You can select records that fall within a range for a given field. For example, select all records that have greater than 60 sales and less than 70 sales by creating two criteria columns (both with the same field name) and entering the **>60** in one column and **<70** in the other, as shown here:

F	G	H	I
	Sales	Sales	
	>60	<70	

Finding Selected Records

Once you have specified both the database range and the criteria range, you can identify selected records in the database range with the Data Find option. When you choose the option, Excel highlights the first record in the database range that satisfies the criteria, and the mode changes to Find. The scroll bars have changed their use—they now take you from one selected record to another. You can find (select) additional records by clicking on the down scroll arrow or return to a record selected earlier by clicking on the up scroll arrow. By clicking on the scroll bar itself, you move to a selected record in the next or previous screen. If you want to return to ready mode you can select Exit Find from the Data menu or click anywhere on the worksheet outside of the database.

You can also use the following keys to continue to select records or to end the process:

Key	Action
DOWN ARROW	Highlights the next record that satisfies the criteria
UP ARROW	Highlights the previous record that satisfies the criteria
ENTER	Moves the active cell within the selected record
ESC	Ends Data Find and returns you to ready mode
LEFT ARROW or RIGHT ARROW	Scrolls the worksheet left or right one column at a time without affecting the selected record

Try the Data Find option with the following instructions (your criteria should still be Sales, >60):

1. Choose Find from the Data menu. The Data Find option changes the mode indicator to Find and highlights the first record that satisfies the criteria, as shown in Figure 8-12.

2. Click on the down scroll arrow or press DOWN ARROW. The second record that satisfies the criteria is highlighted.

3. Click on the scroll bar and up scroll arrow, and try the other keys to become familiar with how they work.

4. Click on the worksheet outside of the database or press ESC to return to ready mode.

Defining an Extract Range

The Data Extract option needs a place to put the records selected from the database range. The extract range is that place. It is defined by the Data Extract option. The extract range, like the criteria range, must have a row containing one or more field names that exactly match the field names in the

8

Figure 8-12.   *First record found with Data Find*

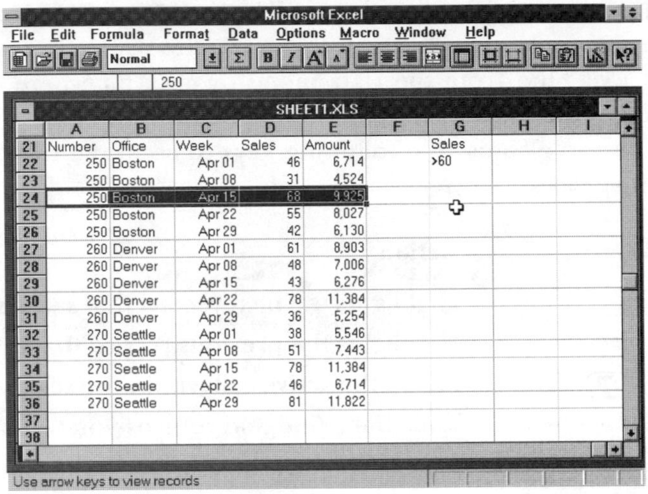

database range. If you want to limit the number of rows that Excel can fill with selected records, then you need to highlight that number of rows in addition to the row of field names when you define the extract range. If you want Excel to define the number of rows it needs, then highlight only the row of field names when you define the extract range. Define an extract range with these steps:

1. Click on G26, type **Office**, press (RIGHT ARROW), type **Week,** and press (ENTER). The labels "Office" and "Week" will be placed in G26 and H26, respectively.

2. Drag G26 through H36 to highlight the range to be used as the extract range, as shown in Figure 8-13.

Extracting Selected Records

The Data Extract option copies the selected records in the database range to the extract range. The selection is based on the selection criteria. Try it now.

1. Choose **Extract** from the **Data** menu. The Extract dialog box opens, as shown here:

The Extract dialog box allows you to select all records that match the criteria or only unique records, thus eliminating duplicates. Here you select all records.

2. Click on **OK**. Data Extract executes, filling a part of the extract range with the selected records, as shown in Figure 8-14.

If Data Extract selects more records than can fit in the extract range, you get an error message to that effect. Enlarge the area or highlight only the field names and repeat the extract.

Be aware, if you specify only a one-row extract range and thereby allow Excel to use as much room as it needs for selected records, any other

Figure 8-13. *Extract range selected*

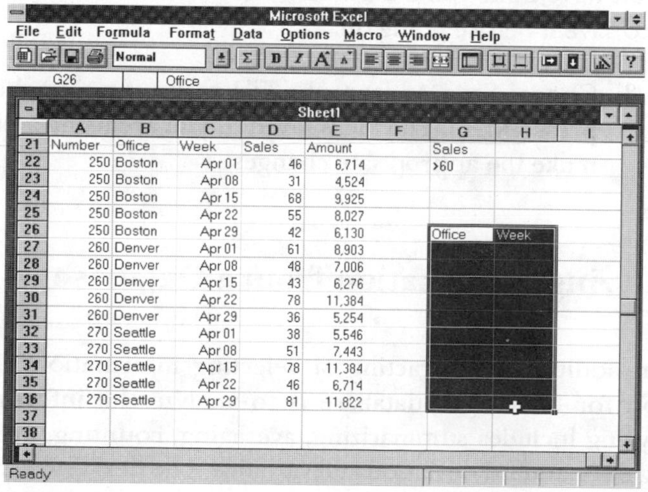

	A	B	C	D	E	F	G	H	I
21	Number	Office	Week	Sales	Amount		Sales		
22	250	Boston	Apr 01	46	6,714		>60		
23	250	Boston	Apr 08	31	4,524				
24	250	Boston	Apr 15	68	9,925				
25	250	Boston	Apr 22	55	8,027				
26	250	Boston	Apr 29	42	6,130		Office	Week	
27	260	Denver	Apr 01	61	8,903				
28	260	Denver	Apr 08	48	7,006				
29	260	Denver	Apr 15	43	6,276				
30	260	Denver	Apr 22	78	11,384				
31	260	Denver	Apr 29	36	5,254				
32	270	Seattle	Apr 01	38	5,546				
33	270	Seattle	Apr 08	51	7,443				
34	270	Seattle	Apr 15	78	11,384				
35	270	Seattle	Apr 22	46	6,714				
36	270	Seattle	Apr 29	81	11,822				
37									
38									

Figure 8-14.   *Results of the Data Extract*

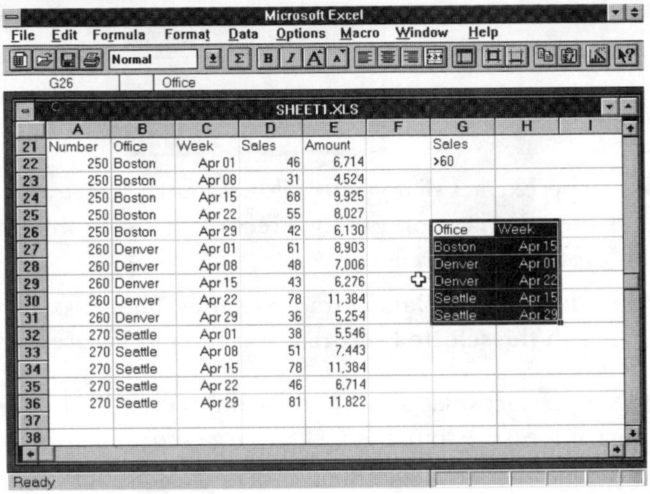

information in the rows under the field names of the extract range is cleared or written over. *All rows below the extract range are cleared, whether or not they are used for extracted data. You cannot undo Data Extract.*

You have done quite a bit of work on this worksheet, so this is a good time to save it before going on.

3. Choose Save As from the File menu, type **c:\sheet\salesapr**, and press (ENTER). The file is saved. If you are using a different directory, make the appropriate changes.

Analyzing Information from a Database

In addition to extracting or selecting information, the other primary reason for building a database is to analyze the information it contains. Analyzing includes summarizing, averaging, counting, grouping, and calculating the standard deviation and variance. The next few sections cover several functions and options within Excel that are used for analyzing information in databases.

Using Database Statistical Functions

In previous chapters, you used the SUM function to add a set of numbers in a range. SUM has the general form, or syntax, of

SUM(*range*)

where *range* is any set of range names or addresses. Other functions include AVERAGE, which calculates the average of a range; COUNT, which counts the number of items in a range; and MIN and MAX, which identify the minimum and maximum numbers in a range. They have similar syntaxes:

AVERAGE(*range*)

COUNT(*range*)

MAX(*range*)

MIN(*range*)

Excel has another set of functions called *database statistical functions.* Among them are DSUM, DAVERAGE, and DCOUNT. They have the same general purposes as statistical functions: they sum, average, and count. Database statistical functions, however, are meant to operate on specific fields in a database and to perform only on records that match criteria. Each database statistical function has a syntax similar to

DSUM(*database, field,criteria*)

where *database* is a range on the worksheet containing the field, *field* identifies a field name or column in the database on which you want to operate (sum, average, count), and *criteria* is a criteria range used to select the particular records you want to use.

The primary differences between SUM and DSUM or between statistical and database statistical functions is that statistical functions operate on a range without any selection. Database statistical functions select both a

8

particular column (field) within a larger range and particular records (cells in the column) on which to operate. DSUM is the same as SUM if the database is a single column you want to sum and the criteria is blank.

All of the information you have learned about database ranges and criteria ranges as they apply to Data options applies to database statistical functions. The *database* can be the addresses of a range on the worksheet including the field names (A21:E36, for example), the name of a range you have defined with Formula Define Name, or the name Database if you have defined a range with the Data Set Database option.

The *field* can be a field name, a field number, or the address of a cell that contains a field name or number. If a field name is used, it should be in quotation marks and should match the field name in the database range exactly. The number determines the column within the database table beginning with the leftmost column as 1. The number for the second column is 2, the number for the third column is 3, and so on.

The *criteria* can be the addresses of a range on the worksheet (G21:G22, for example), a name you have defined with Formula Define Name, or the name Criteria if you have defined a range with the Data Set Criteria option.

All of the following formulas do the same thing: sum the selected sales units in the April Sales database you entered into A21:E36 using the criteria you entered into G21:G22.

```
=DSUM(A21:E36,4,G21:G22)
=DSUM(Database,"Sales",Criteria)
=DSUM(sales,D21,top) if you have defined the names "sales" as
 A21:E36 and "top" as G21:G22.
```

Creating Range Names

You have already named the database and criteria ranges of the April Sales database using the Set Database and Set Criteria options on the Data menu. These options name the ranges Database and Criteria, respectively. Once you have used the options to set the names, you can use them in any Excel function, as if they were any other range name. As you probably guessed, a range name is a name, like Sales, that you define to represent a range of cells on the worksheet. You can have only one range with a given range name, so you can have only one range named Database and one range named Criteria. As you work with database statistical functions, you are going to want to use ranges other than those defined as Database and Criteria. For these other ranges you can use either range addresses or range names.

There are two and possibly three reasons to use range names over range addresses. First, and most compelling, is that a range name always accurately reflects changes you make to a worksheet. When you use a range name in several functions, all those functions are updated when you change the range referred to by the name. Secondly, range names are often easier to remember and almost always more recognizable than the range addresses they represent. Third, in some cases a short range name is easier to enter than a long set of range addresses. Since you will be building several database statistical functions with the same database and criteria ranges, get some practice naming a couple of ranges even though you could use the name already attached to one of those ranges. Use these instructions for that purpose:

1. Highlight the range A21:E36 (the database) and choose Define Name from the Formula menu. The Define Name dialog box opens, as shown here:

    Notice that Criteria and Database are listed as names already existing on the worksheet. Also the range that you highlighted is shown as the range to which the new name you will enter will be attached. Number, which came from the first cell of the highlighted range, is shown as a default name, but you want a different name for the range.

2. Type **Sales** and press (ENTER). The database is now named Sales, as well as Database. This does not conflict with the field named Sales.

3. Highlight the range A38:A39, which you will use as a second criteria range, choose Define Name, type **Loc** (short for location), and press (ENTER) to name the range.

8

Next, prepare an area on the worksheet for entering database statistical functions by entering several titles.

4. Click on A38 and type **Office**. Press (RIGHT ARROW) twice to move to C38 and type **Number**. Press (RIGHT ARROW), type **Total #**, press (RIGHT ARROW), type **Total $**, press (RIGHT ARROW), type **Average #**, press (RIGHT ARROW), type **Average $**, and then press (ENTER).

The bottom few lines of your screen should look like this:

Building the Formulas

Under each of the titles (Number, Total #, and so on) you will enter a database statistical function. (Use Office as a criteria range field, not a title for a database statistical function.) The titles are not necessary for the database statistical functions, but they are informative. After the formulas are entered, their result is all that is displayed. The formulas you enter are DCOUNT, to count the number of nonblank cells in a field in the records in the database range that match the criteria; DSUM, to sum a field in the records of the database range that match the criteria; and DAVERAGE, to average a field in the records of the database range that match the criteria. Initially you leave the criteria blank to select all of the records in the database range.

When you enter a function, do not include spaces anywhere except in a literal enclosed in quotation marks. Also, be sure to include the = symbol and both parentheses. With these rules in mind, enter several database statistical functions with the following steps.

1. Click on C39. The active cell moves to C39.

2. Type **=dcount(sales,"number",loc)** and press (ENTER). The result appears in C39, as shown in Figure 8-15. The DCOUNT function counts the number of nonblank cells in the Number field of the Sales database that match the criteria in Loc.

When typing a function, it is a good idea to use lowercase letters. That way you can tell if Excel recognizes what you are typing. If it does, the

Figure 8-15. *=DCOUNT completed*

functions automatically change to all uppercase, and range names change to leading caps. Excel acts like a spelling checker.

3. Click on cell D39, type **=dsum(sales,"sales",loc)**, and then press (RIGHT ARROW). The result, 802, appears in D39. This DSUM function adds all the numbers in the Sales field of the Sales database that match the criteria in Loc.

4. In the next three cells type the following formulas. Press (RIGHT ARROW) after the first two and (ENTER) after the last.

```
=dsum(sales,"amount",loc)
=daverage(sales,"sales",loc)
=daverage(sales,"amount",loc)
```

5. Drag C39:G39, choose Number from the Format menu, click on #,##0, and click on OK. The row of database statistical functions is formatted with the comma format and no decimal places. Figure 8-16 shows the results.

8

Figure 8-16.   *Database statistical functions entered and formatted*

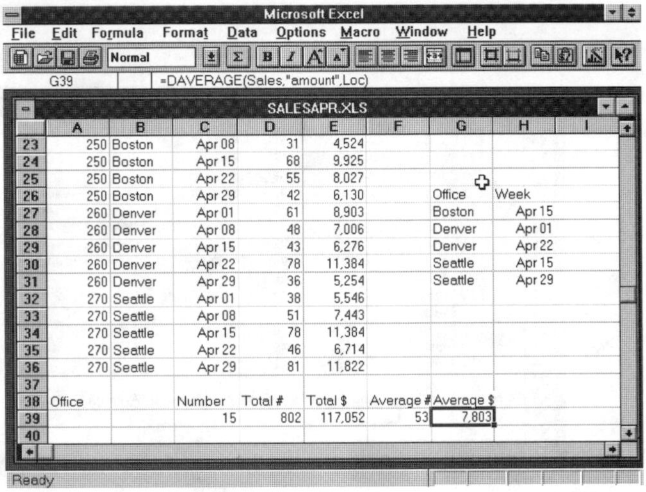

You are now in a position to change the criteria and immediately see the result—called a *what-if* situation. The formulas in C39:G39 reflect the criterion in A39. Enter a new criteria, and the formulas reflect the result. Currently, the blank criteria means that the formulas are utilizing the entire database range. If you enter **Boston** in the criteria range, the formulas utilize only records with Boston in the Office field. Try that next with these instructions:

6. Click on A39, type **Boston**, and press (ENTER). "Boston" is entered in the criteria range, and the formulas recalculate to reflect that, as shown in Figure 8-17. Note that the criteria is not case sensitive. You could enter **boston** or **BOSTON** and get the same results.

Creating a Data Table

As powerful as the criteria-and-formula combination is, Excel has a better way to handle it—a *data table*. A data table shows the results of one or more formulas when one or two variables in the formulas are varied. As an example, a data table can show the results of the five database statistical functions entered in the last section for all of the three sales offices at one time. The variable in this case is the criteria, and the three offices are the variations. This is known as a *one-input data table*.

A one-input data table is a specially configured rectangular range on a worksheet. It can be configured in rows or columns, but rows are most common. For the row configuration, the top row contains as many formulas as you want to use. C39:G39 would be such a row. Then, in the column to the left of the first formula and beginning one row beneath it, you enter as many variables as you want applied to those formulas. Here you will enter the three cities **Boston, Denver,** and **Seattle.** Each formula needs to refer to one cell where the variable is substituted. This is known as the *input cell* and is A39 in this example. Build this data table now, and observe how it works. A39 should still be the active cell.

1. Press (DEL) and then (ENTER). The criterion (Boston) is erased, and the database statistical functions once again show the totals in the database range.

Figure 8-17. *Effects of changing the criterion to Boston*

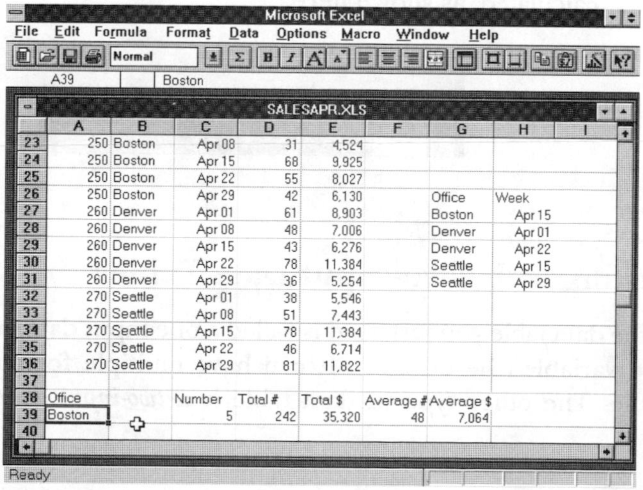

2. Click on B40 and type **Boston, Denver,** and **Seattle,** pressing (DOWN ARROW) after the first two and (ENTER) after the last.

3. Highlight B39 through G42 as your data table range, which is shown here:

4. Choose Table from the Data menu. The Table dialog box opens, as shown here:

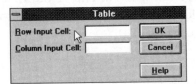

The Table dialog box asks you for either a row input cell and/or a column input cell. Since you have only one variable and it is in a column, you only need to enter a column input cell.

5. Press (TAB) to move from Row Input Cell to Column Input Cell, click on A39 (or type **$A$39**), and click on OK. The data table is then calculated, as shown here:

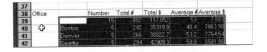

Working with Two-Input Data Tables

The data table you just used is called a one-input data table because there is one variable (the criteria). It can have multiple formulas but only one variable. The other type of data table is a *two-input data table*. It has two variables but only one formula. In a *two-input data table*, one variable is in a column, as the sales offices were in the previous example, and the other variable is in a row. The formula is in the upper-left corner cell that is the intersection between the row variables and the column variables.

For an example of a two-input data table, assume you are a sales manager and want to look at the kind of money your sales people can earn with varying commission rates and varying monthly sales. The formula for this would be monthly sales times the commission rate times 12 to get annual income. The two variables are commission rates, which you want to look at from 3 percent through 6 percent, and monthly sales, which normally fall between $40,000 and $100,000. The steps to build such a table follow:

1. Click on the vertical scroll bar beneath the scroll box. You get a blank area on your worksheet.

2. Click on C45, type **Commission Rate**, press (DOWN ARROW), type **Monthly Sales**, and press (ENTER).

3. Click on B48, type **3%**, press (ENTER), choose Series from the Data menu, type **.5%**, press (TAB), type **6%**, and press (ENTER). The row variables are entered.

4. Highlight B48 through H48, choose Number from the Format menu, click on the one decimal percentage format you built (0.0%), and click on OK. The row variables are now formatted.

5. Click on A48, type **=e45*e46*12**, and press (DOWN ARROW) to enter the formula you want to vary.

6. Type **40,000**, press (ENTER), choose Series from the Data menu, type **10,000**, press (TAB), type **100,000**, click on Columns, and click on OK. The column variables are entered.

7. Highlight A48 through H55, choose Table from the Data menu, click on E45 for the row input cell, press (TAB), click on E46 for the column input cell, and click on OK.

Your commission table is produced, as shown in Figure 8-18. It is equivalent to doing the calculation 49 times (seven rates and seven amounts). As you can see, a data table is a valuable analysis tool.

8

Figure 8-18. *Completed two-input data table*

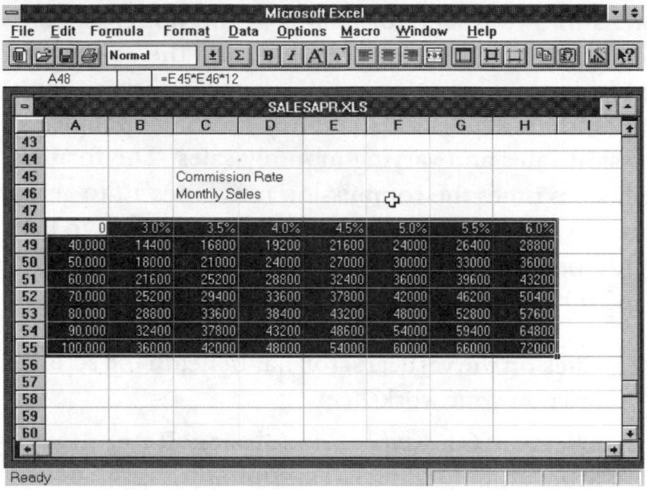

	A	B	C	D	E	F	G	H
45			Commission Rate					
46			Monthly Sales					
48	0	3.0%	3.5%	4.0%	4.5%	5.0%	5.5%	6.0%
49	40,000	14400	16800	19200	21600	24000	26400	28800
50	50,000	18000	21000	24000	27000	30000	33000	36000
51	60,000	21600	25200	28800	32400	36000	39600	43200
52	70,000	25200	29400	33600	37800	42000	46200	50400
53	80,000	28800	33600	38400	43200	48000	52800	57600
54	90,000	32400	37800	43200	48600	54000	59400	64800
55	100,000	36000	42000	48000	54000	60000	66000	72000

Using Crosstabs

A *crosstab* is a table that totals the rows on the right, totals the columns on the bottom, and has a grand total (or *total total*) in the lower-right corner, like this:

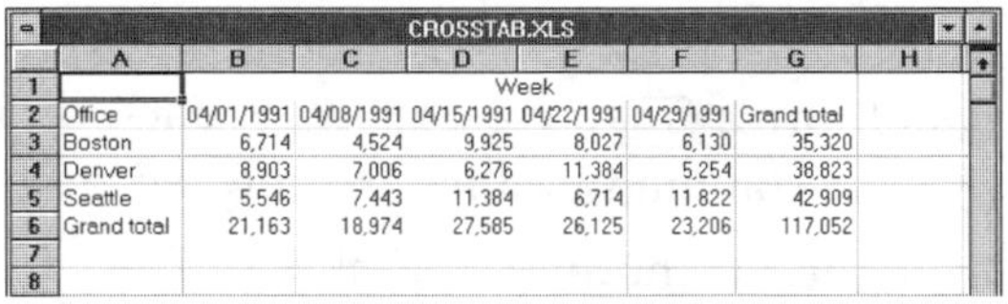

	A	B	C	D	E	F	G
1				Week			
2	Office	04/01/1991	04/08/1991	04/15/1991	04/22/1991	04/29/1991	Grand total
3	Boston	6,714	4,524	9,925	8,027	6,130	35,320
4	Denver	8,903	7,006	6,276	11,384	5,254	38,823
5	Seattle	5,546	7,443	11,384	6,714	11,822	42,909
6	Grand total	21,163	18,974	27,585	26,125	23,206	117,052

Excel 4 has a Crosstab ReportWizard that will help you build a crosstab from a database if you tell the Wizard what the rows and columns are. For your April Sales database, a crosstab report might total each office by week and then total each weekly figure to get the office total for the month. At the same time, you can get a total each week for all sales offices. To do this, you make each row a sales office and each column a week, as shown in the previous illustration. Each cell is the total sales for an office in a week. The total of each row is the total for an office in April, and the total for a column is the weekly total for all sales offices. The grand total is the total sales for all offices for the month.

To make this crosstab report with the Crosstab ReportWizard, you must remove the current criteria, since you want to sum all records, and you must reformat the dates so they can be used with the Wizard (the Wizard cannot recognize the current custom date format you entered earlier in the chapter). Do these two preparatory steps and then see for yourself how the Crosstab ReportWizard works.

1. Click on G22, press (DEL), and click on OK to remove the criteria. If you didn't do this, only the weeks that had more than 60 sales would be included in the crosstab.

2. Select C22:C36, click on Format, Number, Date, and the first date format (m/d/yy) to change the date from the custom date format (mmm dd) to a standard date format.

3. Open the Data menu and choose Crosstab. The Crosstab ReportWizard introductory screen appears as shown in Figure 8-19.

4. Click on Create a New Crosstab. The Crosstab ReportWizard Row Categories screen opens, as you can see in Figure 8-20.

5. Click on Office so that each row will represent a sales office and the total on the right will be the total for a sales office. Click on Add to add the Office field to the Row Categories table, and click on Next to move to the next screen—the Column Categories.

6. Click on Week so that each column will represent a week in April and the total on the bottom will be the total for a week. Click on Add to add the Week field to the Column Categories table, and click on Next to move to the next screen—the Value Fields.

7. Amount is already selected, so the sales dollar amounts will be the values that go into the crosstab and the totals on the right and bottom. Click on Add to add the Amount field to the Value Fields table, and click on Next to move to the next screen—the final Crosstab ReportWizard screen shown in Figure 8-21.

8

Figure 8-19.   *Crosstab ReportWizard introductory screen*

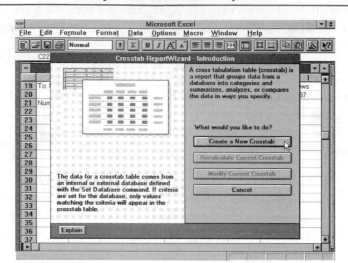

Figure 8-20.   *Crosstab ReportWizard Row Categories screen*

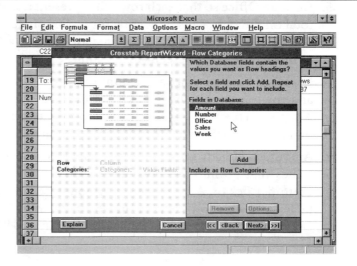

Figure 8-21. *Crosstab ReportWizard Create It screen*

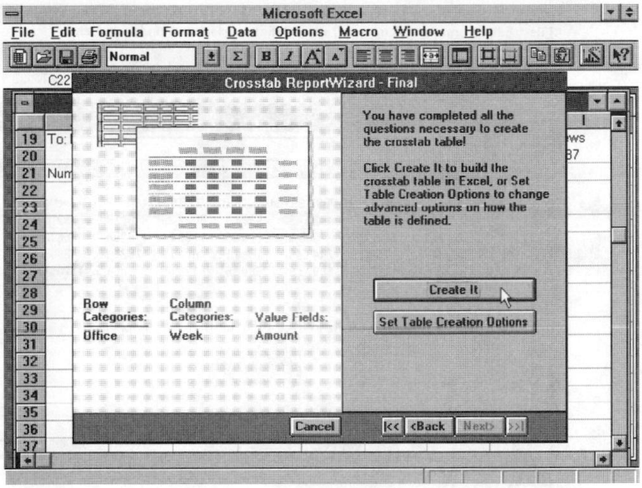

8. Click on Create It. The Crosstab ReportWizard goes to work. You'll see a series of messages in the Message area of the Status bar that tells you what the Crosstab ReportWizard is doing. When the Crosstab ReportWizard has completed its work, a crosstab will be displayed, as you can see in Figure 8-22.

The crosstab report, as it is currently produced by Excel 4, is in outline structure and needs a little formatting. The outline structure allows you to change from the current display to a display of just the totals on the right or on the bottom by clicking on either of the two buttons in the upper-left corner of the Worksheet window. In this case the outline structure does not do much for you. You can turn outlining off by clicking on the Options menu, the Display option, and the Outline Symbols check box.

The dates across the top of the crosstab are text, so you cannot reformat them; if you want to change them, you must reenter them. The numbers in the crosstab can be formatted for better readability. If you use the #,##0 format, you will get the crosstab report shown at the beginning of this section.

8

Figure 8-22.   *Completed crosstab*

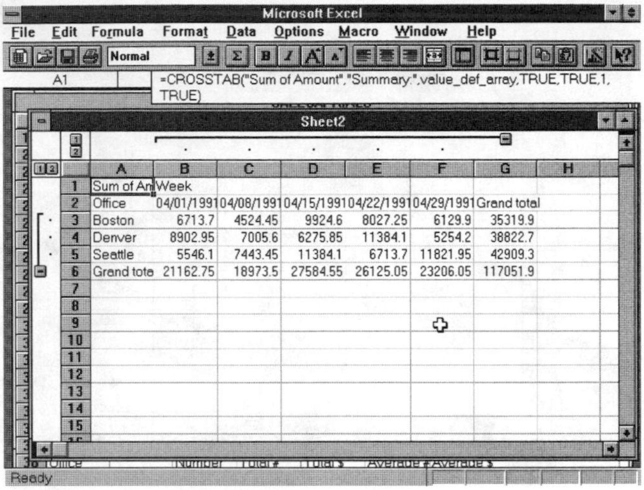

The Crosstab ReportWizard saves you a great deal of work in building what is in essence a summary worksheet. If you want to do that in your work, it would be worthwhile to try the Wizard on your own.

Using Lookup Functions

Excel has two functions that, while not database functions, are related to using databases. These are the horizontal and vertical table lookup functions HLOOKUP and VLOOKUP. Use these two functions to search a two-dimensional range for an item, based on finding a match in another item that is in the first row (horizontal lookup) or the first column (vertical lookup) and an index that tells Excel how many rows down (horizontal lookup) or across (vertical lookup) to move to find the sought-after item. These functions have three arguments:

- A value to look for in the first row or column
- A range or database in which to look
- An index to determine how far down or across to look in the range to find the item sought

The formats of these functions are

HLOOKUP(*x,range,index*)
where *x* is the value to look for in the first row, and

VLOOKUP(*x,range,index*)
where *x* is the value to look for in the first column

Use the vertical lookup function with the second database you built (April Sales) to calculate commissions earned based on the commission rates in the first database you built. The function uses the office number in each record of the second database as the value to search for in the leftmost column of the first database, which is the range of the function. An index of 5 is used since the commissions are in the fifth column. The values in the first column must be in numerical order, so the first step is to re-sort the first database by office number. Do that and then build the formulas with vertical lookup functions using these instructions:

1. Click on the vertical scroll bar above the scroll box until you are at the top of the worksheet and can see the first database you built.

2. Highlight A2 through E7, choose Sort from the Data menu, and click on OK to accept the defaults of sorting by rows on column A. Your database is sorted, as shown here:

	A	B	C	D	E	F
				SALESAPR.XLS		
1	Number	Office	Manager	Quota	Commission	
2	250	Boston	Kauffman	50,000	4.0%	
3	255	Atlanta	Pearson	65,000	4.5%	
4	260	Denver	Fisher	45,000	3.5%	
5	265	Chicago	Colby	70,000	5.0%	
6	270	Seattle	Burke	40,000	3.0%	
7	275	Phoenix	Shepard	60,000	4.5%	
8						

3. Click on the vertical scroll bar below the scroll box and click on F22.

4. Type **=e22*vlookup(a22,a2:e7,5)** and press (ENTER). The formula is calculated with the result of 268.548 (4% of 6,714), as shown here:

F22		=E22*VLOOKUP(A22,$A$2:$E$7,5)					

SALESAPR.XLS

	A	B	C	D	E	F	G
19							
20							
21	Number	Office	Week	Sales	Amount		Sales
22	250	Boston	Apr 01	46	6,714	268.548	>60
23	250	Boston	Apr 08	31	4,524		
24	250	Boston	Apr 15	68	9,925		

The lookup function took the office number, 250, in A22, searched the left column (because you used the vertical function) of the first database (A2:E7), and then, in the row in which it found 250, it went over five cells to find 4%. The 4% was then multiplied by the amount in E22. In searching for the 250 in the first database, Excel picks the first value that equals or exceeds the value for which it is searching. For that reason it is imperative that the range be sorted on the first column or row. The A2:E7 range needs to be absolute because you will be copying it down the database and you do not want it to vary as you do A22 and E22. To complete the April Sales database, format cell F22 and copy it to the remaining entries in the database.

5. Choose Number from the Format menu, click on #,##0, and click on OK. The number is formatted with a comma and no decimal places.

6. Drag the F22 fill handle through F36. The formula is copied down the rest of the database, as shown in Figure 8-23.

To be sure that the lookup function is working, check several of the numbers. For example, Denver's April 8 sales of 7,006 times 3.5% is 245, and Seattle's April 15 sales of 11,384 times 3% is 342. Remember that both the sales amount and the commission are rounded to the nearest whole number. You should find that the vertical lookup function is working perfectly.

Like several other features of Excel's database capabilities, the vertical and horizontal lookup functions are very powerful. As you have seen in the example here, they allow you to combine two databases.

As a final step in this chapter, save your worksheet and leave Excel and Windows by following these steps:

Figure 8-23. *Vertical lookup commission calculation*

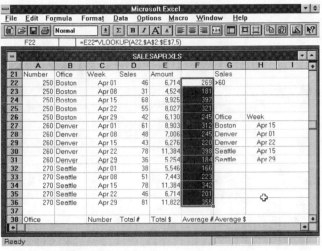

1. Choose Save from the File menu. The file is saved under its current name, replacing the version previously saved.

2. Double-click on both Excel's and the Program Manager's Control-menu box, and click on OK to leave Windows. Excel and Windows close and return you to the operating system.

8

9

Linking Worksheets and Using External Files

Establishing a link to and exchanging information between worksheets is the major topic in this chapter and a highlight of Excel. The chapter covers the process of combining several worksheets into one, including copying from one worksheet to another. Also, exporting and importing non-Excel text and number files is discussed, as is dividing or parsing a non-Excel text file.

Linking Worksheets

If you are building a large worksheet, you can build it in two dimensions by using multiple areas on one worksheet, as shown on the left of Figure 9-1. This can be cumbersome, especially if the multiple areas are segments of a larger entity (as in departments, plants, or stores in a corporation). Unless each segment just fits on one screen, you have to use a combination of several keystrokes to get from one segment to another. Most importantly, if multiple

Figure 9-1.   *A single large worksheet versus multiple worksheets*

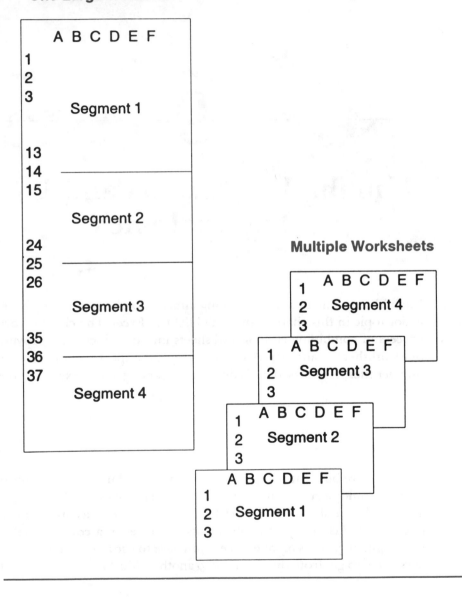

people are maintaining the various portions of the large worksheet, as would be the case with multiple departments or stores in a larger corporation, you have the problem of combining their work.

Excel's answer to this is to allow multiple worksheets to be easily combined either in memory or while on disk, as the right side of Figure 9-1 shows. Each segment, such as a department, is a separate worksheet. To get from one segment to another you simply click on the next worksheet or choose it in the Window menu. Getting around and other range-oriented procedures are much easier with multiple worksheets than they are with a single large worksheet. Also, each department or other company segment can create and maintain their own worksheet, which can then be combined at the corporate level.

Multiple worksheets have a safety aspect. With a single large worksheet you have to worry about what effect inserting and deleting rows and columns will have on surrounding sections of the worksheet. With multiple worksheets you can put different sections on different sheets and forget about them as you insert and delete rows and columns in another worksheet.

The multiple worksheet structure also makes intuitive sense and simplifies the layout of almost any complex worksheet; after all, you are used to turning the pages of a book and putting new or different topics on different pages. The implementation of such a concept in a worksheet is very compelling. Build a multiple worksheet now, and see for yourself.

Creating Multiple Worksheets

In the examples in this chapter you use a set of simple departmental budgets for the marketing area of a corporation. Three departments—customer relations, public relations, and advertising—are summed into the total marketing budget. Each department and the total have exactly the same worksheet format. You can, therefore, build one master worksheet, copy it to the other three, and then come back and customize each of them. Prepare these worksheets now with the following instructions. Your computer should be on, Windows and Excel loaded, and you should have a blank worksheet on your screen.

9

1. Enter and center the titles and column headings across columns A to H as shown here (column A has been widened to 17 spaces, or approximately two normal column widths):

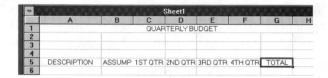

2. Add a top and bottom border in row 6, narrow that row to create a double underline, maximize the worksheet by clicking on the upward-pointing arrow in the upper-right corner of the worksheet, and enter the row headings as shown in Figure 9-2.

These departmental budgets are based on a head count, which varies by department; an assumption (ASSUMP.) for the average cost per head for each of the expense items, which also varies by department; and a quarterly growth percentage, which is common to all departments. The formula, then, for all expense items, is head count times assumption times 1+ growth.

Figure 9-2.   *Row headings and double underline*

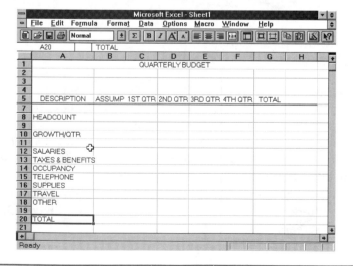

Figure 9-3. *General formula and growth percentages*

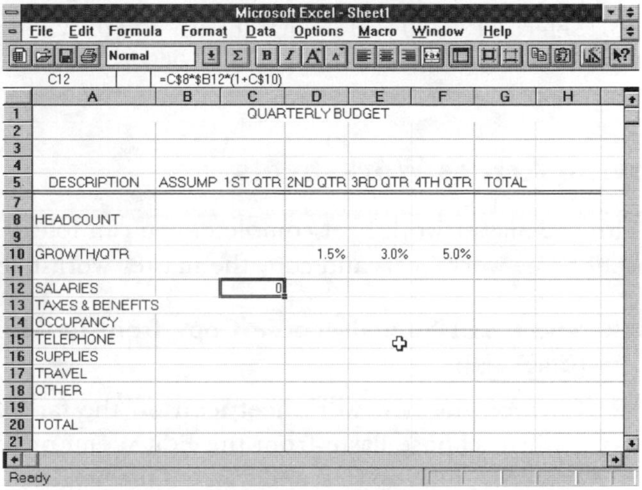

3. Enter the three growth percentages and format them with a single decimal place, as shown in Figure 9-3. Also enter the first formula in C12 as **=C$8*$B12*(1+C$10)**.

Note the mixed references on all the cell addresses. These are very important since you will be copying this one formula to all the other quarters and expense items. Remember that the easiest way to get absolute and mixed references is by pressing (F4) immediately after pointing to or typing a cell address. The first time you press (F4) you get an absolute reference ($C$8), the second time you press (F4) you get a mixed reference with the row fixed (C$8), and the third time you press (F4) you get a mixed reference with the column fixed ($C8). You do not have to remember this because you can continue to press (F4) until you get the reference you want.

4. Select C12:F18 and choose Fill Down and Fill Right from the Edit menu to copy the formula in C12 to the other quarters and expense items.

5. Build the totals in G12:G18 and C20:G20 using the AutoSum button in the Standard toolbar and AutoFill. Do this by clicking on G12,

the AutoSum button, and pressing (ENTER). Drag the fill handle from G12 to G18. Repeat the procedure starting at C20.

6. Select B12:G20 and format it with #,##0. When you are done your master worksheet looks like Figure 9-4.

Copying Across Worksheets

With the master worksheet complete, you can follow these steps to add the other three worksheets and copy the master worksheet to each of them.

1. Select A1:H20 and choose Copy from the Edit menu (or press (CTRL)-(INS)).

2. Click on the new worksheet icon on the far left of the Standard toolbar, choose Paste from the Edit menu or press (ENTER), widen column A to 17 spaces, and shorten the height of row 6 for a double underline.

Figure 9-4.   *Completed master worksheet*

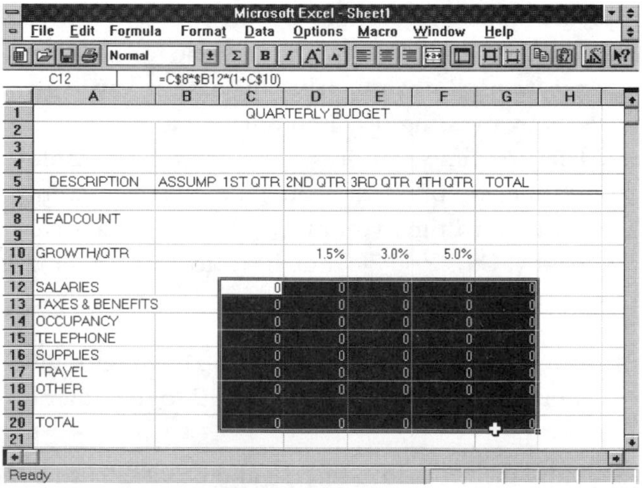

3. Repeat step 2 for a third and fourth worksheet. When you are done, restore your worksheet to normal size; your screen will look like Figure 9-5.

Handling Multiple Worksheets

The display that you have on your screen and that is shown in Figure 9-5 is one of several ways to look at multiple worksheets. This current display is called overlapping worksheets. If you see only one window it is probably because you still have a maximized view. To return to "normal"-size windows (where you can see a smaller amount of each window), click on the Restore button or use the Restore option in the Control menu for the active window (not the Excel Control menu).

Remember that one way to get around with multiple worksheets is by clicking on the sheet you want to go to. The default display, shown in Figure 9-5, provides the ability to click on all the other sheets if you are looking at Sheet4, but you cannot click on any other sheet if you are looking at Sheet1.

Figure 9-5. *Four worksheets with the base information on them*

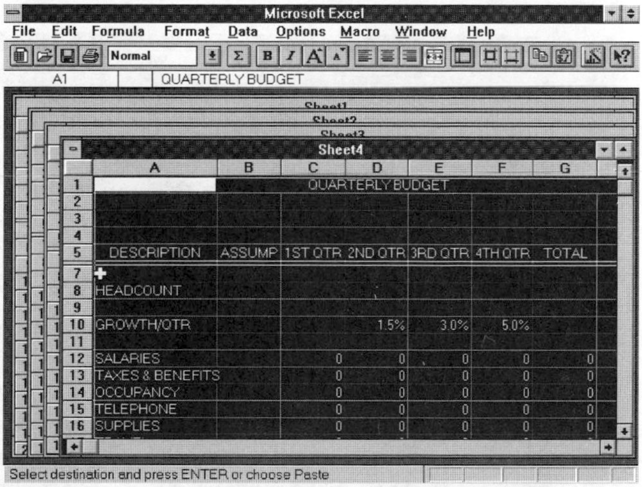

9

The first step, then, is to pull the right edge of each worksheet to the left so they are stair-stepped in the reverse order, as shown in Figure 9-6.

1. Drag the upper-right corner of Sheet3 to the left approximately the width of the vertical scroll bar on Sheet4. Repeat this procedure for Sheet2 and Sheet1, dragging them to the left the approximate width of the previous worksheet's scroll bar. Use the Size option on each worksheet's Control menu to do this operation with the keyboard.

Next try switching between sheets, first with the mouse and then with the Window menu.

2. Click successively on worksheets 3, 2, and 1. Notice how the sheets are now stair-stepped on the right. Had you not done step 1, you would now be looking at only Sheet1.

3. Click randomly on the various worksheets. For example, click on Sheet3, Sheet4, Sheet1, and Sheet2. After a while you can tell which is which by their heights and if they are showing on the left or right.

Figure 9-6. *Stair-stepping the right edge*

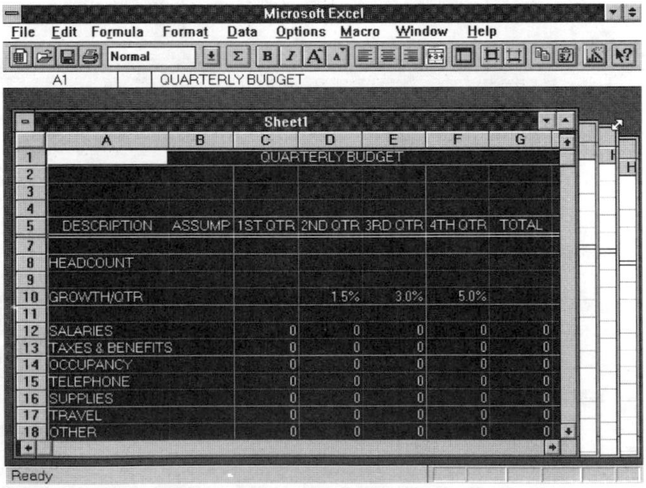

4. Click on the Window menu. Notice how each worksheet is listed, and the last worksheet you clicked on, the *active worksheet*, has a check mark beside it, as shown here:

5. Choose one or two of the worksheet options from the Window menu. Notice how this method works exactly like clicking on a worksheet. The benefits of using the menu are that there is never any question which worksheet you are going to and the worksheet does not have to be visible.

All of your work so far has been with overlapping windows. Another type of window view is called a *tiled view*, which basically gives each window a small part of the screen. Look at that now.

6. Choose Arrange from the Window menu. The Arrange Windows dialog box appears as shown:

7. Click on Tiled in the Arrange list box and then click on OK. The windows are resized so that a portion of all the windows you have open are displayed on the screen, as shown in Figure 9-7.

9

Figure 9-7.   *Tiled view of worksheets*

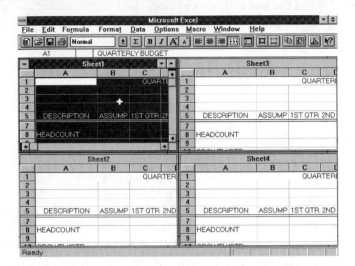

With the tiled view you can easily see what worksheet you want to use, and then you can click on the Maximize button to actually use the worksheet. When you restore the worksheet to its original size with the Restore button or the Restore option on the worksheet's Control menu, you return to the tiled view. The only disadvantage of using the tiled view is that you cannot easily get back to the overlapped view. You must manually move and size each worksheet.

Customizing Individual Worksheets

Using the tiled view, customize each worksheet by following these three steps:

1. Click on Sheet1 to make it the active sheet, and then click on its Maximize button so Sheet1 fills the Excel work area.

2. Enter the title, head count, and assumptions on Sheet1, as shown in Figure 9-8. For the Taxes & Benefits assumption, enter **=14.5%*B12** in place of the amount shown in Figure 9-8. Click on Restore to return Sheet1 to its original size.

Figure 9-8. *Head count and assumptions for Sheet1*

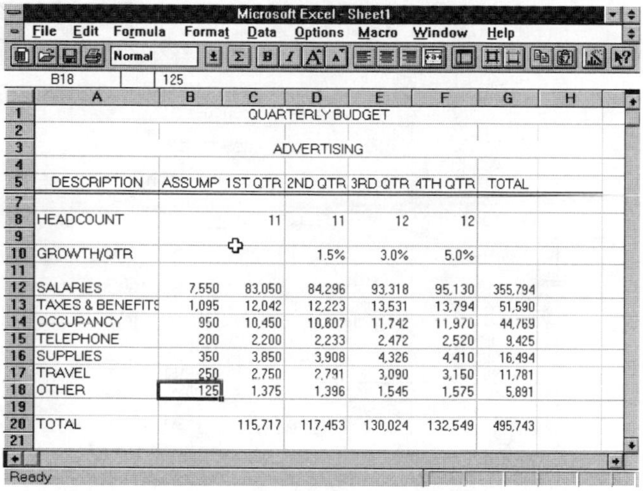

	A	B	C	D	E	F	G	H
				QUARTERLY BUDGET				
1								
2								
3				ADVERTISING				
4								
5	DESCRIPTION	ASSUMP	1ST QTR	2ND QTR	3RD QTR	4TH QTR	TOTAL	
7								
8	HEADCOUNT		11	11	12	12		
9								
10	GROWTH/QTR			1.5%	3.0%	5.0%		
11								
12	SALARIES	7,550	83,050	84,296	93,318	95,130	355,794	
13	TAXES & BENEFITS	1,095	12,042	12,223	13,531	13,794	51,590	
14	OCCUPANCY	950	10,450	10,607	11,742	11,970	44,769	
15	TELEPHONE	200	2,200	2,233	2,472	2,520	9,425	
16	SUPPLIES	350	3,850	3,908	4,326	4,410	16,494	
17	TRAVEL	250	2,750	2,791	3,090	3,150	11,781	
18	OTHER	125	1,375	1,396	1,545	1,575	5,891	
19								
20	TOTAL		115,717	117,453	130,024	132,549	495,743	
21								

3. Repeat step 2 for Sheet2 and Sheet3, using Figures 9-9 and 9-10.

If your Taxes & Benefits quarterly amounts are three or four dollars different than those shown here, you missed changing the assumption to =14.5%*B12.

Creating Linking Formulas

Sheet4 will be the total of the other three worksheets. You therefore want to replace the standard formulas in Sheet4 with formulas that sum the other three worksheets. The tiled view and the mouse make short work of this. Follow these steps:

1. If you are not there already, return to the tiled view so you can see all four worksheets.

Figure 9-9.   *Head count and assumptions for Sheet2*

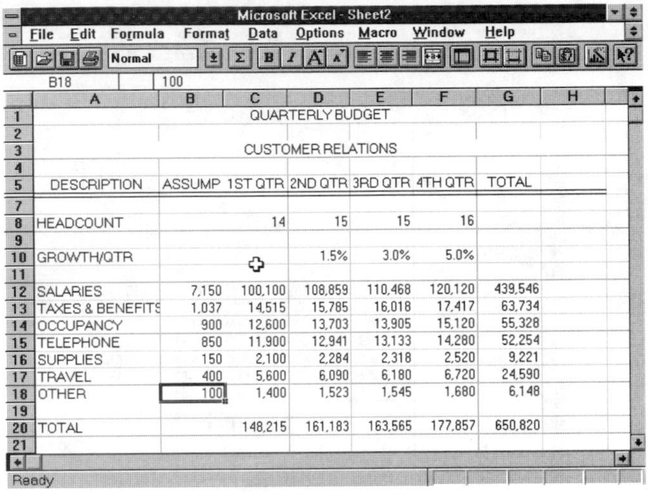

	A	B	C	D	E	F	G	H
1				QUARTERLY BUDGET				
2								
3				CUSTOMER RELATIONS				
4								
5	DESCRIPTION	ASSUMP	1ST QTR	2ND QTR	3RD QTR	4TH QTR	TOTAL	
7								
8	HEADCOUNT		14	15	15	16		
9								
10	GROWTH/QTR			1.5%	3.0%	5.0%		
11								
12	SALARIES	7,150	100,100	108,859	110,468	120,120	439,546	
13	TAXES & BENEFITS	1,037	14,515	15,785	16,018	17,417	63,734	
14	OCCUPANCY	900	12,600	13,703	13,905	15,120	55,328	
15	TELEPHONE	850	11,900	12,941	13,133	14,280	52,254	
16	SUPPLIES	150	2,100	2,284	2,318	2,520	9,221	
17	TRAVEL	400	5,600	6,090	6,180	6,720	24,590	
18	OTHER	100	1,400	1,523	1,545	1,680	6,148	
19								
20	TOTAL		148,215	161,183	163,565	177,857	650,820	
21								

Figure 9-10.   *Head count and assumptions for Sheet3*

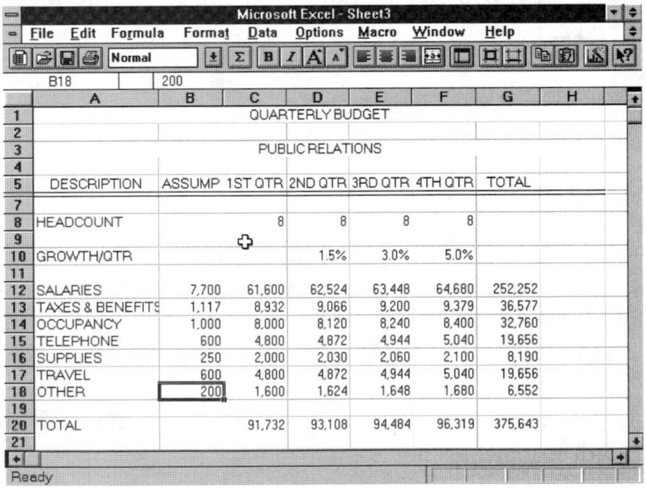

	A	B	C	D	E	F	G	H
1				QUARTERLY BUDGET				
2								
3				PUBLIC RELATIONS				
4								
5	DESCRIPTION	ASSUMP	1ST QTR	2ND QTR	3RD QTR	4TH QTR	TOTAL	
7								
8	HEADCOUNT		8	8	8	8		
9								
10	GROWTH/QTR			1.5%	3.0%	5.0%		
11								
12	SALARIES	7,700	61,600	62,524	63,448	64,680	252,252	
13	TAXES & BENEFITS	1,117	8,932	9,066	9,200	9,379	36,577	
14	OCCUPANCY	1,000	8,000	8,120	8,240	8,400	32,760	
15	TELEPHONE	600	4,800	4,872	4,944	5,040	19,656	
16	SUPPLIES	250	2,000	2,030	2,060	2,100	8,190	
17	TRAVEL	600	4,800	4,872	4,944	5,040	19,656	
18	OTHER	200	1,600	1,624	1,648	1,680	6,552	
19								
20	TOTAL		91,732	93,108	94,484	96,319	375,643	
21								

2. Scroll the worksheets so that the first quarter head count is visible in each window, and click on C8 in Sheet4 to make it the active cell and worksheet, as shown in Figure 9-11.

3. Type **=**, double-click on C8 in Sheet1, and press (F4) three times to make the reference relative. Type **+**, double-click on C8 in Sheet2, and press (F4) three times. Type **+** again, double-click on C8 in Sheet3, press (F4) three times, and press (ENTER).

You have created an *external reference formula,* shown in Figure 9-12. Each part of the equation references a cell in a different worksheet. This is accomplished by including the full sheet name followed by an exclamation point (!) in the reference. You need it to be relative so you can copy the same formula to the other head count and expense cells.

4. Maximize Sheet4 and use AutoFill to copy the equation to the remaining head count cells.

5. With C8:F8 still selected, choose Copy from the Edit menu, select C12:C18 on Sheet4, and press (ENTER) or choose Paste from the Edit

Figure 9-11.   *Scrolling the tiled windows to show head count*

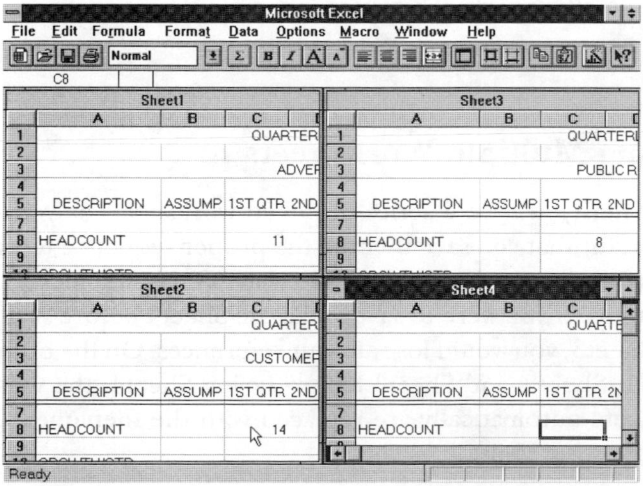

9

Figure 9-12.   *External reference formula*

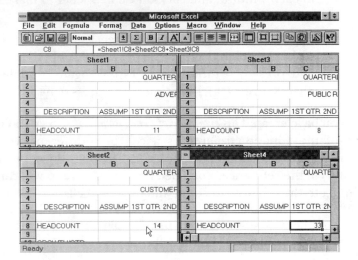

menu. All of the expense cells are filled with the appropriate formula, as shown in Figure 9-13.

6. Type the title **MARKETING DEPARTMENT** in C3 to finish the summary worksheet.

Saving Multiple Worksheets

When you have a series of linked worksheets as you do here, it is very important that you save them in the proper sequence to maintain the linked formulas. Currently, the formulas have Sheet1, Sheet2, and so on for the filenames. If you were to save and close Sheet4 before saving Sheet1, Sheet2, and Sheet3, you would lose all your references. On the other hand, if you save Sheet1, Sheet2, and Sheet3 before saving Sheet4, the worksheet references in Sheet4 automatically are replaced with the filenames. Try that next with the following steps:

Figure 9-13. *Completed summary formulas*

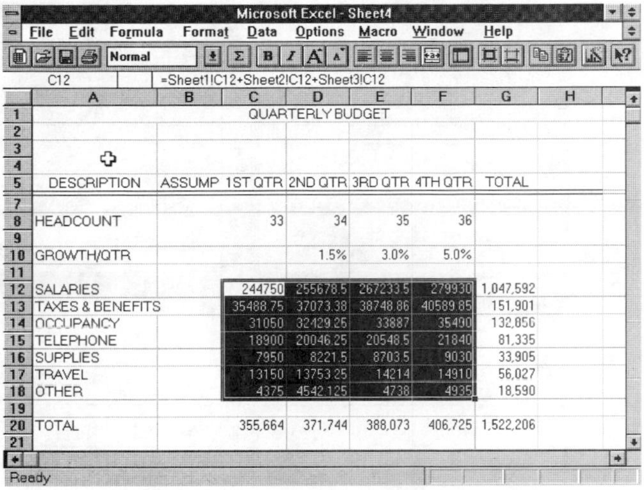

	A	B	C	D	E	F	G
1			QUARTERLY BUDGET				
2							
3							
4							
5	DESCRIPTION	ASSUMP	1ST QTR	2ND QTR	3RD QTR	4TH QTR	TOTAL
7							
8	HEADCOUNT		33	34	35	36	
9							
10	GROWTH/QTR			1.5%	3.0%	5.0%	
11							
12	SALARIES		244750	255678.5	267233.5	279930	1,047,592
13	TAXES & BENEFITS		35488.75	37073.38	38748.86	40589.85	151,901
14	OCCUPANCY		31050	32429.25	33887	35490	132,856
15	TELEPHONE		18900	20046.25	20548.5	21840	81,335
16	SUPPLIES		7950	8221.5	8703.5	9030	33,905
17	TRAVEL		13150	13753.25	14214	14910	56,027
18	OTHER		4375	4542.125	4738	4935	18,590
19							
20	TOTAL		355,664	371,744	388,073	406,725	1,522,206
21							

1. Click on the Restore button or choose Restore in the Control menu to return Sheet4 to its tiled size.
2. Click on Sheet1, choose Save As from the File menu, type **c:\sheet\qtrbudad**, and press (ENTER) to save Sheet1 as QTRBUDAD (your path may be different).
3. In a similar manner save Sheet2 and Sheet3 as QTRBUDCR and QTRBUDPR, respectively.
4. Click on C8 on Sheet4 and look at the formula, which is also shown in Figure 9-14. Notice how the formula has been changed to reflect the new filename.
5. Save Sheet4 as QTRBUDTO.
6. Close each sheet (double-click on the Control-menu box) in the same order (start with QTRBUDAD or what was Sheet1, and then close QTRBUDTO or Sheet4 last).

9

After closing QTRBUDAD (Sheet1) notice that the head count value in QTRBUDTO (Sheet4) remains 33. If you look at the formula in QTRBUDTO

Figure 9-14.   *External reference formula with filenames*

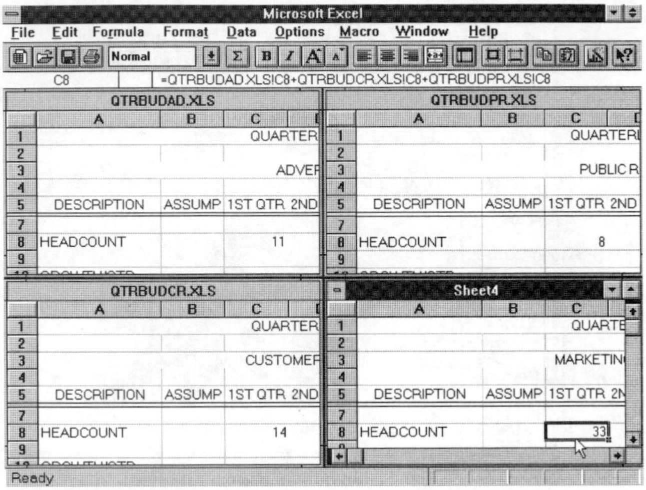

after closing the other two worksheets you see it is still correct and now includes the full path name as well as the filename. All of the values on the worksheet are also still correct, which means they are getting their information off your hard disk.

One consideration with external references is that range names are even more important than they are in other worksheet formulas. External reference formulas are not updated if you insert or delete rows or columns or move or cut cells in the worksheet being referenced. If you use a range name, the range name is adjusted for the changes to the worksheet and the external reference is correct.

Combining Files

There is another way of combining worksheets. Now that you can use complex formulas for that purpose it is not so important as it once was, but it is still an option of which you should be aware.

Excel provides the means to add or subtract a range on one worksheet to or from a similar range on another worksheet using the Paste Special option from the Edit menu. In other words, you can select and copy a range on one worksheet and then, through the Paste Special option, add it to a similar range on another worksheet. The important phrase is *similar range*. More accurately, the two ranges must be exactly alike, cell for cell, because one entire range is overlaid on the other. The two worksheets do have to be in memory together although you can combine six worksheets and only have two of them in memory at one time.

See how this works using the three worksheets created earlier in this chapter with a new total worksheet. Build the new total worksheet first with the normal Copy and Paste options and these steps:

1. Open the advertising department worksheet QTRBUDAD, maximize it, select the range A1:H20, and choose Copy from the Edit menu.

2. Open a new worksheet, press (ENTER) or choose Paste from the Edit menu, widen column A and shorten row 6, delete the formulas in the range B8:F18, change the title to COMBINED TOTAL, and save the new worksheet as QTRBUDCO.

You now have a blank worksheet, as shown in Figure 9-15, with the exact layout of the other three worksheets you built. You can use this new worksheet to add the other three with the Paste Special option.

3. From the Window menu, activate QTRBUDAD, select C8:F18, and choose Copy from the Edit menu.

4. Activate QTRBUDCO, select C8, and choose Paste Special from the Edit menu. The following dialog box opens:

Figure 9-15.   *New worksheet ready for adding others*

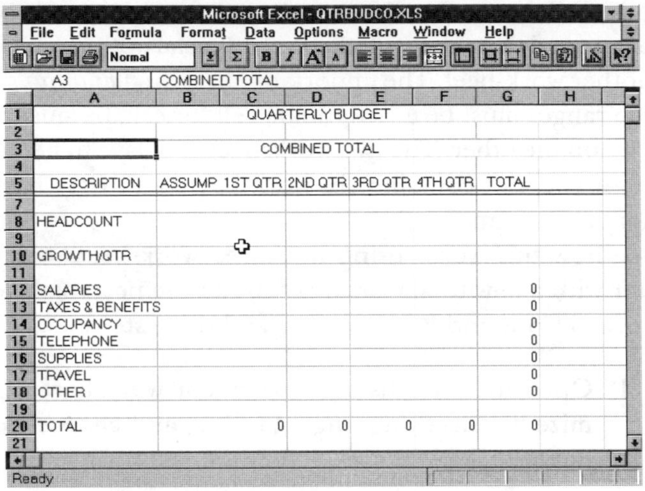

The Paste Special option allows you to paste only parts of the range you copied (the options on the left of the dialog box) and then to add, subtract, multiply, or divide the cells you copied to, from, by, or into the cells being pasted. As you are pasting you can skip blank cells in the copied range so you do not blank the contents of cells in the pasted range, and you can transpose rows and columns. In this case you want to paste only the values, and you want to add them.

5. Choose Values and Add in the dialog box and click on OK. Your QTRBUDCO worksheet now looks like Figure 9-16.

6. To make this example real, close the QTRBUDAD worksheet by activating it and choosing Close from its Control menu.

   Note that you cannot close QTRBUDAD before choosing Paste Special. If you do close QTRBUDAD, Paste Special is no longer available on the Edit menu (it is dimmed).

7. Open QTRBUDCR, select C8:F18, choose Copy, activate QTRBUDCO, make sure C8 is the active cell, choose Paste Special,

Figure 9-16. *Results of pasting the first worksheet*

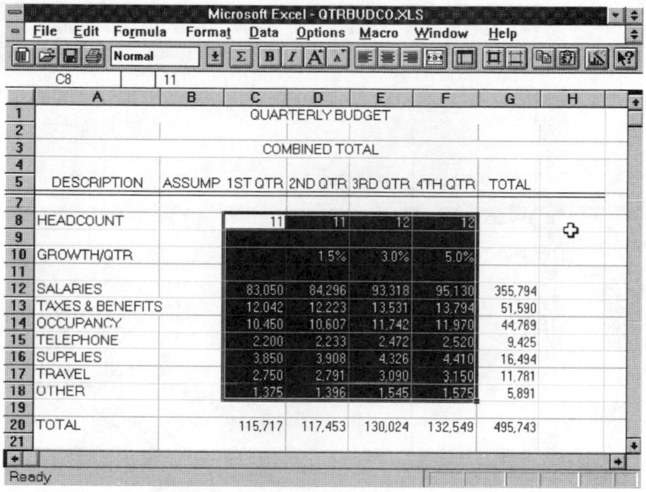

and then choose Values, Add, and OK. The second worksheet is added to the contents of the first.

8. Close QTRBUDCR, open QTRBUDPR, and follow the same procedure outlined in step 7.

9. Delete the range C9:F11 on QTRBUDCO since it contains spurious and unnecessary information. Your final Combined Total worksheet looks like Figure 9-17.

10. Close QTRBUDPR and save QTRBUDCO a second time.

If you compare this QTRBUDCO worksheet with QTRBUDTO in Figure 9-13 (the total built with external reference formulas), you can see they are the same except for the growth percentages, which have been deleted in QTRBUDCO.

For the example in this chapter and for most of your multiple worksheet problems, the external reference formulas are a better solution than using Paste Special. Paste Special should be used only when you are memory constrained. Paste Special is easier in that you do not have to build and copy

Figure 9-17.   *Final Combined Total worksheet*

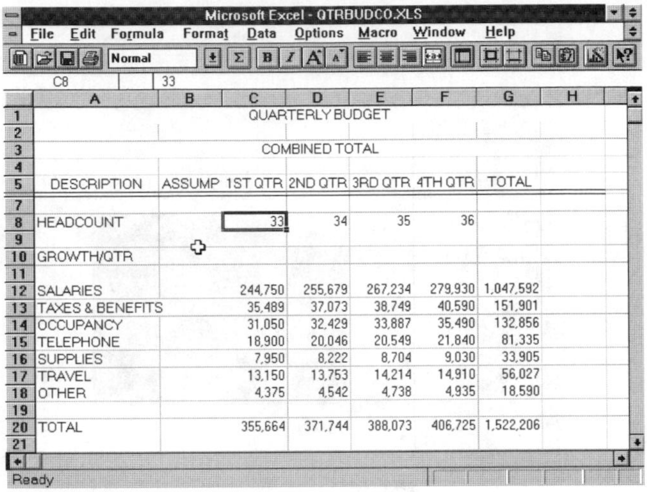

the summing formulas. Of course, the big disadvantage is that the **files must**
have exactly the same file layout. The numbers you want to add must **be in**
the same cell positions on each worksheet.

Dates and times generally should not be combined with **Paste Special; the**
results are not meaningful. Also, blank cells are considered to be 0 by **Paste**
Special unless you select Skip Blanks in the Paste Special dialog box.

The Paste Special option changes the current worksheet by **copying over,**
adding to, or subtracting from its cells. Before using the Paste Special option,
save your current worksheet and carefully position the active cell. Also, if used
soon enough, Edit Undo ((ALT)-(BACKSPACE)) can restore the current worksheet
to its contents prior to executing Paste Special.

Using Workbooks

A *workbook* allows you to organize and manage related documents by
adding worksheets, charts, and other Excel documents into a single source

window. For example, if you were a manager of numerous construction projects, you could create a workbook for each project, add to a workbook its associated worksheets and charts, and then easily access information on each project.

A document can either be saved to a workbook or just appear in one or more workbooks. When a document is saved to a workbook it becomes part of that file. If you want to distribute several files on a related topic, you save them in a workbook, distribute the workbook, and then you are assured all the files have been distributed. A document *listed* in a workbook is available only as long as the document itself is on the disk you are using; it is not a permanent part of the workbook file.

Documents that appear in a workbook can be arranged in any order. This allows you to open them in the sequence most convenient to your needs. The three sequencing icons are located at the lower-right corner of the workbook window, as shown here:

The icons allow you to list and open the workbook files from a shortcut menu, to look at the files in the sequence listed in the workbook window, and finally, to look at the files in the reverse sequence, as listed in the workbook window. Try the following instructions to set up a workbook with the QTRBUDAD, QTRBUDCR, and QTRBUDPR worksheets you previously created.

1. Close QTRBUDCO and open QTRBUDAD, QTRBUDCR, and QTRBUDPR.

2. Choose Save Workbook from the File menu. The File Save As dialog box appears. Type \sheet\qtrbudwk and click on OK to save the workbook to your hard drive. The three files are added to the workbook window, as shown in Figure 9-18.

3. Double-click on QTRBUDAD to open it. Notice the extended filename in the Title bar that now includes the workbook name followed by the filename, as shown in the following illustration:

9

4. Using the right mouse button, click on the Content icon (leftmost) at the lower-right corner of the window, drag the mouse pointer to QTRBUDPR, and release the mouse button. The QTRBUDPR worksheet is displayed on the screen. The three workbook icons are now also at the lower-right corner of the window.

5. Click on the right icon. The workbook window appears. Click on the right icon one more time. The QTRBUDAD worksheet is displayed. The sequence is the reverse of how the files are listed in the workbook window. Click on the last icon to open the worksheets in the sequence listed on the Content shortcut menu.

6. Return to the workbook window. Drag on the workbook icon to the left of the QTRBUDAD filename, until it is below the QTRBUDPR icon. The sequence is now: Workbook, QTRBUDCR, QTRBUDPR,

Figure 9-18.   *Three files added to the workbook window*

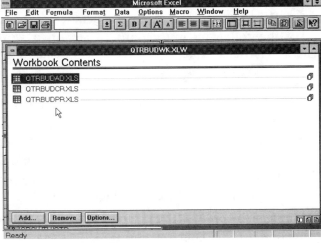

and QTRBUDAD. Click on the Content icon and see the new sequence on the Content shortcut menu.

7. The three files were saved to the workbook in step 2. To list a file in the workbook, highlight QTRBUDAD and click on the Options button. The Document Options dialog box appears, as shown here:

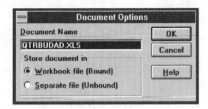

The second choice, Separate file, lists the files in the workbook as separate files.

8. Click on Separate file and OK. The QTRBUDAD file is still listed in the workbook window. Double-click on QTRBUDAD. The filename displayed at the top of the worksheet no longer has the workbook name, QTRBUDWK, attached to it.

9. Click on the Content icon and drag to open QTRBUDWK. Choose Close from the File menu to close the workbook. Close the three individual files and save the workbook. Now, open the QTRBUDCO worksheet.

Saving a Worksheet as a Text File

Sometimes you want to get a range or a complete file out of Excel to use in another program. Most other programs cannot read an Excel file, but they can read a file that is written in the ASCII (American Standard Code for Information Interchange) format. Excel uses the File Save As option to accomplish this. The Save As dialog box has a Save File as Type list box. When opened, the list box displays 18 different file formats in which you can save Excel files. You can see some of them here:

9

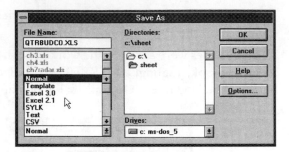

The 18 file formats serve the following purposes:

Normal	Saves a file in the normal Excel 4 file format for use with the Excel program.
Template	Saves a file as an Excel 4 template with the extension .XLT. A template, which is a pattern for future worksheets, forces you to rename the file when you use it so you do not write over the template.
Excel 3.0	Saves a file in the format used by Excel 3.0.
Excel 2.1	Saves a file in the format used by either Excel 2.1 for Windows or Excel 2.2 for OS/2.
SYLK	Saves a file in the SYLK (Symbolic Link) format used to transfer information among Microsoft worksheet packages including Multiplan and Excel for the Macintosh.
Text	Saves a file in the ASCII file format with tabs between columns and carriage returns at the end of each row. This format is primarily used to bring a worksheet into a word processing package. All formulas are replaced by their values and, if a cell has a comma or a tab in it, the cell's value is enclosed in quotation marks.

CSV (Comma Separated Values)	Saves a file in the ASCII file format with commas between columns in place of tabs. Otherwise it is the same as a text file. This is primarily used by database packages. It is sometimes called an *ASCII delimited file*.
WKS	Saves a file in the Lotus WKS format used with Lotus 1-2-3 version 1A.
WK1	Saves a file in the Lotus WK1 format used with Lotus 1-2-3 versions 2, 2.01, and 2.2.
WK3	Saves a file in the Lotus WK3 format used with Lotus 1-2-3 Releases 3.0 and 3.1.
DIF	Saves a file in the Data Interchange Format used by VisiCalc. This format does not transfer formulas, only values.
DBF 2	Saves the currently defined database range in the format used by dBASE II.
DBF 3	Saves the currently defined database range in the format used by dBASE III.
DBF 4	Saves the currently defined database range in the format used by dBASE IV.
Text (Macintosh)	Saves a file in a text format readable on the Apple Macintosh.
Text (OS/2 or DOS)	Saves a file in a text format readable in either OS/2 or DOS.
CSV (Macintosh)	Saves a file in a comma delimited text format readable on the Apple Macintosh.
CSV (OS/2 or DOS)	Saves a file in a comma delimited text format readable in either OS/2 or DOS.

For your purposes here, you want either the Text or CSV format. For use in the body of a word processed document you would use Text and then set

9

tab stops in the word processor to re-create Excel's columns. For use in a database other than dBASE or for mail merging with word processed documents you would use CSV. Save the QTRBUDCO file in both of these formats, and then exit Excel and look at the results by following the next set of instructions (QTRBUDCO should be displayed on your screen as the active worksheet).

1. Choose Save As from the File menu, open the Save File as Type list box, click on Text, and click on OK.

2. Choose Save As from the File menu, open the Save File as Type list box, click on CSV, and click on OK.

You have now created two new files: one in the ASCII text format with the filename extension .TXT and the second in ASCII comma delimited format with the extension .CSV. Next close Excel and look at these files with Windows Write.

3. Double-click on the Excel Control-menu box to close it.

4. If necessary, open the Windows Accessories Group by double-clicking on its icon and then double-clicking again on Write to open that program. Click on the Maximize button to expand Write to full-screen size.

5. Choose Open from the File menu, change the directory to \SHEET\ (or the directory you are using for Excel files), replace the *.WRI in the filename text box with the filename QTRBUDCO.TXT, and click on OK.

6. Choose Convert from the dialog box that asks you if you want to convert to the Write format (although it really does not make any difference). The quarterly budget combined total worksheet opens, as shown in Figure 9-19.

At this point the text file does not look good, but with very little work it can be markedly improved.

7. Choose Replace from the Find menu, type " in Find What, and click on Replace All. This removes all quotation marks. Double-click on

the Control-menu box of the Replace dialog box to close the dialog box.

8. Choose Ruler On from the Document menu, click on the decimal tab icon (the second tab icon with the upward arrow and a period), and click in the space just below the ruler at 1.75", 2.5", 3.25", 4", 4.75", and 5.5" to set decimal tab stops at those locations.

All of a sudden the exported worksheet looks pretty good, as shown in Figure 9-20. Additionally, since it uses tabs instead of spaces, the worksheet can be printed with a proportionally spaced font and not be thrown out of alignment.

9. Choose Save As from the File menu, change the filename extension to .WRI, change the Save File as Type to .WRI, and click on OK. The word processing file will be saved with the normal .WRI Write extension.

10. Choose Open from the File menu, type **qtrbudco.csv**, click on OK, and click on No Conversion. The second text file opens, as shown in Figure 9-21.

Figure 9-19. *Quarterly budget in Text format as displayed by Windows Write*

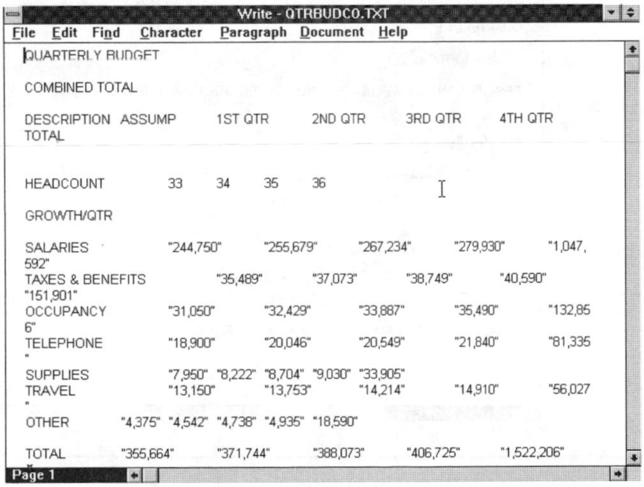

Figure 9-20.   *Worksheet text file in Write after tabs have been inserted*

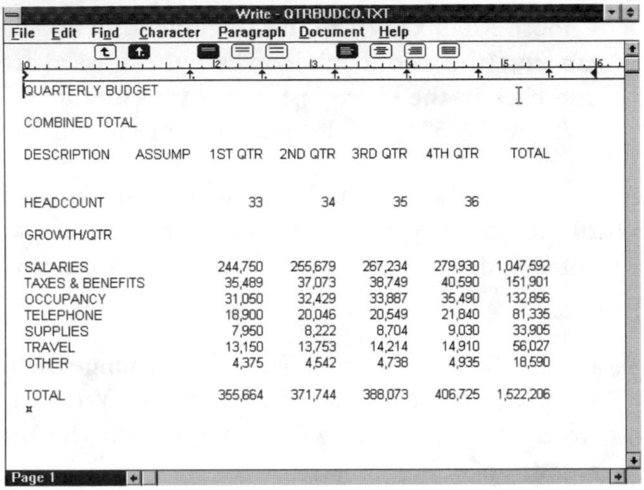

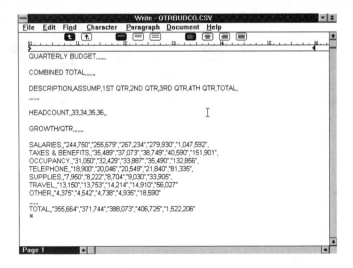

Figure 9-21.   *CSV formatted worksheet in Write*

You can see that the CSV file has replaced tabs with commas, but otherwise it looks very similar to the text file when you originally brought it in. The big difference is that you cannot simply set some tab stops and get a CSV file to line up properly. What you must do is replace the commas with tabs, which will cause a problem with the comma thousands separator in a number. In a word processing package, the CSV format is not very useful except for mail merge. The standard text format with tabs is much more useful. The CSV format is primarily used for transferring files to database packages.

Importing ASCII Text Files

Just as you may need to get data out of Excel for use in other programs, you may need to get data into Excel from other programs in a format other than the Excel standard file format. The most common format is ASCII text in one of two formats: nondelimited ASCII files that are continuous text strings and delimited ASCII files. A delimited ASCII file includes delimiters, usually commas, between fields or columns and often quotation marks around text. Delimiters can also be tabs for Excel's use, but most other programs recognize only commas or semicolons. Using ASCII delimited files with commas and quotation marks is the most common means of exchanging information among database programs. Many word processing programs can also read ASCII delimited files and use them with their mail merge function.

Look at how Excel brings in each of the two text files (both the .TXT and the .CSV files) as well as a nondelimited text. While you are still in Windows Write, create the nondelimited file from QTRBUDCO.CSV, which should still be on your screen.

1. Delete the first seven lines down to but not including the Headcount line (select the lines and use the Cut option on the Edit menu or the (DEL) key), delete the three lines between Headcount and Salaries, and delete the line between Other and Total as well as any leading space in front of Total.

9

2. Select all of the remaining text, open the Character menu, choose Fonts and then select Courier from the Font list box to change from a proportional-spaced font to a fixed-spaced font. Click on OK.

3. Select the full Headcount line, choose Replace from the Find menu, type , (comma) in Find What and press (SPACEBAR) six times in Replace With, and click Replace Selection to replace all commas in the first line with six spaces. Click on Close.

4. Select the remainder of the text below the Headcount line. Using the Replace dialog box, change „" to two spaces. Next change all remaining commas to nothing by typing , in Find What, pressing (DEL) in the Replace With text box, and clicking Replace All. Change " " to two spaces, and change the remaining " to nothing. Click on Close.

5. Add and delete spaces so the numbers line up on their right as shown in Figure 9-22. Then use Save As to save the file as text only with the filename TEST.TXT and change the Save File as Type to Text files.

Figure 9-22.   *Nondelimited ASCII text file in Write after being cleaned up*

6. Double-click on Write's Control-menu box to close it. Finally, double-click on the Excel icon to reopen Excel.

Opening ASCII Delimited Text Files

Both the .TXT and .CSV files that you created are ASCII delimited files. The .TXT file is delimited with tabs, and the .CSV file is delimited with commas. Both files have quotes around numbers that contain comma formatting so the commas will not be treated as delimiters. Bring each of the two delimited files back into Excel and see how well they split up into rows and columns with the following steps.

1. Choose the Open tool from the Standard toolbar and double-click on \SHEET\QTRBUDCO.TXT in the File list box.

    The tab delimited text file is brought in as shown in Figure 9-23. When you check individual cells, you see that everything is in place.

Figure 9-23. *Tab delimited file QTRBUDCO.TXT back in Excel*

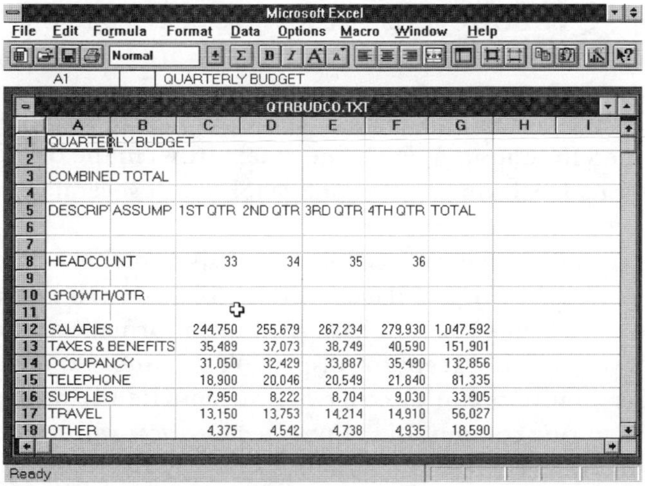

About the only thing you lost was the centering of the titles and column headings, and the extra width in column A.

2. Double-click on the Control-menu box to close the file called QTRBUDCO.TXT, and double-click on \SHEET\QTRBUDCO.CSV in the File menu.

Once again the file is brought in and everything is in its correct cell, with the only loss being the title and column centering and the extra width in column A, as shown in Figure 9-24. The ease with which these files come in is not deceptive. Any ASCII delimited file will come in as easily and as well behaved. If you are using commas as delimiters, use the .CSV extension when saving the file in another application. Excel will not split the text into columns without this extension.

Opening Nondelimited Text Files

Bringing in a nondelimited ASCII text file is a different story: Excel does not split it into columns. See for yourself by bringing in the TEST.TXT file you created in Write.

1. Double-click on the Control-menu box to close the file called QTRBUDCO.CSV, choose Open from the File menu, type \sheet\test.txt, and press (ENTER).

The file comes into Excel as shown in Figure 9-25. Each row is entirely contained in column A. Each line of text (row) in the original file produces a single long label contained in one cell. Look at several cells in column A and then in other columns.

You can see that each cell in column A contains a complete line of text. It looks like the original data, but it is all in one cell instead of occupying a row of cells. While you now have all of the information from the original file, it isn't very useful except for display. You cannot do any arithmetic on the numbers, move them, or otherwise manipulate them; they are just lines of text, all in one column. In the next section, you will see how to divide these lines into discrete text and numbers.

Figure 9-24. *Comma delimited file QTRBUDCO.CSV back in Excel*

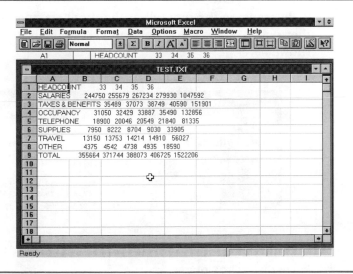

Figure 9-25. *Nondelimited file brought into Excel*

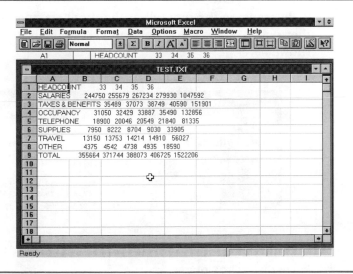

Parsing Nondelimited Text Files

In the previous section you imported a text file in nondelimited ASCII format. Each line of text was contained in a single cell, and the complete file was contained in a single column. To be usable, each line must be divided into text and numbers and placed into individual cells. That dividing or *parsing* of a text line is the function of the Parse option on the Data menu.

Data parsing is particularly useful if you download information from an information service such as CompuServe. For example, when you import current stock market information you get a long label containing the ticker symbol, the volume, and amounts for the high, low, close, and open prices. By itself, the information may make interesting reading, but you cannot do anything with it. Using Data Parse, the stock market information can be divided into its components and used to update a stock portfolio.

Applying the Data Parse option is a multiple-step procedure. First you must select and reformat the information you want to parse so that it is using fixed and not proportional spacing. Then, with the Data Parse option, you must tell Excel where each column break belongs. Finally you do the actual parsing. Carry out those steps with these instructions:

1. Select A1:A9, choose Font from the Format menu, click on Courier, and click on OK.

   By changing the font, all of the numbers line up in columns as they did in Write. The problem is everything is still in column A, as shown here:

A1		HEADCOUNT	33	34	35	36	

				TEST.TXT			
	A	B	C	D	E	F	G
1	HEADCOUNT		33	34	35	36	
2	SALARIES		244750	255679	267234	279930	1047592
3	TAXES &	BENEFITS	35489	37073	38749	40590	151901
4	OCCUPANCY		31050	32429	33887	35490	132856
5	TELEPHONE		18900	20046	20549	21840	81335
6	SUPPLIES		7950	8222	8704	9030	33905
7	TRAVEL		13150	13753	14214	14910	56027
8	OTHER		4375	4542	4738	4935	18590
9	TOTAL		355664	371744	388073	406725	1522206
10							

2. With A1:A9 still selected, choose Parse from the Data menu. The Parse dialog box opens:

The Parse dialog box displays the first line you selected. Excel provides a guess as to where you want the column breaks by entering square brackets ([]) for the beginning and end of each column. You can then change this initial guess.

3. Click the insertion point between the opening square bracket and the "H" in HEADCOUNT. Press (RIGHT ARROW) 16 times and type][. Delete the next two square brackets, move the insertion point to just after the final closing square bracket, remove that bracket, and go back to the final opening bracket. Press (RIGHT ARROW) nine times and type]. Your dialog box looks like this:

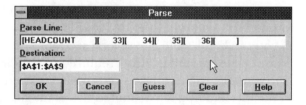

Your brackets should be set with the first interval at 16 characters, the second interval at 7 characters, the next three intervals at 8 characters each, and the final interval at 9 characters.

4. When your brackets are set, click on OK to carry out the parsing of the data. Your results should look like Figure 9-26.

5. Look at several individual cells to assure yourself that the text has been divided over the columns.

If for some reason your parsing did not work, you can use Edit Undo or (ALT)-(BACKSPACE) to return to the unparsed text strings. You can then redo the placement of the square brackets and try again.

9

Figure 9-26.   *Nondelimited data parsed into columns*

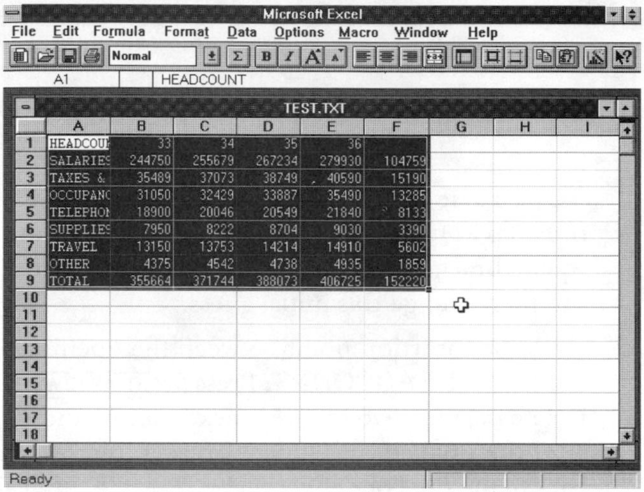

There are two keys to making Data Parse work. First, you change the font into a fixed-spaced typeface like Courier. Second, you line the data up with spaces so that each column is defined and is the same from row to row. If necessary you can break a file into several sections and parse each separately.

You can see the amount of effort required to handle a nondelimited file. Of course, sometimes there is no alternative. When possible, though, a delimited file, preferably a tab delimited file, is far superior.

6. Double-click on the TEST.TXT Control-menu box and click on No to close the worksheet without saving it.

7. Double-click on both the Excel and the Program Manager Control-menu boxes to close them.

Importing 1-2-3 Files

Excel 3 imports 1-2-3 WK3 files, but cannot read the formatting because the formatting is saved in separate files. Excel 4 now reads the formatting files, FMT and FM3, and imports the WK3 files in their entirety.

10

Dates, Functions, and Macros

This chapter brings together three subjects that do not fit easily into any other category: using dates and times, functions, and macros. All three subjects need a forum of their own, and they are the finishing touch—the "icing on the cake" that makes a good worksheet a great worksheet.

Using Dates and Times

From schedules to dates on reports and time-related financial calculations, dates and times are important aspects of the problems Excel addresses. The sections that follow discuss how Excel handles dates and times internally, various ways Excel formats dates and times, and the date and time functions and arithmetic.

Dates and Excel

Dates do not form a nice, neat, linear progression. You cannot add 12 days to April 28th and get May 10th without knowing how many days there are in April. Microsoft has solved this problem by establishing a date serial number scheme. This scheme allocates one number for every day from January 1, 1900 (date serial number 1) to December 31, 2078 (date serial number 65380). Microsoft also provides formatting and formulas to convert the date serial number to a specific calendar date. Internally Excel uses the unformatted date serial number. You can format the date serial number in several ways and get a normal-looking calendar date from a serial number. For example, when formatted with the first Excel date format, the serial number 33343 becomes 4/15/91, as shown here:

In other words, simply typing **33343**, pressing (ENTER), and formatting the number with Format Number m/d/yy produces the date 4/15/91. The following instructions demonstrate several other dates. Your computer should be on, Excel should be loaded, and you should have a blank worksheet on your screen.

1. Select B2:F2, choose Number from the Format menu, select the Date category, the m/d/yy format, and click on OK. The range B2:F2 is formatted as m/d/yy dates.

2. Type **33343** and press (RIGHT ARROW). The date 4/15/91 appears in B2.

3. Type **30638** and press (RIGHT ARROW). The date 11/18/83 appears in C2, as shown in the following illustration:

4. Type **1**, press (RIGHT ARROW), type **65380**, and press (ENTER). The date 1/1/00 appears in D2, and E2 contains 12/31/78.

Note that when you are working in the next century, the two-digit year format can be confusing. Change the format next. E2 should still be the active cell.

5. Choose Number from the Format menu, click after the last "y" in the Code text box, type **yy**, and click on OK. E2 fills with #s because the date is now too big for the cell.

6. Drag on the intersection of columns E and F in the heading for about one tenth of an inch to widen the column. The date 12/31/2078 appears in E2, as shown here:

There is one abnormality in Microsoft's date scheme. The year 1900 was not a leap year, even though the year was evenly divisible by four. Therefore, Excel assigns a date serial number to February 29, 1900, which didn't exist. The only impact of this is that date arithmetic spanning February 28, 1900 through March 1, 1900 is off by one day. All date serial numbers and calculated dates from March 1, 1900 onward are correct.

Times and Excel

Microsoft has also developed a scheme for calculating time: the time is added to the date serial number as a decimal fraction of a 24-hour day.

10

Therefore, midnight is 0.000000, noon is 0.500000, and 11:59:59 PM is 0.999988. When the decimal fractions are formatted with Excel as times, they produce normal-looking time numbers on either a 12- or 24-hour basis. The following steps show how several times are entered.

1. Select B2:E2, press (DEL), click on All, and click on OK to erase both the contents and formats of B2:E2.

2. Choose Number from the Format menu, select the first time format, h:mm AM/PM, and click on OK. The range B2:E2 is formatted with the first time format.

3. Type **.65** and press (RIGHT ARROW). Cell B2 contains 3:36 PM, as shown here:

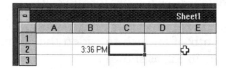

4. Type **.45** and press (RIGHT ARROW). Cell C2 contains 10:48 AM, as shown here:

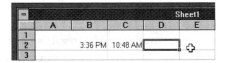

5. Type **0**, press (RIGHT ARROW), type **.9999**, and press (ENTER). Cells D2 and E2 contain 12:00 AM and 11:59 PM, as shown here:

Dates and times are stored in one number. For example, 3:36 PM April 15, 1991, is stored as 33343.65. In a single cell you can display this as a date, as a time, or both, depending on the formatting.

Formatting Dates and Times

There are four date formats, four time formats, and one combined date and time format built into Excel. The date formats use the integer part of a date serial number, and the time formats use the decimal part. The decimal part of a number is ignored by a date format, and the integer part of a number is ignored by a time format. If a date format encounters a number that is negative or greater than 65380, the cell fills with #s. If a time format encounters a negative number, the cell fills with #s.

The nine built-in date and time formats are shown in Figure 10-1. You can, of course, make your own. The components needed to construct your own formats are shown in Chapter 6. Some examples of custom date and time formats are shown in Figure 10-2.

Figure 10-1.   *Built-in date and time formats*

10

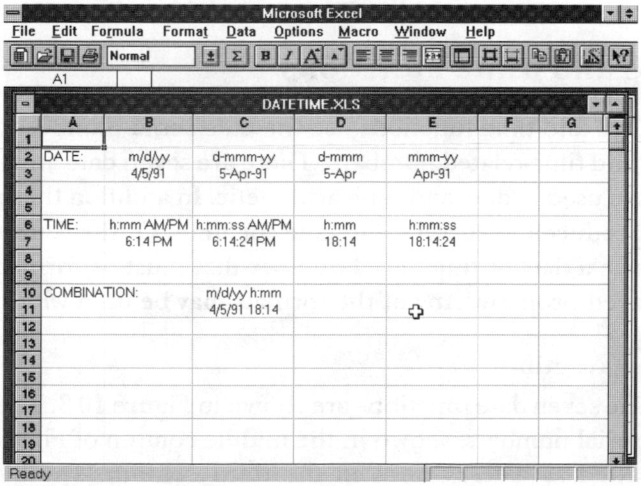

Figure 10-2.   *Examples of custom date and time formats*

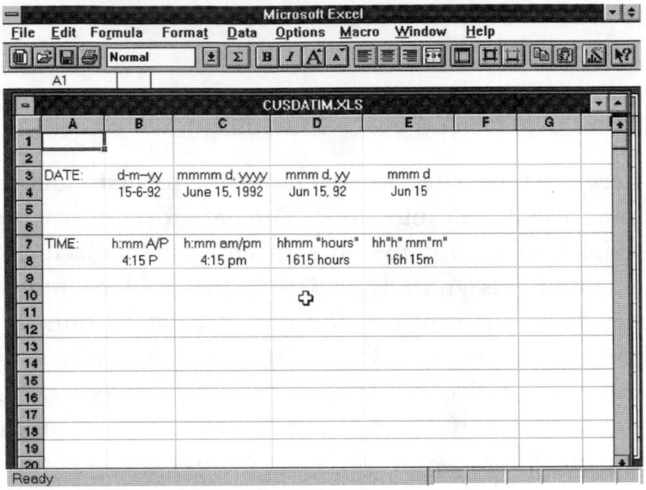

The choice of which format to use is one of personal taste. Some formats require wider columns than others, which may have some bearing on your decision. Also, there is no reason you cannot mix formats in a worksheet.

Date and Time Functions

Date and time functions use the date serial number to calculate various date- and time-related numbers. There are seven date and five time functions that are used in date and time arithmetic. In addition there are two functions that produce the current date and/or time. Of the fourteen functions, five produce a date or time serial number that must be formatted in order to be displayed properly. Any of the formats may be used with the functions.

Date Functions

The seven date functions are shown in Figure 10-3. The first two produce date serial numbers, shown in the middle column of Figure 10-3, that can be formatted as dates, shown in the third column. The next four functions

Figure 10-3.   *Date functions*

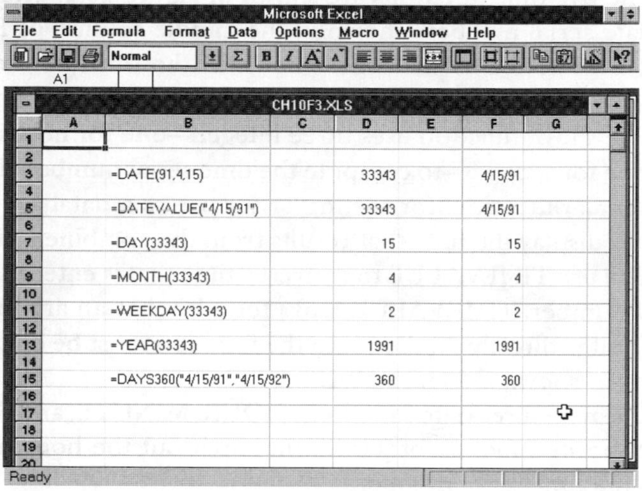

transform a date serial number into part of a date. The last function calculates the number of days between two dates using a 360-day year.

The DATE function takes three integers—one for the year, one for the month, and one for the day—and computes the date serial number. As with all functions, the three arguments (year, month, and day) can be integers that are entered directly into the function, or they can be addresses or range names that refer to cells containing or computing integers suitable for the function. DATE is used when you break out a date to sort or to use as a database criterion and you want to display the date that results from the combined pieces.

DATEVALUE converts a date in text form to a date serial number. DATEVALUE looks for text as an argument. Therefore, a date that is directly entered into the function must be enclosed in quotation marks, as shown in Figure 10-3.

The next four date functions, DAY, MONTH, WEEKDAY, and YEAR, perform the opposite function of DATE: they split out the day, month, weekday, or year from the date serial number. WEEKDAY returns an integer from 1 for Sunday to 7 for Saturday.

10

Time Functions

The five time functions are shown in Figure 10-4. The first two produce the date serial numbers shown in the middle column of Figure 10-4, which can be formatted as the times shown in the third column. The last three functions transform a time serial number into the components of time.

The TIME function uses three integers—one for hours, one for minutes, and one for seconds—to compute the time serial number. TIME is used when you break out a time for sorting or for use as a database criterion and you want to display the time that results from the combined pieces.

You use TIMEVALUE to convert a time that is entered as a label to a date serial number. TIMEVALUE looks for a label as an argument. Therefore, a time that is directly entered into the function must be enclosed in quotation marks, as shown in Figure 10-4.

The next three date functions, HOUR, MINUTE, and SECOND, perform the opposite function of TIME: they split out the hour, minute, or second from the time serial number.

Current Date and Time Functions

The functions used to produce the current date and/or time are NOW and TODAY. Examples of their use are shown in Figure 10-5. These functions use the internal clock-calendar in your computer to determine the current date and time. NOW produces both the integer and decimal components needed for both date and time display. If you are using the current date in a formula or with another function, use TODAY to obtain the integer part of the current date. The decimal (time) part of NOW can cause inaccuracies in date calculations. If you simply are displaying the date, NOW by itself works. Date formats ignore the decimal part of the number.

Entering and Generating Dates and Times

You have just seen how you can enter dates and times either by entering the date serial number (which is not very practical because you don't know what it is in most instances) or by using one of the functions that convert a date or time to the date serial number. Also, you have seen how to generate the current date and/or time. You have two other ways to get dates and times into Excel. First, just typing a date or time on the worksheet in an Excel format

Figure 10-4. *Time functions*

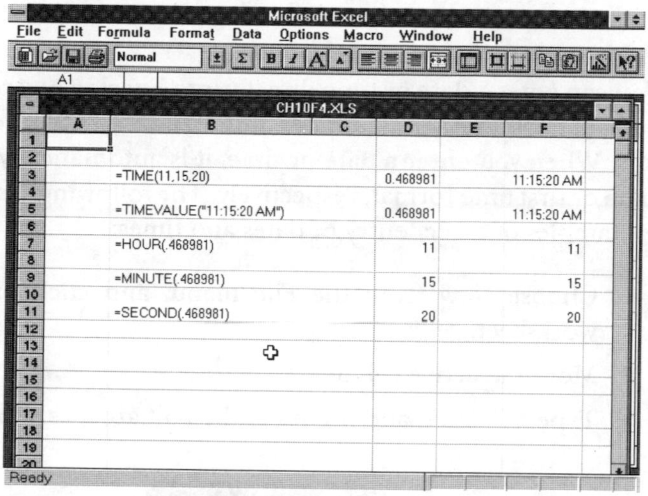

Figure 10-5. *Current date and time functions*

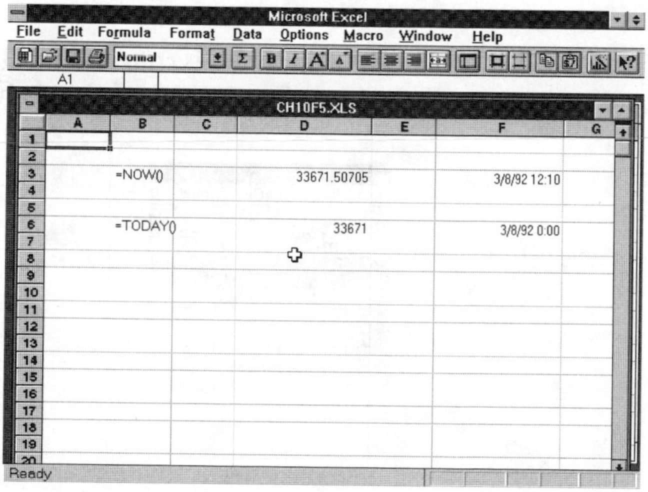

10

produces a date or time serial number. Second, the Data Series option generates a sequence of dates or times.

Direct Entry of Dates and Times

You can enter a date or time directly into Excel in any recognized format and get a date or time serial number. It does not have to be one of the built-in formats. When you enter a date or time, it is automatically formatted as the first date or first time format, respectively. The following instructions provide some examples of direct entry of dates and times:

1. Choose New from the File menu, and click on OK for a new worksheet.

2. Move the active cell to B3.

3. Type **4/15/91**, and it goes in the edit area, as shown here:

4. Press (ENTER). The date, 4/15/91, is converted to 33343, and the cell is automatically formatted as m/d/yy, as shown here:

If you would like to see that 4/15/91 is in fact the date serial number 33343, reformat B3 with the General format. You might also want to do this when you get to time values.

> 5. Click on D3, type **4-15-91**, and press (ENTER). The date is converted to 33343 and automatically formatted as 4/15/91 even though 4-15-91 is not a built-in format.

If you want to enter a formula that looks like a date, you must put an equal sign in front of it.

> 6. Click on B5, type **3:45 pm**, and press (ENTER). The time, 3:45 PM, is converted to .65625, and the cell is automatically formatted with h:mm AM/PM.

> 7. Click on D5, type **3:45 p**, and press (ENTER). The time, 3:45 p, is converted to .65625, and the cell is automatically formatted as 3:45 PM even though 3:45 p is not a built-in format, as shown here:

	A	B	C	D	E
1					
2					
3		4/15/91		4/15/91	
4					
5		3:45 PM		3:45 PM	
6					
7					

Generating a Series of Dates

In Chapter 8, you saw how you can generate dates with the Data Series option, which is a very capable and flexible tool. From any starting date to any ending date within the 178-year range of Excel's date scheme, you can generate as many dates as you can hold in the memory of your computer. If you are generating dates, you can increment them by a number of days, weekdays, months, years, or fractions thereof.

The following steps give several examples of generating dates and times with the Data Series option:

10

1. Choose New from the File menu and click on OK to create a new worksheet.

2. Select B2:F13, choose Number from the Format menu, select Date, the m/d/yy format, and click on OK to format the selected area.

3. Click on B2, type **1/31/92**, press (ENTER), select B2:B13, and choose Series from the Data menu. In the Series in and Type fields, Columns and Date should already be selected. Select Month for the unit and type **12/31/92** as the Stop value. One month is the default Step value, as shown here:

4. Press (ENTER). B2:B13 fills with a series of dates that are one month apart, from 1/31/92 through 12/31/92.

This series provides the actual month end, 1/31, 2/29, 3/31, 4/30, and so on, not just 30- or 31-day intervals. It can be a very useful capability.

5. Click on D2, type **1/31/92**, press (ENTER), select D2:D13, choose Series from the Data menu, and type **7** for the Step value. Seven days or one week is the intended step value, as shown here:

6. Press (ENTER). D2:D13 fills with a series of dates that are one week apart, from 1/31/92 through 4/17/92.

7. Click on F2 and do a third data series, using years as the increment from 1/31/92 to 1/31/2003. You also must reformat the column to display the dates in the next century.

When you are done, your screen should look like Figure 10-6. Column B shows a progression by month, column D shows a progression by week, and column F shows a progression by year.

Generating a Series of Times

Generating times with Excel is not much different from generating dates. While there are no ready-made increments like hours, minutes, and seconds, you can use the standard time notation of hh:mm:ss to indicate a step value.

Figure 10-6.   Date series by month, week, and year

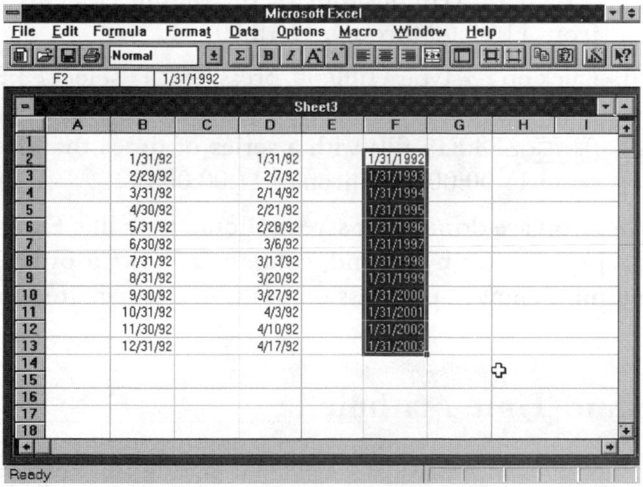

For example, a step value of one second would be 00:00:01, one minute would be 00:01:00, and one hour would be 01:00:00.

The next set of steps demonstrates several data series that produce times:

1. Choose New from the File menu, and click on OK to create a new worksheet.

2. Select B3:F15, choose Number from the Format menu, select Time, h:mm:ss AM/PM, and click on OK. The selected range is formatted with the second time format.

3. Choose Column Width from the Format menu, type **12** for the new width, and click on OK. Columns B through F widen to 12 to handle the full time format.

4. Click on B3, type **11:00:00**, press (ENTER), select B3:B15, choose Series from the Data menu, type **00:00:01** as the step value, and press (ENTER). B3:B15 fills with a series of times that are one second apart, from 11:00:00 through 11:00:12.

5. Click on D3, type **11:00:00**, press enter, select D3:D15, choose Series from the Data menu, type **00:01:00** as the step value, and press (ENTER). D3:D15 fills with a series of times that are one minute apart, from 11:00:00 through 11:12:00.

6. Click on F3, type **11:00:00**, press (ENTER), select F3:F15, choose Series from the Data menu, type **01:00:00** as the step value, and press (ENTER). F3:F15 fills with a series of times that are one hour apart, from 11:00:00 AM through 11:00:00 PM.

When you are done, your screen should look like Figure 10-7. Column B shows a progression by second, column D shows a progression by minute, and column F shows a progression by hour, all formatted for a 12-hour clock.

Date and Time Arithmetic

One of the primary reasons Microsoft developed the date serial number was to allow easy date and time arithmetic. For example, you can add 1 to a date and get the day following, as shown in the next illustration:

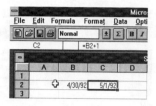

You can add 30 days and get the appropriate day in the next month:

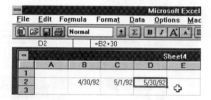

You can also subtract two dates and get the number of days between them.

Figure 10-7.   *Time series by second, minute, and hour*

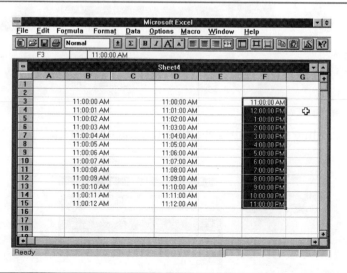

10

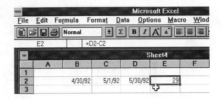

The date functions are useful in date arithmetic. For example, you can use YEAR to determine the number of years between two dates, as shown here:

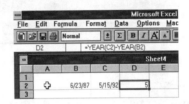

Time arithmetic is a little more complex in that you must add fractions. For example, to add one hour, you must add 1/24th, as shown here:

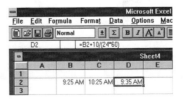

Adding ten minutes requires the fraction 10/(24*60):

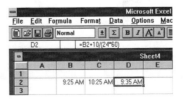

Time functions are useful in time arithmetic. For example, you can determine the number of hours between two times with two HOUR functions, as shown here:

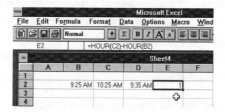

Functions

In earlier chapters you gained some familiarity with statistical functions, database statistical functions, and lookup functions, and you just learned about date and time functions in this chapter. Excel has five other types of functions: financial, informational, logical, mathematical (including matrix and trigonometric), and text. These are discussed here, but first let's look at how functions are used and created.

Using Functions

Functions are ready-made formulas. They perform a previously assigned task that usually involves a calculation but may also include a nonarithmetic operation. Functions always produce a result in the cell in which they are entered. For example, SUM produces a value that is the arithmetic addition of a set of numbers, and UPPER produces a text string that is all uppercase. Functions provide a faster way to accomplish many tasks. For example, using SUM(*range*) is quicker than adding each individual cell in the range if the range contains three or more cells. Functions are the only way some tasks can be accomplished. For example, using NOW or TODAY are the only ways you can read your computer's clock-calendar with Excel.

10

Specifying Arguments

Many functions require pieces of information to perform their task, for example, the range in the SUM(*range*) function. These pieces of information are called *arguments*. The number of arguments in a function varies between 0 and 14, and the length of arguments in a function is limited to 255 characters, including any quotation marks.

Arguments can be numbers, text, arrays, references, and logical or error values, as outlined here:

- Numbers used as arguments in a function can be numerals, numeric formulas, or addresses or range names for cells that contain numbers or numeric formulas.

- Text is any sequence of letters, numbers, spaces, or symbols. Text in a function can be literal text enclosed in quotation marks, a text formula, or an address or range name for a cell that contains literal text or a text formula.

- An array is a rectangular set of values (a range) that is treated in a special way. An array is enclosed in braces ({ }) and has a semicolon between rows. For example, the array {5,6,7;3,4,5;1,2,3} is a 3-by-3 array, with three rows that each contain three columns. Arrays used as arguments in a function can be entered directly, result from a formula that evaluates to an array, or be a set of addresses or range name for a range that contains an array or a formula that evaluates to an array.

- References can be addresses, range names, or any formula that evaluates to an address or range name.

- A logical value is either True or False. You can enter **True** and **False** in either upper- or lowercase letters, but Excel converts them to uppercase. In a function, logical values may be entered directly, result from a logical formula that evaluates to either True or False, or be in a cell referenced by an address or range name. A logical formula is one that contains one of these logical operators:

=	Equal to
>	Greater than
<	Less than

>=	Greater than or equal to
<=	Less than or equal to
<>	Not equal to

- Error values include #DIV/0!, #N/A, #NAME?, #NULL!, #NUM!, #REF!, and #VALUE!. In a function, error values may be entered directly, result from a formula, or be contained in a cell referenced by an address or range name. A brief meaning of each of the error values is given here:

#DIV/0!	You tried to divide by zero
#N/A	Not available
#NAME?	Excel does not recognize a name
#NULL!	Two ranges you expected to intersect do not
#NUM!	Excel has a problem with a number
#REF!	Excel cannot find a cell or range reference
#VALUE!	You used the wrong type of operand or argument

Entering Functions

There are many different functions, but they all have the same structure, or syntax. A *syntax* is a set of rules for consistently doing something in an orderly manner—in this case, entering functions. The syntax for entering functions is as follows:

- Every function begins with the = symbol, unless it is inside a formula (that is, not the first element of the formula) or another function.

- Functions can be entered in either upper- or lowercase letters. They are displayed in uppercase by Excel. If you type a function in lowercase letters and Excel does not change it to uppercase, you know that you misspelled the function name or made some other mistake.

- Spaces cannot occur anywhere in a function, except within a literal string enclosed in quotation marks or immediately after a comma between arguments.

- The arguments of a function must be enclosed in parentheses. If one or more functions are used as arguments for other functions,

10

the parentheses must be nested, with complete left and right sets of parentheses for each function. Even functions that do not have arguments must have a set of parentheses. For example, NOW( ).

- Two or more arguments within a function are separated by commas. You should not have more commas than there are arguments or two arguments without a comma between them.

- Blank cells referenced in a function are assigned the value 0.

- Functions can be used by themselves as a formula or as a part of another formula, function, or macro function.

Functions may be directly entered by typing them in a cell, following the syntax just described, or you can have Excel build the formula using the Paste Function option on the Formula menu. To do the latter, make the cell in which you want the function the active cell, and then choose Paste Function from the Formula menu. The Paste Function dialog box opens, as shown here:

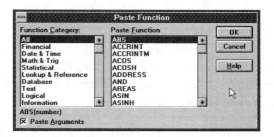

In the Paste Function dialog box, functions are listed alphabetically, within 12 categories including All. You can use the scroll bar to select a function, or you can type the first letter of a function to quickly jump closer to it. Click on the Paste Arguments option box, and Excel provides placeholders for the arguments to remind you what they are. If you choose to paste arguments, you must replace the placeholders with actual arguments. An example of the DDB (double declining balance) function with pasted arguments is shown here:

Additional Functions

The next several sections of this chapter discuss some of the functions that have not been discussed elsewhere. They fall into five groups: financial, informational, logical, mathematical, and text functions. Due to their number, not all of the individual functions are covered here. The following sections contain tips and suggestions for each of the five groups, along with one or two examples of functions within each group.

Financial Functions

Financial functions such as the following calculate amounts used in financing, budgeting, and depreciation. Optional arguments to the functions are in square brackets.

FV(*interest,term, payments*[*,pv,type*])	Returns the future value, given a series of equal payments, the interest rate, and the term. Optionally you can enter the present value and/or whether the payment is made at the end of the period (the default, type = 0) or at the beginning of the period (type = 1).
IRR(*range*[*,guess*])	Returns the internal rate of return for a series of cash flows contained in the range. A guess may speed up the calculation. If you don't enter a guess, Excel uses 10%.
NPV(*interest,range*)	Returns the net present value of a series of cash flows contained in the range at a given interest rate.

10

PMT(*interest, term,*   Returns the payment required for a loan
principal[, *fv, type*])   amount (principal) given the interest rate
and loan term. Optionally you can enter
the future value and/or whether the
payment is made at the end of the period
(the default, *type* = 0) or at the beginning
of the period (*type* = 1).

PV(*interest, term,*   Returns the present value, given a series of
payment[, *fv, type*])   equal payments, the term, and the interest
rate. Optionally you can enter the future
value and/or whether the payment is
made at the end of the period (the default,
type = 0) or at the beginning of the period
(*type* = 1).

SLN(*cost, salvage, life*)   Calculates depreciation expense for an
asset using the straight-line depreciation
method.

When you use financial functions, the term and interest rate must be in the same time units. For example, if you want a result in months, the term must be in months and the interest rate must be in months. (See the first example in the "Examples" section that follows.)

The interest rate can be entered in a financial function as either a decimal (.108) or a percent (10.8%). Also, in many financial functions you must distinguish between cash outflow, which should be a negative number, and cash inflow, which should be a positive number. (See the examples that follow.)

Where a series of payments is used in a function, the payments are assumed to be equal, at regular intervals, and at the end of each period. This is known as an *ordinary annuity*. If you want to change the payment to the beginning of the period, use the optional *type* argument with a value of 1.

Examples   To calculate the prospective monthly mortgage payment on a $140,000 30-year loan at 10.8% interest, use the following function:

```
=PMT(.108/12,30*12,140000)=-$1,312.14/month
```

To calculate the annual rate of interest necessary for a $10,000 investment to grow to $24,000 over 10 years with monthly compounding, use the following function:

```
=RATE(10*12,0,-10000,24000)*12=8.79%/year
```

Informational Functions

Informational functions such as the following provide information about cells and areas of the worksheet, including the number of rows or columns in a range, the formatting of a cell, and whether a cell is blank, contains text, or is a logical value.

COLUMNS(*range*)	Returns the number of columns in a range
ISBLANK(*value*)	Returns the logical value True if the value or cell is blank
ISTEXT(*value*)	Returns the logical value True if the value or cell is text
ROW(*reference*)	Returns the row number (not the number of rows) of the first row in the reference or an array of row numbers for all of the rows in the reference

Example   Often it is helpful to know the column width of a cell. You can choose Column Width from the Format menu, or you can use the function CELL("width"). CELL("width") returns a value that is rounded to the nearest whole number. For example, =CELL("width") returns 8 for the standard cell width of 8.43.

Logical Functions

Logical functions such as the following perform tests to determine if a condition is true.

AND(*condition 1, condition 2,...*)	Returns True if all conditions or logical statements are true
IF(*condition, true-result, false-result*)	Evaluates an equation or condition for true or false and takes one action for a true result and another action for a false result
TRUE	Returns a logical True

10

Example   When you calculate percentages, there are situations that result in dividing by 0 and produce a #DIV/0! error. To replace a possible error value with 0 in the formula =E15/C15, use the following formula in its place:

```
=IF(ISERR(E15/C15),0,E15/C15)
```

Mathematical Functions

Mathematical functions such as the following calculate general, matrix, and trigonometric values.

ABS(*x*)	Returns the absolute value of a number
ATAN(*x*)	Returns the arctangent of a number
MINVERSE(*array*)	Returns the inverse of a matrix or array
RAND( )	Returns a random number between 0 and 1
ROUND(*x*,*n*)	Rounds a number off to a specific number of decimal places
SIN(*x*)	Returns the sine of an angle
SQRT(*x*)	Calculates the square root of a number

Angles used as arguments for COS, SIN, and TAN must be expressed in radians. To convert degrees to radians, multiply the degrees by PI/180. The angle that results from ACOS, ASIN, ATAN, and ATAN2 is in radians. To convert radians to degrees, multiply the radians by 180/PI.

Example   To calculate the length of a guy wire that is supporting a 150-foot-high antenna when the guy wire, attached to the top, makes a 55-degree angle with the ground, use the following function:

```
=150/SIN(55*PI/180) equals 183.12 feet
```

This function returns an answer of 183.12 feet.

Text Functions

Text functions convert, parse, and manipulate text strings. Some text functions are as follows:

CHAR(*x*)	Returns the ASCII character corresponding to the number *x*

EXACT(*string1*, *string2*)	Compares two text strings and returns True if the two strings are the same and False if they differ
LEN(*string*)	Returns the number of characters in a text string
MID(*string*, *start-number,n*)	Returns the specified number of characters from within a text string beginning at a specified position
PROPER(*string*)	Converts the first character in each word of a text string to uppercase and the rest of the characters to lowercase, as in a proper name
TEXT(*x,format*)	Converts a number to text with a given numeric format

The offset number used in string functions always begins at 1. The first character in a string is 1, and the last character is the length of the string. Blank cells in a string function are still considered text, have a length of 0, and do not return an error code.

Example   To convert the date 4/15/92 in A1 to a text string that can be used in a title, use the following function:

```
=TEXT(A1,"mmmm d,yyyy")
```

This function returns April 15, 1992, which is text, not a value.

Macros

A macro is a shortcut. It is a way of accomplishing a set of Excel commands with fewer steps and a way to automate or speed up repetitive procedures. A macro is also a way to guide a less knowledgeable user through a complicated worksheet.

There are two kinds of macros in Excel. A *command macro* is a series of Excel commands, and a *function macro* is a custom function that returns a result. An example of a command macro is one that saves your worksheet, while a function macro example is one that calculates your local sales tax. You can have Excel execute a command macro by pressing two keys. A function macro is executed by putting it in a worksheet cell and recalculating the

10

worksheet. Almost all commands that you can perform from the keyboard, the mouse, or a menu can be stored in a macro and can be activated as you choose. In addition to keyboard and menu commands, a set of *macro functions* lets you perform built-in programming functions, such as repeating a sequence or accepting input from the keyboard. With macro functions you can build custom menus and automate a worksheet. You can see that function macros, which are custom functions that return a result, and macro functions, which supply programming commands to Excel, are quite different.

Anything that you do on a repetitive basis is a candidate for a macro. Macros are stored on a separate sheet called a macro sheet. You can create a library of macros that you can use with many worksheets, which makes macros you create even more useful.

Macro Basics

Few Excel tasks are more repetitive than saving a file. If you take normal precautions, you save your current worksheet several times each hour. To save an existing file, you either choose Save from the File menu, click on the Save tool from the Standard toolbar, or press (SHIFT)-(F12) or (ALT)-(SHIFT)-(F2). Depending on whether you are using a mouse or the keyboard, this takes a varying number of keystrokes or mouse moves—not many, and ones with which you are probably familiar. When you repeat these actions 20 times a day, however, they begin to add up. If you could replace the actions with two keystrokes familiar to you, say (CTRL)-(s), it might encourage you to save your files more often. Saving an existing file, then, is a good candidate for a macro.

Recording a Macro

Built into Excel is the capability to record whatever you are doing on an Excel worksheet and storing those steps on a macro sheet. Once stored, you can "play back" the steps and repeat what you were doing. The steps that are stored on the macro sheet comprise the macro, and playing them back is called running the macro. You turn on the Excel macro recorder by choosing Record from the Macro menu. Do that now and record a Save macro with these instructions:

1. Choose New from the File menu and click on OK to open a new worksheet.

2. Choose Save from the File menu, type **c:\sheet\macro**, and press
   (ENTER). Since you want to build a macro to save a worksheet that has
   already been saved, you must start with a worksheet that has been
   saved.

3. From the Macro menu choose Record. The Record Macro dialog
   box opens, as shown here:

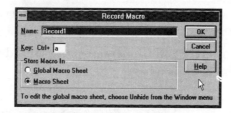

There are two ways you can store macros: on a global macro sheet, or on
a macro sheet you create. The global macro sheet is automatically opened
each time you start Excel. This is generally the macro sheet to use for simple,
frequently used utility macros because Excel will save, name, and open the
sheet for you. If you create a new macro sheet, you will have to manually open
the sheet both to record to it and to run the macros once they are recorded.
You can record a macro by selecting the Macro menu and choosing Record,
or by displaying the Macro toolbar and clicking on the Record Macro tool.
You will create and record a macro using the global macro sheet in this
section.

4. Type **Save.Worksheet** as the macro name, press (TAB) to move to the
   Key field, and type **s**.

5. Click on Global Macro Sheet in the Store Macro In list box and click
   on OK. The dialog box closes, and the Recording status message
   comes on in the Status bar.

The name of a macro can be any legitimate Excel name. It must start with
a letter, can be up to 255 characters long, and can contain any combination
of letters, numbers, periods, and underlines. It should not look like a
reference (either D3 or R3C4) and cannot contain spaces. Since you cannot

10

use spaces, periods or underlines are used as word separators. Periods are used in this book. An Excel name can be entered in either upper- or lowercase letters—Excel does not distinguish between the two.

The shortcut key can be any single upper- or lowercase letter. Upper- and lowercase letters are considered two different characters and will not conflict with one another. You cannot use numbers as shortcut characters.

6. Choose Save from the File menu. This is the step you want to record.

7. Choose Stop Recorder from the Macro menu. The Recording message disappears.

8. From the Window menu, choose Unhide. The Unhide dialog box opens as shown here:

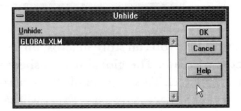

9. Double-click on GLOBAL.XLM. The global macro sheet that was automatically created in the previous steps becomes the active sheet, as shown here:

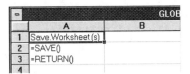

The global macro sheet looks just like a normal worksheet except that the columns look a little wider. The macro itself is in the upper-left corner, in cells A1:A3. A1 contains the name and shortcut key you gave the macro. A2 and A3 are the macro functions that save the current worksheet and return control to you. Macro functions are formulas—they always begin with an equal sign (=). A macro sheet always displays formulas, not the results they produce. Displaying formulas is an option on a normal worksheet, but normally a worksheet displays the results a formula produces. You can use the Options Display option to turn off the formulas display on a macro sheet, but the resulting values are generally not informative. Here is what your global macro sheet looks like with formulas turned off:

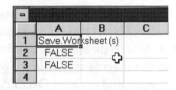

When you are displaying formulas instead of their results, everything on the worksheet is left aligned and you cannot change it with the Format alignment option. Otherwise, all formatting works on a macro sheet as it does on a worksheet.

Documenting a Macro

As you create macros, you may find that after a while you forget what they do. Also, you may want to give one or more macros to someone else to use, and they must know what the macros do. For this reason you must document your macros when you create them.

You can document a macro in several ways. You have used two forms of documentation already—giving the macro a descriptive name and using an obvious shortcut key. Other ways include formatting the macro name on the global macro sheet so it stands out, adding one or more cell notes, and, most importantly, adding some comments beside the macro commands. Add some comments and format the macro name with these steps:

1. With A1 as the active cell, click on the Bold button in the Standard toolbar, and click on OK. The macro name should be made bold.

2. Click on B1, type **Saves current wksht**, and press (ENTER). After slightly widening column A, the upper-left corner of your macro sheet now looks like this:

10

	A	B
		GLOBAL.XLM
1	Save.Worksheet (s)	Saves current wksht
2	=SAVE()	
3	=RETURN()	
4		

Running a Macro

Now that you have a finished and documented macro, you can run it in one of two ways. First and most simply, you can press CTRL-s, the shortcut key. Second, the Run Macro dialog box, reached by choosing Run from the Macro menu, lists all the macros available on open macro sheets, so you can select the macro you want and click on OK. Try both of these methods using the following instructions:

1. From the Window menu, choose MACRO.XLS.

2. Press CTRL-s. The file is saved.

    If you look at the Reference area of the Formula bar or at your disk light, you will see a brief indication that the file was saved. Also, you may see the hourglass wait indicator come on briefly. Press CTRL-s several times until you are satisfied it is working.

3. From the Macro menu, choose Run. The Run Macro dialog box opens, as shown here:

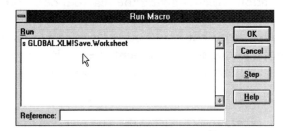

The Run Macro dialog box lists the macro you have just created. On the left is the shortcut key followed by the name of the macro sheet and the macro name. By clicking on the entry in the list box and then on OK you can run the macro.

4. Click on the entry in the list box and on OK (or double-click on the entry). Again you'll notice a brief flicker in the Reference area and in your disk light telling you the worksheet is being saved.

The Run Macro dialog box also serves as a reference if you should forget what the shortcut key is on a particular macro.

If you had any fears about macros, you can now set them aside. You have successfully created and run a macro!

5. Activate the global macro sheet by choosing it from the Window menu.

6. Close the global macro sheet by choosing Hide from the Window menu. When you exit Excel, a dialog box will ask if you want to save changes to the global macro sheet. Click on Yes and the global macro sheet will be hidden, but working, in future uses of Excel.

To edit the global macro sheet, choose Unhide from the Window menu. The Unhide dialog box appears. Highlight GLOBAL.XLM, click on OK, and the file is opened.

If you exit Excel without both hiding the global macro sheet again and choosing Yes to save the change to it, the global macro sheet will appear every time you start Excel until you choose to hide it and to save the change on exiting.

Remember that File Save erases the current file on disk before replacing it with the file being saved. *This means data can be lost.* You may want to create a backup file through the Options command button on the File Save As dialog box. This gives you the added protection of preserving the last file saved.

Repeat the steps you went through to record the Save.Worksheet macro on the global macro sheet, but this time store the macro in a new macro sheet. As a review:

1. Choose Record from the Macro menu.

10

2. Reenter the macro name and key (**Save.Worksheet** and **s**). Choose Macro Sheet and click on OK.

3. Choose Save from the File menu to record it and then choose Stop Recording from the Macro menu.

4. Click on Macro1 in the Window menu and make cell A1 bold.

5. Click on B1 and repeat the documenting of the Save macro.

6. Open MACRO.XLS from the Window menu.

Creating Additional Macros

Create several more simple and general-purpose macros. This time, however, watch the macros being built by reducing the size of the worksheet you are working on and exposing most of the macro sheet, as shown in Figure 10-8. Drag the upper-left corner of the MACRO.XLS worksheet window to reduce it to approximately the size shown in Figure 10-8. When you create a second macro, Excel places it at the top of the next available column of the current macro sheet, unless you tell Excel otherwise with the Set Recorder

Figure 10-8.   *A small worksheet set up for watching macros being created*

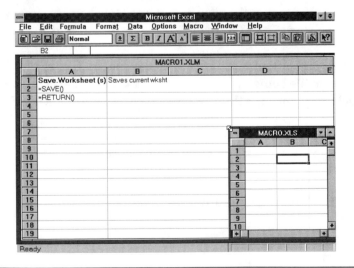

option in the Macro menu. Since you have used columns A and B, the next macro you create is placed in C1.

Copy Macro

Another heavily used option is Copy. While it has a well-defined shortcut key built into Excel, many people find it hard to remember. Create a macro for Copy and assign it the intuitive shortcut key (CTRL)-(c).

1. From the Macro menu, choose Record, type **Copy.Selection**, press (TAB), type **c**, and click on OK. The Recording message comes on in the Status bar, and the name and shortcut key appear in C1 on the macro sheet.

If you cannot see the Copy.Selection macro name on your macro sheet, it is because you left Excel between creating the Save macro and this macro. If you start a new session, even if you open your old macro sheet, Excel creates a new macro sheet to use for macros created in the current session, unless you tell it otherwise. (You will see how in a moment. For now, carry on creating the Copy macro even though you cannot see it.) In step 4, choose the new macro sheet from the Window menu instead of the old one.

2. Choose Copy from the Edit menu. The blinking marquee appears around B2 (or whatever cell you are pointing at) in MACRO.XLS. The macro function =COPY() appears in C2 on the macro sheet.

3. Choose Stop Recorder from the Macro menu. The macro function =RETURN() appears in C3 on the macro sheet. Press (ENTER). Your screen should look like that shown in Figure 10-9.

4. Click on the macro sheet and on cell C1. Click on the Bold tool in the Standard toolbar.

5. Click on D1, type **Copies current select**, and press (ENTER). Your second macro is documented.

Setting a Recording Range

Your next macro would be placed in E1, unless you tell Excel otherwise. Since that is off the screen, tell Excel you want it to begin in A5. You do that either by selecting a starting cell, in which you want the macro to start or by

10

Figure 10-9. *A copy macro added to macro sheet*

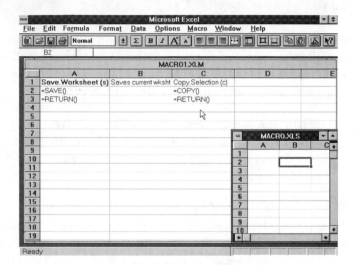

selecting a range you want the macro to occupy and then choosing the Set Recorder option from the Macro menu.

If you select a single cell in which to start the macro, Excel fills as many cells below that cell in the same column as necessary to complete the macro. If the macro reaches the bottom of the column, Excel redirects the macro to the top of the next column with a GOTO macro function, and then continues the macro in the next column. If you select a single cell and the single cell is not blank, Excel finds the last nonblank cell in the column and begins recording immediately below it. If the last nonblank cell has the RETURN macro function in it, RETURN is replaced by the first macro function of the new macro. In this way you can stop recording a macro and then later restart where you left off.

If you select a range in which to record a macro, the range becomes the limits within which the macro is contained. Excel starts the macro in the upper-left corner and continues to the lower-right corner, placing GOTO functions at the bottom of each column. If Excel reaches the limits of the range without completing the macro, you get a message that the range is full.

Unlike selecting a single cell, if you select a range and the first cell in the range is not blank, Excel displays a message saying the range is full and cannot be used. Set the starting cell for recording the next macro with these instructions:

1. Click on A5 of the macro sheet.
2. Choose Set Recorder from the Macro menu.
3. Choose MACRO.XLS from the Window menu to return to your worksheet.

Once you have set where you want to place your next macro, you can start the macro with either the Record or Start Recorder option on the Macro menu. Both options start in the cell you set. The principal difference is that Record is meant to start a new macro and Start Recorder is meant to be used for adding to the last macro you have entered. Start Recorder does not ask you to name or enter a shortcut key for a macro. You can use it only if you have already used Record within an Excel session (since you have most recently started Excel) or if you have used Set Recorder to establish a starting cell. If you have started a macro with Record, you can use Stop Recorder to quit macro recording and then restart with Start Recorder as if you had never quit; you need not use Set Recorder.

Formatting Macro

The custom percent format 0.0% deserves a macro for quick use. Build it next and give it the shortcut keys (CTRL)-(p).

1. Choose Record from the Macro menu, type **Percent.Format**, press (TAB), type **p**, and click on OK. The name and shortcut key appear in A5 of the macro sheet.
2. Choose Number from the Format menu, click on Percentage, select 0.00%, delete one decimal zero in the text box, and click on OK.
3. Choose Stop Recorder from the Macro menu to complete the macro.
4. Click on the macro sheet, click on A5, and make the name bold using the Bold tool. Then in B5 type **0.0% Format**, and press (ENTER).
5. Widen column A by dragging on the intersection between columns A and B so you can see the full format macro function, as shown in Figure 10-10.

10

Date- and Time-Stamp Macro

You will often want to add the date and/or time to a worksheet. Manually you must type **=NOW( )**, format the cell, and then use Copy and Paste Special to convert the function to a permanent value that does not change every time the worksheet is recalculated. It is easier to look at your watch or calendar and type the numbers as text so they do not have to be formatted. A macro takes this process down to two keystrokes that format the cell, enter the function, and convert it to a value. Create the macro following these steps:

1. Click on A9 of the macro sheet and choose Set Recorder.

2. Choose MACRO.XLS from the Window menu and click on A1 if the active cell is not already there.

3. Choose Record, type **Date.Time.Stamp**, press (TAB), type **d**, and click on OK. The name appears in A9.

4. Type **=now( )** and press (ENTER).

5. Choose Number from the Format menu, select the m/d/yy h:mm format, and click on OK.

6. Widen column A of the worksheet by dragging on the intersection between columns A and B until column A is about half again as large.

7. Choose Copy from the Edit menu, choose Paste Special from the Edit menu, click on Values and OK, and press (ESC). The =NOW( ) formula is converted to a value and the copy marquee removed.

8. Choose Stop Recorder from the Macro menu. Click on the macro sheet, make the macro name bold, and document your macro as shown in Figure 10-11.

Now try out this macro.

9. Choose MACRO.XLS from the Window menu, click on B3, and press (CTRL)-(d).

Figure 10-10. *A macro sheet with the Percent macro*

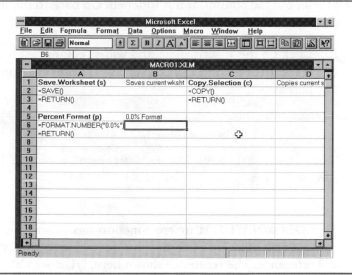

Figure 10-11. *Date/Time Stamp macro*

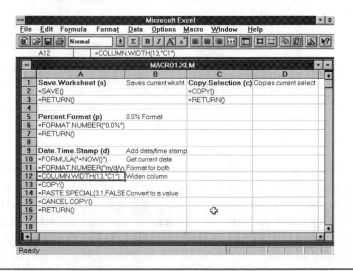

10

The date and time are placed in **B3** and it is formatted (although you cannot tell), but the column is not widened. Go back to the macro sheet and see why.

10. Click on the macro sheet and widen column A, if necessary, until you can see all of the COLUMN.WIDTH macro function, as shown here:

9	Date.Time.Stamp (d)	Add data/time stamp
10	=FORMULA("=NOW()")	Get current date
11	=FORMAT.NUMBER("m/d/y)	Format for both
12	=COLUMN.WIDTH(13,"C1")	Widen column
13	=COPY()	

The COLUMN.WIDTH macro function has two arguments: the width itself (your width may be different due to variation in dragging), and an optional reference. The reference shown here, C1, does not mean column C, row 1, but rather "column 1." This is the problem. To make the Date/Time Stamp macro flexible, you need to remove the column reference. Then the COLUMN.WIDTH macro function refers to the current selection, which is what you want. If your width value is a number with many decimal places, edit it also to round it to an even 12.

11. Click on A12. Edit A12 so that it contains =COLUMN.WIDTH(12).

12. Return to the MACRO.XLS worksheet and try the macro again in B5. It now works the way it should.

Entering Macros

All the macros you have created so far have been recorded. You modified the last recorded macro to give you what you want. You can also directly type in a macro. You can use either an existing macro sheet or create a new one. You simply pick an area on the macro sheet and start typing the necessary macro functions. This, of course, takes some familiarity with the macro functions and their arguments. Once you have written the macro, you can name it with the Define Name option on the Formula menu. Try that next by writing a macro to apply the #,##0 format. You can use the Percent macro as a model.

1. Click on the macro sheet and on C5. Type **Comma.Format(f)** and press (DOWN ARROW).

2. Type **=format.number("#,##0")**, press (DOWN ARROW), type **=return( )**, and press (UP ARROW) twice.

3. Choose Define Name from the Formula menu, click on Command as the macro type, press (TAB), type **f** as the shortcut key, and click on OK. (The name Comma.Format is already in the Name text box.)

4. Format the name on the macro sheet to make it bold, and enter the documentation as shown here:

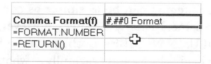

5. Try out the macro by returning to the MACRO.XLS worksheet, typing **62503.60**, pressing (ENTER), and pressing (CTRL)-(f). It works! Next press (CTRL)-(p), since you have not tried that macro, and format the number as a percent. It also works.

You can see that while you can type in a macro, it is much easier to use the recorder. Even if you need to do some heavy modification, building an initial structure with the recorder is a substantial benefit. It not only saves time, but also it gives you the correct macro function name and argument set. It saves you from either having to look these up or use the Paste Function option of the Formula menu.

Rules for Macro Entry

All parts of a macro can be typed in either upper- or lowercase. Excel converts it to uppercase if it is spelled correctly. A macro can occupy as many cells in a column as necessary. You can use both worksheet functions and macro functions. Place one function per cell. This makes the macros easier

10

to read on the screen and easier to edit. As Excel is executing a macro and completes the instructions in one cell, it automatically goes to the cell immediately below and continues macro execution. Excel continues down a column in this manner until it reaches a terminating or redirecting macro function such as RETURN, GOTO, or HALT. During macro execution, Excel ignores a blank cell.

If a macro refers to a range, it is better to name the range than to use addresses. An address in a macro is not updated if the worksheet is changed. A range name, on the other hand, continues to track an address with changes in the worksheet. Also, if you are working with multiple files, it is a good idea to precede a range name with the filename followed by an exclamation point.

Debugging Macros

When a macro does not behave the way you expect, you want to *debug* it, or correct it. Debugging can be as simple as correcting an obvious spelling error in a range name. In many instances, however, the error is not so obvious, as with the COLUMN.NUMBER problem in the Date/Time Stamp macro.

Debugging begins by looking carefully at what happened when the macro was run. Were there any error messages, and what did they say? What happened on the worksheet? Do you get the same result each time you run the macro?

Next, look at the macro itself. Are there any misspellings? Are there missing arguments, periods, or macro functions? If you recorded the macro, did the recorder supply some arguments you do not want? Did you use absolute addressing when you wanted relative or vice versa? Have you defined the range and macro names you are using?

Finally, go back and record the macro again to see if you get the same macro functions a second time. Carefully note all of your actions while you are recording the macro.

In most instances these steps identify the problem. If not, there is one further thing that can be done. You can use the Step command in the Run dialog box to execute a macro one step (one macro function) at a time. Excel will pause after each step so you can see the effects of that step, and continues only when you give the command to do so. The Step command also allows you to permanently halt the macro after any step, so you can more fully explore the partial results of a macro. Try the Step command now by choosing the DATE.TIME.STAMP macro from the Run dialog box. Click on Step and the Single Step dialog box appears. Keep clicking on Step Into to see the macro execute one step at a time.

Macro Functions

A macro function, when executed, performs a predefined function that may be available from the keyboard, the menus, or the mouse. Some macro functions, however, are for purposes of further automating a process and are not available in any other form. These macro functions cause the macro to accept input from the user, wait while the user does something, make a choice among several things, or loop through a set of macro functions multiple times. These are programming macro functions, and Chapter 12 works with them extensively.

Macro functions have a common syntax that must be followed in order for Excel to understand what to do. This syntax is exactly the same as that for worksheet functions described earlier in this chapter.

Function Macros

Function macros are custom functions you create on a macro sheet and then use on a worksheet to return a value or other result. You can distinguish function macros from command macros in two ways. First, command macros take some action like formatting, copying, or saving. Function macros take no action, but rather produce a result, like you might get from a calculation. Second, a command macro is wholly contained on the macro sheet and is executed with either the shortcut key or the Run option on the Macro menu. A function macro is created on a macro sheet, but to use it you must enter the resulting function on a worksheet.

Function macros are generally calculations you have to perform over and over. They have arguments through which you supply values and they use formulas and regular functions to calculate a result based on the values you supply. When you build a function macro, you must use three special macro functions that handle the arguments and the result. These functions, in the order in which they must be used, are as follows:

10

RESULT

The RESULT function is used only if you need to change the data type of the result. The RESULT function has one argument, the data type number. If you have not used a RESULT function to change it, the result is assumed to be a number, text, or a logical value. The possible data type numbers are

1	Number
2	Text
4	Logical
8	Reference
16	Error
64	Array

Data type numbers can be added together except for the reference and array types. For example, the default of number, text, or logical is a type 7 (1+2+4).

ARGUMENT

You must have one ARGUMENT function for each argument in the function macro you are building, and the arguments must be in the order in which they are presented in the function macro. The ARGUMENT function can have up to three arguments: a name, a data type, and a reference. You must have either a name or a reference. Whichever you specify, the other is optional. The data type is always optional. The name must be a legitimate Excel name and becomes defined by the ARGUMENT function. It can then be used by the formulas and regular functions that follow. If you do not specify a data type, Excel assumes it to be a number, text, or a logical value. If the value received by the ARGUMENT function is not a default type and you have not used the data type argument to change that, you will get a #VALUE! error. The reference argument is a cell or range reference on the macro sheet where the value received by the ARGUMENT function is placed. If you use both a name and a reference, the reference is given the name and can be referred to by it.

RETURN

All function macros must end with the RETURN function. The RETURN function has one argument in a function macro—the cell on the macro sheet that contains the result.

The formulas and regular functions to be used in a function macro must be placed after the last ARGUMENT function and before the RETURN function.

Function macros must be directly entered—they cannot be recorded. Build an example to see how they work. The example, call it Tax, calculates sales tax. It has two arguments: the amount on which to calculate the tax and the tax rate. Enter the tax function macro on the open macro sheet in C9.

1. Click on the macro sheet and on C9. Type **Tax** and press (ENTER). Format it as bold.

2. From the Formula menu, choose Define Name. Click on Function and on OK.

3. Click on cell C10. Then type **=argument("amount",1)**, press (DOWN ARROW), and then type **=argument("rate",1)**. Press (DOWN ARROW) again.

4. Type **=amount*rate**, press (DOWN ARROW), type **=return(c12)**, and press (ENTER).

5. Click on MACRO.XLS in the Window menu, and click on A5. (Drag the MACRO.XLS window to the left if you want to see the macro while you are working on the worksheet.)

6. From the Formula menu, choose Paste Function, scroll the Function Category list box and click on User Defined. Then click on the name MACRO1!Tax, and click on OK. You are left with the function in the Edit area and the word "amount" highlighted.

7. Press (DEL) six times to remove the arguments, then type **100,8.1%** and press (ENTER).

The result, 8.1, appears in A5, as shown in Figure 10-12. If an argument is missing when a function macro is used, the ARGUMENT function for that argument passes a value of #N/A to the formulas and functions that follow. To allow for optional arguments, you must trap the #N/A with an IF(ISNA( ))

10

Figure 10-12.   *Function macro for calculating sales tax*

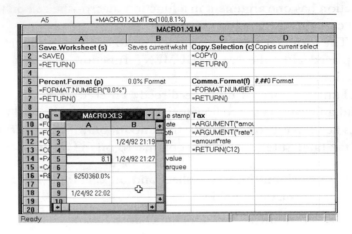

Figure 10-13.   *Tax function macro with an optional argument*

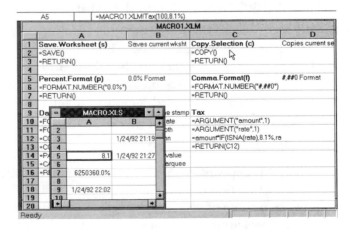

function. For example, if you want to make the tax rate optional in the function macro you just built, you must change the formula in C12 to =amount*IF(ISNA(rate),8.1%,rate). This way, if the rate is not entered, 8.1% would be used, as shown in Figure 10-13.

As you are going back and forth between the macro sheet and the worksheet, be aware that the worksheet is not recalculated by simply activating it. You must either make an entry to or edit a cell, or press (F9), the Calculate Now key.

Depending on who is going to use your macros, especially function macros, you must consider their error-handling capability. If you are the only one who will be using them, they can probably be fairly insensitive to errors. If novice Excel users are going to handle them, the function macros must work with many different error conditions. You are now in the position of a programmer whose hardest job probably is to figure out all the ways someone can use their program. A basic ground rule is that if it can happen, it will, and if it cannot happen, it might anyway. Chapter 12 deals entirely with writing macros to automate a worksheet so a novice can use it (and it does *not* consider every possible error that could occur!).

You are left with a number of open worksheets. Only the macro sheet has potential value. Save it if you want and exit both Excel and Windows by telling Excel you do not want to save the other worksheets.

10

11

Solver and Other Analysis Tools

One of the real powers of an electronic worksheet is the ability to change a number and have that change almost instantly reflected in all related numbers. This makes it possible to look at many alternatives for a given situation. Keeping track of the alternatives and finding the "best" one, though, can still be a difficult job. Excel provides several tools to make analysis easier for you. These tools can help you quickly cycle through and organize different sets of values or scenarios. They can also help you determine what values will achieve a certain result. These tools are:

- *Goal Seek,* which finds a solution for a formula by changing a single variable.

- *What If macro,* which allows you to define multiple sets of values for your variables. The macro then cycles through all possible combinations of the variables and allows you to see the effect on your worksheet.

- *Scenario Manager,* which keeps track of different sets of values for you.

- *Solver,* which finds a solution for a formula by changing multiple variables, and it allows you to set constraints on the variables. Solver also allows you to create several reports.

These tools will help you answer questions such as: How much money should I spend on advertising in order to maximize profit? If I only have a certain amount of dollars to spend on advertising, how should I allocate that money on a monthly basis in order to get the biggest return? What if the monthly growth ratios are different? How will that affect sales and income?
Each of these tools will be discussed in the following sections.

Preparing for Analysis

Before you can use Excel's analysis tools, you need to set up a worksheet on which the tools will operate. The worksheet should contain formulas that express a situation. Make your worksheet as easy to use and as understandable as possible. Write clear formulas and a simple layout. It is helpful to name variables so they are easy to identify.

The worksheet that you created in chapters 5 and 6 can be used after you make a few modifications. You will change the formula for the monthly sales of forms to be dependent on advertising expense and a monthly growth ratio. It is important to have the cells that you are defining as variables and the cell or cells for which you are trying to find values, related either indirectly or directly through formulas. Without this relationship, the analysis tools will not work.

1. Open the worksheet QTR3BUD.XLS. Your screen should look like Figure 11-1.
2. Click on C11. Type the formula **=290*(C3 * 100)*(C23 + 3000)^0.5** and press (ENTER). This formula relates sales of forms (C11) to a monthly growth ratio (C3) and advertising expense (C23). You will change C23 to represent advertising in a minute.
3. Select the range C11:E11.

4. Choose Fill Right from the Edit menu. Cells D11 and E11 will change to zero. You will fix that next.

5. Click on D3. Type **1.4%** and press (RIGHT ARROW). You are entering a monthly growth ratio for August.

6. Type **1.2%** and press (ENTER). This is the monthly growth ratio for September.

7. Select D3:E3. Format as 0.0%.

8. Scroll your screen and click on A23. Indent (press (SPACEBAR) four times), type **Advertising**, and press (ENTER).

9. Click on C23. Type **5000** as the beginning advertising value.

10. Select C23:E23. Choose Fill Right from the Edit menu.

11. Click on the File menu and the Save As option.

12. Type **SOLVEREX** in the File Name box and press (ENTER).

Figure 11-1.   *Initial QTR3BUD.XLS worksheet*

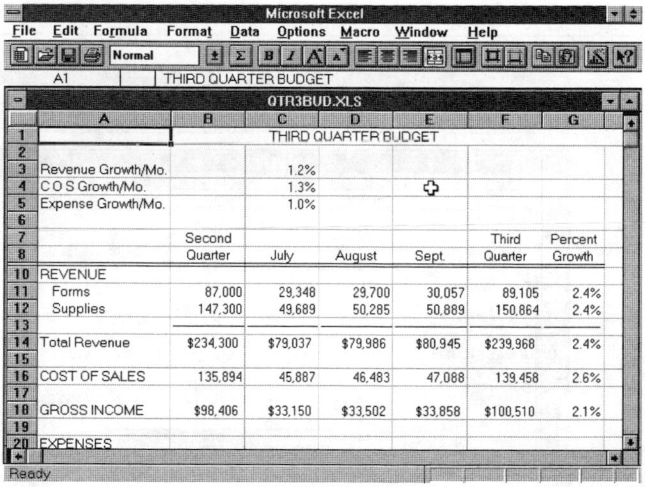

Your worksheet should now look like Figure 11-2. Now that you have prepared your worksheet, with cells related through formulas, you are ready to explore Excel's analysis tools.

Goal Seek

Goal Seek is one of Excel's simplest analysis tools. When you want a formula to equal a particular value, you specify a cell on which the formula is dependent; Goal Seek varies the value of that cell until the formula is the value you want. Goal Seek is useful when you want to solve a formula dependent on one variable. To see how Goal Seek works, use the worksheet you just prepared to find out how much you need to spend on advertising in order to sell $40,000 worth of forms in July. In this case, the variable is cell C23 (advertising expense for July), and the formula we want to equal $40,000 is in cell C11 (sales of forms for July).

Figure 11-2.   *Advertising and new formulas added to your worksheet*

	A	B	C	D	E	F	G
8		Quarter	July	August	Sept.	Quarter	Growth
10	REVENUE						
11	Forms	87,000	31,126	36,314	31,126	98,566	13.3%
12	Supplies	147,300	49,689	50,285	50,889	150,864	2.4%
13							
14	Total Revenue	$234,300	$80,815	$86,599	$82,015	$249,429	6.5%
15							
16	COST OF SALES	135,894	45,887	46,483	47,088	139,458	2.6%
17							
18	GROSS INCOME	$98,406	$34,928	$40,116	$34,927	$109,971	11.8%
19							
20	EXPENSES						
21	Salaries	24,450	8,232	8,314	8,397	24,942	2.0%
22	P/R Taxes	2,322	782	790	797	2,369	2.0%
23	Advertising	14,760	5,000	5,000	5,000	15,000	1.6%
24							
25	Total Expenses	$41,532	$14,013	$14,103	$14,194	$42,311	1.9%
26							
27	Net Income	$56,874	$20,915	$26,012	$20,733	$67,660	19.0%

If you haven't already, scroll your worksheet so you can see cells C11 and C23 simultaneously (like Figure 11-2). Notice that C11 (sales of forms for July) contains the value 31,126. Notice also that C23 (advertising for July) contains the value 5,000.

1. Click on cell C11.

2. Open the Formula menu and choose the Goal Seek option. The Goal Seek dialog box opens, as shown in the following illustration. Set cell is automatically $C$11 because C11 is the active cell on the worksheet.

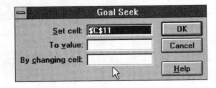

3. Type **40,000** in the To value box.

4. Type **C23** (advertising for July) in the By changing cell box. Click on OK.

5. If necessary, move the Goal Seek Status dialog box so that you can see both C11 and C23.

Notice that C11 now contains the value 40,000, and cell C23 now contains 10,212, as seen in Figure 11-3. You now know that you would have to spend $10,212 on advertising in July to increase your sales of forms to $40,000 (given the formula is valid!).

6. Click on the Cancel button to restore values to what they were before. If you click on OK, the new values are saved on your worksheet. If you choose OK by accident, and you want to restore your old values, immediately choose Undo Goal Seek from the Edit menu.

Goal Seek is useful if you want to know what a single value needs to be in order to cause a single formula to result in a particular value. Solver,

Figure 11-3.   *After running Goal Seek*

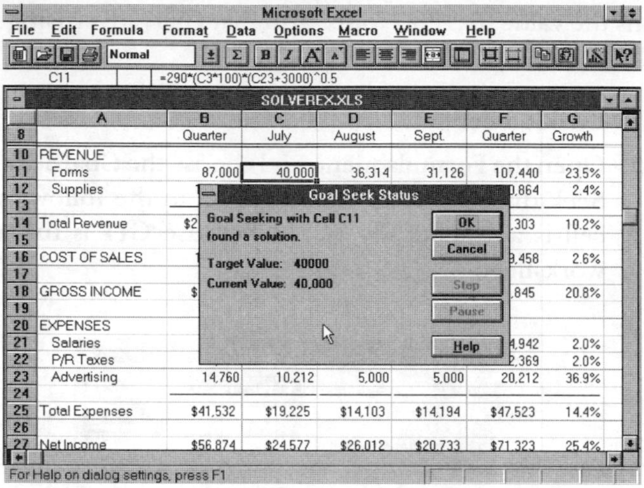

discussed later in this chapter, is useful if you want to solve a problem with multiple variables.

What If Macro

If you want to see the effects of changing the values of multiple cells on your worksheet, Excel has a macro to assist you in doing this. The What If macro allows you to define as many possible values as you want for each variable on your worksheet. The macro then cycles through every combination of the values assigned to the variables so that you can see the effect each set of values has on your worksheet.

For example, say you want to see the effect of different monthly revenue growth ratios. If you define two values for each of the three variables, there are eight different possible combinations of values. Follow these steps to see how this works.

1. Click on the Open file button from the Standard toolbar. Open the file WHATIF.XLA in the C:\EXCEL\LIBRARY directory or in the LIBRARY subdirectory of the directory where you installed Excel. You will not have a What If option on your Formula menu until you open this macro.

2. Select the Formula menu, then choose the What If option.

3. Click on the New button to create a new Data Sheet.

4. Type **C3** (revenue growth ratio for July) in the Reference of Variable #1 box and press (ENTER).

5. Type **1.2%** in the Value #1 for C3 box and press (ENTER).

6. Type **1.1%** in the Value #2 for C3 box, press (ENTER), then click on Done.

7. Type **D3** (revenue growth ratio for August) in the Reference of Variable #2 box and press (ENTER).

8. Type **1.4%** in the Value #1 for D3 box and press (ENTER).

9. Type **1.3%** in the Value #2 for D3 box, press (ENTER), then click on Done.

10. Type **E3** (revenue growth ratio for September) in the Reference of Variable #3 box and press (ENTER).

11. Type **1.2%** in the Value #1 for E3 box and press (ENTER).

12. Type **1.5%** in the Value #2 for E3 box, press (ENTER), then click on Done, and click on Done again (to stop at three variables).

You have now set up the values for the variables and are ready to begin looking at the effect they have on your worksheet.

13. Scroll your worksheet so you can see C3:E3.

14. Press (CTRL)-(SHIFT)-(T).

The first set of variables appears in cells C3:E3. Since they are the same variables as are already there, you will not see a change. When you press (CTRL)-(SHIFT)-(T) a second time, C3 changes to 1.1%, the second value that you assigned to the variable C3. Notice the change the new growth ratio has on sales of forms and income. Keep pressing (CTRL)-(SHIFT)-(T) to cycle through the various values you assigned to the three variables and notice the effect it has on your worksheet.

If you want to change the value of just one of the variables, click on that variable and press (CTRL)-(T). The values you assigned to that variable will be cycled through, but the other variables will remain unchanged. Try this now.

If you would like to see the table of values you entered, you can activate the worksheet where the What If macro stores the values. If you opened Excel just before starting this chapter, you will find the table stored on Sheet2. Figure 11-4 shows the table of values created by the What If macro.

    15. Choose Sheet2 from the Window menu.

The What If macro provides a convenient way of trying out many combinations of variables without having to manually figure out all the possibilities. This feature can save you time and effort. Once you have determined the sets of values that are of interest to you, use Scenario Manager to name and save these sets of data for later viewing.

    16. Choose SOLVEREX.XLS from the Window menu to return to your main worksheet.

    17. Use (CTRL)-(T) to return C3 to 1.2%, D3 to 1.4%, and E3 to 1.2%.

Scenario Manager

Scenario Manager allows you to store different values for variables in your worksheet. In this respect, it is similar to the What If macro, but with Scenario Manager you must explicitly enter all *sets* (specific combinations) of values you want to represent. You can use the What If macro to determine the combinations that are of interest, and then enter those into the Scenario Manager for the easy viewing and reporting capabilities that Scenario Manager provides. Each combination or set of values is a *scenario*. You can have as many different scenarios for your worksheet as you like. Each scenario is named and is a convenient way to organize your sets of values. Once you have entered all the scenarios for your worksheet, you can print a report that

Figure 11-4. *The What If macro worksheet*

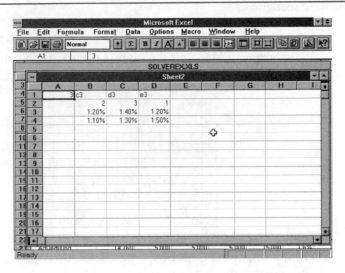

compares the different scenarios by listing all the sets of input values and any affected cells you would like to appear on the report. With this report, you can easily compare the various scenarios you are analyzing. In summary, Scenario Manager allows you to:

- Name and store as many scenarios as you like
- View existing scenarios
- Modify existing scenarios
- Delete scenarios
- Create a summary report of the different scenarios

Creating Scenarios

First, you'll want to create several scenarios for your worksheet. Unlike the What If macro, you must explicitly enter a scenario for every combination of input values you want to examine. Make sure SOLVEREX.XLS is your active worksheet and C3 your active cell, then follow these steps to create three new scenarios:

1. Open the Formula menu and choose the Scenario Manager option. The Scenario Manager dialog box opens, as shown here:

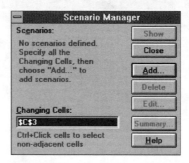

2. In the Changing Cells box, type **C3:E3**, then click on Add. The Add Scenario dialog box opens:

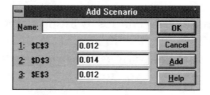

3. In the Name box, type **Scenario1**.

4. Click on Add. The scenario is stored.

5. For the next scenario, type **Scenario2** in the Name box.

6. Type **0.011** in the $C$3 box and click on Add.

7. Type **Scenario3** in the Name box.

8. Type **0.015** in the $D$3 box and click on OK. The Scenario Manager dialog box reappears with the new scenarios that you just defined listed in the Scenarios list box, like this:

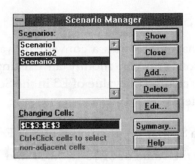

Viewing Existing Scenarios

You just added three scenarios. You can view the different scenarios by choosing the Show option in the Scenario Manager dialog box. When you show a scenario, Scenario Manager substitutes the values associated with that scenario into the variables on your worksheet. Any cells containing formulas dependent on those variables are updated to new values. Follow these steps to see how it works:

1. Click on Scenario2, then click on the Show button.

Watch how the values you assigned to the three variables in Scenario2 affect your worksheet. You may need to move the dialog box. Now look at a different scenario.

2. Click on Scenario1, then click on Show. Examine the results on your worksheet.

3. Click on Scenario3, then click on Show.

4. Practice going back and forth between the scenarios using Show.

You can see how easy it is to substitute sets of values into cells and to examine the effect they have on your worksheet.

Modifying a Scenario

Scenario Manager provides a convenient way of storing and reviewing different scenarios. You can modify an existing scenario very easily. For example, you can change the value of E3 in the Scenario3 you just created by following these steps:

1. Click on Scenario3, then click on the Edit button.

2. Change the value of $E$3 to 0.011 and click on OK.

3. Click on the Show button to see the effect of your change.

Creating a Summary of Your Scenarios

Next create a summary report of your three scenarios. The summary report not only lists your various input values for your variables, it also allows you to specify other cells on the worksheet you want included in the report, such as the cells that will change in each scenario. This gives you a convenient way to compare how different inputs give you different results.

1. Click on the Summary button.

2. The Scenario Summary dialog box appears, as seen here:

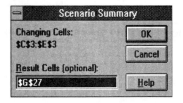

3. In the Result Cells box, type **C11:F11, C27:F27**. These cells, for forms sales and net income respectively, contain formulas that are dependent on the values in cells C3:E3.

4. Click on OK.

A summary report is created on a new worksheet, as seen in Figure 11-5. You can save this summary as a separate worksheet and print it out if you

11

wish. You may want to chart the summary report to give you a comparison between the scenarios. Refer to Chapter 7 for information about how to build a chart. Figure 11-6 shows an example of a chart created from a Scenario Manager summary report. You can see at a glance the relationship between different growth ratios and sales figures.

5. When you have finished looking at the summary, activate SOLVEREX.XLS again.

Creating Other Reports

You can also create reports with the different scenarios using the Print Reports option on the File menu. You can print a single view (or scenario) of your worksheet, or you can print a series of views in one step. Use the following directions to print out a single view of your worksheet using the Print Reports option.

Figure 11-5. *Scenario Manager summary report*

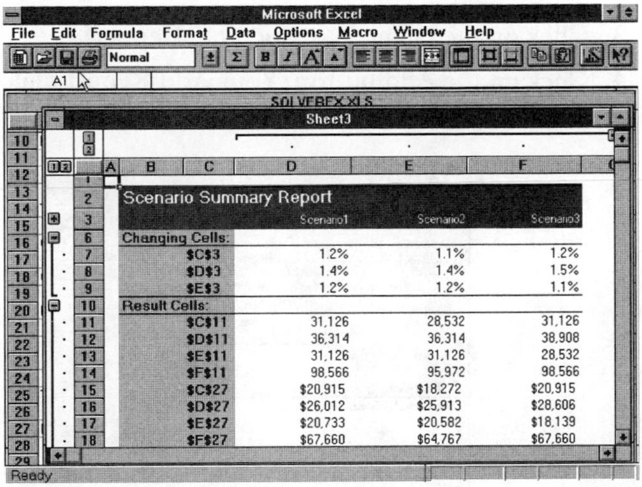

Figure 11-6.   *Chart created from a Scenario Manager summary report*

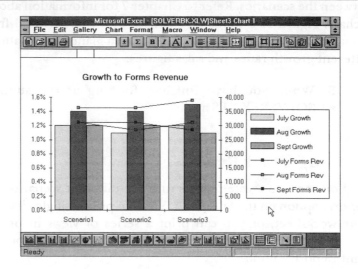

1. Open the File menu and choose the Print Report option.

2. Click on Add, click on the down arrow on the right end of the Scenario box, and click on Scenario1.

3. Click on the Name box, and type **Report1**.

4. Click on the Add button. Your Add Report dialog box should look like this:

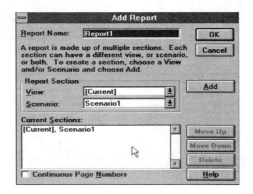

5. Click on OK and click on Print, then click on OK in the Print dialog box and again for the number of copies. A report is generated as shown in Figure 11-7.

6. Click on Close.

The power of the Print Reports feature is realized when you have many scenarios set up for your worksheet, and you want to print out a copy of your worksheet for each scenario. Because this option allows you to print them all at once, it will save you a great deal of time.

Solver

Solver is Excel's most sophisticated analysis tool. If you want to find a solution to a formula that has multiple variables, Solver is the right tool to use. Solver allows you to specify up to two hundred variables. It also allows you to define up to one hundred constraints on those variables. A *constraint*

Figure 11-7.   *Second Scenario Manager report*

THIRD QUARTER BUDGET

	Revenue Growth/Mo.			
Revenue Growth/Mo.	1.2%	1.4%	1.2%	
C O S Growth/Mo.	1.3%			
Expense Growth/Mo.	1.0%			

	Second Quarter	July	August	Sept.	Third Quarter	Percent Growth
REVENUE						
Forms	87.000	31,126	36,314	31,126	98,566	13.3%
Supplies	147,300	49,689	50,285	50,889	150,864	2.4%
Total Revenue	$234,300	$80,815	$86,599	$82,015	$249,429	6.5%
COST OF SALES	135,894	45,887	46,483	47,088	139,458	2.6%
GROSS INCOME	$98,406	$34,928	$40,116	$34,927	$109,971	11.8%
EXPENSES						
Salaries	24,450	8,232	8,314	8,397	24,942	2.0%
P/R Taxes	2,322	782	790	797	2,369	2.0%
Advertising	14,760	5,000	5,000	5,000	15,000	1.6%
Total Expenses	$41,532	$14,013	$14,103	$14,194	$42,311	1.9%
Net Income	$56,874	$20,915	$26,012	$20,733	$67,660	19.0%

limits the values a variable can take on. For example, you could constrain a variable to be an integer, to be greater than zero, or no larger than a certain value. Solver tries to solve the formula to equal the value you specify by trying different values for the variables you defined within the constraints. Instead of specifying a single value you want the formula to equal, you can also indicate that you would like the formula to be a maximum or a minimum value.

The following example shows how to use Excel's Solver to maximize income for the quarter by figuring out how to best spend advertising dollars on a monthly basis. Make sure SOLVEREX.XLS is the active sheet.

1. Scroll your worksheet up, if necessary, click on C3, type **1.1%** if it isn't that value already, and press (RIGHT ARROW).

2. Type **1.2%** and press (RIGHT ARROW).

3. Type **1.4%** and press (ENTER). You just entered three new monthly growth ratios for this exercise.

Your worksheet should now look like the one pictured in Figure 11-8.

Figure 11-8.   *Growth rates to be used with Solver*

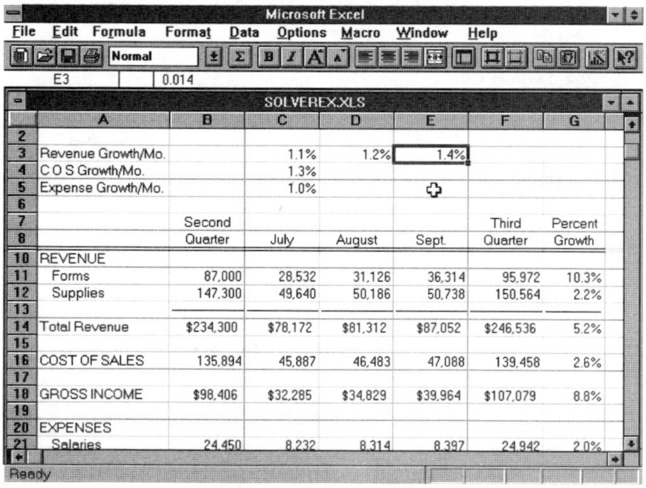

	A	B	C	D	E	F	G
2							
3	Revenue Growth/Mo.		1.1%	1.2%	1.4%		
4	C O S Growth/Mo.		1.3%				
5	Expense Growth/Mo.		1.0%		✛		
6							
7		Second				Third	Percent
8		Quarter	July	August	Sept.	Quarter	Growth
10	REVENUE						
11	Forms	87,000	28,532	31,126	36,314	95,972	10.3%
12	Supplies	147,300	49,640	50,186	50,738	150,564	2.2%
13							
14	Total Revenue	$234,300	$78,172	$81,312	$87,052	$246,536	5.2%
15							
16	COST OF SALES	135,894	45,887	46,483	47,088	139,458	2.6%
17							
18	GROSS INCOME	$98,406	$32,285	$34,829	$39,964	$107,079	8.8%
19							
20	EXPENSES						
21	Salaries	24,450	8,232	8,314	8,397	24,942	2.0%

4. Click on File, then click on Save. If you make a mistake in the following exercises, you can return to this point and start over.

Setting Up Solver

You are now ready to set up Solver.

1. Scroll your worksheet so you can see C23:F23 and cell F27, as shown in Figure 11-9.

2. Open the Formula menu and choose Solver. The Solver Parameters dialog box opens as shown here:

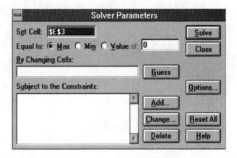

3. Type **F27** (net income for the quarter) in the Set Cell box. You want to maximize net income, and since Max is the default Equal to option button you don't need to change it.

4. Type **C23:E23** (monthly advertising expense) in the By Changing Cells box.

5. Click on the Solve button.

Notice that the values Excel is using to try to solve for in cell F27 appear in the Status bar. Once a solution is found, the Solver dialog box appears as shown here:

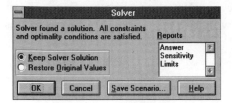

This dialog box allows you to restore the original values, keep the new values, store the values using Scenario Manager, or print reports. For now, you want to look at what happens when you keep the new values.

6. Make sure the Keep Solver Solution button is on, and click on OK.

Your worksheet should now look like Figure 11-10. Compare figures 11-9 and 11-10. Figure 11-9 shows what your worksheet looked like before using Solver, and Figure 11-10 shows your worksheet after using Solver. Pay special attention to cells C11:F11 (sales of forms), C23:F23 (advertising expenses), and cells C27:F27 (income). Because all of these cells are related either directly or indirectly through the formula in cell F27, when Solver maximized

Figure 11-9.   *Worksheet setup for Solver*

	A	B	C	D	E	F	G
8		Quarter	July	August	Sept.	Quarter	Growth
10	REVENUE						
11	Forms	87,000	28,532	31,126	36,314	95,972	10.3%
12	Supplies	147,300	49,640	50,186	50,738	150,564	2.2%
13							
14	Total Revenue	$234,300	$78,172	$81,312	$87,052	$246,536	5.2%
15							
16	COST OF SALES	135,894	45,887	46,483	47,088	139,458	2.6%
17							
18	GROSS INCOME	$98,406	$32,285	$34,829	$39,964	$107,079	8.8%
19							
20	EXPENSES						
21	Salaries	24,450	8,232	8,314	8,397	24,942	2.0%
22	P/R Taxes	2,322	782	790	797	2,369	2.0%
23	Advertising	14,760	5,000	5,000	5,000	15,000	1.6%
24							
25	Total Expenses	$41,532	$14,013	$14,103	$14,194	$42,311	1.9%
26							
27	Net Income	$56,874	$18,272	$20,725	$25,770	$64,767	13.9%

Ready

Figure 11-10. *Initial Solver solution*

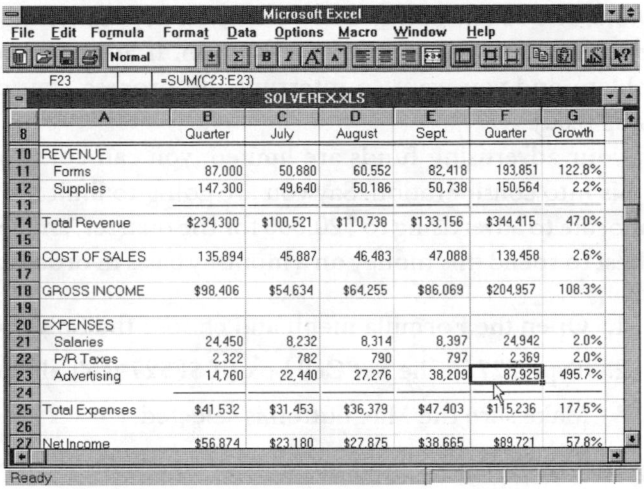

F27 by changing advertising expenses, it also caused the sales for forms to increase. In this example, instead of spending $5,000 a month on advertising, Solver found that you could make the most money if you spend $22,440 in July, $27,276 in August, and $38,209 in September for advertising.

Based on the information you provided in your worksheet, you have just determined how to make the most money possible by spending $87,925 on advertising. You could have used trial and error in order to determine this result, but that would have been a very tedious and time-consuming undertaking, with no guarantee that the answer you found was the optimal solution. Solver is an extremely efficient and accurate problem solver that will provide you with invaluable information.

Constraining Variables

It's nice to say you can make the most money if you spend $87,925 on advertising, but what happens if you don't have $87,925? You need to set an upper limit, a *constraint* on the advertising budget. You can constrain a Solver problem in several ways. You can constrain variables to take on particular values, not to exceed or go lower than certain values, to be integers, or positive numbers, and so on. You can also constrain the problem by limiting the time Solver can take to come up with a solution. If Solver takes too long to solve a problem and you want to interrupt the process, you can stop Solver by pressing (ESC).

If your advertising funds are limited, you can constrain the problem to take this into consideration. Say you are going to limit the amount of money you allocate to advertising to $20,000 for the quarter, and let Solver determine how best to spend this money on a monthly basis in order to maximize profits.

1. Open the Formula menu and choose the Solver option.

2. Type **F27** in the Set Cell box (if $F$27 isn't already there).

3. Make sure the Max button is selected.

4. Type **C23:E23** in the By Changing Cells box (if it isn't there already).

5. Click on the Add button to add a constraint. The Add Constraint dialog box appears, as shown here:

6. Type **F23** in the Cell Reference box. Less than or equal to (<=) is the comparison operator you want, so you don't need to change it.

7. Type **20,000** in the Constraint box. Click on Add to add the constraint.

8. Type **C23:E23** in the Cell Reference box and click on the arrow to display the comparison operators. Select greater than or equal to (>=), type **3,000** in the Constraint box, and click on OK to add the constraint and close the Add Constraint dialog box.

9. Click on the Solve button. Solver searches for a solution. When it finds one, the Solver dialog box reappears.

Your worksheet should now look like Figure 11-11. Notice that Solver determined how to optimally spend your quarterly advertising budget in order to maximize your income. If you don't enter the second constraint (C23:E23 >= 3,000), it is possible that the formulas in C11:E11 will go negative. Since you cannot take the square root of a negative number (the formulas in C11:E11 take the square root), you will get an error condition that will stop the Solver.

Instead of saving the solution on the worksheet, try using the Scenario Manager option instead.

10. Click on the Scenario Manager button.

11. Type **adv20000** in the Name box.

12. Click on OK.

13. Click on the Restore Original Values button, then click on OK.

Figure 11-11. *Constrained Solver solution*

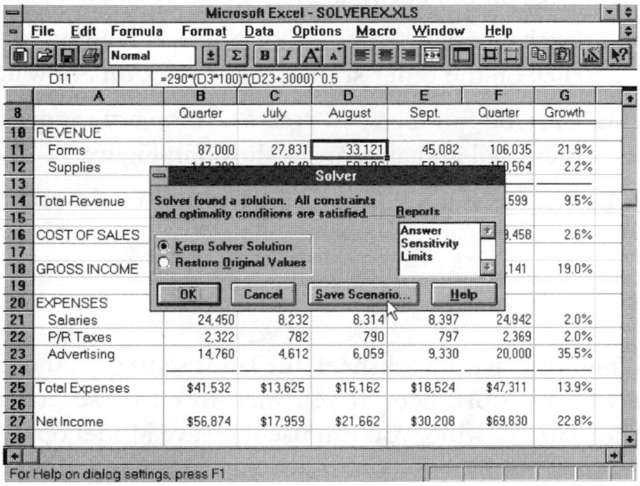

Using Solver and Scenario Manager Together

If you create another scenario, you can see how you can use Solver and Scenario Manager together. Follow the steps below to create an additional scenario where the advertising budget is constrained to $30,000. This example will also show you how to modify an existing constraint.

1. Click on the Formula menu, then click on Solver.
2. Click on the $F$23 <= 2000 constraint and click on the Change button.
3. Type **30,000** in the Constraints box and click on OK.
4. Click on Solve.
5. Once Solver finds a solution, click on the Scenario Manager box.
6. Type **adv30000** in the Name box, then click on OK.
7. Click on the Restore Original Values box, then click on OK.

Now you can take a look at the scenarios you created with the Solver by using the Scenario Manager option.

1. Click on the Formula menu, then click on Scenario Manager.
2. Click on adv20000, then on Show to see one of the scenarios; then click on the other scenario, and click on Show again.
3. Click on Summary to create a summary report. A summary report is created and appears as shown in Figure 11-12.
4. Choose SOLVEREX.XLS from the Window menu to return there.

Saving a Model

When you save a worksheet, the latest settings you defined for Solver are saved with the worksheet. If you want to set up several problems and save them for later viewing, you can use the Save Model option. You must find a range on your worksheet where you can store the settings. Follow these steps to save the current problem.

Figure 11-12. *Summary report of the Solver solution from the Scenario Manager*

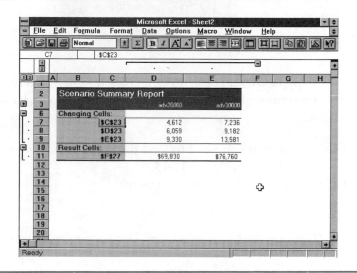

1. Open the Formula menu and choose Solver.

2. Click on the Options button. The Solver Options dialog box opens, as shown here:

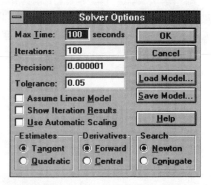

3. Click on the Save Model button. The Save Model dialog box opens, as shown here:

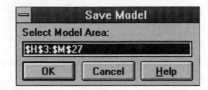

4. Type **I1:O8** and click on OK. Click on OK again to close the Solver Options dialog box, and click on Close to close the Solver dialog box.

The information you need to load the solution has been stored on your worksheet, as shown in Figure 11-13.

To load the model, follow these steps:

1. Open the Formula menu and choose Solver.

2. Click on the Options button. The Solver Options dialog box opens.

Figure 11-13.   *Stored information to reload model*

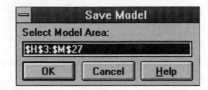

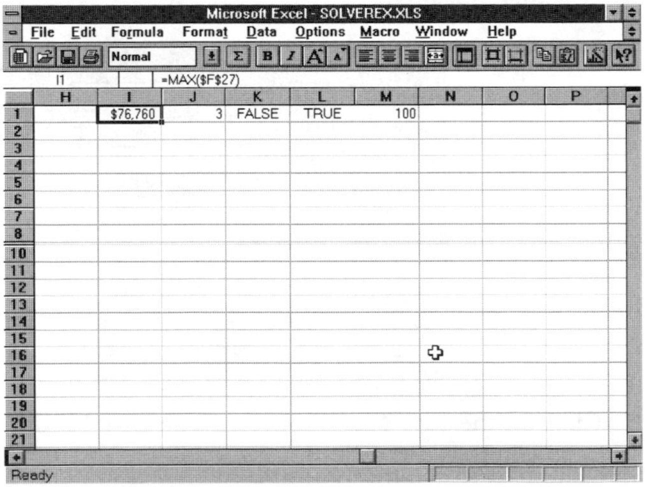

3. Click on the Load Model button. The Load Model dialog box opens:

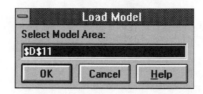

4. Type **I1:O8** in the Select Model Area box and click on OK. Click on OK to "reset previous Solver cell locations" and click on OK again to leave the Solver Options dialog box. The Solver Parameters dialog box opens with all the parameters you set for the model loaded.

5. Click on Close to close the Solver.

Solver is a potent tool with many features—only some of which have been covered here. Along with the other tools presented in this chapter, Solver will help you organize your work, create meaningful comparative reports, solve problems, and save you hours of time.

12

Automating a Worksheet

In this chapter you will build an automated worksheet or application to be used by people who know very little about Excel. This application provides the means of entering, editing, and printing sales orders. All of these functions are complete as they might be in an actual application. At the same time, there are many enhancements you could add to the application to give it even more features. These enhancements are discussed at the end of the chapter.

Building the application takes several steps. The first is to plan it. You must determine what the application will do and how it will be laid out on both the macro sheet and the worksheet. The second step is to build the working part of the worksheet, the title screen, and the report range. Next you build a sophisticated dialog box that will be used for data entry. Finally you build and test the macros necessary to guide a user through the application. The macros produce a custom menu, accept data from the dialog box, update a database, and print the database.

Building an automated worksheet is a detailed process that requires concentration. The reward is to watch the worksheet operate once you finish it. The results in a business can be very powerful. With applications like this you can have people who know very little about Excel doing sophisticated things with it.

Planning an Application

Planning an application entails answering five questions. First, what will the application do—what are the inputs, how is data manipulated, and what are the outputs? Second, how do these requirements translate to functions performed by Excel? Third, how will the worksheet be laid out—which functions will go where on the worksheet? Fourth, what is the logic path of operating the application—how do you logically work through all of its functions and cleanly start and stop it? And fifth, how does the logic path translate into Excel capabilities—dialog boxes, menus, and macro functions?

While all five of these steps are important, most applications built with Excel do not go through such a formal process. They generally result from the "build some, try it out, and when it works, build some more" philosophy. This chapter covers only what the application will do, how that translates to Excel, and how it is laid out on the worksheet.

What It Is Going to Do

Before determining what an application will do, it is important to remind yourself to "keep it simple" and define the minimum set of things that you want to do. It is very easy to describe the Taj Mahal if you ignore what it will take to build it.

Here is the minimum set of things this application should do:

1. Automatically load and prepare the database worksheet.

2. Accept sales orders entered with the customer name, salesperson, product description, quantity, unit price, and sales tax rate.

3. Build a database of these items with the tax calculated and the order totaled.

4. Provide for editing of the database items including changing individual fields and deleting items.

5. Print the database with a heading.

6. Save the worksheet and leave Excel.

This translates well into Excel. You can use a dialog box for entry, a database, and a print range. Excel's Set Print Area handles the selection of an output range for printing, and the Data Form option works well for editing and deleting records in the database. The result is that Excel can handle all of the requirements.

How It Will Be Laid Out

You could lay out this application in a number of ways. You must follow only one rule: don't put anything under the database, so it can grow without interference.

The layout adopted for this example is shown in Figure 12-1. This layout includes a macro sheet and a worksheet. The macro sheet also contains a list of range names. The worksheet can be broken into two vertical segments. The left segment is used for two screens—one that serves as a title screen and the other that serves as a backdrop for entering the sales orders and other activities. The right segment contains the database. As you can see, the one layout rule was adhered to in forming this layout.

Building the Worksheet

There is no right or wrong place to start. Here, you'll start with the screens and then do the database.

Building Screens

The order entry application you will create has two sections of the worksheet that will be used as screens—what the user will see on the screen at various times. The first of the two screens is the title screen that is used at startup and whenever the user completes an operation. This screen is shown

Figure 12-1.   *Layout of the macro sheet and worksheet*

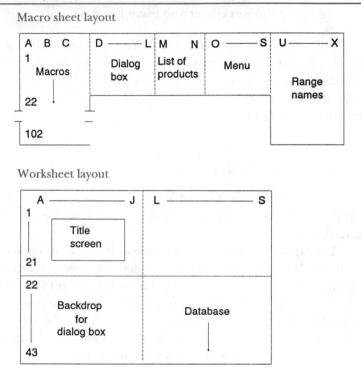

Macro sheet layout

Worksheet layout

in Figure 12-2 in its finished form. The other screen is really a blank screen to be used as a backdrop for other operations.

The normal frame (row and column headings, gridlines, and scroll, Formula, and Status bars) seen on an Excel screen is turned off; it has no bearing on this application. In its place you will construct a new border with Excel's Format Border option and by adjusting the column widths and row heights as shown in Figure 12-3. Your computer should be on, Excel loaded, and a blank worksheet on your screen.

1.   Click on Maximize on the worksheet and then drag the columns and rows to the widths and heights shown in Figure 12-3. It is not necessary that they be precisely as shown since it is only a title screen.

Figure 12-2.    *Title screen in its finished form*

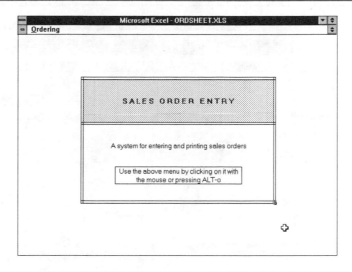

The title box looks off-center in Figure 12-3 because the borders and bars are turned on.

2. Select B3:B19 and I3:I19 at the same time (by pressing and holding (CTRL) while selecting with the mouse), and then select Left and Right from the Format Border option.

3. Select B3:I3, B9:I9, and B19:I19 together, and then select Top and Bottom from the Format Border option. (Ignore the grayed Left and Right boxes. This is telling you that some cells you selected also have Left and Right turned on.)

4. Select C4:H8, then select Shade from the Format Border option, and click on OK.

5. Enter the lines of text shown in Figure 12-3, placing them in C6, C12, D15, and D16. Make the first line bold by clicking on the Bold tool. Highlight each row in turn and center the text across the ranges, C6:H6, C12:H12, D15:G15, and D16:G16. For the title, place one space between each character and three spaces between each word.

Figure 12-3.   *Column widths and row heights for the title screen*

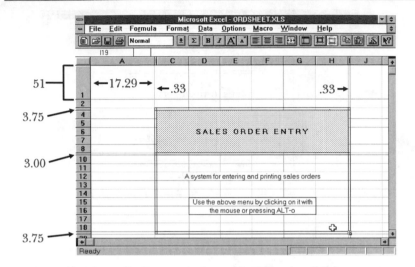

6. Highlight D15:G17. Click on the Outline Border tool (sixth from the right on the Standard toolbar).

For the second screen there is nothing that needs to be done. The only other thing to do on the worksheet is to construct the database.

Preparing for the Database

To prepare for the databases, you need to enter a set of headings and adjust the column widths.

1. Scroll your screen so you can see L21:T40. You want to put the database in this location so you will not run into the short rows or narrow columns used in the title screen. If you cannot get a full 20 rows, make sure you have maximized the worksheet window. If you still cannot get 20 rows, make sure L21 is in the upper-left corner,

and ignore the fact that you have one or two fewer rows on the bottom.

2. Widen columns L and O to 20, and narrow columns P, Q, and R to 7. Again, you can hold down (CTRL) while selecting with the mouse to do L and O together and then do P, Q, and R together.

3. Enter the headings in row 26 that are shown in Figure 12-4 plus a heading of "Total" in S26. Center them, make them bold, and put a bottom border under them using the three respective tools on the Standard toolbar.

Most of the remaining work involves the macro sheet, so as a final step with the worksheet, save it.

4. Click on the Save tool, change to the directory you use to store worksheets (\SHEET here), and name the file ORDSHEET.

Figure 12-4.   *Database area*

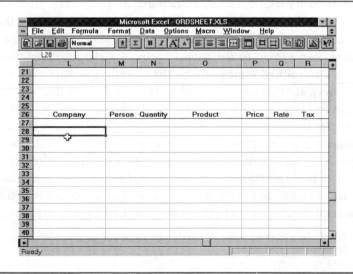

Building the Macros

The next step is to automate the worksheet. This is done through a combination of recording macros and then modifying them. The macros are divided into five sections. In the first section you will build a means to prepare and control the worksheet and the screen. In the next section you will build a dialog box to accept entries for the database and then build the macros to update the database with those entries. In the third section you will record the macros to print the database, save the worksheet, and quit Excel. In the fourth section you will build macros to use Excel's Data Form to edit the database. In the final section you will build a custom menu and a macro that provides access to the rest of the macros. These macros provide the means for entering, editing, and printing data and saving and quitting the application. They also represent the five choices in the menu built in the final section.

While this may sound like a major undertaking, you will find it goes faster than you think. It is not a trivial task either. Remember that you are building a fully operable, complete application that allows a novice to do some sophisticated things with Excel. By working through this application, you should be able to build almost any application of your own.

Think of a series of interconnected macros as a logic path, a set of stepping stones with branches along the way. You start out on the path and come to a branch. You make a choice, branch off, do some task, and then return to the original path. In this application you start out with a menu that provides five choices: entering, editing, printing, saving, and quitting. You choose one, do it, and then return to the menu again to make another choice. Figure 12-5 shows a simplified logic path for the order entry application.

There are two ways to build a series of macros that represent an application: a few large macros or many small macros. Using a few large macros—for example, one macro for each item on the menu—has the benefit of clearly delineating the program flow. Many small macros, which you would combine to perform the menu functions, have two overpowering benefits. First, it is easier to build and test the small macros because they are small. Second, there are small tasks that are required in several of the larger functions. By building one small macro to do these tasks and then calling these macros in each of

Figure 12-5. *Order entry logic path*

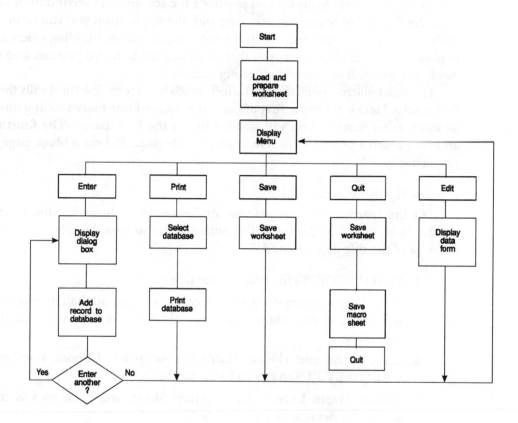

the larger functions, you reduce repetition. Therefore, the instructions that follow have you build many small macros and then combine them to carry out the menu choices.

Preparing and Controlling the Worksheet

Five separate macros are used to prepare and control the worksheet and the screen. The first cleans up and positions the screen. The second undoes what the first did so when you are done with the application you can return to the normal Excel environment. It is important, as you are building macros, to always have *reversing* macros so that when you test a macro you can undo its effects. You will see several reversing macros here.

The third macro opens the worksheet (reads it in from disk) and calls the first macro. Here you see the first of many instances of one macro calling one or more other macros. You will also get to test the first macro. The fourth and fifth macros position the screen on the title page and on a blank page, respectively.

Preparing the Worksheet

The first macro to be created turns off the row and column headings and the gridlines, as well as the scroll, Formula, and Status bars. Finally, it selects the area of the title page desired.

1. Press (CTRL)-(HOME) to return to the title page.

2. Create a new macro sheet, narrow column A to about half its original width, and widen column B so that only columns A, B, and C fit on the screen.

3. Click on B6 and choose Macro Set Recorder. Choose Window ORDSHEET.XLS to return to the worksheet.

4. Choose Macro Record, type **Prepare.Sheet**, and click on OK to accept the default shortcut key "a."

5. Choose Options Display, select Gridlines and Row and Column Headings to turn them off, and click on OK.

6. Choose Options Workspace, click on Status bar, Scroll bars, and Formula bar to turn them off, and click on OK.

7. Choose Options Toolbars and click on Hide to turn off the Standard toolbar.

8. Click on the lower-right intersection of the border to park the active cell.

9. Choose Macro Stop Recorder to complete the first macro, and choose Window Macro1 to switch to the macro sheet.

10. Type the comments shown here:

5			
6	⊹	Prepare.Sheet (a)	
7		=DISPLAY(FALSE,FALSE,FALSE,TRUE,0,,TRUE,FALSE,1)	Turn off grid & border
8		=WORKSPACE(FALSE,,FALSE,FALSE,FALSE,FALSE,"/",FALSE,F	Turn off bars
9		=SHOW.TOOLBAR(1,FALSE)	Turn off toolbar
10		=SELECT("R19C9")	Park active cell
11		=RETURN()	
12			

If for some reason your macro is not the same as the one shown here, turn the Formula back on and edit your macro so it looks like the one here. When you are done, turn off your Formula bar.

11. Click on B1 of the macro sheet, choose Macro Set Recorder, and choose Window ORDSHEET.XLS.

Restoring the Worksheet

Next you need a macro to restore the gridlines, headings, and bars to reverse the steps you just completed.

1. Choose Macro Record, type **Return.Sheet**, press (TAB), type **b**, and click on OK.

2. Choose Options Display, click on Gridlines and Row and Column Headings to turn them on, and click on OK.

3. Choose Options Workspace, select Status bar, Scroll bars, and Formula bar to turn them on, and click on OK.

4. Choose Options Toolbars and click on Show to turn the Standard toolbar on.

5. Choose Macro Stop Recorder to complete the second macro, and choose Window Macro1 to switch to the macro sheet.

6. Type the comments shown here:

12		
13	Return.Sheet (b)	⊕
14	=DISPLAY(FALSE,TRUE,TRUE,TRUE,0,,TRUE,FALSE,1)	Turn on grid & border
15	=WORKSPACE(FALSE,,FALSE,TRUE,TRUE,TRUE,"/",FALSE,FA	Turn on bars
16	=SHOW.TOOLBAR(1,TRUE)	Turn on toolbar
17	=RETURN()	
18		

7. Click on B19 of the macro sheet, choose Macro Set Recorder, and choose Window ORDSHEET.XLS.

Opening the Worksheet

The third macro opens the worksheet and calls the Prepare.Sheet macro.

1. If your screen has been maximized, click on the Restore button or choose Control Restore to reduce it to normal size. Click on Save and choose File Close. That should leave you with the macro sheet as the active sheet.

2. Choose Macro Record, type **Order.Load**, press (TAB), type **c**, and click on OK.

3. Choose File Open, type **ordsheet**, and press (ENTER) to reopen the worksheet.

4. Click on the Maximize button and press (CTRL)-(a) to run the Prepare.Sheet macro.

5. Choose Macro Stop Recorder to complete the macro, and choose Window Macro1 to switch to the macro sheet.

6. Type these comments:

18			
19	⊕	Order.Load (c)	
20		=OPEN("C:\SHEET\ORDSHEET.XLS")	Load Worksheet
21		=WINDOW.MAXIMIZE()	Maximize Window
22		=RUN("Macro1!Prepare.Sheet",FALSE)	
23		=RETURN()	
24			

7. Click on B25 of the macro sheet, choose Macro Set Recorder, and choose Window ORDSHEET.XLS.

Positioning the Screen

Two macros are used to position the screen. The first positions the screen on the title page and the second on the blank page underneath. Build both of these together and then modify the macro to separate them.

1. Choose Macro Record, type **Return.Home**, press (TAB), type **h** for the shortcut key, and click on OK. (The "h" was chosen for "Home," but it could be any letter not already used.)

2. Press (CTRL)-(HOME) and click on the lower-right intersection of the border around the title. That completes the title page positioning.

3. Turn on Scroll Lock, press (PGDN), and press (DOWN ARROW). Turn off Scroll Lock. That positions the blank page.

4. Choose Macro Stop Recorder to complete the macro, and choose Window Macro1 to switch to the macro sheet.

You now need to split this into two macros. Additionally, your macro recorder may not have recorded (CTRL)-(HOME) since you immediately went to I19 (R19C9). The recorder left out what it thought was an unnecessary step since you did nothing at A1. If this happened, you need to add that step because it positions the worksheet on the screen prior to parking the active cell I19.

5. By typing and using Drag and Drop, rearrange the Return.Home macro by adding the Next.Page title and the comments so that it looks like the following illustration. (You may want to turn on the scroll bars and the Formula bar. If so, do it with the Options Workspace option, but turn them off again before going back to the worksheet.)

24			
25	Return.Home (h)		
26	=SELECT("R1C1")		Go home
27	=SELECT("R19C9")		Park active cell
28	=RETURN()		
29			
30	Next.Page (n)		
31	=VPAGE(1)	⇩	Down one page
32	=VLINE(1)		Down one line
33	=RETURN()		
34			

Do not type the (n) after Next.Page until after you have defined the range name in the next step. If you include it in the range name, it will cause problems when the macro is run.

6. Select the cell that contains the Next.Page macro name (B30 in the illustration). Choose Formula Define Name, click on Command macro, press (TAB), type **n** for the shortcut key, and click on **OK**.

7. Click on B35 of the macro sheet (use (PGDN) if necessary), choose Macro Set Recorder, and choose Window ORDSHEET.XLS.

You may be wondering about the R1C1 nomenclature in place of the familiar A1 nomenclature. R1C1, as you probably figured out, stands for row 1, column 1. When you record a macro, this is the system used by Excel. When you write your own macros, you may also use this system, making sure the R1C1 is enclosed in quotation marks, or you may use A1 without quotation marks but preceded with an exclamation point (!). For example, =SELECT("R1C1") is the same as =SELECT(!$A$1). The R1C1 is interpreted as an absolute reference, equivalent to $A$1. If you want a relative reference, to move the active cell relative to its current position, place [] around the numbers. For example =SELECT("RC[2]") moves the active cell two columns to the right, and =SELECT("R[-2]C[3]") moves the active cell up two rows and to the right three columns.

Testing and Debugging Your Macros

You now have five macros: Prepare.Sheet, Return.Sheet, Order.Load, Return.Home, and Next.Page. Because of their small size, using the recorder to create them, and looking at the illustrations in this book, they are probably error free. You still need to prove that by trying them out. Do so now.

1. Choose File Close and click on No to not save any changes.

2. Press (CTRL)-(c) to execute the Order.Load macro. This macro calls the Prepare.Sheet macro, so you actually are testing two macros in one.

You should get the title screen displayed with nothing other than the Title bar and Menu bar at the top of your screen, as shown in Figure 12-6. If you did not get that, first study what you did get. Repeat the macro several times to observe what is going on. Look at any error messages. Often with macros you get an error message that tells you the line number on the macro sheet of the erroneous macro function. If you type in macro functions, spelling errors are frequently the cause. After looking at what happens when you execute the macro, go over to the macro sheet and look carefully at the offending macro. Look at spelling, parentheses, quotation marks, and macro function arguments. Compare what you see with the illustrations shown here. These illustrations produced operating macros (really!).

3. Press (CTRL)-(n) to position the blank page on your screen. Except for the Title and Menu bars (and the mouse pointer) you should have a blank screen.

4. Press (CTRL)-(h) to position the title page on your screen.

5. Press (CTRL)-(b) to return to normal Excel display mode.

You should now have five proven macros. If you do not, fix them before going on.

Figure 12-6.   *Title screen*

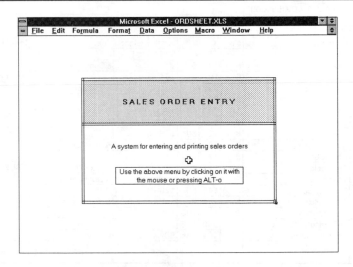

Building the Data Entry Tools

The data entry tools consist of a data entry dialog box and two macros—
one for viewing the database and one for updating it. You also need to enter
some formulas on the worksheet.

Building a Dialog Box

Building a dialog box is a fairly complex task. You start out with a blank
rectangle on the screen and add buttons, list boxes, check boxes, text boxes,
and text, and then you size and position each item. Figure 12-7 shows the
completed macro sheet specification for the dialog box used in this application, shown in Figure 12-8. Thankfully, Microsoft includes the Dialog Editor
as a separate program with Excel. The Dialog Editor allows you to build dialog
boxes on the screen interactively by sizing and dragging the components. That
way you can see what you are doing as you are doing it. Without the Dialog
Editor you would have to take a stab at the specifications, execute the macro
on the worksheet, observe the results, come back to the macro sheet to make
a correction, and then try it again.

Figure 12-7.   *Completed dialog box specification*

	D	E	F	G	H	I	J	K	L
1	Orders.Dialog (d)								
2	=DIALOG.BOX(E6:K22)								
3	=RETURN()								
4									
5	Field Type	No.	X	Y	Width	Height	Text	Init/Res.	Name
6	Dialog Box				505	161			
7	Text Field	5	10	6			&Company:		
8	Text Box	6	10	21	254			American	Company
9	Text Field	5	300	8			&Product:		
10	Text box (linked)	6	300	24	192			9.5x13 Cla	Product
11	List box (linked)	16	300	48	192	84	Orders.XLM!Produc	4	
12	Text field	5	12	44			&Salesperson:		
13	Text box	6	12	60	116			Tom	Person
14	Number box	5	12	84			&Quantity:		
15	Check box	8	12	100	116			5	Quantity
16	Text field	13	12	124			&Taxable?	TRUE	Taxable
17	Text field	5	144	44			&Tax Rate:		
18	Number box	8	144	60	120			0.081	Rate
19	Text field	5	144	84			&Unit Price:		
20	Number box	8	144	100	120			6.75	Price
21	OK button (default)	1	300	136			Enter		
22	Cancel button	2	404	136	88		Cancel		
23									
24									

Figure 12-8. *The working dialog box*

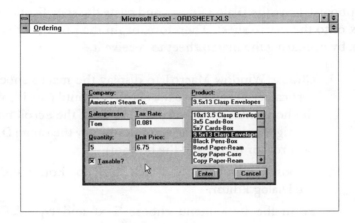

You load the Dialog Editor through the Control menu Run option. When started, the Dialog Editor presents a blank dialog box on the screen and its own menus. Two of the menus, File and Edit, are fairly standard, but the third menu, Item, is unique to the Dialog Editor. The Item menu, shown here, allows you to choose from among the various types of items that you can place in a dialog box.

You choose an item, and then place and size it in the blank dialog box. If there is text involved, you can type the text. After you have placed an item, or at any time, you can use the Edit menu to edit all of the specifications for the item, including its size and placement. This is really the best of both worlds. You can see on the screen how you want to size and align items, and with the Edit Info option you can see the specific coordinates to determine if items are truly lined up.

When you are done constructing a dialog box, you copy it to the Clipboard, leave the Dialog Editor, and paste the specifications for the dialog box onto the macro sheet. Therefore, begin the process of creating a dialog box by preparing the macro sheet to receive it.

1. Choose Window Macro1 to display the macro sheet. Click on the vertical scroll bar above the Scroll box until row 1 is visible. Click on the horizontal scroll bar to the right of the Scroll box and then on the right-pointing scroll arrow to display the range D1:H21 (this can be a row or two less at the bottom).

2. Choose Control Run, and click on Dialog Editor and on OK to load the Dialog Editor.

3. From the Item menu choose Text and type **&Company:**. The ampersand (&) places the underline under the letter that follows the & ("C" in this case)—the underline appears later, not while you are entering it. If you want to include an ampersand in the text, enter two of them.

4. Choose Item Edit Box and click on OK to accept the default Text Box. A text box appears under Company. Drag the right edge of the text box to the right about three quarters of an inch. Look at Figure 12-8.

5. Choose Item Text and type **&Salesperson:**.

6. Choose Item Edit Box and click on OK to accept the default Text Box. A text box appears under Salesperson. Drag the right edge of the box to the left about three quarters of an inch.

7. Choose Item Text and type **&Quantity:**.

8. Choose Item Edit Box and click on Number and on OK to create a number box. A number box appears under Quantity. Drag the right edge of the box to the left about three quarters of an inch.

9. Choose Item Button, and click on Check Box and on OK.

10. Choose Edit Info, type **4** and **123** in the text boxes opposite X and Y, respectively, and type **&Taxable?** in the Text text box and **True** in the Init/Result text box, as shown here:

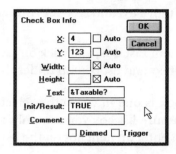

The Init/Result field contains the initial value and the result of anything entered in the dialog box. By saying "TRUE," you are saying that the check box should, by default, be checked, and that a sale is by default taxable.

11. Click on OK to close the Check Box Info dialog box. Then drag the bottom edge of your dialog box down about one quarter of an inch and drag the right edge outward about an inch as shown in Figure 12-9. Do not worry about absolute precision. It is not important and you will do some correcting later on the macro sheet.

Figure 12-9.   *Dialog box under construction*

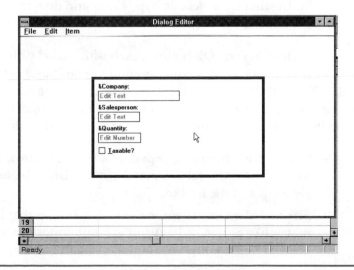

12. Choose Item Text and type **&Product:**. Drag this text to the upper right.

13. Choose Item List Box, and click on Linked and on OK. If necessary, drag the text and list box up under the Product text.

A linked list box is one in which the selected item in the list appears in the text box. On a pure list box you can only select items on the list. With a linked list, you can enter an item not on the list by typing it into the text box.

14. Choose Item Text and type **&Tax Rate:**. Drag it into place opposite Salesperson.

15. Choose Item Edit Box, and click on Number and on OK to create a number box. A number box appears under Tax Rate (if not, drag it there). Drag the right edge of the box to the left about one inch—so the right edge lines up with the Company text box.

16. Choose Item Text and type **&Unit Price:**. Drag it opposite **Quantity**.

17. Choose Item Edit Box, and click on Number and on OK to create a number box. A number box appears under Unit Price (if not, drag it there). Drag the right edge of the box to the left about one inch—so the right edge lines up with the Tax Rate and Company text boxes.

18. Choose Item Button and click on OK to produce an OK command button that is the default. Type **Enter** and drag the button under the left edge of the list box.

You can have several OK buttons, each with a label different than OK on them. One of the buttons is considered the default and activates when you press (ENTER). All OK or Cancel buttons close the dialog box. The OK buttons use the information entered into the dialog box to update the Init/Result area in the macro sheet. The Cancel buttons do not update the Init/Result area.

19. Choose Item Button, accept the default of Cancel, and click on OK to produce a Cancel command button. Drag the button under the right edge of the list box.

20. Size and align each item in the dialog box so that it looks approximately like Figure 12-10. Again, it is not important to have the dialog box be an exact duplicate of the one shown here.

12

21. Choose Edit Select Dialog to select the entire dialog box. Choose Edit Copy to copy the dialog box specifications to the Clipboard.

22. Minimize the Dialog Editor. Click on E6 on the macro sheet and choose Edit Paste. The specifications appear on the macro sheet. The specifications on your macro will probably be different than what is shown here.

23. Narrow the columns and add the column headings shown in Figure 12-11.

Dialog Box Settings

There are eight columns in a dialog box's specifications (columns E through L in Figure 12-11). The first contains a number that specifies the type of item in the dialog box (see the list that follows). The second and third columns are the x and y coordinates on which the upper-left corner of each item is located. The fourth and fifth columns are the height and width of each item. You can get the position of the lower-right corner of each item by adding the width to the x coordinate and the height to the y coordinate. Measurement starts in the upper-left corner of the dialog box. The sixth column contains any text associated with them. The character preceded by an ampersand (&)

Figure 12-10.   *Finished dialog box in the Dialog Editor*

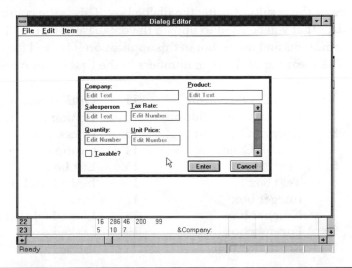

Figure 12-11.   *Dialog box settings with headings*

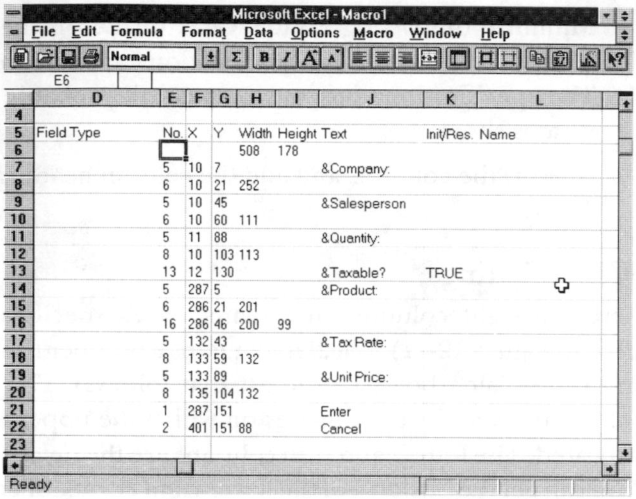

has an underline placed beneath it and, during operation of the dialog box, that item can be accessed by pressing (**ALT**) and the underlined character. In the case of a list box, the text column eventually contains the reference to the list that is used in the box. The Init/Result column contains either initial values or the results of using the dialog box. This is the column that contains the data that will be used to update the database. The final column is meant for comments and notes, but in this application it is used for the range name.

The meaning of the type numbers in the first column are as follows:

1	Default OK button	11	Option button group
2	Normal Cancel button	12	Option button
3	Normal OK button	13	Check box
4	Default Cancel button	14	Group box
5	Text	15	List box
6	Text box	16	Linked list box
7	Integer box	17	Icon
8	Number box	18	Linked File list box
9	Formula box	19	Linked drive and directory
10	Reference box		list box

20	Directory text	23	Picture button
21	Drop-down list box	24	Help button
22	Drop-down edit/list box		

The first row contains the specifications for the dialog box itself. From then on, most items take two lines—one for the text label and the second for the text edit box. The order in which items are listed is the order in which they will be addressed. It is the order in which you would proceed if you pressed (TAB) on each field. There is one change to this order that is worthwhile—to move the product text, text box, and list box (three rows) up under the company text box. Move the product rows and enter the field types and range names next.

1. Insert three rows above the Salesperson text. Remember to insert across all seven columns that are being used, but not across the columns to the left that contain the macros.

2. Drag and drop the three product rows (D17:K19) to the newly created rows, and delete the original product rows.

3. Enter the field types in column D and the range names in column L, as shown in Figure 12-12.

4. Select K8:L20, choose Formula Create Names, click on Top Row to turn it off, on Right Column to turn it on, and on OK. The names to the right of the Init/Result column name some of the cells in the Init/Result column. For example, K8 is named Company and K13 is named Person.

5. Scroll the screen to the right, click on M5, type **Products**, press (DOWN ARROW), and continue to type the list of products shown in Figure 12-13. This is the list of products that will be displayed in the list box in the dialog box.

6. Select the full list, choose Formula Define Name, modify the range referred to as $M$6:$M$16, and click on OK to accept the defaults presented and name the list Products.

7. Click on J11 (the text field for the product list box) and enter **Orders.XLM!Products** to tie the new list to the list box in the dialog box.

Figure 12-12. *Items and range names on the dialog box specifications*

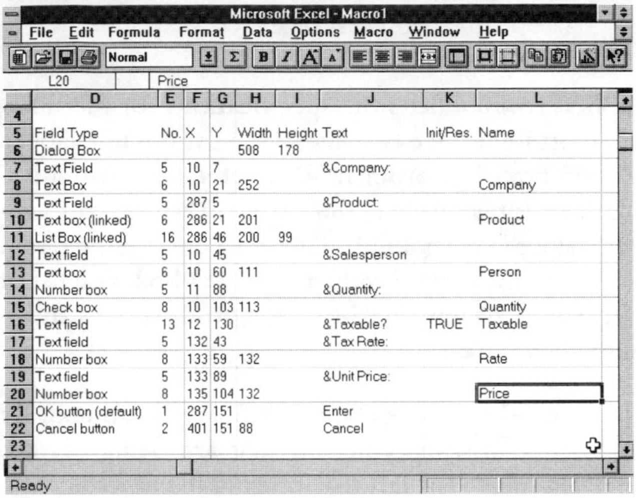

	D	E	F	G	H	I	J	K	L
4									
5	Field Type	No.	X	Y	Width	Height	Text	Init/Res.	Name
6	Dialog Box				508	178			
7	Text Field	5	10	7			&Company:		
8	Text Box	6	10	21	252				Company
9	Text Field	5	287	5			&Product:		
10	Text box (linked)	6	286	21	201				Product
11	List Box (linked)	16	286	46	200	99			
12	Text field	5	10	45			&Salesperson		
13	Text box	6	10	60	111				Person
14	Number box	5	11	88			&Quantity:		
15	Check box	8	10	103	113				Quantity
16	Text field	13	12	130			&Taxable?	TRUE	Taxable
17	Text field	5	132	43			&Tax Rate:		
18	Number box	8	133	59	132				Rate
19	Text field	5	133	89			&Unit Price:		
20	Number box	8	135	104	132				Price
21	OK button (default)	1	287	151			Enter		
22	Cancel button	2	401	151	88		Cancel		
23									

This completes the dialog box specifications. Now you need only create a small enabling macro and try out your dialog box.

8. Scroll your screen so D1 is visible, click on D1, and type these three macro lines (remember not to type the (d) after the Orders.Dialog until after step 9):

	D	E	F
1	Orders.Dialog (d)		
2	=DIALOG.BOX(E6:K22)		
3	=RETURN()		
4			

9. Select the macro name (Orders.Dialog), choose Formula Define Name, click on Command, press TAB, type **d**, and click on OK.
10. Save the macro sheet with the name ORDERS.XLM.

Next try the dialog box and see what happens.

11. Press CTRL-d. The dialog box should open as shown here:

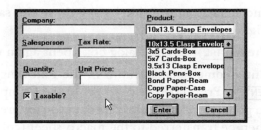

12

Your dialog box may have a few small glitches. For example, the Quantity number box may be too large or the Unit Price label may be too small. Fix any problems your dialog box may have, and then try entering some data.

12. Click on Cancel or press (ESC) to close the dialog box, and then change the width of the Quantity number box (H15) to 104, like the Salesperson text box width.

13. Adjust the X, Y, and width specifications of the other items so items that are over one another have the same X coordinate and width,

Figure 12-13. Product list

	Microsoft Excel - Macro1					
File Edit Formula Format Data Options Macro Window Help						

M18 — Red Pens-Box

	I	J	K	L	M	N
4						
5	Height	Text	Init/Res.	Name	Products	
6	178				10x13.5 Clasp Envelopes	
7		&Company:			3x5 Cards-Box	
8				Company	5x7 Cards-Box	
9		&Product:			9.5x13 Clasp Envelopes	
10				Product	Black Pens-Box	
11	99				Bond Paper-Ream	
12		&Salesperson			Copy Paper-Case	
13				Person	Copy Paper-Ream	
14		&Quantity:			HB Lead-Box	
15				Quantity	Mechanical Pencil	
16		&Taxable?	TRUE	Taxable	No.10 Envelopes	
17		&Tax Rate:			No.2 Pencils-Box	
18				Rate	Red Pens-Box	
19		&Unit Price:				
20				Price		
21		Enter				
22		Cancel				
23						

Ready

and items that are side by side have the same Y coordinate. See Figure 12-14.

14. Press (CTRL)-(d). The dialog box opens again with your corrections.

15. Enter some data as shown in the following illustration and press (ENTER). Press (TAB) twice to get to the Company field and use (TAB) to go from field to field. The data you entered in the dialog box will then be transferred to the macro sheet (column K) as you can see in Figure 12-14.

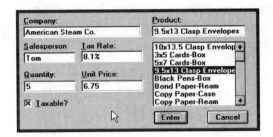

That completes the dialog box. You are now ready to build the macros that will take data placed in column K of the macro sheet and update the database on the worksheet.

Viewing the Database

Next, you need to build a macro that allows you to view the database.

1. Scroll the macro sheet so you can see B35. Click on B35, choose Macro Set Recorder, and choose Window ORDSHEET.XLS.

2. Choose Macro Record, type **View.Database**, press (TAB), type **v** for the shortcut key, and click on OK.

3. Press (CTRL)-(a) to prepare the worksheet.

4. Turn on Scroll Lock, press (CTRL)-(PGDN) and (RIGHT ARROW) to move horizontally, and press (PGDN) to move vertically. Turn off Scroll Lock.

5. Click on the Company name heading on the worksheet. Choose Macro Stop Recorder. Choose Window ORDERS.XLM.

6. Document your new macro as shown here:

12

34		
35	View.Database (v)	
36	=RUN("ORDERS.XLM!Prepare.Sheet",FALSE)	Prepare worksheet
37	=HPAGE(1)	Position worksheet
38	=HLINE(1)	
39	=VPAGE(1)	
40	=SELECT("R26C12")	Upper left DB corner
41	=RETURN()	
42		

7. Click on B43, choose Macro Set Recorder, and choose Window
   ORDSHEET.XLS.

The next step is to build the formulas for transferring the orders from
the macro sheet to the worksheet.

8. Press (CTRL)-(b) to return to the normal Excel screen. Scroll the screen
   so you can see and click on L22.

9. Beginning in L22, type the external reference formulas to match the
   field names in row 26. The first is **=ORDERS.XLM!Company**.
   Repeat this process for the Person, Quantity, Product, Price, and
   Rate fields.

Figure 12-14. *Data transferred from the dialog box*

	D	E	F	G	H	I	J	K	L
4									
5	Field Type	No.	X	Y	Width	Height	Text	Init/Res.	Name
6	Dialog Box				508	178			
7	Text Field	5	10	6			&Company:		
8	Text Box	6	10	21	252			America	Company
9	Text Field	5	286	6			&Product:		
10	Text box (linked)	6	286	21	200			9.5x13 Cl	Product
11	List Box (linked)	16	286	46	200	99	Orders.XLM!Prod	4	
12	Text field	5	10	45			&Salesperson		
13	Text box	6	10	60	111			Tom	Person
14	Number box	5	10	88			&Quantity:		
15	Check box	8	10	103	111			5	Quantity
16	Text field	13	10	130			&Taxable?	TRUE	Taxable
17	Text field	5	133	45			&Tax Rate:		
18	Number box	8	133	59	132			0.081	Rate
19	Text field	5	133	88			&Unit Price:		
20	Number box	8	133	104	132			6.75	Price
21	OK button (default)	1	287	151			Enter		
22	Cancel button	2	401	151	88		Cancel		
23									

Microsoft Excel - ORDERS.XLM

File Edit Formula Format Data Options Macro Window Help

Normal

E6

Ready

10. For Tax (R22), enter the formula,

```
=if(orders.xlm!taxable=true,n22*p22*q22,0)
```

and for Total (S22) enter

```
=n22*p22+r22
```

The first formula calculates the tax by multiplying the quantity (N22) times the price (P22) times the tax rate (Q22), if the sale is taxable, or returns 0 if the sale is not taxable. The second formula calculates the Total Sale by multiplying the quantity (N22) times the price (P22) and adding the tax (R22). To format all future database entries, you'll next format entire columns.

11. Click on the column heading N and format the column with the #,##0 format. Click on the column heading P, hold down the (CTRL) key and click on the column headings R and S, and format all three columns with the #,##0.00 format. Click on the column heading Q, and format the column with the 0.0% custom format.

12. Select L22:S22, choose Edit copy, select L27:L28, choose Edit Paste Special, click on Values, and click on OK. Press (ESC) to turn off the marquee. You now have the beginnings of the database.

13. Select L26:S30 (be sure to include the two blank lines—one is mandatory and the second is insurance so you can add records to the database and maintain the Database range), and choose Data Set Database to establish the database range. Your screen should look like the one shown in Figure 12-15.

Updating the Database

You are now ready to build a macro that updates the database.

1. Choose Macro Record, type **Add.Record**, press (TAB), type **r** for the shortcut key, and click on OK.

2. Press (CTRL)-(v) to execute the View.Database macro.

3. Press (CTRL)-(DOWN ARROW) and then (DOWN ARROW) again, and press (SHIFT)-(RIGHT ARROW) seven times. You have now selected the first blank line underneath the last record in the database. Pressing

CTRL-DOWN ARROW is an important step because it gets you to the bottom of a database of any length.

4. Choose Edit Insert, make sure Shift Cells Down is selected, and click on OK.

5. Choose Formula Goto, type **L21**, and click on OK. Select the full database record you are creating in L22 (Company name) through S22 (Total sale) by pressing DOWN ARROW and then pressing CTRL-SHIFT-RIGHT ARROW.

6. Choose Edit Copy, click on Company in the heading (that is, cell L26), press CTRL-DOWN ARROW and DOWN ARROW again. Choose Edit Paste Special, click on Values, and click on OK.

7. Press ESC to clear the marquee, press CTRL-h to return to the title screen, and press CTRL-n to display the blank screen.

8. Choose Macro Stop Recorder and choose Window ORDERS.XLM. Your Add.Record macro should look like the one shown in Figure 12-16.

Figure 12-15. *The database range*

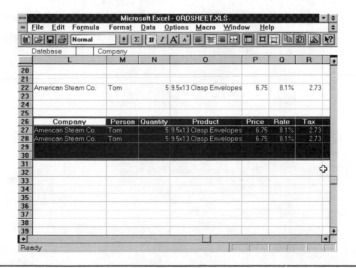

This macro has two problems as it is recorded. Notice that the fourth line (row 46), =SELECT("R29C12:R29C19"), and the eleventh line (row 53), =SELECT("R29C12"), are absolute references. These work only once; the next time you use the macro to add a record, it copies over the record you just added. The references need to be changed to be relative to the current active cell. You will recall that this means that the commands should be =SELECT ("R[1]C:R[1]C[7]") and =SELECT("R[1]C").

9. Change line four and line eleven (row 46 and row 53) to =SELECT("R[1]C:R[1]C[7]") and =SELECT("R[1]C"), respectively, and add the comments shown in Figure 12-17. (You need to turn on the Formula bar by choosing Options workspace and clicking on Formula Bar.)

10. Click on B60 (scroll the screen if necessary), choose Macro Set Recorder, and choose Window ORDSHEET.XLS. Also, if you have not already, choose Options Workspace and turn off the Formula bar.

Figure 12-16.   *Add.Record macro as recorded*

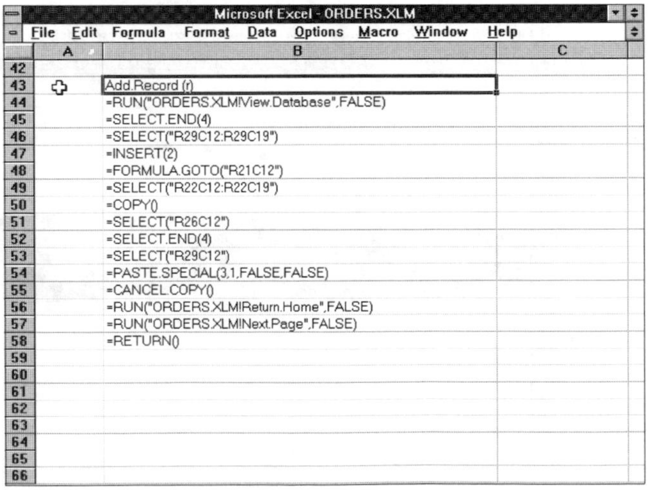

Figure 12-17. Corrected Add.Record macro

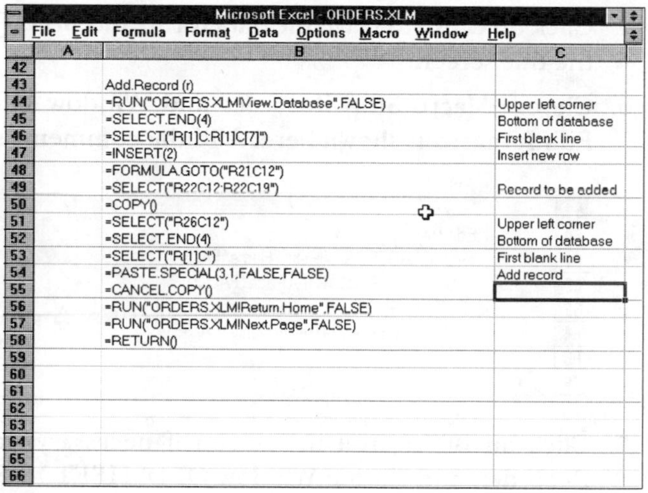

Using Data Form for Editing

With a database in place, you now need to be able to edit and delete records. Excel has a built-in capability for this in the Data Form option. Build a macro to use this feature next.

1. Choose Macro Record, type **Edit.It**, press (TAB), type **e** ("e" may already be the default), and click on OK.

2. Press (CTRL)-(h) and (CTRL)-(n) to assure that the worksheet is positioned correctly.

3. Choose Data Form. Excel's data form is displayed, as shown in Figure 12-18.

With the data form you can edit individual fields of a record, add and delete records, and find records based on criteria you enter. Yes, you could have used this in place of the dialog box you built, but then you would not have had such an excellent opportunity to build a dialog box.

4. Click on the scroll bar to go from record to record, or use the Find buttons.

5. Click on Close to leave the data form, and press (CTRL)-(h) to display the title screen.

6. Choose Macro Stop Recorder and Window ORDERS.XLM. The Edit.It macro is shown here. Add the comments shown.

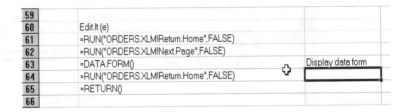

59		
60	Edit.It (e)	
61	=RUN("ORDERS.XLM!Return.Home",FALSE)	
62	=RUN("ORDERS.XLM!Next.Page",FALSE)	
63	=DATA.FORM()	Display data form
64	=RUN("ORDERS.XLM!Return.Home",FALSE)	
65	=RETURN()	
66		

7. Click on B67 (scroll the screen if necessary), choose Macro Set Recorder, and choose Window ORDSHEET.XLS.

Figure 12-18.   *Excel's data form*

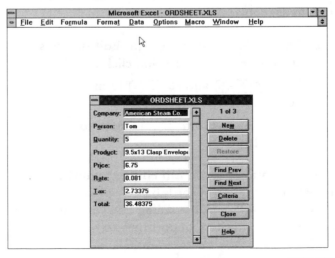

Printing, Saving, and Quitting

You next need to be able to print and save your worksheet and leave Excel. Build macros for those purposes now.

Building a Printing Macro

The printing macro is actually two macros: one to select and set the print area and the other to do the printing. Build both of these next.

1. Choose Macro Record, type **Select.Database**, press (TAB), type **f** (if necessary) for the shortcut key, and click on OK.

2. Press (CTRL)-(v) to execute the View.Database macro.

3. Press (SHIFT)-(CTRL)-(RIGHT ARROW) and (SHIFT)-(CTRL)-(DOWN ARROW) to select the database.

4. Choose Options Set Print Area to define the print area.

5. Choose Macro Stop Recorder and Window ORDERS.XLM.

6. Change the third line (B69) to read

    =SELECT("ORDSHEET.XLS!DATABASE")

    and add the comment shown here:

66	
67	Select.Database (f)
68	=RUN("ORDERS.XLM!View.Database",FALSE)
69	=SELECT("ordsheet.xls!Database")
70	=SET.PRINT.AREA()
71	=RETURN()
72	

(with comment: Select database)

7. Click on B73 (scroll the screen if necessary), choose Macro Set Recorder, and choose Window ORDSHEET.XLS.

8. Choose Macro Record, type **Print.It**, press (TAB), type **p** for the shortcut key, and click on OK.

9. Choose File Page Setup, click on Header, and click on the date button to left align the date. Then press (TAB) and type **ORDERS** to center the filename. Next, press (TAB), type **Page**, skip one space, and click on the page number button to right align the page number. Click on OK to return to the Page Setup dialog box, click on Footer,

press (TAB), press (DEL) to remove the center-aligned page number, and click on OK to return to the Page Setup dialog box. Turn off the row and column headings if they are on and click on OK.

10. Press (CTRL)-(f) to set the print range, choose File Print, and click on OK in the Print dialog box. The result is shown here:

3/12/92			ORDERS				Page 1
Company	**Person**	**Quantity**	**Product**	**Price**	**Rate**	**Tax**	**Total**
American Steam Co.	Tom	5	9.5x13 Clasp Envelopes	6.75	8.1%	2.73	36.48
American Steam Co.	Tom	5	9.5x13 Clasp Envelopes	6.75	8.1%	2.73	36.48
American Steam Co.	Tom	5	9.5x13 Clasp Envelopes	6.75	8.1%	2.73	36.48

11. Press (CTRL)-(h) to return to the title page.

12. Choose Macro Stop Recorder and Window ORDERS.XLM.

13. Enter the comments shown here:

72		
73	Print.It (p)	
74	=PAGE.SETUP("&L&D&CORDERS&RPage &P","",0.75,0.75,1,1,F,	Set header, margins
75	=RUN("ORDERS.XLM!Select.Database",FALSE)	
76	=PRINT(1,,,1,FALSE,FALSE,1,FALSE,1,180)	Print database
77	=RUN("ORDERS.XLM!Return.Home",FALSE) ⇩	
78	=RETURN()	
79		

14. Click on B80 (scroll the screen if necessary) and choose Macro Set Recorder.

Saving and Quitting

The saving and quitting macros are trivial by comparison to what you have already done. Build them here.

1. Save the macro sheet, choose Window ORDSHEET.XLS, and save the worksheet. Now if something goes wrong, you do not lose anything.

2. Choose Macro Record, type **Save.It**, press (TAB), type **z**, and click on OK.

3. Press (CTRL)-(h) to ensure you are on the title screen and choose **File Save.**

4. Choose **Macro Stop Recorder** and **Window ORDERS.XLM.**

5. Click on B85 (scroll the screen if necessary), choose **Macro Set Recorder,** and choose **Window ORDSHEET.XLS.**

6. Choose **Macro Record,** type **Quit.It,** press (TAB), type **q,** and click on **OK.**

7. Press (CTRL)-(b) to return to the normal Excel display, and press (CTRL)-(z) to save the worksheet.

8. Choose **File Close** and then **File Save** to save the macro sheet.

9. Choose **Macro Stop Recorder.**

One macro function needs to be added to the Quit.It macro: QUIT(). This is the function you use to actually leave Excel.

10. Move the last =RETURN() down one row and type **=QUIT().**

11. Add the comments shown in Figure 12-19.

Figure 12-19.   *The Save and Quit macros*

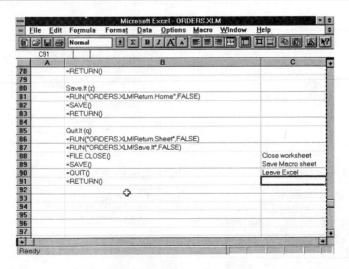

12. Click on B93 (scroll the screen if necessary) and choose Macro Set Recorder.

Building and Using a Menu

To tie together all of the macros you have built into a system with a menu, you need three macros and the menu specifications. One of the macros displays the menu, the second automatically loads the worksheet, and the third is used to combine the data entry and update functions. You also need a macro to return to normal Excel menus. Build these items next beginning with the menu.

1. Scroll the macro sheet so at least O1:S20 is displayed (maximize your window if necessary).

2. Adjust the column width and type in the macros and text shown in Figure 12-20.

Figure 12-20.   *Menu specifications and macros*

	O	P	Q	R	S
1				Display.Menu	
2				=ADD.BAR()	
3				=ADD.MENU(R2,O12:S19)	New menu in O12:S19
4				=SHOW.BAR(R2)	
5				=RETURN()	
6					
7				Excel.Menu (I)	
8				=SHOW.BAR(1)	Display full menus
9				=RETURN()	
10					
11					
12	&Ordering				
13	&Order Entry	Orders.xlm!Enter.It		Enter a new order	
14	-				
15	&Print Database	Orders.xlm!Print.It		Print the list of orders	
16	&Save Database	Orders.xlm!Save.It		Save the Orders database	
17	&Quit Ordering	Orders.xlm!Quit.It		Save database and quit Excel	
18	-				
19	&Edit Database	Orders.xlm!Edit.It		Edit database with Excel Form	
20					

The lower part of the five columns, beginning in row 12, is the menu specification. The first column contains the menu name in O12. The & says to place an underline under the following letter. The remaining items in column O are the options on the menu, again with underlined letters specified. Column P contains the macros that are called when you choose a menu option, column Q is not used, column R contains the comments that are displayed in the Status bar, and column S may contain calls to custom help messages.

The Display.Menu macro creates a new Menu bar in R2, adds a new menu to the Menu bar defined in R2, based on the specification in O12:S19, and shows the Menu bar defined in R2. The Excel.Menu macro returns you to the full Excel Menu bar. The SHOW.BAR (1) argument stands for full menus. The other alternatives are

2	Full Chart menus
3	Nil menus (File only)
4	Info menus
5	Short menus
6	Short Chart menus

Now to continue with building the menu:

3. Click on R1, choose Formula Define name, click on Command, type **m** for the shortcut key, and click on OK. Also click on R7, choose Formula Define name, click on Command, type **1** (lowercase *l*) for the shortcut key, and click on OK.

4. Scroll back to A1 on the macro sheet and enter the Auto_Open macro shown here:

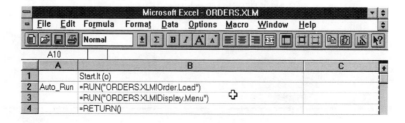

The Auto_Open macro automatically loads the worksheet when you load the macro sheet. That is why the macro sheet has the name ORDERS while the worksheet has the harder to remember name.

5.   Use Formula Define Name to define the macro name Start.It with the shortcut key "o" for "open." Also use Formula Create Names Left after selecting A1:B4 to define Auto_Open.

6.   Insert a new row above the three columns, A17:C17, and type **=show.bar(1)** in B17. With this added macro function, the Excel menus are restored with the Return.Sheet macro.

The final step is to tie the dialog box together with the Add.Record macro and an IF function to see if the user wants to enter additional records.

7.   Create the macro functions shown in Figure 12-21. This can be done by typing the functions and defining the macro name. Alternatively, you can go over to the worksheet; turn on Record; enter the macro

Figure 12-21.   *The Enter.It macro*

	A	B	C
93			
94		Enter.It (i)	
95		=RUN("ORDERS.XLM!Prepare.Sheet",FALSE)	
96		=RUN("ORDERS.XLM!Next.Page",FALSE)	
97	Again	=RUN("ORDERS.XLM!Orders.Dialog",FALSE)	
98		=RUN("ORDERS.XLM!Add.Record",FALSE)	
99	Answer	=INPUT("Do you want to enter another order? y/n",2,"Ordering","y")	
100		=IF(Answer="y",GOTO(ORDERS.XLM!Again))	
101		=RUN("ORDERS.XLM!Return.Home",FALSE)	
102		=RETURN()	
103			

name and shortcut key; press (CTRL)-(a), (CTRL)-(n), (CTRL)-(d), (CTRL)-(r), and (CTRL)-(h); turn off Record; and then come back to the macro sheet, insert two blank lines before running the Return.Home macro, and type the INPUT and IF functions. In either case, select A97:B99 and use Formula Create Names Left to define the two names there.

The Enter.It macro uses the INPUT and IF macro functions to determine if you want to continue to enter orders. The INPUT function, which displays a small dialog box, has this format:

INPUT(*prompt,type*[,*title,default,x,y*])

Title, default, and x and y are optional. *Prompt* is text that is displayed in the dialog box. *Type* is the data type, which has these possible values:

0	Formula
1	Number
2	Text
4	Logical
8	Reference
16	Error
64	Array

You can sum the types. The default, for example, is 7, which is the sum of Formula, Number, Text, and Logical. The title is displayed at the top of the dialog box, the default is a proposed response to the question being asked, and the x and y coordinates are for positioning the dialog box.

The IF macro function has a format similar to a normal IF function:

IF(*condition,true response*[,*false response*])

Condition is a logical statement that evaluates to either True or False. If the condition is True then *true response* is returned; otherwise, *false response* is returned. With a macro function, responses may be GOTO functions, as in the Enter.It macro.

Testing and Correcting the Macros

The normal testing process is primarily one of trying out the macros and seeing what happens. Then, based on what you have seen, you can make the necessary corrections. To speed up that process, print out your macros and the range names, and then compare the results to figures 12-22 and 12-23. Sometimes "desk checking" like this can eliminate the majority of errors, which are usually typographical, before you ever run the macros.

If you haven't done it already, it is a good time to turn on the Status bar, Formula bar, scroll bars, and the Standard toolbar. Use these instructions to print out the macros and the range names:

1. Select A1:C102 on the macro sheet, choose Options Set Print Area, and choose File Print. The result is shown in Figure 12-22.

2. Scroll your macro sheet so T1:X22 is visible. Click on U2, choose Formula Paste Name, and then select Paste List.

3. Type the headings and narrow the columns, as shown in Figure 12-23.

4. Select U1:X33, choose Options Set Print Area, choose File Print, and click on OK. The range names are printed.

5. Compare your printouts to figures 12-22 and 12-23 and make the necessary corrections.

6. If B23 still reads =RUN("Macro1!Prepare.Sheet",FALSE), change Macro 1 to ORDERS.XLM. Also, if any of your macro function names have an underline followed by a letter, for example "Next.Page_n," you defined the range name with the shortcut key in parentheses after the name. In these cases, you will need to redefine the name without the shortcut key after the name.

Working Through the Application

The next step is to execute each part of the macro and see what happens. Use the following steps for that purpose.

Figure 12-22. *Macro listing*

	A	B	C
1		Start.It (o)	
2	Auto_Ru	=RUN("ORDERS.XLM!Order.Load")	
3		=RUN("ORDERS.XLM!Display.Menu")	
4		=RETURN()	
5			
6		Prepare.Sheet (a)	
7		=DISPLAY(FALSE,FALSE,FALSE,TRUE,0,,TRUE,FALSE,	Turn off grid & bord
8		=WORKSPACE(FALSE,,FALSE,FALSE,FALSE,FALSE,"/",	Turn off bars
9		=SHOW.TOOLBAR(1,FALSE)	Turn off toolbar
10		=SELECT("R19C9")	Park active cell
11		=RETURN()	
12			
13		Return.Sheet (b)	
14		=DISPLAY(FALSE,TRUE,TRUE,TRUE,0,,TRUE,FALSE,1)	Turn on grid & bord
15		=WORKSPACE(FALSE,,FALSE,TRUE,TRUE,TRUE,"/",FA	Turn on bars
16		=SHOW.TOOLBAR(1,TRUE)	Turn on toolbar
17		=SHOW.BAR(1)	
18		=RETURN()	
19			
20		Order.Load (c)	
21		=OPEN("C:\SHEET\ORDSHEET.XLS")	Load Worksheet
22		=WINDOW.MAXIMIZE()	Maximize Window
23		=RUN("ORDERS.XLM!Prepare.Sheet",FALSE)	
24		=RETURN()	
25			
26		Return.Home (h)	
27		=SELECT("R1C1")	Go home
28		=SELECT("R19C9")	Park active cell
29		=RETURN()	
30			
31		Next.Page (n)	
32		=VPAGE(1)	Down one page
33		=VLINE(1)	Down one line
34		=RETURN()	
35			
36		View.Database (v)	
37		=RUN("ORDERS.XLM!Prepare.Sheet",FALSE)	Prepare worksheet
38		=HPAGE(1)	Position worksheet
39		=HLINE(1)	
40		=VPAGE(1)	
41		=SELECT("R26C12")	Upper left DB corn
42		=RETURN()	
43			
44		Add.Record (r)	
45		=RUN("ORDERS.XLM!View.Database",FALSE)	Upper left corner
46		=SELECT.END(4)	Bottom of database
47		=SELECT("R[1]C:R[1]C[7]")	First blank line
48		=INSERT(2)	Insert new row
49		=FORMULA.GOTO("R21C12")	
50		=SELECT("R22C12:R22C19")	Record to be adde
51		=COPY()	

12

Figure 12-22. *Macro listing (continued)*

	A	B	C
52		=SELECT("R26C12")	Upper left corner
53		=SELECT.END(4)	Bottom of database
54		=SELECT("R[1]C")	First blank line
55		=PASTE.SPECIAL(3,1,FALSE,FALSE)	Add record
56		=CANCEL.COPY()	
57		=RUN("ORDERS.XLM!Return.Home",FALSE)	
58		=RUN("ORDERS.XLM!Next.Page",FALSE)	
59		=RETURN()	
60			
61		Edit.It (e)	
62		=RUN("ORDERS.XLM!Return.Home",FALSE)	
63		=RUN("ORDERS.XLM!Next.Page",FALSE)	
64		=DATA.FORM()	Display data form
65		=RUN("ORDERS.XLM!Return.Home",FALSE)	
66		=RETURN()	
67			
68		Select.Database (f)	
69		=RUN("ORDERS.XLM!View.Database",FALSE)	
70		=SELECT("ordsheet.xls!Database")	Select database
71		=SET.PRINT.AREA()	
72		=RETURN()	
73			
74		Print.It (p)	
75		=PAGE.SETUP("&L&D&CORDERS&RPage &P","",0.75,0.	Set header, margin
76		=RUN("ORDERS.XLM!Select.Database",FALSE)	
77		=PRINT(1,,,1,FALSE,FALSE,1,FALSE,1,180)	Print database
78		=RUN("ORDERS.XLM!Return.Home",FALSE)	
79		=RETURN()	
80			
81		Save.It (z)	
82		=RUN("ORDERS.XLM!Return.Home",FALSE)	
83		=SAVE()	
84		=RETURN()	
85			
86		Quit.It (q)	
87		=RUN("ORDERS.XLM!Return.Sheet",FALSE)	
88		=RUN("ORDERS.XLM!Save.It",FALSE)	
89		=FILE.CLOSE()	Close worksheet
90		=SAVE()	Save Macro sheet
91		=QUIT()	Leave Excel
92		=RETURN()	
93			
94		Enter.It (i)	
95		=RUN("ORDERS.XLM!Prepare.Sheet",FALSE)	
96		=RUN("ORDERS.XLM!Next.Page",FALSE)	
97	Again	=RUN("ORDERS.XLM!Orders.Dialog",FALSE)	
98		=RUN("ORDERS.XLM!Add.Record",FALSE)	
99	Answer	=INPUT("Do you want to enter another order? y/n",2,"Order	
100		=IF(Answer="y",GOTO(ORDERS.XLM!Again))	
101		=RUN("ORDERS.XLM!Return.Home",FALSE)	
102		=RETURN()	

Figure 12-23.   *List of range names*

	U	V	W	X
1	Range Name	Range	2=Macro	Key
2	Add.Record	=$B$44	2	r
3	Again	=$B$97	0	
4	Answer	=$B$99	0	
5	Auto_Run	=$B$2	0	
6	Company	=$K$8	0	
7	Display.Menu	=$R$1	2	m
8	Edit.It	=$B$61	2	e
9	Excel.Menu	=$R$7	2	l
10	Next.Page	=$B$31	2	n
11	Order.Load	=$B$20	2	c
12	Orders.Dialog	=$D$1	2	d
13	Person	=$K$13	0	
14	Prepare.Sheet	=$B$6	2	a
15	Price	=$K$20	0	
16	Print.It	=$B$74	2	p
17	Print_Area	=$A$1:$C$102	0	
18	Product	=$K$10	0	
19	Products	=$M$6:$M$16	0	
20	Quantity	=$K$15	0	
21	Quit.It	=$B$86	2	q
22	Rate	=$K$18	0	
23	Recorder	=$B$94:$B$16384	0	
24	Return.Home	=$B$26	2	h
25	Return.Sheet	=$B$13	2	b
26	Save.It	=$B$81	2	z
27	Select.Database	=$B$68	2	f
28	Start.It	=$A$10	2	o
29	Taxable	=$K$16	0	
30	View.Database	=$B$36	2	v
31				

12

1. Save and close both the worksheet and the macro sheet. **Choose File Open, select ORDERS.XLM, and click on OK. The macro begins by** displaying the title screen with the single Ordering menu, **as shown** in Figure 12-24.

2. Select the menu, and it should open as shown here:

3. Choose Order Entry, and a dialog box opens in which you can enter the database information.

Figure 12-24.   *Title screen with menu*

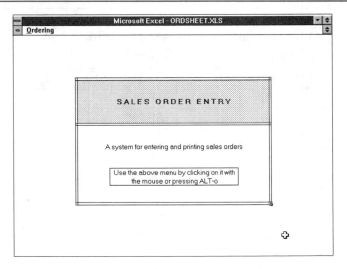

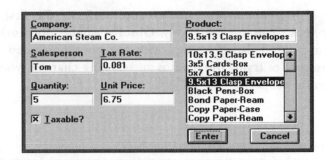

4. Enter a record. What you put in the fields does not matter. Use (TAB) to go from field to field and (ENTER) to complete the entry.

   When you press (ENTER) (or click on the Enter command button) you should see the database being updated. Then the second dialog box appears, asking if you want to enter another record:

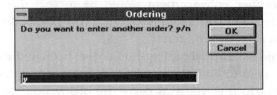

5. Click on OK to accept the y default, and enter another item. Follow the same procedure outlined in step 4. When you get to the "Do you want to enter another order?" prompt, type **n**.

6. Choose Edit Database from the menu and try out the various options on Excel's Data Form.

7. Choose Print Database. The output you get should be similar to that shown earlier in the "Building a Printing Macro" section.

8. Choose Save Database. You should see some indication of that worksheet being saved.

9. Finally, choose Quit Ordering. You should be returned to Windows.

If your macros did not execute perfectly the first time, take heart—it happens to almost everybody. Observe what is not working right. Compare your printed list of macros with the ones presented here. Within a few iterations of trying the macros and making changes, you should get them to operate properly.

Future Enhancements

A large number of improvements can be made to enhance this application.

One easy enhancement is to stop the screen flashing during macro execution by inserting ECHO(FALSE) macro functions at the start of the Prepare.Sheet, Add.Record, and Print.It macros and then an ECHO(TRUE) at the end of each of those macros. This prevents Excel from updating the screen during those macros.

Another enhancement would be to sort the orders by customer and prepare statements from the results. Also, by sorting on the product you can look at sales by product.

One enhancement that should have been in the original product is to add a date field to both the database and the data entry dialog box. Should you want to do this, you can paste the dialog box specifications back into the Dialog Editor, make the changes, and then paste it back on the macro sheet.

You now have an exceptionally powerful tool at your disposal. You can make of it just about whatever you wish.

A

Installing Windows and Excel

Windows and Excel can operate with many combinations of computers, disks, displays, and printers. As a result, providing installation instructions might have become a complex process were it not for the Setup programs that come with both Windows and Excel. These programs do most of the work for you. You have only to determine what equipment you have and then run the Setup programs, answering the questions they ask you.

This appendix describes how to start and use both Windows and Excel Setup programs. In addition, it discusses how you prepare to store the data you create in Excel and how to start and leave the Windows and Excel programs.

The minimum requirements to run Windows 3.1 and Excel 4 are an Intel 80286 or higher processor and 2MB of memory. Of course, you will achieve much faster performance and be able to take full advantage of the multitasking abilities of Windows 3.1 with an Intel 80386 or 80486 processor, and increased memory. Also, you will need at least 10MB of free hard disk to load Windows, and an additional 11MB for a full Excel setup. Additionally, MS-DOS or PC DOS versions 3.1 or higher are required.

There are two options that you need to use to get the most out of Excel. A mouse is highly recommended, though technically not required. Both Excel and Windows are written with the mouse as a primary means of maneuvering through their many windows, menus, and features. Keyboard commands, in most instances, should be looked at as secondary alternatives to using the mouse. A printer is the other option not absolutely necessary for Windows and Excel to run, but you will find it very frustrating not to be able to see your work on paper. Most popular printers are supported by Windows and Excel.

This appendix is written for Windows 3.1 and Excel 4. While most of what is said here may be true for other versions of either product, you need to be on the lookout for differences.

Preparing to Store Data

When you use Excel, you will create documents that you will want to come back and use again at a later time. To preserve this data, you store it in files on a disk. The files are preserved when you turn the computer off. The programs that comprise Windows and Excel are also stored in files on a disk.

With a hard-disk-based system, you also have a floppy disk drive. Therefore, you can store the data on either floppy or hard disks. From the standpoints of both speed and ease of use, it is best to store data, in addition to the programs, on your hard disk. Since hard disks store so much information, they should be divided into directories, which are arbitrarily named areas that you establish for particular purposes. To prepare to store the data you create with Excel, you should create one or more directories.

Creating Directories on a Hard Disk

To store the program files on a hard disk, the Windows and Excel Setup programs automatically create directories for you or use directories you create or already have. The default name for the Windows directory is \WINDOWS and for Excel it is \EXCEL.

You can use existing Excel directories to hold your data files without concern, but it is easier to locate and access your data files if you create separate directories to organize your work. If you want to create your own data directory to hold the Excel data files used in this book, use the following instructions. Your computer should be turned on and you should be at an operating system prompt such as C> or C:\>.

1. Type **cd** and press (ENTER) to make sure you are in the root directory.

2. Type **md\sheet** (short for worksheet) and press (ENTER) to create a directory named SHEET. (If you want to create a directory with a name different than SHEET, replace SHEET with the name you want to use, but this book assumes SHEET is the directory for your data files.)

Copying Your Disks

To protect the original floppy disks that contain the Windows and Excel programs, you need to make a copy or backup of these disks before installing the programs (the Microsoft licenses allow you to make one copy for this, and only this, express purpose). You will need the same number of new or reusable disks as there are disks in the original programs. (The number of disks depends on whether you are using 5 1/4-inch or 3 1/2-inch disks.) You will need to make a copy of each of the original disks, and each disk will be copied onto its own separate backup disk.

You can copy floppy disks in several ways. Since you need only a single floppy drive to run Windows and Excel, instructions are given for using a single floppy drive to copy the original disks. If you wish to use a different method of copying, do so.

The DISKCOPY command used here permanently removes all information on the disk. When reusing a disk, make sure you do not want any information that may be on it.

1. Count the number of disks that came with both Windows and Excel and note their type: 5 1/4-inch 360KB, 5 1/4-inch 1.2MB, 3 1/2-inch 720KB, or 3 1/2-inch 1.44MB—360KB and 720KB disks are labeled DSDD (double-sided double-density) and the 1.2MB and 1.44MB are labeled DSHD (double-sided high-density). Obtain and have handy

the same number and type of new or reusable disks. (Remember, if you use reusable disks you must be willing to get rid of all information currently on them.)

2. If necessary, turn on your computer. You should have already installed DOS on your hard drive and have a basic understanding of how to enter commands from your keyboard, of the size capacity of your disk drives, and of how your disk drives are labeled (A, B, C, and so on).

3. You should be at the DOS prompt (for example C> or C:\>) and in the root directory. If you have been using your computer and/or don't know which directory you are in, type **cd** to return to the root directory.

4. Be sure your backup disks (the ones you are copying onto) are the same size as the disks that came with Windows and Excel. Insert the first Excel or Windows disk to be copied into the floppy disk drive. It is assumed for the remainder of this appendix that this is drive A. If you are using a drive other than A, use your drive letter in place of A (a, a:, or A:) in the instructions that follow.

5. At the DOS prompt, type **diskcopy a: a:** and press (ENTER). You'll see the message "Insert SOURCE diskette in drive A:, Press any key when ready." The "SOURCE diskette" is the Excel or Windows disk being copied. Since it is already in the drive, press (ENTER) to confirm it.

6. When you see the message "Insert TARGET diskette in drive A:," remove the Excel or Windows disk and insert the first new or reusable disk to which you wish to copy. If the disk is a new, unformatted disk, you will see a message, "Formatting while copying," telling you that the disk is also being formatted.

7. Soon you'll again see "Insert SOURCE diskette in drive A:." You must remove the first new or reusable disk and reinsert the first Excel or Windows disk. Then you'll see "Insert TARGET diskette in Drive A:" telling you to remove the first Excel or Windows disk and

reinsert the first new or reusable disk. This will be repeated a couple of times.

Remember that "SOURCE" refers to the disk from which you are copying and is the original Excel or Windows disk, and "TARGET" refers to the disk to which you are copying and is the new or reusable disk that will hold the backup copy. The disk copying process takes several passes, so you must insert and remove each of the disks several times.

8. After several passes, you will see the message "Copy another diskette (Y/N)?" Type **y** and press (ENTER).

9. Once again, you will see the message "Insert SOURCE diskette in drive A:." Remove the disk from drive A that is now the copy of the first Excel or Windows disk, label it similarly to the original disk, insert the second Excel or Windows original disk in drive A, and press (ENTER).

10. Repeat steps 6 through 9 until you have copied all of the disks that came with your Windows and Excel packages.

11. When you have copied all the disks, type **n** in response to "Copy another diskette (Y/N)?" and press (ENTER). You will be returned to the DOS prompt. Remove the last copied disk from drive A and label it.

When you have completed copying all disks, protect the new disks to prevent them from being changed or infected with a virus. A 3 1/2-inch floppy disk is protected by first turning it on its back so you can see the metal hub in the center. Then, with the metal end away from you, slide the small black plastic rectangle in the lower-right corner toward you or toward the outer edge of the disk. This will leave a hole you can see through. A 5 1/4-inch disk is protected by placing an adhesive tab over the notch on the upper right (if you are looking at the disk from the front). Once a disk is protected, it can't be changed until you reverse the protection process.

Place your original Windows and Excel disks in a safe location and use the copies you made for the installation process that follows. Use the original disks only to make additional copies.

A

Running Windows Setup

Running the Windows Setup program is very simple. As a matter of fact, you do it with only a few instructions (assuming your computer is turned on and you are at a DOS prompt—C> or C:\>):

1. Place the Windows Setup disk in drive A or any other floppy disk drive you have and close the door.

2. Type **a:** and press (ENTER) to make drive A current. (If you are using a different drive, type that drive letter in place of A.)

3. Type **setup** and press (ENTER) to start the Setup program.

4. Press (ENTER) again to begin Setup.

5. Press (ENTER) one final time to start the Express Setup.

Express Setup is a quick and easy way of installing Windows. If you are an experienced user who wants to control how Windows is installed, you can choose Custom Setup by typing **c**. Express Setup is sufficient for most users.

Windows Express Setup will begin copying files. Follow the instructions on your screen.

You can install as many printers as you have available, but the first one you choose will be the default—the one automatically used unless you instruct otherwise. When you have selected a printer (by using (DOWN ARROW) to move the highlight to it), click on the Install button or press (ALT)-(I). Then click on the computer port to use (LPT1, COM1, and so on), or use (DOWN ARROW) to move the highlight to it, and click on Install or press (ENTER) to complete installing your first printer.

Use Printers in the Main group Control Panel to install a second or third printer.On some printers—laser printers in particular—you also must set them up. To do that, choose Setup from the Printers dialog box (click on Setup or press (ALT)-(S)). Change the Printer setup options to suit your needs.

You will be asked if you want to run a tutorial on how to use Windows and the mouse. If you are a new user of Windows, you may want to take a break in the setup to run the tutorials. If you choose to continue the setup, you can always run the tutorials later from the Program Manager Help menu. Assuming that to be the case, complete the setup by clicking on Skip Tutorial.

Figure A-1.   *Initial Windows screen*

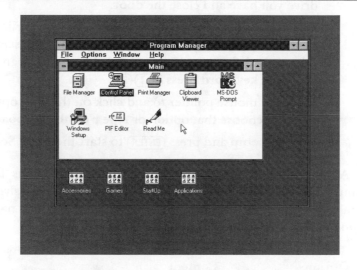

Starting Windows

When you complete Setup, you are asked if you want to reboot your computer or return to DOS. Click on the Reboot icon and type **win** at the DOS prompt to load Windows.

When Windows is loaded, the screen shown in Figure A-1 appears.

The initial screen shows the Main group of Windows system applications under the Program Manager. Your next task is to run Excel Setup.

Running Excel Setup

The Excel Setup program must run under Windows—Windows must be running for Excel Setup to run. Given that, use these instructions to install Excel (Windows should be running from the steps performed in the last section):

1. Place the Excel Disk 1 ("Setup") in drive A or any other floppy disk drive you have and close the door.

2. Move the mouse pointer until it is on the word "File" on the left of the Menu bar (the second bar from the top of the screen). Press and release the left mouse button to "click on" and open the File menu. From the keyboard press (ALT)-(F).

3. Move the mouse pointer to and click on the Run option of the File menu to choose that option or type **r** on the keyboard.

4. Type **a:\setup** and press (ENTER) to start the Excel Setup program.

As in Windows Setup, you have installation options for Excel. The Complete Installation is the easiest and most comprehensive. The Custom Installation allows you to change the directory path and name and install optional files. The options and contents are as follows:

Option	Content
Microsoft Excel	Excel programs and the ReadMe and Help files.
Excel Tutorial	Files used to run the Excel lessons.
Dialog Editor	An application that helps you build dialog boxes.
Macro Translator	An application for translating 1-2-3 macros into Excel macros. This is not discussed in this book.
Macro Library	A library of ready-to-use macros. This is not discussed in this book.
Excel Solver	An application for goal-seeking analysis.
Q+E	An application used to bring information from external database tables into Excel. This is not discussed in this book.

You can get additional information on each optional file from the Setup Information window. The Minimum Installation installs the programs and files needed to run just Excel. Since you don't install the options, you save approximately 6MB of disk space. This book assumes you will perform a complete installation. The next series of steps will complete the installation of Excel.

5. Click on the Complete Installation icon. Excel and all of its sub-directories and files are installed in C:\EXCEL.

6. Click on No when asked if you want to know about Lotus 1-2-3 usage in Excel. You can view this information from the Help menu after you have loaded Excel.

7. Click on Update to have Excel added to the PATH statement of your AUTOEXEC.BAT file.

8. When Setup is complete you will get a message to that effect. Click on OK or press (ENTER). A new group window will appear on the screen entitled "Microsoft Excel 4.0," as shown in Figure A-2.

Starting Excel

To start Excel you must open the Excel group icon. Since you no longer need the Main group window, you'll close it first.

Figure A-2. *Excel group window*

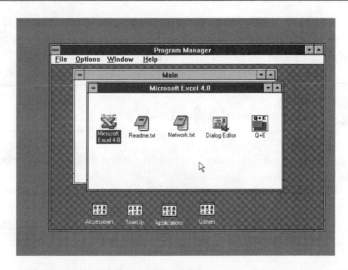

1. Make the Excel group smaller by dragging the lower-right corner of the Excel group window to the upper left until you can see the Main group. Then, click on the Main group window to activate it.

2. Click on the Minimize button in the upper-right corner of the Main group window. Alternatively, from the keyboard you can press (ALT)-(SPACEBAR) and (RIGHT ARROW) to open the Main group's Control menu and then type **n** to choose Minimize.

3. To start Excel, double-click on the Excel application icon or press (ENTER) if it is already highlighted. If Excel is not already highlighted, press (LEFT ARROW) or (RIGHT ARROW) to move the highlight to the Excel application icon.

4. When you start Excel for the first time, you are offered three short lessons:

The Basics	Provides the necessary steps to get you using Excel 4 quickly
What's New	Provides an overview of Excel 4's new features
For Lotus 1-2-3 Users	Shows how to use Lotus 1-2-3 skills in Excel

Click on a lesson button if you want to view that lesson, or click on the Exit to Microsoft Excel button at the bottom of the screen to go directly to the normal Excel screen shown in Figure A-3.

Leaving Excel and Windows

When you wish to leave Excel and return to the DOS prompt, do so with these instructions:

1. Double-click on the bar in the upper-left corner of the Excel window (not the Sheet1 window), or press (ALT) and (SPACEBAR) and type **c**. You will leave Excel and return to Windows.

Figure A-3.   *Normal Excel 4 screen*

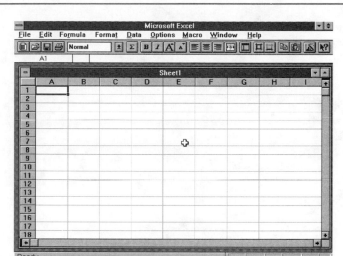

2. Double-click on the bar in the upper-left corner of the **Program Manager** window (not the Excel group window), or press (ALT) and (SPACEBAR) and type **c**.

3. You are asked if you want to end your Windows session. If you exit Windows now, the layout and content of the final **Program Manager** window will be saved. The default is to save changes. If you don't want to save changes to the Program Manager window, the default can be changed by selecting the Options menu and clicking on the Save Changes option. From this point on any changes made to the Program Manager windows will be lost, unless you change the default. Click on OK or press (ENTER). You are returned to DOS.

B

Toolbars

Toolbars provide a quick and easy way to access many of Excel's more frequently used features. There are a total of nine toolbars available for your use, with the Standard toolbar being the default toolbar present when you first install Excel. You can choose to display as many toolbars as you wish, and you can customize the existing toolbars or create your own by adding and deleting individual tools.

Each of the toolbars and their tools are described in the following sections. Tools are listed from left to right across each toolbar.

Standard Toolbar

The Standard toolbar is present when you first install Excel. You can turn it off, replace it with one of the other toolbars, or customize the tools it contains. The Standard toolbar provides a general set of tools covering file handling, formatting, and editing. It has broad applicability to much that you do with Excel.

Tool	Function
New worksheet	Creates a new worksheet.
Open file	Allows you to open an existing document; displays the Open dialog box.
Save file	Saves the active document.
Print	Prints the active document.
Style box	Selects and applies styles to selected cells or defines a new style based on the style of the selected cells.
AutoSum	Creates a SUM function in the active cell with a reference to the contiguous range of numbers either in the column above or in the row to the left.
Bold and Italic	Applies or removes bold or italic type styles to selected cells.
Increase font size	Increases the selected text by one font size.
Decrease font size	Decreases the selected text by one font size.
Left, Center, Right Alignment	Applies left, center, or right alignment to selected cells.
Center across columns	Horizontally centers text from one cell across selected columns.
AutoFormat	Applies cell formatting to ranges of cells.
Outline border	Applies a border around selected cells.
Bottom border	Applies a border on the lower edge of selected cells.
Copy	Copies the selected cell or range to the Clipboard.
Paste Format	Transfers the formatting from the Clipboard to the selected cell or range.
ChartWizard	Assists you in creating or editing charts.

Tool	Function
Help	Displays a question mark for the mouse pointer. When clicked on a command or screen area, context-sensitive help is provided.

Formatting Toolbar

The Formatting toolbar provides the means to quickly apply many different types of formatting. It is very handy if you do a lot of formatting. You can customize the tools it contains, including adding customized formats you use often.

| Normal | ± | MS Sans Serif | ± | 10 | ± | **B** | *I* | U | ⫶ | ≣ | **$** | **%** | **,** | +.0 .00 .00 +.0 | ⊡ | ⊞ |

Tool	Function
Style box	Allows you to select an existing style or name the formats of a selected cell or range to a new style.
Font name box	Displays a list of available fonts.
Font size box	Displays a list of font sizes according to the font selected in the Font name box.
Bold and Italic	Applies or removes bold or italic type styles to selected cells.
Underline	Underlines selected text.
Strikeout	Creates a line through selected text.
Justify align	Changes the spacing between words to fill a line.
Currency style	Changes selected cells to a currency style, for example, $100.00.
Percent style	Changes selected cells to a percent style, for example, 33%.
Comma style	Changes selected cells to a comma style, for example, 1,234.00.

Tool	Function
Increase decimal	Adds a decimal place to a number's display.
Decrease decimal	Takes away a decimal place from a number's display.
Light shading	Adds light shading to selected cells.
AutoFormat	Formats a selected range or worksheet from a list of existing formatting combinations.

Utility Toolbar

The Utility toolbar is a catchall for tools that don't fall in some other category. Included in this toolbar are editing and outlining tools, tools for sorting and checking of spelling, as well a number of others.

Tool	Function
Undo	Allows you to negate your previous action.
Repeat	Repeats the last action.
Paste value	Transfers values from the Clipboard to a selected cell or range.
Zoom in	Increases the magnification of the displayed document.
Zoom out	Decreases the magnification of the displayed document.
Sort ascending	Arranges a selected range in an ascending order.
Sort descending	Arranges a selected range in a descending order.
Lock cell	Ensures the contents of a selected cell or range (in a protected document) are not changed.
Promote	Increases by one level the selected rows or columns in an outline.

Tool	Function
Demote	Decreases by one level the selected rows or columns in an outline.
Show outline symbols	Creates outlining symbols, or displays existing outlining symbols.
Select visible cells	Selects visible cells, but does not show hidden rows or columns.
Button	Assigns a macro to a button you draw with a crosshair pointer.
Text box	Allows you to type text into a box you draw with a crosshair pointer.
Camera	Takes a "picture" of a selected cell or range and allows you to copy and paste the picture to a new document.
Check spelling	Spell checks document or Formula bar text.
Set print area	Establishes the boundaries of the print area.
Calculate now	Calculates document or Formula bar formulas.

Chart Toolbar

The Chart toolbar is automatically placed on the screen when you use a chart window, either by creating a new chart or opening an existing chart. The Chart toolbar provides the means to select the type of chart you will build, or to add legends, arrows, gridlines, or text boxes by simply clicking on a tool.

Tool	Function
Area chart	Creates a chart that shows the magnitude of change over time.

Tool	Function
Bar chart	Creates a series of horizontal bars that allow comparison of the relative size of two or more items at one point in time.
Column chart	Creates a series of vertical columns that allow the comparison of the relative size of two or more items, often over time.
Stacked column chart	Creates a column chart that displays the relative size of two or more items as a whole.
Line chart	Creates a chart that shows trends over time.
Pie chart	Creates a chart that is best used for comparing the percentages of a sum that several numbers represent.
Scatter (XY) chart	Creates a chart that shows the relationship between pairs of numbers and the trends they present.
3-D area chart 3-D bar chart 3-D column chart 3-D perspective column chart 3-D line chart 3-D pie chart	Creates a three-dimensional view of the basic chart.
3-D surface chart	Creates a chart that resembles either a rubber sheet or wireframe stretched over a 3-D column chart.
Radar chart	Creates a chart that shows how data changes in relation to a center point and to each other.
Line/column combination chart	Creates a chart that combines a column and line chart.
Data series combination chart	Creates a chart that combines a column and line chart with three data series, for example, high, low, and close stock prices.

Tool	Function
Preferred chart	Sizes an area where the preferred chart is displayed.
ChartWizard	Helps you create or edit a chart.
Horizontal gridlines	Adds or removes horizontal gridlines to or from a chart.
Legend	Adds or removes a legend to or from a chart.
Arrow	Adds an arrow to a chart that you can drag where you want.
Text box	Allows you to type text that you can drag anywhere on a chart.

Drawing Toolbar

The Drawing toolbar provides the tools to draw lines, arrows, rectangles, ovals, and arcs as well as work with the objects that are drawn. When you use a drawing tool the mouse pointer becomes a crosshair and allows you to perform the functions of the selected tool.

Tool	Function
Line	Draws a line.
Arrow	Draws an arrow on a worksheet or macro sheet, or adds an arrow to a chart.
Freehand line	Draws a freehand line.
Rectangle	Draws a rectangle or square.
Oval	Draws an oval or circle.
Arc	Draws a portion of a circle.
Freehand polygon	Draws a combination of freehand and straight lines.

B

Tool	Function
Filled rectangle Filled oval Filled arc Filled freehand polygon	Fills in the basic design with the window's background pattern.
Text box	Allows you to type text into a box you draw with a crosshair pointer.
Selection	Allows you to select a graphic object.
Reshape	Changes the shape of a polygon.
Group	Combines multiple selected graphic objects into one graphic object.
Ungroup	Splits a grouped graphic object into its individual graphic objects.
Object to front	Puts the selected graphic object in front of all others.
Object to back	Puts the selected graphic object behind all others.
Color	Cycles the foreground color of the selected cell or graphic object to the next one in the color palette. Press (SHIFT) and click this tool to reverse the direction.
Drop shadow	Displays a shadowed rectangle around selected cells.

Microsoft Excel 3.0 Toolbar

The Excel 3.0 toolbar allows you to have the exact toolbar that was used with Excel 3.0 if you are wedded to that. Like the Excel 4 toolbars, you can customize this if you wish.

Tool	Function
Style box	Selects and applies styles to selected cells, or defines a new style based on the style of the selected cells.
Promote	Increases by one level the selected rows or columns in an outline.
Demote	Decreases by one level the selected rows or columns in an outline.
Show outline symbols	Allows you to create outlining symbols or display existing outlining symbols.
Select visible cells	Selects visible cells, but does not show hidden rows or columns.
AutoSum	Creates a SUM function in the active cell with a reference to the contiguous range of numbers either in the column above or in the row to the left.
Bold and Italic	Applies or removes bold or italic type styles to or from selected cells.
Left, Center, Right alignment	Applies left, center, or right alignment to selected cells.
Selection	Allows you select a graphic object.
Line	Allows you to draw a line with a crosshair pointer.
Filled rectangle Filled oval	Allows you to draw the basic design, which is then filled with the window's background pattern.
Arc	Allows you to draw a portion of a circle with a crosshair pointer.
Chart	Allows you to draw an embedded chart with a crosshair pointer.
Text box	Allows you to type text into a box you draw with a crosshair pointer.
Button	Allows you to assign a macro to a button you draw with a crosshair pointer.

B

Tool	Function
Camera	Takes a "picture" of a selected cell or range and allows you to copy and paste the picture to a new document.

Macro Toolbar

The Macro toolbar provides a set of tools to create and run macros. It is handy when you are doing extensive work with macros.

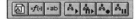

Tool	Function
New macro sheet	Allows you to create a new macro sheet.
Paste function	Displays the Paste Function dialog box.
Paste names	Displays the Paste Name dialog box.
Run macro	Starts the selected macro.
Step macro	Displays the Step Macro dialog box.
Record macro	Starts macro recording.
Resume macro	Pauses, and then with a second click, resumes macro recording.

Macro Recording Toolbar

The Macro Recording toolbar provides one tool which allows you to use a single mouse click to stop recording.

Tool	Function
Stop recording macro	Stops recording the current macro.

Macro Pause Toolbar

The Macro Pause toolbar provides one tool which allows you to use a single click to pause macro recording and then with another click, resume it. If a PAUSE function is executed in a macro, this toolbar is automatically displayed.

Tool	Function
Resume macro	Continues a macro after it was paused or pauses a macro if it is running.

Adding, Moving, Copying, and Deleting Tools

You can easily change the tools on the nine toolbars to any combination you desire. The Customize dialog box, available from either the Toolbars option from the Options menu or the Tool Shortcut menu (click the right mouse button on the toolbar), provides a categorized listing of all the tools offered by Excel. (The Customize dialog box must be open to delete, move, or copy a tool.) Simply drag the tool you want to add to a displayed toolbar and Excel will rearrange the tools to make room for the addition. In many cases, the last tool on the right side of the toolbar will be pushed out of view. To delete a tool, which will then make room for any added tools, drag the tool anywhere off the displayed toolbar. To move a tool from one toolbar to another, display both toolbars and drag the tool from one to the other.

Copying tools is the same as moving except you must press (CTRL) while dragging.

Creating a New Toolbar

If you find the toolbars provided by Excel do not meet your needs, you can create a totally new toolbar and customize it with the tools of your choice. From Options Toolbars, name the new toolbar in the Toolbar Name text box, and choose either Add or Customize. The new toolbar is displayed in the upper-left corner of the worksheet. You can now move or copy tools from either the tool category listing or from a displayed toolbar. When you are done, choose Close and drag the new toolbar to the toolbar area. The new toolbar is added to the list of toolbars and can be displayed when needed.

Moving and Sizing Toolbars

You can display toolbars in their normal position in the toolbar area above the Formula bar, or you can move them to any position in the application area. When moved from the toolbar area the toolbar becomes a standard window that can be moved and sized. To move from the toolbar area, point on any empty area of the displayed toolbar and drag the toolbar to the application area. The toolbar can now be moved and sized as you choose. As you drag the toolbar near the toolbar area, it returns to its normal display.

Customizing Tools

You can customize individual tools in a number of ways. The most useful customization allows you to create a tool and assign a macro to it. Also, you can assign the macro to an existing tool, thereby changing the tool's function. The tool's appearance can be created or changed by importing a graphic image or by copying from another tool.

A Tool Shortcut menu is available to assist in tool customizing. To display the menu you have to be in either the Toolbars or Customize dialog box, point on a tool, and press the right mouse button.

To assign a macro to a custom tool, you have to choose one of the tool examples from the Custom category in the Customize dialog box. Drag the tool to the location on the toolbar where you want it. The Assign to Tool dialog box opens and allows you to choose from any open macros or record a new one. Additionally, to change the function of a tool (existing or custom), from the Customize dialog box, click on the tool you want to change, choose Assign Macro to Tool from the Macro menu or Tool Shortcut menu, and choose from any open macros or record a new one.

To change the appearance of a custom tool, copy a graphic image to the Windows Clipboard (use either bitmap or picture format), switch to Excel, and from the Toolbars or Customize dialog boxes, click on the tool you want to change. Then choose Paste Tool Face from the Tool Shortcut menu. You can also copy the face on one tool to another. From the Toolbars or Customize dialog box, click on the tool face you want to copy from a toolbar, choose Copy Tool Face from the Tool Shortcut menu, click on the destination of the tool face, and then choose Paste Tool Face from the Tool Shortcut menu.

Custom tools, unlike the Excel supplied tools, can only be displayed on their respective toolbars. If you try to drag one from a toolbar to the Customize dialog box or to another toolbar, it will be permanently deleted.

B

Index

B

C

M

X

Y

Z

Excel 4 Command Card

Shortcut Keys

Option	Shortcut Key
Absolute/mixed/relative	F4
Add to current selection	SHIFT F8
Array formula	CTRL SHIFT ENTER
Bold style	CTRL B or CTRL 2
Calculate active document	SHIFT F9
Calculate all documents	F9 or CTRL =
Cancel	ESC
Clear	DEL
Clear formula	CTRL DEL
Close active document	CTRL F4
Copy	CTRL C or CTRL INS
Create names from cell	CTRL SHIFT F3
Cut	CTRL X or SHIFT DEL
Define names	CTRL F3
Delete contents (Clear)	DEL
Delete selection	CTRL -
Edit cell	F2
Edit note	SHIFT F2
Exit find	ESC
Extend selection	F8
Fill down	CTRL D or CTRL < or CTRL SHIFT .
Fill right	CTRL R or CTRL > or CTRL SHIFT .

Option	Shortcut Key
Fill selection	CTRL ENTER
Find dialog box	SHIFT F5
Find next cell	F7
Find previous cell	SHIFT F7
Format commas	CTRL ! or CTRL SHIFT 1
Format currency	CTRL $ or CTRL SHIFT 4
Format date	CTRL # or CTRL SHIFT 3
Format general	CTRL ~ or CTRL SHIFT `
Format percent	CTRL % or CTRL SHIFT 5
Format scientific	CTRL ^ or CTRL SHIFT 6
Format time	CTRL @ or CTRL SHIFT 2
Formula/value display	CTRL `
Goto	F5
Help in context	SHIFT F1
Help window	F1
Hide columns	CTRL 0
Hide rows	CTRL 9
Info window	CTRL F2
Insert AutoSum formula	ALT =
Insert cells	CTRL + or CTRL SHIFT =
Insert date while editing	CTRL .
Insert formula above	CTRL :
Insert time while editing	CTRL ; or CTRL SHIFT :

Excel 4 Command Card

Shortcut Keys

Option	Shortcut Key
Insert value in cell above	CTRL " or CTRL SHIFT '
Italic style	CTRL I or CTRL 3
Maximize/restore document window	CTRL F10
Minimize document window	CTRL F9
Menu	F10 or ALT or /
Move document window	CTRL F7
New chart	F11 or ALT F1
New line in formula bar	ALT ENTER
New macro sheet	CTRL F11 or ALT CTRL F1
New worksheet	SHIFT F11 or ALT SHIFT F1
Next pane	F6
Next window	CTRL F6
Normal style or font	CTRL 1
Note entry edit	SHIFT F2
Open file	CTRL F12 or ALT CTRL F2
Outline border	CTRL & or CTRL SHIFT 7
Paste	CTRL V or SHIFT INS
Paste argument in function	CTRL A
Paste function	SHIFT F3
Paste name	F3
Previous pane	SHIFT F6
Previous window	CTRL SHIFT F6
Print selection	CTRL SHIFT F12 or ALT CTRL SHIFT F2

Option	Shortcut Key
Quit Excel	ALT F4
Remove all borders	CTRL _ or CTRL SHIFT -
Repeat	ALT ENTER
Restore document window	CTRL F5
Save	SHIFT F12 or ALT SHIFT F2
Save as	F12 or ALT F2
Select column	CTRL SPACEBAR
Select entire worksheet	CTRL SHIFT SPACEBAR
Select number style	CTRL S or ALT '
Select region	CTRL * or CTRL SHIFT 8
Select row	SHIFT SPACEBAR
Shortcut menu	SHIFT F10
Show document/info	CTRL F2
Size document window	CTRL F8
Strikethrough	CTRL 5
Summation formula	ALT =
Underline	CTRL U or CTRL 4
Undo	CTRL Z or ALT BACKSPACE
Unhide columns	CTRL (or CTRL SHIFT 9
Unhide rows	CTRL) or CTRL SHIFT 0